South Asian Diasporic Cinema and Theatre

South Asian Diasporic Cinema and Theatre

Re-visiting Screen and Stage in the New Millennium

Edited by
Ajay K. Chaubey
Ashvin I. Devasundaram

RAWAT PUBLICATIONS
Jaipur • New Delhi • Bangalore • Guwahati • Kolkata

ISBN 978-81-316-0907-1

Published by
Prem Rawat for **Rawat Publications**
Satyam Apts, Sector 3, Jawahar Nagar, Jaipur 302 004 (India)
Phone: 0141 265 1748/7006 Fax: 0141 265 1748
E-mail: info@rawatbooks.com
Website: www.rawatbooks.com

New Delhi Office
4858/24, Ansari Road, Daryaganj, New Delhi 110 002
Phone: 011 2326 3290

Also at *Bangalore, Guwahati* and *Kolkata*

Typeset by Rawat Computers, Jaipur
Printed at Nice Printing Press, New Delhi

Contents

Section B
Typology of Indian Cinema: An Accentuated Journey of Hundred Years

Section C
Theatricality of South Asian Diasporic/Indian Theatre: A Critical Reception

Section D
Partitoned Lives in Cinema and Theatre: Recent Perspectives

Preface and Acknowledgement

This edited volume ushers the scholarly study of South Asian cinema and theatre into the contemporary arena. This is an epoch characterised by a crisscross of constant reconfigurations and information flows traversing the globe at the speed of digital bytes. The trajectory of Cultural Studies, particularly cinema and drama, often reaches a stage where repetition, stagnation and stasis become accepted with a resigned sense of inevitability. Indeed, quiescence, obsolescence and validation of status quo in the cultural sector of scholarly analysis are symptoms that stress the need for decisive and often disjunctive interventions. These interruptions are a *sine qua non* to shake the roots and branches of complacent epistemological constructions of culture. This anthology, therefore, suggests the reinvigoration of a corpus of study that has arguably become etiolated and typecast.

This volume seeks to affirm heterogeneity and difference, celebrating multi-dimensional modes of looking at the same canvas. This is aptly reflected in the cornucopia of individual papers on a variegated canon of film and drama. Their integration into the architecture of this volume is designed to galvanise a holistic, inter-textual and multi-vocal interaction. This co-mingling of multiple voices, articulating the new, topical and sometimes radical dimensions of South Asian film and drama, intends to breach the boundaries of the book's containing covers, reaching out to establish a stimulating and thought-provoking rapport with its readers. In addition, this compendium is conceived as a mediator between earlier volumes on this topic whilst extrapolating future trends germane to cinema and theatre thematically centering on the South Asian sub-continent. Ultimately, this volume seeks to act as a bridge, dissolving borders and boundaries, addressing often specious cultural pre-conceptions, and forging a cultural studies causeway across the largely reductionist duality of South Asian 'diasporic' and 'domiciled' visual arts.

We unfalteringly concede the selfless action of the following scholars who have overtly contributed to this volume and have written their essays afresh. They are: Pragya Shukla, Irum Alvi, Shilpa Daithota Bhat, Subrata Kumar Das, Rajesh James, D. Sudha Rani, Manjinder Kaur Wratch and Anindya Raychaudhuri.

No volume is supposed to be accomplished until it gets some of the essays from the scholars representing the East in the West and the Western scholars working on the multiple themes of the East. The editors and the publisher duly acknowledge the following reputed critics and incipient scholars for their prompt permission to reproduce their essays in this volume:

Sanjena Sathian for her essay entitled 'Gender and Nation in the South Asian Diaspora: Transnational Cultural Spaces in Bollywood Cinema' published in the *Columbia Undergraduate Journal of South Asian Studies*, Vol. II.I, Fall 2010. 22–41.

Rekha Sharma for her essay 'Desi Films: Articulating Images of South Asian Identity in a Global Communication Environment' published in *Global Media Journal*, Vol. 4.1. 127–143.

E. Anna Claydon for her essays entitled 'British South Asian Cinema and Identity-I: Nostalgia in the Contemporary British Cinema and the South-Asian Diaspora' and 'British South Asian Cinema and Identity-II: Representing America in the films of Gurinder Chadha' published in the *SACS* Vol. 2.1 (26–38) and Vol. 2.2 (47–58) respectively.

Ana Cristina Mendes for her paper entitled '*Bride & Prejudice* and the Post National Cinema Debate' published in Carlos Ceia and Isabel Lousada (eds.), *Novos Caminhos da*

História e da Cultura. Lisbon: FCSH, Universidade Nova de Lisboa, 2007, 95–103.

M.M.K. Sardana for his critical essay 'Bollywood on the Wings of Technology and its Contribution to Economy: Hundredth Year of Indian Cinema' published on line as ISID Discussion notes. The same can be viewed at.

Nandi Bhatia for her one of the popular essays entitled 'Diasporic Activism and the Mediations of "Home": South Asian Voices in Canadian Drama' published in *Studies in Social Justice*, Vol. 7, Issue 1 (2013): 125–141.

Neilesh Bose for his critically acclaimed essay entitled 'Sharuk and Shylock: The Creation of a South Asian American Aesthetic' published in the *South Asian Popular Culture*, Vol. 7, No. 3, October 2009. 195–209.

Priyam Basu Thakur for her essay 'Theater for Development in Indian Context: An Introspection' which was originally published in *Global Media Journal*, Winter Issue, December 2013, Vol. 4, No. 2, 1–12.

We thank and appreciate the aforementioned authors, editors and publishers for their kind consent to reproduce their (respective) essays in this volume. We acknowledge the substantial support, erudite remarks and ethical values imbibed in us from our family and friends. We remain obligated, as usual, to our teachers, mentors, scholarly friends and friendly scholars. Pranit Rawat as well as his team for the Rawat Publications is solely thanked for bringing this volume well in time.

We also thank all the contributors of this volume, in general, and Shilpa Daithota Bhat, and Subrata K. Das, in particular, for proofreading 'Introduction' and few other essays. Their suggestions and comments mean a lot to us.

Finally, we will remain attentive to acknowledge the permission if someone is missed inadvertently. All errors are our own.

Ajay K. Chaubey
Ashvin I. Devasundaram

South Asian Diasporic Cinema and Theatre

A Critical Introduction

AJAY K. CHAUBEY AND ASHVIN I. DEVASUNDARAM

Cinema and theatre serve as multidimensional apparatuses to depict that which is not depicted, to raise a voice for the voiceless and to unpack the packed. These properties often inform a wide spectrum of the visual and performing arts. Iconic play *The Mousetrap* could be cited as an example of multiform meaning, with its intertextual and subtextual consanguinity with Shakespeare's *Hamlet*. Performative texts have always been fluid and culminate at the intersection point of heightened audience perception; where people begin to think beyond the texts. Performative art forms possess the ability to imagine and re-imagine the unimagined psychosomatic issues related to society, politics, economy, industry, de-politicization, de-colonization, not to mention internal-colonization that is instrumentalized with the assiduous assistance of political forces and capitalists; the Bhopal Gas Tragedy and its subsequent ramifications is a case in point. Performative texts, as emissaries of popular culture, have expanded across global geographical and linguistic precincts and have become common cultural currency in a diverse array of nations and languages. Importantly, such performative texts are used as a 'vehicle for cultural articulation and debate'.[1]

We are immersed in a paradox-ridden global digital age. On the one hand, ethno-cultural boundaries seem to be melting away, dissolved by the speedy transmission of information-redolent internet megabytes. On the other hand, inward-looking nationalism, intolerance towards alternative narratives and 'strangers' (Loshitzky, 2010: 4) seem increasingly ascendant. In the latter scenario, socio-cultural identities are susceptible to becoming homogenised and mythologised. This process buttresses exclusionary notions of historically ordained ethno-cultural purity and imagined national uniformity (Anderson, 2006), where diversity is the actual extant reality.

In this contradictory situation, where local and global collide and coalesce, charting the ever-changing trajectory of the South Asian diasporic experience can constitute a challenging prospect. In this regard, cinema and theatre are integral implements to understand identity formation and cultural perceptions. However, it must be noted that these sectors of the visual and performing arts are not inoculated from or neutral to the designs and dictates of capital (Piketty, 2014) and ideology, which manifest in several shape-shifting twenty-first century avatars. With these vectors in mind, this volume takes on the monumental vision of anthologising a polymorphous canon of South Asian cinema and drama.

Whilst broaching these themes it is crucial not to compartmentalise South Asian cinema and theatre into hermetic blocks, sealed off from each other. Instead, the two dimensions are always-already interlocked in a protean dialogic, a conversation that is itself continued with multitudinous spheres, vectors and discourses. The synergy between cinema and drama in a South Asian scenario is epitomised by new British Asian playwrights, such as Ayndrilla Singharay, whose theatre production *Unsung* (2014), adapted from a Rabindranath Tagore's short story 'Punishment', is currently being transformed into an eponymously titled film. South Asian theatre is being invigorated in new and distinct modes in fresh arenas of cultural interosculation. For example, Bashabi Fraser's poem 'From the Ganga to the Tay', adapted into a theatrical dance performance, imagines a cultural confluence between Scotland and India, as represented through the two nations' iconic rivers. Samir Bhamra's Indianised dramatic rendition of Shakespeare's

Cymbeline is another case in point. There is also an accentuated permeation of South Asian themes into the work of established non-Asian British playwrights. These include David Hare's *Behind the Beautiful Forevers* (2014–15), about garbage collectors in a Mumbai slum, Howard Brenton's *Drawing the Line* (2013), tracing the provenance of India's Partition, and the incisive political drama *Stowaway* (2014–16) conceived by young writers from Analogue Theatre Productions, registering the perilous journey of an Asian refugee, concealed in the wheel-arch of an airplane.

In the Indian sub-continent, current repressions of rationalism in a retrogressive arena of religiosity places into context the meditations of diasporic Indian scholars on new developments in cinema and drama. National grand narratives and their global cultural proponents, such as Bollywood, are being interrogated through alternative and heterodox micro-level interpretations of modern India (Devasundaram, 2016). Indian cinema is currently undergoing a transformative overhaul where urban audiences hyperlinked to the world via technological networks and new media are fomenting change from within. Similarly, marking '100 years of Indian cinema' inaugurates new idioms, modes and angles of appraising and evaluating structural changes in Bollywood and the other forms of Indian cinema that have for too long remained inadequately represented in western scholarly examinations. A recent example is *Haider* (2014), Indian filmmaker Vishal Bharadwaj's inventive indigenisation of Shakespeare's *Hamlet*, addressing exigent themes of geopolitical conflict and providing a transdiscursive contestation of dominant systems of power. Overall, looking through a multi-perspective contemporary lens, this volume addresses the points raised so far and apportions equal scope and importance to film and theatre in the book's various sections.

In the aforementioned labile global milieu, where capital casts its universalising cloak, there can be a nebulising of synchronic nuances, particularities and heterogeneities that are conveniently collapsed into the appellation 'South Asian'. This volume seeks to reveal some of these specificities through the looking glass of film and drama. This is a time when scholarship in the broader area of South Asian Studies is asking searching questions about the continued efficacy of established theoretical paradigms to interpret arts, culture and politics in a postcolonial field (Chibber, 2013). Perhaps it is possible to circumvent the jeopardy of reinforcing academic fossilisation by reframing, remapping and recuperating the scholarly examination of South Asian arts and culture, in concordance with the shape-shifting realities of the digital age.

In this regard, it becomes necessary to revitalise the reading of South Asian films and theatre in this millennium by departing from enervated modes of mediation, interpretation and representation that often inform essentialised reproduction and stereotypical regurgitation, both by western and South Asian proponents. On the same lines, one could consider the possibility of recasting the dominant pedagogy of nation often underwritten or subconsciously validated, even in scholarly South Asian diasporic interventions. It may be timely to stake a claim for a refurbished critical analysis of the region's recent cinematic and theatrical trajectory, detached from the restrictive talons of long-distance nationalism (Anderson, 1998, 2007), nostalgia, self-exoticisation and self-valorisation. These often-defensive hermeneutic modes may have outlived their utility as templates or touchstones in an era where urgent and pressing geopolitical developments demand a more immersive, introspective, and rational approach.

In the current time, several South Asian nations are countenancing critical questions, particularly India, Bangladesh and Sri Lanka, where politico-religious dogmatism has transmogrified to phantasmagoric proportions. This has largely precipitated a parlous state of affairs that places self-expression, secularism and civil liberties in peril. In this situation, it is worth asking how does diasporic perceive and address domicile? How can we depart from the etiolated and otiose centre-periphery, outside-inside model? South Asian diasporic cinema and theatre runs the risk of being perceived through distant, vicarious and hence detached modes of negotiating geopolitical lived experience. Is it possible to revivify the region's discursive cinematic and dramatic past in the context of the present, keeping an eye on the future? Can we succeed in creating a multilogue from the binaries of non-resident and resident, interiority and exteriority, local and global, endogenous and exogenous, allochthonous and autochthonous?

Rather than fashion a specious harmony across the socio-political, cultural and economic, spatio-temporal particularities that inflect the South Asian diasporic and South Asian endemic experience, it may be useful to acknowledge difference. It is this very property that at once positions this volume's mapping of twenty first century cinema and theatre not only as a timely intervention but also as an inclusive one. Acknowledging the diversity of films and drama thematically orientated around South Asia would serve as a pertinent reminder of recent disconcerting reorientations in the region that bear ramifications for cinema and theatre. The thrust towards ethno-religious 'purity' and drive towards a mythologised homogeneity of nation based on imagined religious sameness conceals in its design the catastrophic consequences of social fracture and discord. The rise of socio-religious tensions stemming from divisive politics invokes the era of Partition, a theme witnessing reengagement in new films such as *Qissa* (2014). Such cinematic conjuring of the spectres of traumatic and tumultuous historical events exemplify how past discourses continue to be reinterpreted and reframed in contemporary South Asian cultural conduits. Cinema and theatre from a South Asian diasporic standpoint, rather than being distantiated, needs to be articulated from within its area of address; wherever this may be – South Asia, UK, USA or other domains. By identifying convergences, departures and imbrications in interstitial zones between the local, national and global, this volume is well-placed to evaluate, interrogate and contest dimensions of discourse from multi-angle vantage points.

Section A of the volume provides an in-depth critical insight into films from the new millennium. The essays in this segment ask compelling questions on gender and identity, which continue to constitute moot points in South Asian Studies in general. The scholarly investigations look at South Asian films and their arbitration on questions of identity in the larger context of cultural overlaps in a latticed global network environment. The recent emergence of new independent Indian cinema ushering an era of female directors, such as Kiran Rao and Anusha Rizvi from India, and Pakistan's Oscar-winning Sharmeen Obaid Chinoy, presents an opportunity to re-examine the oeuvre of British-Asian directors such as Gurinder Chadha. Extending the ambit to dimensions beyond the archetypically Indian construction of 'desi', this volume presents important insights into the Afghan diaspora and diasporic domains in relation to the relatively recondite Afghanistan cinemascape.

Section B is streamlined to represent a compendious and multifaceted study of the vicissitudes characterising the 100 years of Indian cinema. Rapid technological innovation and digitisation of the creative process in Bollywood addresses reorientations in the nation's dominant cinematic form. Invoking alternative filmic articulations of marginal voices from below provide a counterpoint from the perspective of subalterns, through Hamid Naficy's notion of 'accented' cinema. Issues of suppression of sexual freedom, particularly in relation to women and LGBT communities are a topical source of polemic in India. In this regard, authoritarian imposition of religious rituals, conventions and practices invoke a re-reading of Canadian-Indian filmmaker Deepa Mehta's seminal films on these subjects. Continuing this strand, examining the conventions of queerness as represented in 1990s Malayalam films draws into focus the protracted legal battle waged by liberal campaigners to repeal the nation's continued adherence to the British colonial law, Section 377, outlawing homosexuality in India. Performing the pedagogical mythic narrative of nation (Bhabha, 1994) raises the possibility of altering it with every iteration and interpretation. Cinema and theatre are indispensable instruments in the endeavour to constantly interrogate, re-orientate and renegotiate dominant narratives of representation and push boundaries of artistic agency. In this regard, cultural and academic voices emerging from within the South Asian diaspora could be located as key players and stakeholders in the reformulation of self-representation.

The perennially contentious question of who represents whom continues to be raised in discourse surrounding ethnic minority representation, particularly in the USA and Britain. The concerted call for enhanced levels of diversity in British television, theatre and film is a case in point. In a postmodern socio-cultural constellation, it is conceivable that the demise of the author has been enacted and now constitutes a fait accompli. Although the rise of demographically demotic digital intermediaries through social media and the internet have indeed decentred the omnipotence of the film/drama critic, diversity and inclusion in the creative process behind stage and screen remains a critical question. The diversity debate cannot be silenced by the tick-box culture still extant in Britain and the USA where in temporary appeasement, token ethnic minority characters are planted in front of proscenium arch and film frame. This stated, films such as the Cannes award-winning *Dheepan* (2015), fronted by three relatively unknown Sri Lankan actors are indexical of a possible drive towards change through greater representation of non-Caucasian narratives, film actors and dramatis personae.

It would be inimical to advocate a totalising system of ethnic self-representation in cinema and theatre where only members of certain communities are authorised to represent themselves. This would result in the redrawing of new isolationist borders and vitiate intercultural cohesion, communication and co-operation. South African playwright Yael Farber's *tour de force* theatre production *Nirbhaya*, performed at the Edinburgh Festival 2013, is a powerful example of how international creative collaboration transcending boundaries can constitute compelling and life-transforming works of art. This drama about the 2012 Delhi bus gang rape features oral testimonies of five Indian women, who themselves are real life victims of domestic violence. Overall, *Nirbhaya* underscores how theatre without boundaries can act as a torchbearer for social change.

This eclectic and multi-hued anthology of twenty first century South Asian diasporic cinema and theatre comes at a time witnessing instances of parochial and uninformed vilification of polemical artworks, solely on the basis of their not being authored by ethnic minorities. This arguably defeats the possibility of a constructive and conciliatory multilogue that dispenses with erstwhile dialectics of white/black, occidental/oriental, and coloniser/colonised. These antiquated binaries must be superseded not reversed, particularly in the visual and performing arts, if there is to be a realistic attempt to accelerate equal representation, progressive attitudes, cultural miscegenation and hybrid acculturation. The transglobal success of Ritesh Batra's *The Lunchbox* (2013), a film co-produced by India, USA, France and Germany inter alia, aptly encapsulates the future direction of a pan-global synthesis in film production.

To reiterate an earlier point from a theatre perspective, South African artist Brett Bailey's 2014 *Exhibit B* could be called to attention. This was a travelling *tableaux vivant* exhibition castigating Victorian colonial attitudes that viewed indigenous African cultures as sub-human species that could be displayed in vitrine 'zoos' for the viewing wonderment of 19th and early 20th century white Anglo-Saxon audiences. It could be argued that *Exhibit B* discursively enacts a disassembling of the colonial master plan through the live art exhibition's subversive postcolonial mimicry of colonial atrocities. The tableaux features black actors frozen in mimetic poses of enslavement and brutalisation tracing the trajectory of past colonial oppression that still reverberates in current neo-colonial structures. Successfully received at the 2014 Edinburgh Festival, the subsequent London performance of *Exhibit B* was forcefully disrupted by mainly ethnic minority campaigners who eventually caused host venue, the Barbican, to capitulate and cancel the show. This was largely based on allegations that Bailey, as a white South African was inappropriately representing and even reproducing exploitative colonial discourse. The fact that a preponderance of the protestors including academics had not even witnessed the exhibition before demanding its proscription is a minor point (Blacker, 2014). This scenario recalls Birmingham Repertory Theatre's cancellation of British Asian playwright Gurpreet Kaur Bhatti's *Behzti* (2004), following violent protests by the local Sikh community and death threats to Bhatti, who is Sikh herself (Branigan and Dodd, 2004). More recently in 2015, the UK's

National Youth Theatre fearing controversy, cancelled *Homegrown*, a play by director Nadia Latif and playwright Omar El-Khairy, about Islamic radicalism in London schools, prompting allegations of a new 'culture of caution in the arts' (BBC News, 2015).

These examples in Britain to some extent mirror the more pervasive blind censorship of art and culture in the South-Asian sub-continent where battles are fought by filmmakers and dramatists against contraventions on the freedom of expression. It could be argued that levels of objectivity and self-reflexivity from within South Asian communities could be accentuated whilst broaching self-representation in film, drama and other arenas of expression. This volume hopes to step forward in that direction by creating a synergy of self-appraisal, one that does not recoil from contesting dominant narratives whilst delving into new dimensions of South Asian identity and the diasporic experience.

Essays in this Volume

Section A: *Filming South Asian Diaspora: Critical Essays in the New Millennium*

South Asian diasporic cinema is more pervasive in the new millennium than in the preceding century. Indian cinema is an established phenomenon not only in South Asia but also in the wider Asian continent. It has traversed across the globe, gaining popular appeal thanks to the immense presence of the Indian/South Asian diaspora. New emerging alternative forms of Indian cinema are articulating new micro level stories and subversive narratives that are engaged with contemporary lives, society and politics. This section, the longest in the volume, offers a synchronic analysis of performative texts in the backdrop of South Asian, South Asian American or South Asian British cinema. The following essays, enclosed in the section, meticulously trail the trajectory of diasporic cinema in the present century, which sometimes receive greater response overseas than in India. The essays critically map the unmapped nuances of gender, nation, identity, nostalgia, inter-cultural relations, cultural tourism and film adaptation of canonical text/s.

Sanjena Sathian's inaugural essay entitled 'Gender and Nation in the South Asian Diaspora: Transnational Cultural Spaces in Bollywood Cinema' chronologically explores the development of depictions of females in the Indian diaspora in five major Bollywood films: *Pardes*, *Dilwale Dulhania le Jayenge*, *Kabhi Khushi Kabhie Gam*, *Salaam Namaste* and *Love Aaj Kal*. In the last three decades, Bollywood cinema has shifted from projecting anti-colonial understandings of moral and sexual female boundaries to emphasizing a more liberated, diasporic female figure. The essay further explores that 'the genre (which) has traditionally found ways to restrict feminine sexuality within the confines of a nation-state', and only in a post-nation-state world, within transnational cultural spaces, can the female figure achieve some degree of liberation.

Rekha Sharma's essay '*Desi* Films: Articulating Images of South Asian Identity in a Global Communication Environment' examines Indian diasporic films as a vehicle for cultural articulation and debate. First, it provides a theoretical foundation of hegemony and resistance with regard to notions of ethnicity and immigrants' articulations of identity in interstitial zones. Second, it discusses sources of hegemony from Indian and Western media. Third, it explores the creation of a hybrid identity as reflected in Indian diasporic films, pointing out some of the themes and conventions of this emerging genre. This exploration of desi films addresses such broad questions as 'Who determines the images of "Indianness" outside of India, especially in a global communication environment?' as well as 'How are Indians being portrayed in this global media environment, and how do those images differ from earlier media portrayals in Indian and Western media?'

E. Anna Claydon's critical essay 'British South Asian Cinema and Identity–I: Nostalgia in the Contemporary British Cinema and the South Asian Diaspora' centres upon the concept of nostalgia as it is represented in three films which epitomise the way in which contemporary, hybrid, British cinema has tackled issues of diasporic identities and the South-Asian diaspora. The essay seeks to establish a discourse upon British South-Asian films and filmmakers, which recognises the subtleties of representation which are, for many, difficult to articulate and to broach, illustrating how the hybridity of contemporary British cinema is not simply a matter of cross-cultural representation but is the complex combination of the small details which belong to many homes and which adapt to create another.

E. Anna Claydon's 'British South Asian Cinema and Identity–II: Representing America in the films of Gurinder Chadha' is a complementary essay to the previous one. Claydon articulates 'following on from my discussion in the previous issue of nostalgia in contemporary British South-Asian cinema, this article continues by focusing on the films of British South-Asian and Sikh filmmaker Gurinder Chadha.' Gurinder Chadha first rose to prominence with her 1989 documentary 'I'm British But...' an insight into identifications British South-Asians make with their multicultural influences. This was followed by *Bhaji on the Beach* in 1993 and later *Bride and Prejudice* (2005), an adaptation of Austen's novel, *Pride and Prejudice* wherein Chadha deals with both the adaptive processes of intercultural relations and a British text engaging with post-colonialism. Consequently, the dilemmas of America and Britain are evident in considering the 'truths' of identity in Chadha's adaptation and what has been 'lost' at 'home', can be found again elsewhere wherever that might be.

The next paper is '*Bride and Prejudice* and the (Post-) National Cinema Debate' by Ana Cristina Mendes who asserts that from the outset, the novelty of Gurinder Chadha's film *Bride and Prejudice* (2004) lies in its inclusion of twenty first century Indian culture into a British canonical text, *Pride and Prejudice*. This is visible not only in the Bollywood-styled musical interludes but also in issues raised, such as the economics of cultural tourism resulting in the tourist-driven 'India without all the Indians', in the protagonist Lalita's words. Nonetheless, in the context of this essay, Mendes is not preoccupied with a thematic reading of *Bride and Prejudice*, but rather the *debate* around the film, to focus on the ways in which critical discourses intersect to classify the film as a national and/or diasporic cultural product. Discussing a film that is defined by its filmmaker as British but categorised by critics as South Asian diasporic stimulates a consideration of debates about identity, community, belonging, and nation in cinema studies.

The next chapter, 'Hanif Kureishi's *My Son the Fanatic*: Anxiety in Assimilation' by Pragya Shukla, different from the aforementioned essays, offers an incisive critique of secularism and fundamentalism. The former is suspended in a state of undecidability, often as a conscience-inducing utopian imaginary that is never quite reified or concretised in society. This is then counterpoised with the latter, depicting religious intolerance and orthodoxy that is framed in the British setting of the film as an unpatriotic and anti-national activity/ideology. The plot revolves around a Pakistani born taxi driver, Parwez, and his son Farid. Parwez is a secular Muslim whose life takes a jolt when his son converts to fundamentalist Islam and this, in turn, gives way to family breakdown and communal conflict. The paper penetratingly studies the multifarious aspects of diaspora, nostalgia and assimilation of identity in the host nation.

Irum Alvi's essay entitled 'Afghan Diaspora and Diasporic Spaces in the Cinematic Landscape of Afghanistan and Iran' focuses on the need for belonging to a place, a home, a country and a family, which has momentous implications especially for the diasporic population. This paper follows on from recent research and posits that despite increasingly geographically dispersed Afghan diasporas, the sense of place is still a strong indicator of individuality and is fundamental to the Afghan diasporic community's knowledge and understanding of themselves and 'others'. Combining the delineation of Afghan diasporic characters in films made by Afghans with the socio-political scenario in Afghanistan, the paper posits that along with identity the notion of place that the Afghan diasporic community has left behind are strong, deep-rooted and multi-faceted factors. In essence, the narrative of the Afghan diaspora is constantly imbued with a sense of belonging to the place where they grew up, the wider country – the *watan* and the nation – the *Qawm*.

Since Indian cinema, of late, has completed its odyssey of one hundred years, it is our academic obligation to include a dedicated section on the typology of Indian cinema in this volume.

Section B: *Typology of Indian Cinema: An Accentuated Journey of Hundred Years*

This segment focuses unswervingly on the Indian cinema, which as stated earlier has accomplished its journey of hundred years in this millennium. Indian cinema commenced its long trajectory in 1913 with Dadasaheb Phalke's iconic *Raja Harischandra*. Since then, Indian cinema has grown exponentially, engendering multiple genres and competing with other concurrent and contemporary major film-industries around the globe. The essays included in this section cogently cover subtle nuances of the Indian cinema celebrating its centennial voyage. The chapters deal with a wide gamut of theoretical contours of technological shifts and economic contributions to the nation by Bollywood, divulging its 'accented' journey, multifarious tropes, regional sense and sensibility. The essays in this section also offer multiple interdisciplinary perspectives through theoretical delineations of literature and cinema.

M.M.K. Sardana's essay 'Bollywood on the Wings of Technology and Its Contribution to Economy: Hundredth Year of Indian Cinema' studies Bollywood – as the mainstream Hindi language film producing industry is popularly known as – is the largest producer of films in India, though regional cinemas compete both in terms of quantity and quality of film production with the mainstream cinema. Bollywood film industry is as old as Hollywood. Since 1960, India has been holding the record of producing the maximum number of commercial films and has attracted the maximum number of viewers; yet it stands nowhere near Hollywood in terms of quality and from the point of revenue generation.

The next essay of this snippet entitled 'Bollywood Dreams Hand-in-Hand with the Canadian Movie Business: Interplay of Diasporic Cinema with Emotions, Creativity and Money' by Shilpa Daithota Bhat is complementary to the previous essay as it investigates the business dimension of this gargantuan industry, Bollywood, in the context of Indo-Canada bilateral association. Several Canadian film companies have opened branches in India and have benefitted commercially owing to abnormally high film consumption levels in India. Bhat D. is of opinion that 'business and economic relations affect and trigger new cultural streams and films create a space wherein there is articulation and amalgamation of multiple perspectives.' Hence, this paper focuses on how this area is characterized by perpetually broadening opportunities. This also seeks to analyse the business of films and India and Canada relationship in the context of culture.

Subrata Kumar Das's chapter entitled 'Subalterns' Voices through 'Accented Cinema(s)': A Study of Deepa Mehta's *Fire* and *Water*' studies women as 'subalterns' and explores how such 'subalterns' raise 'voices' to get 'spaces' in mainstream social phenomena through Mehta's *Fire* and *Water*. Since last two decades, some Indian diasporic feminist auteur have tried to deconstruct the image of 'scopophilia' from the traditional Hollywood and Bollywood films for 'male gaze' (Laura Mulvey). These 'Accented Cinema(s)', in Hamid Naficy's words, give two sites for marginalized women–a site of resistance for the films' characters and the other being the site for the expression of that resistance for the filmmakers. These filmmakers try to eradicate the subaltern status of women and allow them a 'space' to be heard in mainstream societal phenomena. Das holds the view that 'feminist "Accented Cinema(s)" not only project strong-willed and sexually-assertive women but also telescope women as agents of progressive, revolutionary, egalitarian social thinkers who openly show their free spirits of resistance and challenge' and further asserts that the women characters in these films raise their voice against different social taboos and repressions meted out to them by a patriarchal society.

The next paper 'Queer Tropes in Post 1990s Malayalam Cinema' by Rajesh James foregrounds the unheard queer narratives in the post-90s reel space of Malayalam Cinema. Malayalam Cinema, since its inception, has arguably been ideologically homophobic. The aesthetics and politics of such cultural artifacts marginalized queerness in all its contours. The concept of poly spaces as a common niche was largely not considered. However, the fact of such absences and closetedness now foregrounds its underground cinematic existence. Though Malayalam cinema is still a powerful medium that spins around heterosexual, patriarchal, masculine, racial and moral codes, there are subversive attempts from the margins to topple the heteronormative cultural products and its ideological formulations.

Cinema came into existence afterwards while theater has been popular ever since the classical era owing to royal patronage and encouragement. There are convergences, divergences and imbrications between cinema and theatre through theme, structure, content, design, treatment and audience reception. The next section focuses on theatre through a South Asian lens.

Section C: *Theatricality of South Asian Diasporic/ Indian Theatre: A Critical Reception*

Theatre, a tool to engage with the everyday lived experience of diverse societies, is a strong medium to explore the unexplored, to render articulate the inarticulate, to motivate the demotivated and to develop hitherto underdeveloped themes and concepts through explicit and implicit representation. According to Shakespeare, 'theatre is a mirror of highlighting man's humanity and also a tool for understanding why man also finds it so easy to transgress that same humanity' (quoted in Priyam Basu Thakur's essay in this volume). This section engages with research explorations in this field that cover multifarious manifestations such as – 'home and spaces' in multicultural Canada'; 'plays written and performed by South Asian community'; 'Anglophone plays that attempt to negotiate the messy, painful and often horrifically traumatic transnational history of partition' and 'the history of theatre in international and Indian context and with the origin and nature of development communication in third world perspective.'

Nandi Bhatia in her paper entitled 'Diasporic Activism and the Mediations of "Home": South Asian Voices in Canadian

Drama' analyzes how the networks between home and spaces of residence in multicultural Canada come alive on theatre stages through visual motifs, actors, props, and photographic collages, which confront the different trajectories of 'home' that resurface in these plays. Through live scenes of imagination that speak to spectators, several plays under discussion in this essay expose how, while providing emotional sustenance for some, the baggage of 'home' may also pose challenges in the home of residence. So the questions I raise are: How does home appear? To what end? In addition, what does returning 'home' teach us about the inequalities and injustices underlying the current global order?

The next essay entitled 'Sharuk and Shylock: The Creation of a South Asian American Aesthetic' by Neilesh Bose examines the landmark play, Shishir Kurup's *Merchant on Venice* and its premiere production in Chicago in 2007, in order to initiate a historical discussion of South Asian American theatre history. Through an examination of this adaptation of Shakespeare's *Merchant of Venice*, its relationship to the original together with its distinctive literary qualities and a consideration of its performative manifestation, this essay argues that Kurup's play heralds the coming of a South Asian American theatre aesthetic through engagements with language and inclusion of South Asian American cultural and historical specificity into the American theatre.

D. Sudha Rani's essay entitled 'South Asian Diasporic Theatre: A Critical Overview' attempts to do keen scrutiny of the plays produced by this stratum of society and comprehend the issues related to the South Asian community which is spread across the globe with their prominent presence in countries like the USA, the UK, Canada and South Africa. South Asian diasporic society is vibrant in production of literature, which is a significant branch of world literature. Among other genres of literatures, theatre is the younger genre. The South Asian playwrights in the above-mentioned countries are writing about diverse issues ranging from socio-political issues to psychological separation from homeland to issues, which are important to their counter parts in their homelands.

Priyam Basu Thakur in her paper 'Theatre for Development in Indian Context: An Introspection' introspects the role of theatre in development communication. Theatre is a very effective and responsive tool for foster the growth of development procedure. The paper convulses the history of theatre in international and Indian context and with the origin and nature of development communication in third world perspective. The paper also attempts to espouse the liaison between theatre and development by using Paulo *Freire & Augusto Boal's* analysis. In developing India, theatre left its impact on issues like the agriculture, literacy campaign, social harmony, girl trafficking, child labour, gender discrimination, religious tolerance, women empowerment, prevention of HIV-AIDS, family planning, pulse polio, nutrition, environment and pollution, etc. The paper concludes that theatre plays a crucial role in conflict resolution, cultural identification, community development, social protest and in spreading mass awareness to the grass root level. Few of the issues are concurrently illustrated in cinema and theatre.

Section D: *Partitioned Lives in Cinema and Theatre: Recent Perspectives*

The 'holocaust' of Partition and its representations in cinema and theatre has drawn the attention of researchers, media and academia. Several creative writers, poets, novelists and critics have offered manifold accounts of Partition-induced trauma and decimation in the aftermath of the 'great divide'. Two prominent literary figures – William Dalrymple and Pankaj Mishra – have opined respectively that this (Partition) is 'bloody legacy'[2] of India and Pakistan and '… 1947 has yet to come to an end'[3]. The section explicitly posits the multiple propositions of Partition, which forms the backdrop of several performative texts across India and world. Mapping the trajectory of Partition's 'trauma' is in no way a stress-free task to accomplish in a single academic effort. As far as the inclusion of essays on 'Partition' is concerned, the objective is not only to record the pain, agony, trauma and alienation of transplanted individuals and communities but also to capture the rubric of the nation in its essentialised binary of divided/undivided. This constitutes the rationale of this shortest segment to be included in this volume.

The introductory essay, 'Partitioned Lives and the Cinematic Quest for Redressal' by Manjinder Kaur Wratch, studies 'the psychobiography of the three nations India, Pakistan and Bangladesh,' communally devastated by partition and war. The paper critically surveys cinematic texts, based on the aftermath of partition, from *Lahore* (1949) to *Khamosh Pani* (2003) to *Pinjar* and *Parzania* (2005) and offers a comprehensive conclusion that 'cultural recall exposes traumatic experiences of the Partition to critical interrogation thereby opening new vistas of social transformation.' The paper also discerns how state-sponsored divisive politics culminating in communal violence devastates the camaraderie of ordinary folks who want to live in peace and bonhomie. It explores how religious violence ripped apart communities, plunging victims into an abyss of alienation, making them 'exiles' in their own land and dragooning them into painstakingly woeful lives on the margins of society.

The next paper entitled 'Do They Want to Turn Partition into a Gilbert and Sullivan Opera?: Performing Partition as Uncanny Farce' by Anindya Raychaudhuri deals with a selection of Anglophone plays – *Blood* by Harwant S. Bains, *Final Solutions* by Mahesh Dattani, *A Shaft of Sunlight* by Abhijat Joshi, *A Tainted Dawn* by Sudha Bhuchar and Kristine Landon-Smith, *Child of the Divide* by Sudha Bhuchar and *Drawing the Line* by Howard Brenton. Raychaudhuri studies how these plays 'dramatise the history of partition, and the politics that are at stake in so doing.' Through his study of these plays, he aims to challenge some of the assumptions of this reading, asking whether this narrative does have great dramatic potential or does it risk reinforcing a deeply problematic political narrative.

The abovementioned critical essays on cinema and theatre engage in critical conversations espousing heterogeneous themes. They are written by young scholars from India and abroad who have largely transcended the hegemony of established and ossified norms and structures of research in literature and film studies. These eminent contributors have assisted in bringing this volume to fruition, extending a productive and prolific scholarly output that will benefit imminent scholars around the world. It is confidently expected that this anthology, feasibly maiden in its kind, will be useful for both research students and academicians.

Notes

1. Please see Chapter 2 by Rekha Sharma (in this volume) for more details.
2. http://www.newyorker.com/magazine/2015/06/29/the-great-divide-books-dalrymple. Accessed on August 18, 2015.
3. http://www.newyorker.com/contributors/pankaj-mishra. Accessed on August 18, 2015.

Works Cited

Anderson, Benedict. *The Spectre of Comparisons*. London: Verso, 1998. Print.

——. 'EuroTopics - Benedict Anderson On Diaspora Nationalism'. *Eurotopics.Net*. Web. 7 Oct. 2015. <http://www.eurotopics.net/en/home/medienindex/media_articles/archiv_article/ARTICLE19423-Benedict-Anderson-on-diaspora-nationalism>

——. *Imagined Communities*. 3 ed. New York: Verso, 2006. Print.

BBC News. *Homegrown: Scrapping radicalisation play 'shuts down' debate - BBC News. Web. 7 November 2015. <http://www.bbc.co.uk/news/entertainment-arts-33949056 >*

Bhabha, H. *The Location of Culture*. London: Routledge, 1994. Print.

Blacker, T. *It's not just the censorship of Exhibit B which proves that the stupid are winning*. *Independent*. Web. 7 October 2015. <http://www.independent.co.uk/voices/comment/its-not-just-the-censorship-of-exhibit-b-which-proves-that-the-stupid-are-winning-9760951.html>

Branigan, T., V. Dodd. *Writer in hiding as violence closes Sikh play*. *Guardian*. Web. 7 October 2015. <http://www.theguardian.com/uk/2004/dec/21/religion.arts>

Chibber, V. *Postcolonial Theory and the Specter of Capital*. New York: Verso, 2013. Print.

Devasundaram, Ashvin. *India's New Independent Cinema: Rise of the Hybrid*. London: Routledge, 2016. Print.

Loshitzky, Y. *Screening Strangers*. Bloomington: Indiana University Press, 2010. Print.

Piketty, T. *Capital in the Twenty-first Century*. London: The Belknap Press of Harvard University Press, 2014. Print.

Section A

Filming South Asian Diaspora: Critical Essays in the New Millennium

1

Gender and Nation in the South Asian Diaspora

Transnational Cultural Spaces in Bollywood Cinema

SANJENA SATHIAN

Modern Hindi popular cinema has undergone distinctive shifts as India increasingly finds its place in a globalized world. Mass migrations and economic integration in the global economy produce a confused cultural space in cinema; now Bollywood filmmakers must cater not only to audiences in Mumbai and Delhi but also to Indians scattered across the diaspora, from Singapore to Australia, from the United Kingdom to the United States. The result is a creation of a new genre within Bollywood: the diasporic film, which includes films catering to a non-resident Indian or 'NRI' audience. But a category of Bollywood cinema is rapidly emerging which goes beyond merely creating a story that those in the diaspora can relate to: films which use the diaspora for more than mere spectacle. These films are set in the diaspora and portray the lives of Indians living abroad, creating a new, dynamic cultural space in which the South Asian diaspora is ascribed specific characteristics. These characteristics are problematized, however, by their source: the diaspora is imagined through a uniquely Indian lens.

This paper will explore the representation of the diasporic woman figure in Bollywood films, following the progression of the representation of women in five films made between 1995 and 2009. Using a combination of theories of gender traditionally applied to the analysis of Bollywood cinema as well as sociological and anthropological arguments about the creation of 'cultures of imagination' in a globalized world, I will argue that Bollywood has moved from an anti-colonial interpretation of morality and sexuality to a postcolonial acceptance of the diaspora as a new cultural sphere, which thereby allows women in Bollywood to move marginally away from representing explicitly patriarchal values.[1] The readings of these films are not specifically feminist but simply attempt to approach criticism of the films' representations from an unattached standpoint, so as to avoid the pitfalls of putting too much emphasis on a single-perspective ideology. I will investigate these portrayals in a chronological order, attempting to understand whether Bollywood cinema has developed enough in the past 14 years to allow for a diasporic woman to exist as a cosmopolitan figure similar to her male NRI counterpart.

Before delving into a filmic analysis, however, it is imperative to understand the context through which these films should be understood. Popular cinema is an element of mass media that is particularly insidious in creating culture between the homeland and the diaspora; these 'texts-in-motion' are some of the most volatile sites in a battle waged between the traditionalism of the homeland and the modernity of the West.[2] Too many issues are involved in this fight to fully understand Bollywood's representations of the diaspora, but gender can be seen as emblematic of the problem at large. The woman in Bollywood cinema is a projected space onto which the anxieties of the masculine NRI, lost in modernity, aims to rediscover tradition.

The first major Bollywood film involving an NRI figure was *Purab Aur Paschim* (1970), which portrayed the NRI as morally depraved and in need of a 'Mother India' to reinstate him with his Hindustani values.[3] This was the pattern of depiction that most older films involving NRI characters followed: the NRI was either the Indian who had travelled West and grown rich, but sought the values and love of the homeland, or the NRI who had disowned the homeland and become depraved by Western society.[4] Distinct changes in the functioning of the global economy have changed the East/West dichotomy since the production of these films, however. Beginning in the early 1990s, India saw the beginnings of the effects of economic globalization, the results of liberalization that began in the 1970s.[5] The NRI figure, who re-emerged in Indian cultural narratives in the 1990s, therefore became much more complex.

This new NRI is an identity undergoing a constant process of re-negotiation, and much of this renegotiation occurs within the filmic space.[6] Physical place and space are important in constructing identity, but in the absence of a state to propagate an identity across a physical space, the cultural element of the state, the 'nation' must de-couple from the state; the political alone can no longer unite a scattered nation.[7] Instead, 'cultural spheres' of ethnicity become the foundation for identity and the texts through which we can examine ethnography.[8] In true Deleuzian fashion, the reality of identity becomes changeable, and the site for this constant mutation is the media of diaspora.[9] The identities created within Bollywood are merely constructions of diaspora, however, and the Spivakian subaltern, in this case the female NRI, has no space to speak within Bollywood's frameworks of anti-colonialism.[10]

This is similarly the case within the actuality of the diaspora: such cultural spaces encounter enormous troubles in attempting to maintain ideals of tradition and the feminine. Scholar of modernity Arjun Appadurai notes this:

> Because both work and leisure have lost none of their gendered qualities in this new global order but have acquired ever subtler fetishized representations, the honor of women becomes increasingly a surrogate for the embattled communities of males, while their women in reality have to negotiate increasingly harsh conditions of work ... deterritorialized communities ... may enjoy the fruits of ... capital and technology, (but) have to play out the desires and fantasies of these new ethnoscapes, while striving to reproduce the family as microcosm of culture.[11]

This argument notes a constant tension between ideals of femininity and the reality of a constantly modernizing woman; such a discursive tension epitomizes the conflict between

Bollywood's representations of female figures and the actuality of modern South Asian women.

However, before invoking Appadurai in his entirety, I must respond to his overarching argument that diasporas are cultural spaces in which transnationalism can arise. This argument may be too simplistic to account for the interactions between Bollywood and the diaspora. Jigna Desai's interpretation of cultural globalization is more focused on the politics of the Indian nation and therefore a preferable framework for understanding Bollywood.[12] He argues that critiques and studies of postcolonial nations are characterized by a tension between creating identity through anti-colonial or post-colonial lenses; Desai defends a postcolonial critique as preferable because it allows for a deconstruction of colonial Eurocentric logic, and abandons the 'binary logic ... of elite nationalisms'.[13] Such a simplistic logic is visible in Bollywood's early construction of the diaspora, and this anti-colonialism prevents the Indian diaspora from truly engaging or creating new cultural spaces. In particular, anti-colonial conceptions of gender prevent women from becoming effective citizens of such new cultural spaces.

The anti-colonial Indian identity that Bollywood exports ensures that certain patriarchal or traditional gender constructs are perpetuated.[14] South Asian diasporic identity is constructed based not on tangible elements of shared histories but rather on essentialist conceptions of 'some shared South Asianness ... based on an Orientalist and anti-colonial nationalist formulation of Indian or South Asian difference'.[15] This essentialism manifests itself in an over-fetishization by Bollywood of certain things deemed 'Indian' or characteristic of 'Indian-ness' – these include notions of tradition, of the value of the physicality of the nation-state (which, for the case of South Asian identity, must remain hyphenated until true transnational cultural spaces can be formed), and familial loyalty. Each of these elements of supposed 'Indian culture' projects itself onto gender in a distinct way, and in the context of Bollywood films, shackles South Asian diasporic females to such notions. This paper aims to determine whether cinematic representations of the female NRI figure have allowed Bollywood to evolve into a transnational cultural space, by reaching a post-national, postcolonial discourse, or rather if they simply re-inscribe notions of an essentialist and simultaneously patriarchal Indian society.

A Brief Discussion: Constructions of the Feminine in Hindi Cinema

Before attempting to deconstruct representations of the female NRI in the diaspora, it is necessary to outline basic characteristics of Bollywood's historical representation of women. Shoma Chatterji identifies four characteristics of what she considers to be the central characteristics of the traditional cinematic woman.[16] First and most importantly comes the value of female chastity; secondly, if the woman suffers, it must serve a metaphorical purpose to create a resultant new reality; third, her sons must fight for her, and in the absence of sons, characters who play surrogate sons must fight for her; lastly, a fight for justice usually translates to a defense of her honour and chastity.[17] Mythological conceptions of a woman also inform Bollywood's representation of 'ideal woman' figures; these conceptions extend to interpretations of not only benign figures like Sita, Ram's obedient and docile wife, but also the powerful (Kali; Shakti). These two extremes in Hindu notions of femininity create an uncomfortable dichotomy for women: since women are either passive or excessively powerful, meaning they have to either be worshiped or tamed.[18]

Stuart Hall's ideas about conceptions of cultural identity through film are important to this understanding of the feminine as well: he argues that identity is the product of multiple representations, each of which are formed by unique contexts, and that these cultural identities can be thought of in two distinct ways: first, that there is 'one true self' residing as a common spirit among all members of the same ethnicity, and second, that cultural identity is not a question of 'are' but rather of 'becoming'.[19] The latter mode of understanding cultural identity negates essentialist theories of identity, and is the conception Appadurai demands from participants in a transnational cultural space; however, Bollywood's inherent essentialism, particularly in the context of not only South Asian identity but especially South Asian *female* identity, has traditionally placed it in the first camp.

Such an essentialist interpretation of South Asian femininity imagines the ideal woman adorned in a *sari*, her forehead dotted with a red *bindi* and hair pulled back in a plait – beautiful but sexually constrained.[20] This repressed sexuality is the crux on which constructions of women in Indian cinema operate. Violation of the woman's chastity is a violation of her honour – which implicates the male in control of her, her husband or father, rather than the woman herself.[21]

Such repressions of sexuality mirror real-life suppressions of aspects of many women's experiences in the diaspora. It is important to compare the reality of these women's lives to their filmic counterparts; because the subaltern is given no place to speak in Bollywood cinema, the true voice of the diasporic woman must, and has come, from external sources.[22] Some scholars have noted that providing a voice to women in cinema can rupture the dominant narrative of patriarchy.[23] But it must be understood that the voice Bollywood gives to the diasporic women does *not* do this; this voice is instead a construction of so-called 'essential' Indian identity.

The true female NRI creates her own ideas of womanhood through 'private spaces' and ultimately abandons the nation-state's definition of Indian femininity.[24] Prema Kurien notes in the results of a sociology study of migrated Indian graduate students that the modern diasporic woman (if she has chosen to migrate on her own, without a male counterpart) in reality is often quite transgressive and hails from a more progressive family.[25] However, Bollywood's traditional representation of women relies on depictions of diasporic women in marriages, as opposed to such independent NRI women. Marriage in Indian culture is traditionally disempowering for the women, particularly in the case of arranged marriages.[26] For most Indian women it means leaving home to serve a new family – but with the advent of migration it goes even further to imply migrating across continents for a new husband in hope of a new life.[27] Brides 'imported' from India are brought abroad in hopes that they can serve as vessels for the transportation of Indian values.

Therefore, in reality, we see two diasporic women: one who travels independently and is therefore fiercely non-conformist, and the other who travels to follow and is subordinate to her husband. Bollywood traditionally prefers to represent the latter as the desirable diasporic woman, but in more recent films has allowed the first type to play the protagonist, perhaps indicating a slow acceptance of female autonomy in the diaspora.

Essentialism in the 1990s: The (Re)-Birth of the Diasporic Film in *DDLJ* and *Pardes*

Dilwale Dulhania Le Jayenge (1995) is, perhaps, the foundational text for modern diasporic films. The film is a clear departure from original monolithic classifications of the NRI as either longing for the homeland or morally depraved: Shahrukh Khan as Raj represents an NRI figure who has, to a degree, negotiated the straddle of being both Indian and English. Raj has adopted some 'immoral' Western traits – which we first see when he tricks Amrish Puri's character Baldev, the main character's father and a migrant from India to London, into selling him beer; he flirts with Simran (Kajol), Baldev's daughter, and flaunts his sexual exploits to his friends. But Raj reasserts his Indian-ness to the audience in a scene when a drunk Simran falls asleep in his bed and awakens wearing his clothes. Terrified, she asks what happened the night before. Raj reminds her that he is *Hindustani* and understands the value of an Indian girl's honour.

Raj assures Simran, and more importantly an audience concerned about the translation of values across oceans, that he remains morally 'Indian', and in doing so, immediately changes the story from an innocent love story to a love story infused with the traditional values of the homeland. In doing so, Raj inscribes what Patricia Uberoi calls the 'tyranny of tradition' into the story.[28] Though he was fully in control of Simran's body the night before, he benevolently spared her – solely because he understands what an *Indian* girl's *honour* means. These are the two central elements of womanhood as defined by Bollywood – the nation and feminine sexuality – and Raj, in recognizing their inviolability, reinforces Bollywood's essentialist interpretation of the woman. He protects Simran, yes, but by protecting Simran's sexual purity, he robs her of the ability to protect herself.[29]

Two scenes in the film between Simran and her mother further illustrate the re-inscription of patriarchy in the film. The first occurs once Simran is engaged to an Indian man whom she has never met. The match is arranged by her father and she blithely accepts the practice, even defending it to a baffled Raj. In order to take her trip to Europe (where she and Raj meet) with friends after graduation, she prepares her home with elements of the homeland, dresses in Indian garb, and asks her father for permission to take this month-long trip so she can have one month of 'her own life' between being a daughter and becoming a wife to this unknown man. But in Europe, Simran meets Raj and falls in love – and despite this, Simran returns home to continue with the preparations for the wedding, though she cannot rid herself of the memory of her love. Raj, who loves her as well, accompanies her to India where she is to be married, but refuses to elope with her. Simran's mother tells her to give up on the hope of being with Raj:

> When I was a little girl, my grandfather used to tell me that there is no difference between a man and a woman. Both have the same rights. But once I grew up, I understood that it was not the case. My education was stopped … . I sacrificed my life; first as a daughter and then as a daughter-in-law. But when you were born I took a vow that you would never have to make the same sacrifices as I did. I wanted you to live your own life … . Women are born to make sacrifices for men, but not the other way round. I beg you, give up your happiness and forget him (the boy). Your father will never allow it.

This is one of the only places in the film when we are permitted to hear the voice of a woman; but though she speaks up against tradition, she silences herself and begs Simran to re-submit herself to the order of patriarchy. Some scholars argue that this scene suggests a transgression of traditional lines of morality in Bollywood, but its transgression is barely noticeable.[30] The woman barely has time to speak against patriarchy before she immediately re-submits not only herself but also her daughter to its authority.

In a second scene, Simran's mother changes her mind and grants permission for Raj to take her daughter away, hoping to give her daughter the kind of freedom she never had. Raj is humbled by her gesture but pointedly ignores it, holding out for

Simran's father, Baldev, to provide his blessing. Again, *DDLJ* reinforces the patriarchal authority of the Indian diasporic family. Though women in *DDLJ* are allowed a voice with which to criticize patriarchal power structures, they are robbed of their agency – in giving up their dreams they acquiesce to a system within which they have no other options.[31]

Raj, on the other hand, can be seen simply as self-sacrificing, and not as the victim of tradition, because as a male he holds the rein to that system of traditions. In making his choice to respect tradition he is a hero-figure, the NRI who has not only found prosperity in the diaspora but has maintained the essence of India within him abroad. Simran, in contrast, is continually defined as a character only in relation to the men to whom she 'belongs' – in London, despite having grown up abroad, she and her sister speak perfect, unaccented Hindi, and are thoroughly Indian down to their very body language.[32] She knows well enough to turn off the British pop music and replace it with Indian songs when her father enters the home, and even remains faithful to her arranged engagement when defending it to Raj. And yet – Simran is the one who desires to elope with Raj, indicating that a woman's sexual impulses, when let free, have the ability to run wild if not checked by a male counterpart; this demonstrates a severe lack of autonomy for her character as she is pulled between father and husband-to-be with little to no space for her own life.

The NRI, central in negotiating the unidentified cultural space spanning the diaspora and India, is defined in terms of two distinct gender roles: the male NRI is wealthy, an archetypal knight in shining armour, and most importantly, he protects female sexuality from the moral gropings of the Western world – his female counterpart is simply chaste and often lacking personality.[33] Though Simran's sexuality is not eliminated – instead, it is veritably flaunted in scenes where she dons a short skirt and dances sexually in the rain – it is acceptable only because it exists beneath the authority of men.

Most critics have treated *DDLJ* as a film somewhat radical for its time, arguing that it treated the diaspora not as a place of total moral depravation where the Indian spirit goes to die, but as a potentially new cultural space in which Indian values can be transported and negotiated by a willing NRI.[34] However, this negotiation is only possible for the male NRI – not only does *DDLJ* disallow a space for the female NRI to negotiate this new cultural space, but in fact indicates that the *only* reason the male NRI can exist as this cosmopolitan figure is because of the suppression of the woman and the overt 'protection' of her sexual purity.[35] Robina Mohammad argues this with dexterity:

> Bollywood reinforces the notion that Indian men's cultural authenticity remains predicated on their ability to control their women ... . Baldev's control is central to his mission to keep Hindustan alive in London, which has depended on and is manifested in his ability to control his daughters. At the core of Raj's Indian values lies the notion that Indian women remain the property of men, demonstrated by his insistence that irrespective of Simran's own desires he will accept her only if and when her father places her hand in his.[36]

On a metaphorical level, this need for female chastity in the diaspora speaks to the metaphor of woman as a site for the valorization of the Indian nation – a concept that dates back cinematically to the iconic *Mother India* (1957). Threats to the Indian woman are threats to the nation itself; Indian womanhood represents the 'nation, religion, God, the Spirit of India, culture, tradition, family'.[37] The essence of India must remain alive away from the homeland, and the male NRI is the soldier protecting it. This interpretation of Indian femininity can be seen clearest in *Pardes* (1997), a film made two years after *DDLJ* and starring two of the same actors: Amrish Puri as the father and Shahrukh Khan as the good male NRI figure.

Pardes, meaning 'foreign land', lacks whatever subtlety *DDLJ* managed to include in its narrative. The film hearkens back to the 1970s era portrayal of the diaspora in some ways, wherein its central conflict is between the nation and the West.[38] The cultural space negotiated by *DDLJ* for the male NRI to easily exist economically and physically in the West but morally in the East is strained and threatened. The storyline revolves around Kishorilal (Amrish Puri), an immigrant Indian who has made a fortune in the States but whose heart yearns for India. His yearning is painfully obvious and drilled into the viewer's mind in an early set of conversations where he lauds the beauty of India, down to her very soil, and in the song sequence 'I Love My India', in which he declaims, 'I saw London, I saw Paris, I saw Japan ... there isn't another India in the whole world'.

As in *DDLJ*, the site for negotiating the interaction between East and West is through male-female relationships. Kishorilal asks for the hand of his Indian friend's daughter, Ganga, on behalf of his NRI son, Rajiv. 'We NRIs need girls like her very badly', he says, 'we've pushed our kids so deeply in English books and manners that somewhere or the other even after seeing so much success we feel as if we're failures'. This comment swiftly negates the economic value of travelling out of India to find one's fortune and instead berates the NRI for abandoning the moral centre of the nation. Kishorilal is hardly an NRI – simply a businessman away from his country – so the true male NRI narrative occurs through Rajiv and his foster brother Arjun (Shahrukh Khan).

Pardes represents a clearly patriarchal logic – Ganga is given away in arranged marriage to a man she does not love, who sexually assaults her before they are married, and is 'saved' by the man who genuinely loves her, Arjun. Like in *DDLJ*, the possibility that Ganga and Arjun had an affair behind Kishorilal's back implicates Kishorilal more than Ganga herself.[39] Ganga's character is undeniably an allegorical one, representative of the purity and holiness of the nation – represented by her name, which she shares with the holy and pure Indian river Ganges. When Rajiv takes Ganga to a Vegas hotel room and attempts to have sex with her before marriage, this potential violation of her purity threatens the purity of the nation. As in *Mother India*, in order for the woman to be the nation, she must be explicitly de-sexualized; the woman can only be represented as a metaphorical and allegorical figure, as the nation in *Pardes* or as representative of the ideals of Indian femininity in *DDLJ*.[40] Ganga is even described as India herself in the film: 'you wished to nestle an Indian girl; India itself – in America?'

According to Mankekar, the narratives of 'essentialist conceptions of nation and Indian culture converge with discourses of gender and female sexuality'.[41] The implication for such allegorical representations of the diasporic woman as a holding space for the nation abroad is that diasporic Bollywood is still haunted by both essentialist notions of Indian 'culture'.[42] Bollywood, then, remains trapped within a discourse of anti-colonial nationalism, even its diasporic representations, and this anti-colonialism is inherently limited by the specter of the colonial.[43]

But within a diegetic space so wedded to nationalism, is there a space for transnationalism? More fundamentally, is there space for the creation of new imagined cultural spaces, for the political entity of the state to de-hyphenate from the cultural entity of the nation?[44] In the case of India, some scholars have found that internationalism manifests itself not in intermingling or integration of cultural spaces but rather in a re-entrenchment of nationalism through seeking distinct recognition of the state on an international scale.[45] If this re-entrenchment of nationalism is truly occurring, it gives rise to another question: is there space for a female figure to escape the bounds of nationalist allegory and to become a cosmopolitan figure herself?

The male NRI figure is genuinely Indian – Raj in *DDLJ* is the epitome of the mantra 'phir bi dil hai Hindustani',[46] and Arjun in *Pardes* is essentially Indian in values (preserving Ganga's chastity until he can truly call her 'his') and actions (composing the 'I Love My India' song). But, significantly, these characters are also *wealthy*. They have joined the West in one of the most noteworthy ways: through the elimination of Hindu hierarchy (the caste system) and its replacement with socioeconomic rankings (where they comfortably reside in the upper-middle class). At the end of the 1990s, with *DDLJ* and *Pardes* in perspective, neither Bollywood's male nor female NRI had negotiated the expanded world of cultural globalization – both, in the imagination of Bollywood, remained beholden to anti-colonial representations. The distinction, however, is that the male NRI was evolving to become a transitionally cosmopolitan figure while the female NRI figure maintained her purely allegorical persona, as the nation, as ideal woman, and as the vessel through which India could remain with the male NRI as he embraced the diaspora.

The New Millennium Rung In: *K3G* Approaches Cultural Cosmopolitanism

Four years after *Pardes*, Karan Johar's film *Kabhi Khushi Khabie Gam* (2001) – popularly referred to as *K3G* – brought prominence to the translation of the family drama genre into the diaspora. *K3G*, as it was nicknamed, marks a turning point in diasporic film because its storyline is not entirely dependent on the use of the diaspora – rather, the world outside India seems a natural continuation of the lives of the rich, cosmopolitan Raichand family. This new cosmopolitanism makes way for two new female figures to appear on screen. While the characters of Simran in *DDLJ* and Ganga in *Pardes* both lack autonomy, the two central female characters in *K3G*'s diaspora have distinctive personalities. Importantly, however, this change does not divorce either Anjali (Kajol) or Pooja (Kareena Kapoor) from the realm of patriarchy. Though some argue that *K3G* is a change from *Pardes* and *DDLJ*, its shift is limited, as it ultimately re-entrenches the same values of the 1990s films.[47]

Rahul Raichand (Shahrukh Khan), the adopted son of Yash Raichand (Amitabh Bhachchan), falls in love with Anjali, a girl from the less-than-wealthy Delhi district of Chandni Chowk. Furious that Rahul could transgress his carefully drawn class lines, Yash refuses to give his blessing to the couple. The home, a sacred space in Hindi cinema and in Indian society, is broken, as Rahul and Anjali take their leave. The scene in which the two leave is particularly melodramatic – Yash's wife Nandini (Jaya Bachchan) is left staring longingly after her son while Anjali hysterically begs for Rahul not to leave until Yash gives his blessing.

Rohan (Hrithik Roshan), Rahul's much younger brother, is unaware of this family drama until he finishes boarding school. Upon discovering the schism, Rohan convinces his father to let him go to England under the guise of attaining an MBA. Rohan's arrival in England lacks the intensity of the female NRI's arrival in the diaspora as seen in *Pardes*; Ganga watches the sights and sounds of New York City unfold around her, noticeably brighter, louder, and busier than the fields of Punjab she has grown up in. She seems overwhelmed, above all – but there is no trace of such emotion in Rohan as he arrives. 'Vande Mataram' plays as the camera pans shots of London, first focusing on tourist attractions like the Eye and Big Ben and then on the sheer wealth of the city by showing shots of designer stores. In the middle of London, Bharatanatyam dancers appear behind Rohan as he smiles jauntily, and he dances in front of White women wearing the green and orange hues of the Indian flag. The message here is not entirely subtle: Rohan is the 'super-Indian' who is genuinely Indian but can easily find his way through the diaspora.[48]

The two diasporic female NRIs are introduced when Rohan finds his way to Rahul's house by revealing himself to Anjali's younger sister, Pooja. Rahul's English home is enormous, sleek, and clearly lacking the true essence of a home: the elders. In the absence of parental blessings, Rahul and Anjali have placed on their wall an enormous photo of Yash and Nandini, who smile benevolently on the younger generation's unfulfilled life abroad.

The home space, however, is carefully tended to by our first female NRI figure: Anjali, or the faithful wife, whose only purpose is to *be* India in England. Anjali only wears saris and even shoots nasty words at their White English neighbour in Hindi right in front of her face; she bemoans the 'English' nature of the son she and Rahul have raised in England. In one particular scene, Krishna, their son, is due to sing a British song at a concert put on by his school but instead bursts into the Indian national anthem. As Anjali weeps with joy at seeing her son in his Indian skin, the British parents rise and put their hands on their hearts in recognition of the Indian nation. The scene contains all the absurdities common to family melodramas in Bollywood but is further complicated by the convergence of nation and woman. Though Anjali is colourful and spunky in ways that neither Simran nor Ganga are allowed to be, she remains simply a vessel for the nation in the diaspora.

Ashish Rajadhyaksha's arguments about the exportation of 'Indian nationalism, now commodified and globalized into a 'feel good' version of 'our culture' and Aswin Punathambekar's revisions of the argument to account for a 'transitive logic' of 'complex interactions between a) the diaspora, b) Bollywood, and c) India' are both valid theories in an analysis of *K3G*.[49] To some degree, Kajol is representative of Indian nationalism as Rajadhyaksha says, but Punathambekar's arguments account for the increasingly transnational and multicultural nature of cultural spaces, which contribute to 'diasporic public spheres' as new cultural spaces in themselves.[50] *K3G* is not simply an example of transporting 'Indian culture' to the diaspora; the interaction is subtler – the film uses Indian national sentiment not for explicitly political reasons, but rather for moral and familial reasons.[51] Anjali is concerned with providing her son with Indian 'values' and translating the cultural *spaces* of the nation to the diaspora, not translating 'culture' itself.[52] This distinction is not liberating to the female NRI, however; *K3G*'s use of Anjali as a vessel for Indian cultural elements still hampers her to anti-colonial interpretations of the feminine and the nation.

Though Anjali's sexuality is not explicitly implicated in the same way Simran's and Ganga's are, her sister Pooja's entire character is dependent on sexuality. The first time we are introduced to an adult Pooja we see her dancing in skintight, revealing clothes to the song 'It's Rainin' Men'. She is perpetually the butt of jokes and of Rahul's disdain on account of her risqué clothing, and we see that she leads boys on and manipulates her sexuality. This is a new diasporic female protagonist – but her sexuality is soon disciplined. The cosmopolitan male easily imposes tradition, pushes out the modern and saves Pooja's sexuality. When Pooja falls for Rohan, he immediately begins pulling her towards his cultural space, having her sing 'Om Jai Jagdish' in the morning prayer with him and encouraging her to dress in a more modest salwar-kameez; she additionally fasts for him on the Karva Chauth festival. Pooja, like Simran, is simply tugged between cultural spaces, unable to command them both the way the male NRI can. While certainly Pooja enjoys more autonomy and is not treated as a singular possession the way Simran and Ganga are, she is still not afforded the humanity to exist in multiple cultural spaces.

K3G is the logical continuation of *DDLJ*'s suggestion that Indian values can find a home in the diaspora; while *DDLJ* implies this through Raj's character (and *Pardes* negates it), *K3G* outlines what exactly must be done for this translation to comfortably occur. This is the major shift between *DDLJ* and *Pardes* in *K3G*: we begin to see some acceptance by Bollywood that globalization is not merely economic. *K3G* includes at least an acknowledgement by Bollywood of the female NRI's *desire* to be cosmopolitan – she is given some agency, and indeed, some personality in the characters of Anjali and Pooja; ultimately, in reiterating the traditional values of familial relations, Johar simply reinforces patriarchy in a manner that is perhaps more insidious than previously. *K3G* allows the female NRI to not only go to the diaspora but also to test her lifestyle limits within it – and then reinstates her into her 'rightful' place in the family, grounding this in tradition.

K3G lies somewhere between an anti-colonial and a postcolonial text: though it still recognizes elements of inherent 'Indian-ness' and translates them to the diaspora, two major changes occur here. First, though this 'culture' is essentialist and projects itself onto female sexuality, the act of projecting it into a diasporic space inherently makes the film more transnational. *DDLJ* fixes the East and West with specific characteristics and, though it suggests the possibility of a conciliatory existence of the two through Raj, it indicates that Simran has to lose herself in order for such a reconciliation to occur. *K3G*, on the other hand, allows Pooja to adopt some elements of Western society – though her sexuality is ultimately re-subjugated to the same notion of 'culture' as Simran, the fact she is afforded some integration of East and West at all is a change from the essentialism of *DDLJ* and *Pardes*. Whereas *DDLJ* and *Pardes* demanded that broken families return to India to become truly whole once more, *K3G* brings the homeland to the diaspora, allowing the Raichands to unite in England.[53] *K3G* does not yet reach postcolonialism – such a narrative is only recognizable through its liberation of femininity, since female sexuality is the object onto which anti-colonial discourse is projected.

Transnational Spaces in Perspective in *Salaam Namaste*, *Love Aaj Kal*

In the past decade, the number of Bollywood films set in the diaspora is increasing. The setting of these films is not coincidental; though more recent diasporic films do not often make use of the diaspora to explicitly contrast East and West, such contrasts subtly persist and are still indispensable parts of any diasporic film. In addition, the diaspora has become the site for untouchable issues in India to find a narrative voice – extra-marital affairs, pre-marital sex, casual dating, drinking, and homosexuality. Though in recent Bollywood films even set in India (such as *Fashion* (2008) and *Wake Up Sid!* (2009)), independent female characters are becoming more prevalent, these female characters are more significant when placed in the diaspora, because it means making a concession that the very vessel of the nation abroad has come to espouse different values than those 'essential' Indian ones.

In order to interpret these films through the same lens as those discussed earlier, it is important to note the representation of three central elements: the presence of the substantive 'culture' of the nation in influencing characters' actions and the values of the film, the presence and importance of 'cultural' elements of the nation, and the portrayal of female sexuality as the subject onto which both 'culture' and 'cultural' characteristics are explicated.

In many modern films, especially *Salaam Namaste* (2005) and *Love Aaj Kal* (2009), sexuality manifests itself in the development of a more equal male-female relationship as opposed to within the hierarchy of a patriarchal system.[54] In these two films, which follow a popular Western genre of romantic comedies, the female NRI figure at last achieves autonomy from the nation as an oppressive force; these films are postcolonial by nature because they ignore the existence of a colonial past – even of the motherland in some instances – and therefore the woman is no longer the subject of essentialist interpretations of the nation or cultural elements. This is not to say that these films are female-empowering, nor do they reject patriarchal norms altogether: that would be inaccurate and a sweeping argument to make – however, they do help sculpt Appadurai's new cultural space, in which the diaspora can exist for its own sake, with this cinema as a site for negotiation of the diaspora's own problems.

Salaam Namaste and *Love Aaj Kal* share elements of multiculturalism and recognize transnationalism. In place of an ideology of overt Indian nationalism we see a multicultural logic beginning to take hold, through an endorsement of an entirely separate diasporic cultural space. However, this cultural space is not fully transnational in that it exists as an 'Indian bubble' within the diaspora. In *Salaam Namaste*, Ambar (Preity Zinta) works her way through medical school by DJ-ing on a radio programme called 'Salaam Namaste', where she speaks only in Hindi to a presumably Indian audience in Australia. She speaks to her romantic counterpart Nikhil Arora (Saif Ali Khan) – who goes by 'Nick' in an attempt to westernize himself – in Hindi, even yelling at him about how he should identify more with his Indian culture. Despite the fact that the film operates almost entirely in Hindi, ignoring the English that would presumably be spoken all around this Hindi bubble, Nick and Ambar are allowed to move in and out of the bubble, almost picking and choosing what aspects of the West and of the East they would like in their lives. They have White friends (around whom they often still speak Hindi, inexplicably) – but most importantly, they are explicitly progressive characters.

Despite remaining culturally Indian, Nick and Ambar make moral choices that are distinctly Western, but the film does not operate as a source of discipline, and the consequences are substantially less dire than they would be in the homeland. Ambar is alone in Australia, having left her family (and been subsequently disowned by them) for refusing to marry. Without the institution of the family ready to contain the female sexually and morally, Ambar is able to act more freely. She and Nick move in together and have pre-marital sex, a rarity even for modern Bollywood, but when Ambar becomes pregnant, Nick breaks up with her. But because they are still living together, they continue encountering one another and eventually come together just in time for the baby. The institution of family concludes the film, but not through the logic of the nation-state: because *Salaam Namaste* is allowed to exist in a multicultural space, and more importantly, because Ambar is a character, and not an allegory, because she breaks with traditional institutions that contain female sexuality within the bounds of national morality, she is a freer character than her historical counterparts.

In *Salaam Namaste*, elements of the homeland are still transported to the diaspora, and these are reminiscent of aforementioned private spaces, the spheres used by diasporic Indians to form their own communities abroad.[55] These spaces are not transnational; they are distinctly reminiscent of the nation, however, they have achieved the de-coupling of the nation-state. Through these constructions, Bollywood recognizes both a logic of postcolonialism and elements of cultural globalization because, though the new diasporic spheres of Indians are not fully integrated with the rest of society, they are cultural spaces that exist in fluidity, truly as 'cultural' rather than 'culture', and simply as a recognition of love for the homeland rather than the imposition of morality by the homeland.

In *Love Aaj Kal* (significantly translating to 'Love These Days'), Jai (Saif Ali Khan) and Meera (Deepika Padukone) live a modern life together in London; their relationship is portrayed as casual and they easily break up when they decide the time has simply come for it to end. Like *Salaam Namaste*, the characters are placed in a multicultural setting where the Hindi bubble can continue to exist (Jai and Meera come together by flirting in Hindi in an ostensibly English nightclub), but their 'Indian-ness' is not essentialized. Instead, it is restricted to cultural elements of their everyday life choices – namely, speaking in Hindi to each other. Though the two break up, they continue talking to each other and remain, we assume, in love, as they move all around the world. Finally, risking Meera's engagement to another man and Jai's relationship with a Swiss girl, they come together – but in order to do so, Meera must break an engagement and violate the rules of the familial and marriage institution. The ease with which she leaves her fiancé represents an enormous change from what Simran and Ganga saw in the 1990s – but, like *Salaam Namaste*, the film must conclude with Indian cultural elements tying it together: they come together only and finally on Indian soil. All the while that Jai and Meera's story is being told, Khan plays a double-role as a young Punjabi man, Veer Singh, decades earlier, fighting for his love, a girl named Harleen, against her family and a rival fiancé. The contrast is clear: in the past, men and women had to win the right to be together, reaching across long distances and dealing with moral and social codes, but today, Jai and Meera have only their own stubbornness and the troubles of modern communication in a too-big world to blame for their problems.

The film is not judgmental about Jai and Meera's modern lifestyles. Still, the double storyline reminds the audience that some cultural elements of India should be transported to the diaspora to be integrated into modern life. *Love Aaj Kal* recognizes Meera's independence to live a free lifestyle, just as Jai does, but still ends the relationship on Indian soil. This is not a logic of nationalism nor does it represent the tyranny of tradition; though Jai and Meera give up their free lifestyle for the sake of being together, they do so based on mutual personal choice. The two travel the world and enjoy their own lives before coming together – the fact that it occurs on Indian soil does not necessarily link the nation with the state but rather implies that the nation in essence – though fragmented – can survive globalization. The traditional story of Veer Singh is a backdrop to the trials and tribulations of modern love, but its terminal purpose is ultimately to compare love across the ages, and to show its essence is the same, not to extract morality from the traditional and impose it onto a transnational modern space.

Conclusion

Bollywood's construction of the diaspora has evolved since its original conceptions of a strict dichotomy between East and West. Originally, anti-colonial notions of nationality projected themselves onto the female figures in these films and prevented the diasporic films from being true texts of transnationalism. However, as Bollywood has evolved in modern times, newer films have treated the diaspora as an acceptable space – and traditional notions of morality and sexuality attached to anti-colonial nationalism has been abandoned in these spaces. More recent texts have achieved a degree of postcolonial transnationalism. This is not to say that these texts are integrative or accept the intermingling between India and the diaspora itself – only the existence of Indians in the diaspora. The move away from endorsement of particularly patriarchal values does not mean Bollywood is free from the shadow of a male-dominated society; however, the films continue to objectify women's bodies as sex objects, and often only deal with the female subject through the lens of a relationship rather than as an independent subject. This paper does not attempt to deal with the gaze of the audience, only the morality within the diegetic space of the film. Nor can we assume that, because women have enjoyed more sexual freedom in newer Bollywood films, the diasporic woman's voice is now adequately heard or represented here. These constructions are still from the perspective of the 'East' and include distinct elements of love for the nation, if not overt nationalism. The subaltern has not yet found her voice in the space of Hindi popular cinema – but the growing transnational nature of these films has created awareness and grudging acceptance within Bollywood that a separate cultural space exists, in which elements of India can be integrated with elements of the West in a conciliatory, rather than combative fashion.

Notes

1. Based on Arjun Appadurai's thesis of cultural globalization as outlined in *Modernity at Large*, 1996, and off various responses to this thesis.
2. Appadurai, Arjun. *Modernity at Large: Cultural Dimensions of Globalization* (Minneapolis: University of Minnesota Press, 1996), 9.
3. Brosius, Christian and Yazgi, Nicolas. 'Is there no place like home?: Contesting cinematographic constructions of Indian diasporic experiences'. *Contributions to Indian Sociology* 41 (2007): 353.
4. Desai, Jigna. 'Bollywood Abroad: South Asian Diasporic Cosmopolitanism and Indian Cinema'. In *New Cosmopolitanisms*, edited by Gita Rajan and Shailja Sharma (Stanford: Stanford University Press, 2006), 24.
5. Oza, Rupal. 'Showcasing India: Gender, Geography, and Globalization'. *Signs* 26 (2006): 1071.
6. Mishra, Vijay. *Bollywood Cinema: Temples of Desire*. (New York: Routledge, 2002), 238.
7. Bhattacharjee, Anannya. 'The Habit of Ex-nomination: Nation, Woman, and the Indian Immigrant Bourgeoisie'. *Public Culture* 5 (1992): 34–35.
8. Appadurai, *Modernity at Large*, 54.
9. Karim, Karim Haiderali. *The Media of Diaspora*. (London: Routledge, 2003), 9.

10. Spivak, Gayatri. 'Can the Subaltern Speak?' *Marxism and the Interpretation of Culture*. Ed. Cary Nelson and Lawrence Grossberg. (Champaign: University of Illinois, 1988), 275.
11. Appadurai, *Modernity at Large*, 45.
12. Appadurai, *Modernity at Large*; Desai, *Beyond Bollywood*.
13. Desai, Jigna. Beyond Bollywood: The Cultural Politics of South Asian Diasporic Film. (New York: Routledge, 2004), 10.
14. This paper is not large enough in scope to delve into differences between post-colonialist and anti-colonialist discourses. I will rely on Desai's assertions that post-colonialism is a social condition and intellectual movement seeking to critique anti-colonialist notions of nationalism; while anti-colonialism re-engages the specter of the colonial, post-colonialism seeks to create a fully new identity. Desai, *Beyond Bollywood*, 10.
15. Desai, *Beyond Bollywood*, 19.
16. Roots can be traced to goddesses or goddess-like women: ex. Sita in the Ramayana.
17. Chatterji, Shoma. Subject: *Cinema, Object: Woman – A Study of the Portrayal of Women in Indian Cinema*. (Calcutta: Parumita, 1998), 29–30.
18. Rayaprol, Aparna. *Negotiating Identities: Women in the Indian Diaspora*. (Delhi: Oxford University, 1997), 123–125.
19. Harindranath, Ramaswami. *Perspectives on Global Cultures*. (New York: Open University Press, 2006), 44–45.
20. Chatterji, *Subject: Cinema, Object: Woman*, 65.
21. Chatterji, *Subject: Cinema, Object: Woman*, 136.
22. This paper does not attempt to provide an exhaustive understanding of these other sources, but film examples include Deepa Mehta's *Fire*, Mira Nair's *Mississippi Masala* and Gurinder Chadha's *Bend it Like Beckham* and *Bhaji on the Beach*.
23. Datta, Sangeeta. 'Globalization and Representations of Women in Indian Cinema'. *Social Scientist* 28 (2000): 71–82.
24. Bhattacharjee, 'The Habit of Ex-Nomination', 38–40; Lessinger, Johanna. 'Indian Immigrants in the United States: the emergence of a transnational population'. In *Culture and Economy in the Indian Diaspora*, edited by Bhikhu Parekh. (London: Routledge, 2003).
25. Prema Kurien's argument is based off of a small sociological study with a sample size of only 30 people, many of whom are graduate students, so this should not be taken as a sweeping generalization. Kurien, Prema. 'Gendered ethnicity: creating a Hindu Indian identity in the United States'. *The American Behavioral Scientist*. 42 (1999): 648–673.

26. Palriwala, Rajni and Patricia Uberoi. 'Marriage and Migration in Asia: Gender Issues'. *Indian Journal of Gender Studies* 12 (2005): vi-ix.
27. Palriwala and Uberoi, 'Marriage and Migration in Asia', ix.
28. Uberoi, Patricia. 'The Diaspora Comes Home: Disciplining Desire in DDLJ'. *Contributions to Indian Sociology* 32 (1998): 322.
29. Mankekar, Purnima. 'Brides who Travel: Gender, Transnationalism, and Nationalism in Hindi Film' *Positions* 7 (1999): 739.
30. Uberoi, 'The diaspora comes home', 324.
31. Uberoi, 'The diaspora comes home', 325.
32. Mishra, *Bollywood Cinema*, 251.
33. Mankekar, 'Brides who travel', 750–51; 754.
34. Mankekar, 'Brides who Travel', 742; Mohammad, 1033; Rajan and Sharma, 'New Cosmopolitanisms', 129; Uberoi, 'The Diaspora Comes Home', 326.
35. Mankekar, 'Brides who Travel', 749; Sharpe, Jenny. 'Gender, Nation and Globalization in Monsoon Wedding and Dilwale Dulhania Le Jayenge'. *Meridians* 6 (2006): 66; Uberoi, 'The Diaspora Comes Home', 322, 332.
36. Mohammad, Robina. '*Phir Bhi Dil Hai Hindustani* (Yet the Heart remains Indian): Bollywood, the 'Homeland' Nation-State, and the Diaspora'. *Environment and Planning D* 25 (2007): 1035.
37. Bhattacharjee, 'The Habit of Ex-Nomination', 31.
38. Uberoi, 'The Diaspora Comes Home', 326.
39. Uberoi, 'The Diaspora Comes Home', 320.
40. Chatterji, *Subject: Cinema, Object: Woman,* 36–37; Oza, 'Showcasing India', 1081.
41. Mankekar, 'Brides who Travel', 739
42. Appadurai, *Modernity at Large*, 12–15. I use the noun 'culture' in quotes here in reference to Arjun Appadurai's notion of 'cultural' in the adjectival form as preferable (Appadurai 1996). He argues that the noun 'culture' implies an essentialist substance of culture whereas 'cultural' denotes a more changeable element, more appropriate to the new imagined spaces created by globalization.
43. Desai, *Beyond Bollywood*, 11
44. Appadurai, *Modernity at Large,* 39. These questions are emblematic of Appadurai's central struggle between primordial identity and modernity, outlined in Appadurai, 139–40.
45. Oza, 'Showcasing India', 1076.
46. 'His heart is still Indian'.

47. The scholarship I refer to here is that of Aswin Punathambekar, who calls *K3G* 'the co-existence of tradition and modernity'. Punathambekar, Aswin. 'Bollywood in the Indian-American Diaspora: Mediating a Transitive Logic of Culture Citizenship'. *International Journal of Cultural Studies.* 8 (2005): 151–173.
48. Punathambekar, 'Bollywood in the Indian-American Diaspora', 162.
49. Punathambekar, 'Bollywood in the Indian-American Diaspora', 164.
50. Appadurai, *Modernity at Large*, 147.
51. Brosius and Yazgi, 'Is There No Place like Home?' 373.
52. Again, I refer to Appadurai's distinction of 'culture' as essentialist and 'cultural' as moveable. While *Pardes* and *DDLJ* treat India within essentialist framings; Indian 'culture' *is* a certain way but in *K3G*, a new space becomes available for trans-cultural flows to create their own diasporic public sphere.
53. Punathambekar elaborates this concept as a movement of homelands as well: *DDLJ* and *Pardes* are the diaspora seeking the homeland, while *K3G* is the homeland seeking the diaspora. Punathambekar, 'Bollywood in the Indian-American diaspora', 162.
54. These two films were chosen because of their particular awareness of their diasporic nature – five other films from the period between 2003 and 2009 were studied in writing this paper and all of them displayed subtler versions of the same trends observed in these two films.
55. Bhattacharjee, 'The Habit of Ex-Nomination', 38–40; Lessinger, 'Indian Immigrants', 170.

Works Cited

Appadurai, Arjun. *Modernity at Large: Cultural Dimensions of Globalization*. Minneapolis: University of Minnesota Press, 1996. Print.

Bhattacharjee, Anannya. 'The Habit of Ex-Nomination: Nation, Woman, and the Indian Immigrant Bourgeoisie'. *Public Culture,* 5 (1992): 19–44. Print.

Brosius, Christian and Nicolas Yazgi. 'Is There No Place like Home?: Contesting Cinematographic Constructions of Indian Diasporic Experiences'. *Contributions to Indian Sociology* 41 (2007): 353–384. Print.

Chatterji, Shoma. *Subject: Cinema, Object: Woman – A Study of the Portrayal of Women in Indian Cinema*. Calcutta: Parumita, 1998. Print.

Datta, Sangeeta. 'Globalization and Representations of Women in Indian Cinema'. *Social Scientist* 28 (2000): 71–82. Print.

Desai, Jigna. *Beyond Bollywood: The Cultural Politics of South Asian Diasporic Film*. New York: Routledge, 2004. Print.

——. 'Bollywood Abroad: South Asian Diasporic Cosmopolitanism and Indian Cinema'. *New Cosmopolitanisms*. Eds. Gita Rajan and Shailja Sharma. Stanford: Stanford University Press, 2006. 115–137. Print.

Harindranath, Ramaswami. *Perspectives on Global Cultures*. New York: Open University Press, 2006. Print.

Karim, Karim Haiderali. *The Media of Diaspora*. London and New York: Routledge, 2003. Print.

Kurien, Prema. 'Gendered Ethnicity: Creating a Hindu Indian Identity in the United States'. *The American Behavioral Scientist*, 42 (1999): 648–673. Print.

Lessinger, Johanna. 'Indian Immigrants in the United States: The Emergence of a Transnational Population'. *Culture and Economy in the Indian Diaspora*. Ed. Bhikhu Parekh. London: Routledge, 2003. Print.

Mankekar, Purnima. 'Brides who Travel: Gender, Transnationalism, and Nationalism in Hindi Film'. *Positions*, 7 (1999): 731–762. Print.

Mishra, Vijay. *Bollywood Cinema: Temples of Desire*. New York: Routledge, 2002. Print.

Mohammad, Robina. 'Phir Bhi Dil Hai Hindustani (Yet the heart remains Indian): Bollywood, the 'homeland' nation-state, and the diaspora'. *Environment and Planning D: Society and Space* 25 (2007): 1015–1040. Prnt.

Oza, Rupal. 'Showcasing India: Gender, Geography, and Globalization'. *Signs*, 26 (2006): 1076–95. Print.

Palriwala, Rajni and Patricia Uberoi. 'Marriage and Migration in Asia: Gender Issues'. *Indian Journal of Gender Studies*, 12 (2005): v-xxix. Print.

Punathambekar, Aswin. 'Bollywood in the Indian-American Diaspora: Mediating a Transitive Logic of Culture Citizenship'. *International Journal of Cultural Studies*. 8 (2005): 151–173. Print.

Rayaprol, Aparna. *Negotiating Identities: Women in the Indian Diaspora*. Delhi: Oxford University, 1997. 123–125. Print.

Sharpe, Jenny. 'Gender, Nation and Globalization in Monsoon Wedding and Dilwale Dulhania Le Jayenge'. *Meridians*, 6 (2006): 58–81. Print.

Spivak, Gayatri. 'Can the Subaltern Speak?' *Marxism and the Interpretation of Culture*. Eds. Cary Nelson and Lawrence Grossberg. Champaign: University of Illinois, 1988. 271–313. Print.

Uberoi, Patricia. 'The diaspora comes home: Discriplining Desire in DDLJ'. *Contributions to Indian Sociology* 32 (1998): 305–36. Print.

2

Desi Films

Articulating Images of South Asian Identity in a Global Communication Environment

REKHA SHARMA

As scholars examine cultural exchange via processes such as acculturation, assimilation, and isolation, immigrants' communication systems and preferred content types will be important areas of concentration. That is, while the trend toward globalization has allowed people to travel and communicate more easily, it has also resulted in a multiplicity of homelands. Individuals who trace their heritage to a specific region or nation increasingly have had to negotiate a sense of belonging and cultural tenure that takes into account the locations of their ethnic backgrounds as well as their daily lives. The idea of cultural hybridity addresses the dialectical tension of negotiating an identity based on living in or between two cultures (Berghahn, 2006). Immigrants create hybrid identities that reflect individual identity as well as macro-level commonalities that arise from straddling the values and norms of Eastern and Western societies. Therefore, their self-selected representations in media indicate their need to participate in social discourse and make their voices heard in a global dialogue. Some researchers have investigated immigrants' use of media from their homeland to maintain cultural ties (Hur and Jeffres, 1980; Lee, 2004) or from the land in which they have settled to learn about their new environment (Lee and Tse, 1994; Reece and Palmgreen, 2000; Viswanath and Arora, 2000). But scholars are only beginning to understand the ways second- and third-generation immigrants negotiate a permanent interstitial existence.

Although generations of immigrants around the world have had to balance cultural values and manage their representation in media, people of Indian ethnic origin exemplify such issues within a larger rubric of globalization. In the past decade, non-resident Indians (NRIs) have drawn the attention of businesses and political candidates due to their economic clout, social contributions, and visibility in communities in the United States, Canada, the United Kingdom, and elsewhere (Luce, 2007). As a minority group, NRIs have helped to create a sense of 'Indianness' outside of India.

The children of those immigrants who elected to make their homes outside of South Asia are referred to as *'desis'*, an abbreviation of the Hindi word *'pardesi'*, meaning 'foreigner'. The term illustrates one of the many labels created to discuss hybridized identity. In a global context, the term 'South Asian' differentiates people from the Indian subcontinent from Native American groups as well as unifies people sharing similar practices, beliefs, religions, or languages. Geographically, South Asia includes the countries of India, Pakistan, Bangladesh, Bhutan, the Maldives, Nepal, Sri Lanka, and Tibet (Desai, 2004). However, the convenience of the South Asian label belies the diversity of people from these regions.

Although India itself has been a source of information about Indian identity for Western audiences, a specialized genre of *desi* media has garnered more recognition in recent years. Cinema has been instrumental to the development of a shared South Asian identity and to the communication of *desis'* particular cultural issues to the larger world (Desai, 2004). *Desi* films – movies created by, about, and primarily for South Asian immigrants – are capable of reaching large numbers of people regardless of their education, economic status, or linguistic proficiency. Most are produced in English and are accessible in theatres, video rental stores, libraries, or via the Internet.

This paper examines Indian diasporic films as a vehicle for cultural articulation and debate. These *desi* films most clearly exemplify resistance to hegemonic messages conveyed by Indian and Western media sources, as they carve out a unique niche of expression that refers and challenges notions of what it means to be Indian in a global context. Under this lens, this exploration of desi films addresses such broad questions as 'who determines the images of 'Indianness' outside of India, especially in a global communication environment?' as well as 'how are Indians being portrayed in this global media environment, and how do those images differ from earlier media portrayals in Indian and Western media?'

To better understand the themes of cultural hybridity in *desi* films, it is also important to understand cultural identity as it is depicted in media of home and host cultures. Thus, this paper begins with a theoretical foundation of hegemonic discourse and resistance with regard to cultural notions of ethnicity and immigrants' new articulations of identity in interstitial zones. Second, this paper will provide background regarding sources of hegemony from media in the Indian subcontinent and from Western countries. Third, it will explore the creation of a hybrid or hyphenated identity as reflected in Indian diasporic films, pointing out some of the themes and conventions of this emerging genre. For ease of analysis, the films in this sample relate to people of Indian heritage specifically. Consequently, the term 'Indian' will be used unless a more specific term is warranted for accuracy. As this is only an exploration of the topic, the analysis is limited to a small sample of Indian diasporic movies from the years 2001 to 2007 produced in the US, UK, and Canada. This analysis does not contrast the differences across US, UK, and Canadian *desi* films, mainly because the audience for the *desi* films discussed here spanned all three countries, and all of the films were accessible there. Instead, this analysis deals primarily with broader East-West distinctions regarding cultural identity issues discussed in the films.

An Overview of Media Hegemony

Scholars have acknowledged that 'globalization' is a widely used but vaguely defined term (Edwards, 2007; Hoover and Stokes, 2003; Yue, 2003). Stohl (2005) explained that contemporary globalization theories address the worldwide increase in economic interdependence as well as the rapid communication of ideas, values, and materials due to new technologies. Moreover, globalization impacts the creation of new identities that challenge existing classifications and roles (Stohl, 2005). Appadurai (1990) noted dimensions of global flow that are especially pertinent here. He referred to 'ethnoscapes' to describe shifting patterns of migration among groups of people such as immigrants, refugees, and guest workers (7). He also explained that:

> Mediascapes ... tend to be image-centered, narrative-based accounts of strips of reality, and what they offer to those who experience and transform them is a series of elements (such as characters, plots, and textual forms) out of which scripts can be formed of imagined lives, their own as well as those of others living in other places. (9)

Cultural production processes are a subset of globalization research. In contrast to other historical agents of globalization such as imperialism and colonialism, the idea of hegemony is useful for framing a discussion of less unidirectional transfers of people, ideas, and information across national boundaries. Although cultures may be impacted by military occupation, government dictatorship, or corporate expansionism, hegemony captures more subtle aspects of cultural exchange. Hegemony is not a matter of overt domination of the masses from a large authoritarian force, but a continuous struggle to win support for the rule of a dominant class of 'organized intellectuals' (Storey, 2006: 50).

One of the seminal theorists of hegemony, Gramsci (1973), described the State not as a political society that controls people through coercion, but as a balance between political and civil society. According to Gramsci (1973), the hegemony of one social group over an entire nation would be exercised through private institutions such as schools, trade unions, or the Church. He also argued that the intellectual strata of administrators, scientists, scholars, philosophers, and other individuals whose professions centre on 'intellectual elaboration' would serve as functionaries of the State (Gramsci, 1971: 9). The idea of hegemony rests on the notion of consensus, wherein subordinate classes appear to support the cultural and political meanings as well as the values, ideals, and objectives of the prevailing social group. Thereby they are incorporated into the group's power structures (Storey, 2006).

Extending these ideas of cultural acquiescence, Carragee (1993) described media hegemony as a framework for examining mass media and power, highlighting the relationship of media messages to sociopolitical change. Altheide (1984) summarized a Gramscian explanation of media hegemony as referring to 'the dominance of a certain way of life and thought and to the way in which that dominant concept of reality is diffused throughout the public as well as private dimensions of social life' (477).

Hegemonic Discourse from the East and the West

Edwards (2007) noted that despite the proliferation of new communication venues such as blogs and Internet chatrooms, it is important to study more traditional forms of communication such as cinema as well: 'When "older" media are chosen by artists as means of expression, we may see a cultural shift in a variety of ways, both thematically and stylistically, as well as the changed environment within which such traditional media now operate' (291). Films contextualize globalization and provide a window to view images and experience emotion in meaningful ways; viewers in a home country can watch films to learn about life abroad, and immigrants in other countries can look back at the heritage they wish to preserve (Kao and Rozario, 2008; Srinivas, 2005).

Films have been studied as mediated forms of diasporic discourse across many cultures. For example, literature exists on films about Caribbean migration to London (Guha, 2009), depictions of Italian and Jewish diaspora communities (Marx and Cohen, 2010), and the work of émigré directors of Algerian (Higbee, 2007) and Martinican descent (Demissie, 2008). Scholars have addressed feelings of alienation and loneliness among Italian immigrants in Australia (Rando, 2007) and of Australasian immigrants' disenchantment with life in the diaspora (Smaill, 2008), as well as comedic, melodramatic, and documentary treatments of female immigrants in Spain (Ballesteros, 2005). Contrasting themes of assimilation in immigrant films or of separation in exilic films, Klein (2004) differentiated diasporic discourse in film as that which highlights accommodation processes required to negotiate communities and identities between the home and host lands.

Bollywood Heroes and Heroines

To the more pertinent discussion of cinematic portrayals of Indian culture, Bollywood has become synonymous with the Indian film industry for audiences around the world. In actuality, the Indian film industry contains a great deal of linguistic variation, with five major centres of regional film production reflecting eight primary languages (Chapman, 2003). India has produced an average of 700 commercial films annually (Chapman, 2003; Dasgupta, 1996), and completed five times more full-length feature films than Hollywood in 1990 (Chapman, 2003). The 'Bollywood' nickname given to Hindi commercial films is indicative of the industry's centre in Mumbai, formerly known as Bombay. The popular Bollywood formula combines family-drama, romance, action, song, and dance (Dasgupta, 1996). At their most basic level, Bollywood movies could be characterized as morality plays pitting good against evil (Gokulsing and Dissanayake, 2004). For Indians living in India as well as NRIs living in diaspora communities, the conflict is often perceived as one between traditional Indian values and Western values (Deprez, 2009).

Bollywood films about the diaspora often express immigrants' desire to return to or maintain an affiliation with their home country, often manifesting fear of losing cultural values or nostalgia for a remembered past or mythologized heritage (Deprez, 2009; Kaur, 2002). Nevertheless, Bollywood movies depict the life of NRIs with glamorized images of consumerism that coincide with free market reforms in India and the promise of prosperity through globalization (Kaur, 2002; Srinivas, 2005). In these films, NRIs are portrayed as wealthy urbanites who 'use English phrases, cell phones and computers, celebrate Valentine's Day and frequent exercise clubs and shopping malls' (Srinivas, 2005: 321).

The issue of gender provides an example of some of the hegemonic messages regarding Indian identity in Bollywood movies. Males and females in Bollywood fall into expected patterns of behaviour based on their status as heroes or heroines. Frequently, these characterizations are based on Hindu religious archetypes. Although a more complete analysis of Bollywood cinema is beyond the scope of this paper, it is important to note that portrayals of Indian men and women that do not align with the traditional Hindu archetypes are often seen as negative and even threatening to the social stability of the country. The 'bad' woman in Bollywood films often equates to individualism, hedonism, and duplicity, concepts often conveyed symbolically by an association with Western decadence: smoking, drinking, dancing in night clubs, and promiscuity (Gokulsing and Dissanayake, 2004). Feminist critiques of Bollywood movies have illuminated many such stereotypes, but less research has been done on the cinematic standards for male characters.

Representations of India in the West

For decades, the majority of cinematic depictions of India in the movies of the US and Great Britain were told from Christian, Caucasian, and colonialist perspectives. Many such movies conveyed outright racism via stereotypes of Indian culture as exotic and dangerous (Muraleedharan, 1996). The undercurrent of these films centred on imperialist narratives of passivity and power. Vann (2002) argued that colonialism and racism could not be separated, and that in colonialist films, the colonized land is a 'passive receptacle that the energy of the colonizer must fill', just as the colonized person is a mere entity meant to be moulded by the colonizer (188). The resurgence of British colonialist films about India in the 1980s marked a sort of nostalgia for colonial power borne of uncertainty in a modern England of rising poverty rates and other social instabilities (Eliason, 1984).

Aside from racist and otherwise negative constructions of Indian identity in Western cinema, Indians were simply not represented for many years in films and television of the US, Canada, and the UK. Mastro and Robinson (2000) called this a nonrecognition phase in which a minority group is rendered invisible, usually until it is recognized through ridicule. Similarly, Durham (2001) discussed the returned gaze, a dramaturgical concept that allows the object being portrayed to resist hegemonic discourse by forcing observers to examine themselves through their interaction with the media message. Essentially, in viewing the South Asian depiction, the Western audience would become the object of the returned gaze as they became aware of the act of observing in the context of the image being portrayed. Being aware that one has observed the object in the media message allows one to confront beliefs about the portrayal. Yet without significant depictions of South Asian characters or concerns in Western media for so many years, Indians in the US, Canada, and the UK had no ability to return the gaze to the audience, and hence, no way to counter hegemonic influences.

Resistance and Creation of a New Hybrid Identity

While new immigrant groups may establish a community with its own identity, successive generations must maintain a symbolic ethnicity (Rex, 1996). By the 1990s, the diversification of Western societies due to global movements of people, the widespread accessibility of communication tools, and the availability of funding allowed filmmakers from minority groups to begin constructing mediated images and asserting their own identities (Smith, 1996). Desi films have represented Indian immigrants' creation of a hybridized ethnic identity in a medium that has the potential to reach audiences around the world. Indian diasporic filmmakers have articulated narratives of their experiences, struggles, choices, and values that reflect their existences in interstitial cultural zones. In so doing, they have given South Asian immigrants of several generations a chance to counter the hegemonic media messages of their home countries and their host countries.

Overcoming Stereotypes

Diasporic films draw upon and challenge normative limitations of Indian culture as well as the oversimplifications and stereotypes of Indians in Western media messages. Dasgupta (1996) described the bulk of Hindi commercial films as reinforcing attitudes that 'good' Indian women are submissive and self-sacrificing while 'bad' women are individualistic and sexually aggressive, despite feminist filmmakers' efforts at resisting patriarchal characterizations. In the media of the US, Canada, and the UK, South Asian people have been discussed according to particular stereotypes or ignored altogether (Durham, 2001). For example, in a study of US magazine advertising, Paek and Shah (2003) found evidence supporting a 'model minority' stereotype of Asians as successful workaholics. However, they also noted that Asian-Indians – another term used to differentiate NRIs from the American Indians indigenous to North America – were relatively invisible. Since the terrorist attacks of 11 September 2001, many Americans have come to associate South Asian immigrants with negative stereotypes of Middle Eastern and Muslim people (Mitra, 2005).

Because immigrants have the experience of being exposed to the cultural values of their home and host countries, they are uniquely positioned to process particular hegemonic media messages actively rather than passively consume them. Immigrants are forced to interpret media messages more consciously simply because they must evaluate which ones to accept or reject as expressions of their own interstitial existence. In effect, immigrants create an entirely new culture that references cultural norms of their home and host countries and filters them through a lens of global awareness and direct experience.

Media Use Motives and Patterns

Immigrants use media to accomplish a wide range of culture-production and cultural maintenance functions. Media-used motives are often a function of an immigrant's length of stay in the host country. Therefore, they differ widely depending on whether an individual is trying to cope with cultural change for a short time or establish a new sense of self and home. Reece and Palmgreen (2000) studied the cultural adjustment of sojourners, specifically Indians temporarily residing in the United States. The researchers examined need for acculturation among Indian graduate students, comparing respondents' media use in India and in the US. Surveillance emerged as a highly important motive for television viewing in both environments, but in the US, respondents mainly watched national news. The researchers accounted for this pattern by noting the usefulness of understanding US politics and current events in the cross-cultural adaptation process. Knowing more about the US allowed Indian sojourners to understand their new environment and make comparisons with their homeland.

To better understand the linkages between media use and the adaptation process of second-generation immigrants in diaspora communities, however, Durham (2004) conducted in-depth interviews with focus groups of South Asian, adolescent girls. The author found that a common complaint of the daughters of South Asian immigrants had to do with their inability to take part in coming-of-age rituals in American society. Parents were fearful of allowing their daughters to participate in social events such as attending the high school prom because of sensationalized media portrayals of Western dating and sexual practices. Although second-generation females did not believe mass media messages accurately reflected life in the US, their NRI parents formed perceptions of social reality based on observations of sexuality and decadence in Western media sources. As a result, they tried to instill traditionally Indian values in their daughters to dissuade them from adopting certain aspects of Western culture.

In addition to studies of the use of media from the host country, communication researchers have also studied immigrants' motives for seeking ethnic media from their home countries. Much of this research hinges on the idea of cultural maintenance. Lee (2004) found that first-generation Korean immigrants believed satellite TV was useful for cultural maintenance because it offered immediate and convenient exposure to both news and entertainment. Shi (2005) argued that individuals often used ethnic media strategically to obtain culture-specific knowledge, perhaps to appear authoritative or to secure inclusion in a particular group. Even the isolation of some members of diaspora communities may not indicate a rejection of the host culture, so much as a need to preserve a sense of cultural distinctiveness and plurality.

The consumption of media from immigrants' home countries could also ground displaced people. This is especially true for sojourners, who need to clarify their identity in new environments, sometimes without knowing whether their host country will become a permanent place of residence. Sampedro (1998) interviewed international students who read newspapers affiliated with their countries of origin. Students said these newspapers helped them preserve ties to their friends, family, and culture by informing them of events and issues their loved ones would read about at home.

Immigrants as 'Global Citizens'

Globalization has required immigrants to take on multiple labels of self-identification. Their identities span discrete categorizations of ethnic origin and place of residence, instead reflecting lives that bridge the intellectually convenient boundaries of nation, race, and religion and defy the simplistic indicators of mother tongue or style of dress. The *desi* Indian in diasporic cinema is just one example of the immigrant taking on the mantle of the global citizen. For second- and third-generation immigrants, the boundaries between home and host culture blur significantly. This is due to having been brought up in a culture that is considered one's home while trying to retain aspects of one's ethnic heritage. As a result, each person's cultural experience is a unique amalgam of choices, experiences, and values. So *desis* have had to establish a sense of commonality and community. Sampedro (1998) noted that immigrants' ontological insecurity stimulated them to engage in cognitive and affective rituals, such as seeking certain kinds of media. This is because the development of a shared cultural narrative requires engagement of the individual on emotional and intellectual levels.

Desi films have the potential to cultivate such a narrative, combining the idiosyncrasies of individual cultural adjustments with larger themes about immigration and cultural production processes. South Asian diaspora filmmakers have illustrated these issues not only for immigrants and their children who are negotiating hybrid ethnic identities, but also for viewers in the world at large:

> Unlike the work of their western predecessors, their films give priority to class, race, and gender issues, concentrating on the

> gritty realism of daily existence and focusing on the position of marginalized outsiders, the urban underclass of the western metropolis, much of which is made up by people of color, prodominantly from the former colonies of Britain in Asia and Africa. But the new historical project does not occur in a vacuum. It works in combination with a new ethnic assertiveness, arising out of feelings of injustice at being denied access, or worse, being misrepresented in the public sphere. (Rajgopal, 2003: 51)

Thus, diasporic cinema has become a forum for exchanging ideas about globalization on large and small levels, as well as an important catalyst for dialogue about issues that separate some groups of people and unite others.

Central Themes of *Desi* Films

Indian diasporic filmmakers have often struggled to get funding from major studios in the US, Canada, and the UK because topics of interest to *desis* were not considered mainstream enough to guarantee commercial success (Smith, 1996). With no way to reach a widespread audience, diasporic filmmakers were limited in their ability to resist hegemonic discourse regarding the notion of 'Indianness' in a global environment. Consequently, many of the most popular *desi* films were produced independently, marketed largely through word-of-mouth publicity, and circulated in limited release. Nevertheless, *desi* films have been gaining more attention from media conglomerates and more exposure to audiences beyond Indian diaspora communities.

The political, economic, and social dimensions of globalization have formed the basis of cinematic discourse in the Indian diaspora. Desai (2006) noted that postcolonial migration in general and residence in the US after the 11 September attacks in particular have created contradictory positions of power for South Asian minority groups. Thus, the author explained, South Asian filmmakers have tended to examine a need for belonging due to geographic displacement. Additionally, characters in Indian diasporic films have been crafted to highlight the tensions of cosmopolitanism (Desai, 2006).

Contrast Between East and West

Chief among these tensions is the sheer contrast between the everyday lives of people from Eastern and Western cultures. Many *desi* films address this issue to show that globalization is not only a term used for macro-level trends among societies but also a phenomenon that affects people in minute yet profound ways. For example, the movie *American Desi* (Katdare and Pandya, 2001) opened with a montage of images and sounds meant to contrast the lifestyle of American-born Kris (short for 'Krishna') Reddy from that of his Indian immigrant parents. As Kris, wearing a baseball jersey, prepares to leave for college, the audience sees the American flag and hears his rock 'n' roll music in his bedroom. Kris speaks in English to his Caucasian friend, using the slang and casual profanity typical in media depictions of American teens. Meanwhile, his sandal-clad father prepares *chai* in the traditional way Indians make their tea. His mother, wearing a *sari*, speaks to him in Hindi and asks him to participate in a Hindu religious ceremony before he leaves the house.

The contrasts between Eastern and Western culture depicted through differences in food, clothing, music, social customs, and religion underscore the cultural adaptation processes Indian immigrants and their children must negotiate in their daily lives. Diasporic filmmakers have also highlighted this concept by showing *desi* characters interacting with people from the dominant Western culture of the host country. In *The Namesake* (2007), director Mira Nair not only used climate, choices of first names, and music to show cultural contrast, but also showed the main character Gogol (also known as Nikhil) being introduced to a Caucasian woman at a dinner party. Although it is only their first meeting, she immediately asks him about how old he was when he emigrated. In *American Chai* (MacCrae and Mehta, 2001), Indian-American college student Sureel flashes back to his childhood, when children on the playground asked him questions such as 'are you Jewish or Christian?' and 'what tribe are you from?' These encounters not only reflect experiences many Indians living in diaspora communities have faced, but also the challenges they have dealt with in articulating their ethnic identity to themselves and to people originally from the host culture.

Director Gurinder Chadha expounded on this theme of contrast in *Bend it Like Beckham* (2002) not only by illustrating differences between Indian and British cultures, but by showing commonalities as well. As the main character, Jess (short for 'Jesminder') pursues her dream of playing professional soccer, she must deal with the cultural expectations of femininity. However, just as her Indian parents prefer that their daughter cook well rather than kick well, the other girls on the team must deal with stereotypes about women who play sports. According to the film, athletic females in general have had to handle taunts about their style of dress, their interests, their ability, and even their sexuality. Jess also encounters racism when a rival player mutters a negative epithet at her during a match. In explaining this to her coach, he responds by telling her that as a person of Irish heritage, he has too encountered racism.

This message is particularly important as globalization forces diverse groups of people together. Although it is important to address ethnic differences between groups, it is also vital that people relate to each other as individuals with a shared sense of humanity. From a media standpoint, messages about commonality make it easier for audiences to relate to the narratives in *desi* films, thereby increasing their commercial appeal. Yet this also empowers Indian diasporic filmmakers to resist hegemonic discourse and carve out a hybrid identity for people who live in the interstitial zones between East and West. It also brings to light the accuracy of media depictions of Indians living abroad and opens the door for dialogues about immigration, acculturation, and other issues related to globalization.

Multiplicity and Range of Identities

In creating a hybrid identity for Indians living in diaspora communities, the makers of *desi* movies have had to challenge the stereotypical portrayals of Indians in Western societies. One way to do this has been to present a range of *desi* identities that represent a spectrum of balances between Eastern and Western cultures. According to Chacko (2010), 'No single identity can sufficiently articulate the concept of self as each individual occupies multiple subject positions or identities simultaneously' (84).

In *American Desi* (2001), Kris confronts his own feelings about his Indian heritage when he begins to date a *desi* girl who embraces her Indian culture and interacts with other Indians even though she has grown up in the US. To further exemplify the diversity of the *desi* experience, each of the Kris' Indian roommates are shown to be coming from different Indian states and are of different religions, yet behave in stereotypical ways. Jagjit is a Punjabi Sikh, easily identifiable by his beard and turban. He embodies the enthusiasm and awkwardness of the 'FOB', or 'fresh off the boat' Indian who has recently come to the US. Similarly, Salim is an Indian Muslim obsessed with a Bollywood actress and anxious to avoid *desi* girls, whom he believes to have been corrupted by their time in the United States. Finally, A.J., whose name is actually Ajay, is an American-born *desi* of Gujarati descent who dresses and talks in ways that align more with the African-American hip-hop subculture.

All of these stereotypes are explained or addressed later in the film. Jagjit wants to pursue a career as an artist rather than as an engineer, as his parents have desired. As a recent immigrant, he encounters the same pressures and expectations that second-generation Indians entrenched in American life have faced. Salim becomes enamoured with a Muslim girl who was raised in the US. She informs him that she is not corrupt, and that she has maintained her religious beliefs, her respect for her parents, and even her ability to cook traditional Indian food. A.J. teaches Kris how to perform a *garba,* a style of dance popular in Gujarat, and explains that he feels that Indians and Africans share a common ancestry since the two continents were once geographically united. Essentially, he argues that culture transcends location.

Director Deepa Mehta also addressed the multiplicity of the *desi* identity in *Bollywood/Hollywood* (2002). In this film, the female lead, Sunita, introduces herself to the male lead, Rahul, as 'Sue' and quotes lines of Spanish poetry as the two dance together in a bar. Rahul concludes that Sunita is a call girl of Spanish descent and proceeds to educate her about Indian customs when he recruits her to pose as his fiancée. Throughout the film, then, Sunita keeps characters and audience members guessing about whether she is a prostitute or an escort and whether she is Latina or Indian-Canadian. When she recognizes Rahul's chauffeur as a well-known drag queen, she promises to keep his secret identity under wraps by telling him, 'I'm kind of partial to multiple identities'. This line of dialogue crystallizes the movie's themes about people taking on an array of personas, labels, and modes of behaviour to adapt to situations and achieve goals. A primary motive for this multiplicity is the need to resist societal boundaries and negotiate between cultural expectations and individual desires for personal fulfillment.

Freedom versus Obligation

The spectrum of *desi* identities and the negotiation of the balance between Eastern and Western cultural values have also been shown in Indian diasporic films as a tension between pursuing one's own objectives and honouring the obligations of one's ancestral culture. As a consequence of this tension, covert rebellion and outright deception have been key plot devices in *desi* films. In many *desi* movies, this kind of resistance takes place when Indian parents demand that their children accept arranged marriages or follow certain career paths.

In *Bollywood/Hollywood* (2002), Rahul hires Sunita to pose as his future wife because his family has rejected his relationship with a New Age pop star and because his mother has threatened to cancel his younger sister's wedding unless he could find a more suitable (Indian) bride. Sunita herself has rebelled against her parents' plans to arrange her marriage to a Punjabi wrestler and the expectation that she will oblige as a docile daughter. In *American Desi* (2001) and *American Chai* (2001), characters hide the fact that they would prefer to establish a career in the arts because professions such as engineering and medicine are more acceptable to their parents.

But a corollary to the theme of rebellion in these Indian diasporic films is optimism about the power of open communication. In *Bend it Like Beckham* (2002), Jess bristles at the idea of keeping her pursuit of a soccer career secret from her parents and eventually reveals her activities to them. Explaining that she was happy when she didn't have to sneak away to practices and lie about her whereabouts, she tells them, 'I really want to play, and if I can't tell you what I want now, then I'll never be happy, whatever I do'. In *American Chai* (2001), Sureel compares his own need for freedom with his father's motive for emigrating to the United States. In both films, the *desi* children are able to resolve the tension with their parents by discussing it openly. Moreover, they gain the blessings of their parents to leave home, travel abroad, and pursue their dreams. Although these resolutions might resolve the conflicts rather simplistically, the filmmakers succeed in showing the value of open dialogue on individual and societal levels. The characters achieve a positive balance between their individual needs and their familial and cultural obligations through direct communication. On a societal level, the filmmakers convey the idea that the way to resolve racial, religious, and ethnic tensions is to confront them on a global stage.

Embracing Globalization

Indian diasporic films also carry the theme that globalization is something to be accepted rather than denied. Again, this idea applies to the attitudes of individual characters as well as to audiences' beliefs about interplay between cultures. The departure of characters in *American Chai* (2001) and *Bend it Like Beckham* (2002) sends the message that global travel and the potential for intercultural communication expand intellectual horizons and provide opportunities for betterment. But other *desi* films convey a similar advocacy of globalization in more subtle ways.

In *Bollywood/Hollywood* (2002), Sunita's alcoholic father sings songs from old Bollywood movies, and Rahul's grandmother sprinkles quotations from Shakespeare into everyday conversations. These parental figures symbolize an adherence to the past and to perhaps antiquated traditions meant to preserve culture. At one point, Rahul tells Sunita that she must exhibit knowledge of Indian customs to his family because they are 'caught in a time warp trying to preserve what (they) can of the home country'. When Sunita's father and Rahul's grandmother have a change of heart at the end of the movie, audiences can also interpret the resolution as a positive message about the diasporic blend of Indian tradition and Western adaptation. The movie conveys that if cultural isolation is about excessive dependence on the past, then cultural adaptation is about negotiation in the present and preparation for the future.

In *The Namesake* (2007), Gogol's father tells him of his own time as a young man, when a fellow passenger on a train told him to travel abroad. When Gogol deals with the changes in his life and the dispersal of his family, he remembers his father's words: 'See the world. You will never regret it, Gogol'. Gogol's mother, Ashima, whose name quite purposefully means 'no boundaries', welcomes an interstitial existence between resuming her classical music training and life in India for six months and returning to the US to be with her children for the remainder of the year. The characters embrace their status as global citizens and are able to find a sense of stability and identity that is not tied to a geographic locus.

Conclusion

Globalization highlights the flows of people and information via processes of immigration, technological development, and access to different media. Viewed this way, globalization opens the possibility for challenges to dominant ways of perceiving people and their cultural beliefs. However, to develop meaningful dialogues about differences and commonalities between groups of people, it is necessary to recognize the diversity of the individuals who make up those groups and avoid the temptation to place them into simplistic categories. In the years ahead, it will be interesting to see whether a pan-Indian or South Asian identity will erase regional differences in global discourse, or whether a hybrid *desi* identity can be established that celebrates common experience while honouring the spectrum of experiences, beliefs, and ideals held by Indians and other cultural minorities living abroad.

This paper was intended to shed light on the messages about cultural articulatiòn and intercultural debate in the films of the Indian diaspora. By referencing and resisting hegemonic messages in Indian and Western media sources, these *desi* films have allowed people who have been geographically displaced due to globalization-related forces and events to develop a new sense of self and community. By reflecting the experience of living in interstitial cultural zones, these films give a voice to marginalized groups and communicate revised notions of 'Indianness' to audiences around the world.

Future research should expound upon the ideas addressed in this exploratory analysis. For instance, researchers could look for more themes common to films of the Indian diaspora by expanding the number of countries involved in the analysis or the range of release dates under consideration. Feminist scholars could look at the possibility of a double standard regarding females in diaspora communities and the amount of rebellion that is considered socially acceptable within the realm of filmic discourse. It would also be intriguing to compare the types of messages about ethnic identity construction and cultural exchange in Bollywood movies and in *desi* films. Researchers could also examine resistance to hegemony in other types of *desi* media. Books, songs, television shows, newspapers, magazines, blogs, and websites provide a wealth of messages to form a basis for studies of news media, popular culture, and politics.

Communication scholars should also employ a variety of perspectives and methodologies. Critical analyses could provide rich detail crucial to uncovering rhetorical strategies and layers of meaning in polysemic texts. At the same time, quantitative studies employing techniques such as content analyses could reveal patterns across genres or media types as well as data about how messages related to diasporic identity or acculturation processes have changed over time.

Communication researchers would do well to devote attention to immigrant communities and the networks of interpersonal and mass communication they have established to preserve, maintain, and shape their identities. Immigrants and their children in diaspora communities are uniquely situated to negotiate identities that span sets of values and avoid the intellectual binaries that separate East and West. Understanding how this happens in subcultures could eventually reveal a wealth of information about how societies may cope more successfully with the uncertainties of globalization in large and small ways.

Ultimately, achieving this level of comprehension could empower people to direct globalization processes rather than merely respond to them.

Works Cited

Altheide, David L. 'Media Hegemony: A Failure of Perspective'. *Public Opinion Quarterly* 48 (1984) 476–490. Print.

Appadurai, Arjun. 'Disjuncture and Difference in the Global Economy'. *Public Culture: Bulletin of the Project for Transnational Cultural Studies* 2 (1990): 1–24. Print.

Ballesteros, Isolina. 'Embracing the Other: The Feminization of Spanish "Immigration Cinema".' *Studies in Hispanic Cinemas* 2. (2005): 2–14. Print.

Berghahn, Daniela. 'No Place like Home? Or Impossible Homecomings in the Films of Fatih Akin'. *New Cinemas: Journal of Contemporary Film* 4 (2006): 141–157. Print.

Carragee, Kevin M. 'A Critical Evaluation of Debates Examining the Media Hegemony Thesis'. *Western Journal of Communication* 57 (1993): 330–348. Print.

Chacko, Mary A. '*Bend it Like Beckham:* Dribbling the Self through a Cross-Cultural Space'. *Multicultural Perspectives* 12 (2010): 81–86. Print.

Chadha, Gurinder. (Producer/Director). *Bend it like Beckham* (Motion picture). United Kingdom: Bend It Films. 2002.

Chapman, James. *Cinemas of the World: Film and Society from 1895 to the Present.* London: Reaktion Books Ltd, 2003. Print.

Dasgupta, Shamita D. 'Feminist Consciousness in Woman-Centered Hindi films'. *Journal of Popular Culture* 30 (1996): 173–189. Print.

Demissie, Fassil. 'Navigating the African Diaspora through Film: Interview with Euzhan Palcy'. *African and Black Diaspora: An International Journal* 1 (2008): 101–110. Print.

Deprez, Camille. 'Comparative Reflections on Hong Kong and Indian cinema: Identity, Diaspora and Cosmopolitanism'. *China Perspectives* 3 (2009): 87–96. Print.

Desai, Jigna. 'Bollywood Abroad: South Asian Diasporic Cosmopolitanism and Indian Cinema'. Eds. Gita Rajan and Shailja Sharma. *New Cosmopolitanisms: South Asians in the US*. Stanford, CA: Stanford University Press, 2006. 115–137. Print.

——. *Beyond Bollywood: The Cultural Politics of South Asian Diasporic Film*. London: Routledge, 2004. Print.

Durham, Meenakshi G. 'Constructing the "New Ethnicities": Media, Sexuality, and Diaspora Identity in the Lives of South Asian Immigrant Girls'. *Critical Studies in Media Communication* 21 (2004): 140–161. Print.

——. 'Displaced Persons: Symbols of South Asian Femininity and the Returned Gaze in U S Media Culture'. *Communication Theory* 11 (2001): 201–217. Print.

Edwards, Brian T. '*Marock* in Morocco: Reading Moroccan Films in the Age of Circulation'. *The Journal of North African Studies* 12 (2007): 287–307. Print.

Eliason, Marcus. 'Debate over Film Portrayals of India'. *Associated Press*. 7 April 1984. Print.

Gramsci, Antonio. *Letters from Prison*. New York: Harper and Row, 1973. Print.

——. *Selections from the Prison Notebooks of Antonio Gramsci*. New York: International Publishers, 1971. Print.

Guha, Malini. "Have You been Told, the Streets of London are Paved with Gold': Rethinking the Motif of the Cinematic Street within a Post-Imperial Context'. *Journal of British Cinema and Television* 6 (2009): 178–189. Print.

Hamilton, David. (Producer) and Deepa Mehta, (Director). *Bollywood/Hollywood* (Motion picture). Canada: Bollywood/Hollywood Productions, 2002.

Higbee, Will. 'Locating the Postcolonial in Transnational Cinema: The Place of Algerian Émigré Directors in Contemporary French Film'. *Modern and Contemporary France* 15 (2007): 51–64. Print.

Hoover, Michael and Lisa O Stokes. 'Hong Kong in New York: Global Connections, National Identity, and Filmic Representations'. *New Political Science* 25. 4 (2003): 509–532. Print.

Hur, K. Kyoon and Leo W. Jeffres. 'Preservation of Ethnicity through Communication'. *Communication* 9 (1980): 175–192. Print.

Katdare, Deep, (Producer) and Piyush D. Pandya (Director). *American Desi* (Motion picture). United States: American Desi Productions, 2001.

Kao, Kai-Ti, and Rebecca-Anne D Rozario. 'Imagined Spaces: The Implications of Song and Dance for Bollywood's Diasporic Communities'. *Continuum: Journal of Media and Cultural Studies* 22. 3 (2008): 313–326. Print.

Kaur, Ravinder. 'Viewing the West through Bollywood: A Celluloid Occident in the Making'. *Contemporary South Asia* 11(2002): 199–209. Print.

Klein, Christina. 'Crouching Tiger, Hidden Dragon: A Diasporic Reading'. *Cinema Journal, 43*, 18–42. Print.

Lee, Changho. 'Korean Immigrants' Viewing Patterns of Korean Satellite Television and its Role in their Lives'. *Asian Journal of Communication* 14 (2004): 68–80. Print.

Lee, Wei-Na., and David K. Tse. 'Changing Media Consumption in a New Home: Acculturation Patterns among Hong Kong Immigrants to Canada'. *Journal of Advertising* 23(1994): 57–70. Print.

Luce, Edward. *In Spite of the Gods: The Strange Rise of Modern India*. New York: Doubleday, 2007. Print.

MacCrae, Taylor. (Producer) and Mehta, Anurag. (Director). (2001). *American Chai* (Motion picture). United States: Fusion Films.

Marx, Lesley, and Robin Cohen. 'Cinematic Representations of Diaspora: Italians and Jews'. *Crossings: Journal of Migration and Culture* 1 (2010): 5–23. Print.

Mastro, Dana E. and Amanda L. Robinson. 'Cops and Crooks: Images of Minorities on Primetime Television'. *Journal of Criminal Studies* 28 (2000): 385–396. Print.

Mitra, Ananda. 'Creating Immigrant Identities in Cybernetic Space: Examples from a Non-Resident Indian website'. *Media, Culture and Society* 27 (2005): 371–390. Print.

Muraleedharan, Tharayil. 'Women/Migrants/Victims in the Male Empire: The Redeployment of Racist and Patriarchal Notions in Raj Cinema'. *Critical Arts Journal* 10 (1996): 91–104. Print.

Paek, Hye Jin and Hemant Shah. 'Racial ideology, model minorities, and the "not-so-silent partner": Stereotyping of Asian Americans in U. S. Magazine Advertising'. *The Howard Journal of Communication* 14 (2003): 225–243. Print.

Pilcher Lydia D. (Producer) and Nair, Mira. (Director). *The Namesake* (Motion picture). United States: Fox Searchlight Pictures. 2007.

Rajgopal, Shoba S. 'The Politics of Location: Ethnic Identity and Cultural Conflict in the Cinema of the South Asian Diaspora'. *Journal of Communication Inquiry* 27 (2003): 49–66. Print.

Rando, Gaetano. 'Liminality, Temporality, and Marginalization in Giorgio Mangiamele's Migrant Movies'. *Studies in Australasian Cinema* 1 (2007): 209–221. Print.

Reece, Debra, and Philip Palmgreen. 'Coming to America: Need for Acculturation and Media Use Motives among Indian Sojourners in the US'. *International Journal of Intercultural Relations* 24 (2000): 807–824. Print.

Rex, John. 'National Identity in the Democratic Multi-Cultural State'. *Sociological Research Online* 1.2.1996. Web. 13 November. 2002. <http://www.socresonline.org.uk/socresonline/1/2/1.html>

Sampedro, Victor. 'Grounding the Displaced: Local Media Reception in a Transnational Context'. *Journal of Communication* 48 (1998): 125–143. Print.

Shi, Yu. 'Identity Construction of the Chinese Diaspora, Ethnic Media Use, Community Formation, and the Possibility of Social Activism'. *Continuum: Journal of Media and Cultural Studies* 19 (2005): 55–72. Print.

Smaill, Belinda. 'Affective authorship: Contemporary Asian Australian documentary'. *Studies in Australasian Cinema* 2 (2008): 157–170. Print.

Smith, Allan. 'Seeing things: Race, image, and national identity in Canadian and American movies and television'. *Canadian Review of American Studies* 26 (1996): 367–391. Print.

Srinivas, Lakshmi. 'Communicating Globalization in Bombay Cinema: Everyday Life, Imagination and the Persistence of the Local'. *Comparative American Studies: An International Journal* 3.3 (2005): 319–344. Print.

Stohl, C. 'Globalization theory'. *Engaging Organizational Communication Theory: Multiple Perspectives*. Eds. S.K. May and D. K. Mumby. Thousand Oaks, CA: Sage, 2005. 223–262. Print.

Storey, John. *Inventing Popular Culture: From Folklore to Globalization*. Melden, MA: Blackwell Publishing, 2006. Print.

Vann, Michael G. 'The Colonial Casbah on the Silver Screen: Using 'Pépé le Moko' and 'The Battle of Algiers' to Teach Colonialism, Race, and Globalization in French History'. *Radical History Review* 83 (2002): 186–192. Print.

Viswanath, K. and Arora, Pamela. 'Ethnic Media in the United States: An Essay on Their Role in Integration, Assimilation, and Social Control'. *Mass Communication and Society* 3(2000): 39–56. Print.

Yue, Ming-Bao. 'There is No Place like Home': Diasporic Identifications and Taiwan Cinema of the 1960s and 1970s'. *Postcolonial Studies* 6. 2. (2003): 207–221. Print..

3

British South Asian Cinema and Identity–I

Nostalgia in the Contemporary British Cinema and the South Asian Diaspora

E. ANNA CLAYDON

This chapter, one of two articles originally published in 2008 and 2009 in *South Asian Cultural Studies*, set out my theories regarding identification in a series of successful British South Asian hybrid films from *East is East* to *Bride and Prejudice*. This chapter centres upon the concept of nostalgia as it is represented in three films which epitomize the way in which contemporary, and hybrid, British cinema has tackled issues of diasporic identities, in these cases, that of the South Asian diaspora. The second article developed these ideas further by discussing the tensions between the aspirations towards American success and specifically Indian familial identities and how these are problematized throughout Gurinder Chadha's British South Asian films. In collecting these two articles together, as twin sequels to my work on *Bhaji on the Beach* in *Picturing South Asian Culture in English* (2003), I want to establish a discourse upon British South Asian films and filmmakers which recognizes the subtleties of representing issues which are for many difficult to articulate and to broach. I also seek to illustrate how the hybridity of contemporary British cinema is not simply a matter of cross-cultural representation or fulfilling the 'ethnic minority' criteria by which the Arts Council seem to solely define 'diversity' in recent times but that it is, like all art, the complex combination of the small details which belong to many homes and which adapt to create another. That, in a sense, contemporary British cinema is inherently driven by diasporic and intertextual sensibilities which persistently allude to something lost, 'homelike', in the past.

Nostalgia in the Post-National

In this article, I shall discuss three comparatively recent films about the experience of the South Asian diaspora in Britain; two of which are set in the 1970s (but in very different communities) – *East is East* (Damien O'Donnell, 1999) and *Anita and Me* (Metin Hűsyein, 2003) – and, the third, contemporarily set, *Bend it Like Beckham* (Gurinder Chadha, 2002). Each of these films explores the diasporic experience quite differently and represents distinct sub-cultural inflections based upon religion, region and period. However, one of the significant factors in these diaspora films is that they are also rooted deeply in the generic and narrative traditions of British cinema. I shall begin by examining the theoretical frameworks behind recent thinking upon diaspora cinema, the post-national and nostalgia and then move on to analyse the films themselves, seeking to answer the following question through linking the narratives to the generic conventions the films adhere to: why are recent British films, and especially those about the South Asian community more rooted in the iconographies and ideologies of the past?

Films which represent the South Asian and other postcolonial diasporas have been little examined as a body for their diasporic properties. Rather, as part of the critical appraisal of the mid-1990s and as a part of the renaissance of new British cinema, they have been analysed, limitedly, in terms of a reshaping of the British national cinema. Which is what John Hill claims still exists, albeit transformed by changes in society:

> (We should not) underestimate the possibilities for a national cinema to re-imagine the nation, or rather nations within Britain, and also to address the specificities of a national culture in a way that does not presume a homogeneous and 'pure' national identity. (Hill, 1997: 252)

However, the very term 'national cinema' makes certain assumptions about commonality and national characteristics, which can be problematic for contemporary British cultural forms. 'Traditional assumptions about national identity and unity (...) have become less and less tenable', wrote John Corner and Sylvia Harvey over a decade ago:

> For increasing access to education in the post-war period and the circulation of information and ideas by a public service broadcasting system committed (at its best) to the principles of free enquiry, have created social space for the/recognition of differences of language, of culture, of class experience and values, of family and domestic life experienced as differentially restful or laborious. (Corner and Harvey, 1991: 12–13)

In the last few years, these challenging assumptions have contributed towards a debate surrounding the nature of a British national cinema and what it means to discuss British culture more widely. These debates are not, however, local to Britain but can be seen as part of the wider mobility in societies, which is the result of centuries of encroaching globalization. Globalization is a term that has a particular postmodernist flavour to it, referring to the pastiche cultures of the West and McDonaldization. It is a term which expresses concern with the Americanization of the world as an economic, military and cultural 'superpower' and recognizes the colonization of global cultures which Americanization has achieved. However, globalization should be understood as one system by which the Western cultures have overridden Eastern cultural tropes through waves of Empire building. Consequently, there is a certain irony in Britain's concerns about national identity as the Empire culture it shaped is overtaken by another and the vestiges of the Empire have come calling:

> The long history of colonialism and imperialism has brought large populations of migrants and refugees from the Third to the First World. Whereas Europe once addressed Africa and Asia across vast distances, now that 'Other' has installed itself within the very heart of the western metropolis. Through a kind of reverse invasion, the periphery has infiltrated the colonial core. The protective filters of time and space have disappeared, and the encounter with the 'alien' and the 'exotic'

is now instantaneous and immediate. (Kevin Robbins, in Corner and Harvey, 1991: 32)

Thus, the cultural influence of the diaspora from South Asia, in Britain, over the last 50 years, should be seen as being just as significant in contemporary British cultural forms as any Americanization of British youth sub-cultures. Which is why the assumptions surrounding national identity and a national cinema, a homogeneous society and British stereotypes have not only weakened any argument about national cinema and its tropes but have also been built upon false grounding. If there is one thing British cinema has always revealed, even when there have been no characters who might be designated racially 'Other', it is that what makes Britain work as an entity, become more than its component nations, is the co-operation of disparate peoples for a common purpose. Take, for example, the British war films upon which Andrew Higson (1995), Marcia Landy (1991) and Sarah Street (1997) build their arguments for a British national cinema which represented a shared and homogenized culture, such as *This Happy Breed* (David Lean, 1944): many of these films actively use Otherness of class and region, if not nationality, to show how the *system* of Britain is an Empire across its own societies as well as those in South Asia or Africa. Consequently, the cinema which Britain has produced has always been more and less of a national cinema. It has been imperial, post-imperial and, as postmodernism fragments identification with anything other than an American, again a false, national identity; rather, it becomes post-national.

The concept of post-national cinema is a comparatively new way of thinking about British cinema but can be traced back to the mid–1990s with the beginnings of a more critical analysis of what has become known as 'heritage cinema' (films such as those made by Merchant Ivory, especially their E.M. Forster adaptations). This criticism reached a peak in the label 'anti-heritage cinema', which was applied to *Sense and Sensibility* (Ang Lee, 1996) and *Elizabeth* (Shekhar Kapur, 1998) by writers such as Pamela Church-Gibson (2000), Higson (2000) and Street to describe the changes in political, narrative and editing styles which could be seen in the British costume dramas of the *new*

British cinema. These films were less reverent of their source material, be that Jane Austen's novel or the historical records surrounding Elizabeth I, and, like *Shakespeare in Love* (John Madden, 1998), were more contemporary in their critique of past beliefs through the heightening of proto-feminist characters into visionaries of the future. Also, in purely filmic terms, the pace of editing and use of hand-held cameras was increased, making the films, whilst still visually impressive, less about place or space and more about the individuals which filled it. Thus, the 'anti-heritage cinema' set about negating the narrative components of nationhood in the costume drama in favour of a hybrid which was more closely related to the Gainsborough and 20th century melodramas of the 1940s than the biographies and epic landscape films made from the early 1970s to *Howard's End* in 1992. The hybrid components were contemporary editing and politics, often non-British directors, a pastiche of the past and a focus upon character. The pastiche of the past, however, was not about nostalgia but about a postmodernist, symbolic, imitation of heritage, which made it ironic and more active within the film mise-en-scène than it had previously been. Consequently, the post-national, as part of the anti-heritage dialectic of contemporary British dramas, seeks to use a pastiche of the past to question the present and is central to any debate-surrounding heritage and identity.

The place of the nostalgic within the post-national, however, should be understood as performing another function in terms of the British cinema and those films made from within the diaspora. The term nostalgia means 'homesickness' (Tana Wollen in Corner and Harvey, 1991: 182) and is not the temporally specific term we use it as most of the time to mean love of the past or the old. Therefore, nostalgia can be witnessed in most films about diasporas from all exoduses. The form this homesickness takes in diaspora films can vary a great deal. It can manifest itself through a literal longing for the home which has been left, an emphasis upon comparing the new and old homes, and a clinging to the iconographies and beliefs of home which is less about any cultural superiority and more about a community which can be said to still share a common culture. Thus, in narrative terms, the key structural devices used to represent nostalgia are memory and formal hybridity. This is one reason why two of the most popular films about British South Asians have been set in the past, in the early 1970s, at a time when *most* adult South Asians in Britain were immigrants and their children the first to battle with cultural conflicts born from generational differences. British South Asian diaspora films *are* hybrid, Higson's chief identifier of a post-national cinema in his 2,000 essay 'The Instability of the National'. They manifest a complex of mixture of cultural influence through style (British social realism and Bollywood fantasy, for example in *Bhaji on the Beach* – Chadha, 1993), content (the generation divide over religions, as in *My Son the Fanatic* – Udayan Prasad, 1997) and genre (British kitchen-sink, Restoration farce and Road Movie – again *Bhaji on the* Beach) but they are a cinema of immigration and immigrants. These films, made by directors, writers and actors born in Britain but of South Asian (or Other) extraction, reflect the cultural emphasis, within the diaspora cultures, of the spiritual, if not the literal, 'home'.

Anita and Me and the Peacocks

In approaching the concept of 'home' in the South Asian diaspora movie, it is useful to examine the most recent of the three films I referred to in the introduction, Metin Hűsyein's *Anita and Me*. Based upon Meera Syal's successful and semi-autobiographical book of the same title (1997), *Anita and Me* is set in the Black Country village of Tollington in the early 1970s, which is described by the protagonist, Meena (played by Chandeep Uppal), as 'the jewel of the Black country'. Meena's summer is spent obsessing about the slightly older, blonde and sassy Anita (Anna Brewster), worrying about taking the 11plus and finding a voice as a writer, inspired by Anita, 'the Yeti' hidden in the big house and her grandmother's stories, in a language Meena does not know, of India. There are certain echoes within the narrative of Toni Morrison's novel *The Bluest Eye* (1990) as Meena wishes she was blonde and writes to Jackie magazine about the problem of being 'brown' but the abusive family is not her own, ruled by the 'film star' and the 'princess', her father and mother, but that of Anita and Anita's mother

(Kathy Burke) runs of with a carpet salesman from Cannock, away from the never seen husband who beats her. The sadness within Meena's family (and the extended family, which includes her Auntie Shyla, played by Syal) is instead caused by the frustrations of fighting for recognition as immigrants in a racist country. As Shyla says to Meena and the other children: 'You kids, you don't know what we were'. Meena's mother, meanwhile, played by Ayesha Dharker, spends sad hours looking at the moon ('It is the same moon, isn't it?' She asks her husband for consolation) and dreaming of the peacocks in her home village.

> *Meena's mother:* Where I grew up I pulled sugar cane straight from the fields for my breakfast and squirted milk straight from the goat into my tea. We had a cobra underneath the people tree and peacocks on the roof. Meena (incredulously): A cobra? Peacocks?
>
> *Meena's mother:* We were a bad combination back there. Too much brains and no rich parents. At least here there are no bribes to pay to get by and ... no peacocks.

Meena refuses to believe her mother's story of the peacocks because, to Meena, they seem fantastic; something from her mother's imagination of home which has little to do with reality. Meena's response to the garden (which she wishes was full of flowers and not herbs) is similar to her vision of herself: she wants to be an English rose, like Anita, and be decorative, whilst her mother sees the beauty in the practicalities of the garden they can eat.

As with many diaspora films, food becomes an important marker of culture and the emphasis placed by Meena's mother upon the edible garden as a memory of home is further emphasized by Meena's pleading for fish fingers and chips rather than a curry or *dahl* on her dinner plate; to which Meena's mother responds: 'English food is easy, you just boil it and it tastes of nothing but this, this fills more than just your tummy'. Thus, for Meena's mother, the food, the garden and even the sight of the same moon, all become signifiers of home and triggers for happier memories as 'the princess' and the 'film star', the teacher and the philosopher, struggle for equality.

The fact that the film is set in the past, is purporting, especially as a semi-autobiographical text, to represent Meena's life as a approximation of South Asian lives of the early 1970s. Therefore, to represent 'history' is one of the key reasons that the homesickness is be elaborated on fully within the narrative and the novelty of the South Asian immigrant in Britain is experimented with. Indeed, the presence of one South Asian family in a village which contains variants of British stereotypical characters (the shop keeper, the layabout, the caring but ineffective vicar) is a useful metaphor enabling the film to become a 'state of the nation' text. These 'historical' qualities within the film are principally within the mise-en-scène and the interaction of the Kapoor family, and other characters, with wider issues of the time, such as racial violence, a hippy culture greatly influenced by Indian religions and changes in the British landscape. They are aspects that are written into the text to establish period and political context. As Tana Wollen says:

> History belongs to writing. Memory on the other hand is produced by recollection and belongs to the oral transmission of personal or local identities which do not require public or written forms of verification. Whereas history is 'work', and for some a profession, memory in non-selective, it can belong to everyone. (Wollen, 1991: 187)

Thus, the visual cues of *Anita and Me*, the costumes and other de-politicized elements, just as with the repeating motif of the Space Hopper in *East is East*, are part of the film's attempt to elicit a memory-based response from the spectator, the temporal understanding of nostalgia to which I referred earlier. Consequently, the mixing of historical and memory-based visual imagery within the film confuse what is written and what is remembered. Wollen continues:

> This is why film and television fictions matter politically, especially when issues of national identity are at stake. How then can we locate screen fictions along these distinctive routes to the past: are they history or memory? Since they are not writing, do they belong to the oral tradition preserved by memory? (*Ibid*, 187).

There is a certain quality of film spectatorship which can be said to rely upon an oral tradition, or retelling the film narrative to those who cannot go to see the film themselves for whatever reason. It is somewhat similar to reading newspapers to those who cannot read or interpreting the stories the *Police Gazette* of the 1880s was like telling about Jack the Ripper to an avid audience but the orality within the film's nostalgia is vital in *Anita and Me* as Meena listens to her mother or, in dreamlike state, seems to understand her grandmother finally as she passes on another story about the peacocks' cries on the village rooftops. The oral aspects of the film's narrative are, however, limited to the scenes where memory is being recollected. Indeed, the medias of history, documents, letters, newspapers are carefully used by the film to subvert memory and South Asian cultural tropes. Two key examples illustrate this: when the vicar (Mark Williams), 'Uncle Alan', brings a newspaper to Meena's parents with a report on their engineer friend's murder (by Anita's boyfriend on a night of 'Paki-bashing' and chips), it triggers a brief breakdown for Meena's mother; and later, when Meena and the family return from their neighbours' wedding at the end of the film to discover Meena's 11plus results and another envelope, it is the second, addressed to Sharon de Beauvoir which Meena opens first and jumps in joy to having had a story accepted by Jackie magazine.

In *Anita and Me*, whilst Meena is confused and struggles against her cultural heritage (which is beautifully emphasized by her description of Diwali to her mother in a rote-learnt tone), she is not the character who suffers great homesickness and the nostalgia within the film emanates from the adults, the immigrants. As Meena's mother says to Shyla of their view across the countryside, 'The sky and the trees is the closest we get to home, Shyla'. Nevertheless, as the narrative progresses over about a year and Meena matures, realizes her adoration of Anita was built upon a false grounding, and learns to understand her parents more, so her own sense of cultural identity becomes more secure and the home her mother has created for her the cure for her own sickness, wanting to be blonde.

The film opens with Anita and Meena falling off a slippery lakeside into dirty waters as Anita's white shoe floats away. It is somewhat of a MacGuffin, a red herring to encourage the spectator to think a dark ending, despite the comedy is in store, especially when Meena learns who was responsible, in part, for the engineer's murder. The image, leads you into an expectation that the film may perhaps be more like Peter Jackson's 1994 *Heavenly Creatures* in which two girls form an unhealthily close relationship and murder one of their mothers to stay together (which was based upon a real case); but by the time the film's analeptic narrative comes full circle (which is not quite at the film's conclusion) the fall becomes an accident as a result of a fight: and it also becomes the point at which Meena crystallises who she is in relationship to those around her, the point at which she is both culturally secure and individually independent. Anita says to her, trying to explain, 'You're not like the others'. To which Meena replies 'I am the others'.

The vision of the early 1970s explored in *East is East* is somewhat different to that in *Anita and Me*, as is its exploration of otherness and the protagonists' tense relationship with British White society and it is to this fill I shall now turn to discuss a different model of nostalgia framed by British Asian diasporic film.

East is East and Half A Cup of Tea

Whilst *Anita and Me* is set in a mining village outside 'Brum', *East is East* is set in the very different urban sprawl of Salford terraces. However, as in Tollington, the Khans, led by the patriarch George (Om Puri) are the only Asian family in a predominantly White neighbourhood illustrated with posters of Enoch Powell. What is different about this family, compared to the other two films in this paper, is that the Khans are a mixed-race family and the difficulties of cultural conflict are magnified by the half English, half Pakistani children. At the root of these conflicts, however, is George's desire that his wife and family follow Muslim practices and traditions, from arranged marriages to the cultural conformity that a move to Bradford might represent.

George never tires of voicing how his family *should* behave but he is a hypocrite in his censures as this scene emphasizes, and the narrative elsewhere tells the spectator that George has been married twice. He came to Britain to *escape* an arranged marriage to 'the first Mrs Khan'. At the time of the film's release, the characterization of George was attacked for being so negative, stereotypical and demonising the Muslim father but the writer, Ayub Khan-Din responds, emphasizing the autobiographical (again) qualities of the films, that:

> I'm sure people will have some criticism about how I portray my father. But at the end of the day, I'm portraying my father; he's not a Pakistani everyman. To a certain extent, this is a man who abandoned his culture and married an English woman, and then decided that his children should marry Pakistanis. So you know, there was huge hypocrisy there.

In the sense of 'a man who abandoned his culture', George Khan could reasonably be said to be not very homesick but his hypocrisy does demonstrate a certain variant of nostalgia that I outlined earlier on, the clinging onto iconographies and beliefs not out of respect for them but out of loneliness (hence George's violence born from frustration and his eulogising of Bradford).

Yet George is, like his children, struggling with cultural confusion, but on a less obvious scale than running from the Mosque bus when it calls. There are three key points to consider: George's name, the epitome of Englishness in many ways (but ironically we should remember that St. George wasn't anymore English than George Khan); the chip shop, 'George's English Fish and Chips'; and, finally, George's beloved 'half a cup of tea'. Every single one of these signifiers of Englishness is imported; the Jewish and Italian diasporas lay claim to introducing fish and chips, tea came from India and China, and St. George was Czech. In other words, these signifiers of English culture, the film emphasizes, are like George's children, the hybrid results of Empire or other cultures. Thus, *East is East*, set in 1970, in Salford, represents the post-national and anti-heritage argument within British cinema to just as much of an extent as the contemporary setting of *Bend if Like Beckham* or the costumed delirium of *Elizabeth*. In this sense, there is a difference set up in *East is East,* which contrasts greatly with *Anita and Me*. In Hűsyein's film, there is a clear sense of 'them' and 'us' established throughout in the dialogue. Interestingly, this is emphasized on both sides of the cultural divide as whilst overt physical violence comes only from White characters (in the shape of the engineer's murder), the family, especially Shyla, discuss the differences between English and Indian households with disdain if not disgust and Meena's line, 'I am the others', places her firmly on the side of her family. In *East is East*, however, because the family literalizes the racial dialectic, what is interesting is the extent to which the children view their South Asian culture negatively (for example when Sajid cries, running to the door, 'the Pakis are coming!') and how his sister Meenah loathes wearing the sari her aunt has sent her from Pakistan.

Nevertheless, George seems out-of-date to contemporary audiences and it is perhaps right to question the extent to which Ayub-Din's critical representation of his father may have damaged more realistic representations of what many Western cultural critics consider, within their own prejudices, a potentially already harmful patriarchal culture.

In the last section of this analysis, I shall examine how these anachronisms extend into Gurinder Chadha's 2002 film *Bend it Like Beckham* and how this anachronistic approach to characterization, especially within the contexts of father-figures modelled on the writers' own fathers, is another, perhaps even more complex, form of nostalgia.

Bend it Like Beckham and the Anachronistic Father

Bend it Like Beckham is the one contemporaryf ilm within this article but it is also the one which raises most questions about nostalgia, memory and diaspora filmmaking. The protagonist of the film, Jess (Parminder Nagra), wants to play football professionally, dreams of playing with Manchester United and confides her most secret thoughts to a poster of David Beckham on her bedroom wall. She is invited to join the Hounslow Harriers' women's football team, after being spotted by their captain, the blonde, athletic Jules (Keira Knightley) whilst playing with her male friends in the park. However, she fails to tell her parents, knowing they will disapprove of what they deem immature and unladylike and so ensues a narrative in which the chief momentum is created by find and not-be-found scenarios, and misunderstandings around lesbianism; all of which finally culminate in a wedding, a football match and Jess and Jules being picked by an American coach to move to a US college scholarship programme.

In many ways *Bend it Like Beckham* is a film which represents the same themes as *East is East* (the struggle for individualism in the potentially smothering family, the frustrated father, the representation of religion at the heart of familial beliefs). However, unlike *East is East*, *Bend it Like Beckham* does not ridicule religion. If anything, the female lead, Jess (Jasminder) is keen not to offend her family or its religious beliefs and the film goes out of its way to parallel Jess's family's problems with those of her White friend, Jules's family. Thus, whilst *East is East* is a film which literalizes multiculturalism in the family unit at a time when multiculturalism meant less of a mixing of cultures together and more the presence of many cultures, *Bend it Like Beckham* seeks to represent the multicultural society we wish we had through the commonalities between Joe, Jess and Jules, whilst revealing the prejudices of all sides through the families and thus, the lack of integration and hybridity.

One of the techniques the film uses, consciously or unconsciously, to represent the lack of integration and the prejudices from both families is the anachronistic and stereotypical representation of the parents of both Jess and Jules parents. Juliet Stevenson's cringe-worthy mother to Jules is rather more like Alison Steadman's grotesque in *Abigail's Party* (Mike Leigh, 1976) than any real working-class Hounslow housewife with an accent you could scrape down a blackboard and she initially responds to Jess as Jules's 'exotic' friend, littering her small-talk with references to 'your people' and curries. Later, when she thinks Jules and Jess may be lesbian lovers she becomes even funnier in her mistakes and Malapropisms – but she is still an out-of-date stereotype which you would never see in Hounslow (which has one of the largest Asian communities in the South-East and, incidentally, the highest rates of protests against marriages in the country) today. Jess's father, meanwhile, is depicted as a kindly, if sometimes stern, figure and is another autobiographical father, with the film overall dedicated to Chadha's late parent. Given that *Bend it Like Beckham* is set contemporarily and *East is East* 30 years earlier, the question raised about Jess's father is: should he not be more like the rebelling sons of George? However, it is in answering this question that comprehending diaspora filmmaking emphasizes the political heart of films about the South Asian community. These are not films about assimilation, adaptation of settlement, but about the immigrant experience and how difference is sustained and repeated rather than broken down (making it a horrific repetition if Kristeva's theories of abjectivity from *Powers of Horror* (1982) are adapted to this scenario). In this sense, this is how diaspora films fit firmly into the tradition of British social films about class and a film such as Jack Clayton's 1959 *Room at the Top,* with a few changes, could be remade with a Black or a South Asian lead. As Karen Alexander reminds us in her essay 'Black British Cinema of the '90s' (Alexander, 2000: 113), *The Full Monty* was originally about a group of Black men.

Jess's father's sadness at his treatment overwhelms the argument that has been taking place before his monologue after the wedding but the film does end on an optimistic note with him, Joe (the Harriers' coach) and others playing cricket on the grass in front of their houses.

Cinemas of the British Others

In his 1994 essay, 'National Cinema and Cultural Identity: Ireland and Europe' (McLoone, 1994: 157–158), Martin McLoone sets out a series of coherent 'overlapping themes' which I believe can, with adaptation, be as accurately applied to South Asian diaspora films of Britain as, like the cinemas of Ireland, Wales and Scotland, a minority cultural expression. To open out the potential use of these themes, I shall discuss each of the core themes and how they can be applied to the diaspora cinema produced by British South Asians.

First, McLoone lists 'an interrogation of the rural mythology which underpinned cultural nationalism and its encapsulation in the use of landscape' as a core thematic concern within Irish film. When Irish films such as *Waking Ned* (Kirk Jones, 1998), albeit filmed on the Isle of Man, are considered within this context, and against the stereotypical imagery of Ireland as countryside of white thatched cottages, it is easy to see how rural mythologies are important to any representation of Ireland. However, in diaspora films, the rural mythology needs to be adapted to the situation of the South Asian communities because the mythology of British spaces leads to a space in which the South Asian immigrant can only ever situate themselves as Other. The, in particular, English spaces of the farmed land, Yorkshire dales and football pitch (seen in each of the three films) are as potent an evocation of cultural nationalism within the landscape as the green hills of Eire and Ulster: and as such, they are further politicized as spaces in which the young protagonists of the film feel a freedom from the origin culture with which they tussle.

The second point which McLoone raises is 'a new concern (of Irish cinema) to represent urban experience which was largely submerged and ignored by this rural mythology'. Admittedly, some of the adaptations in place above for the diaspora film address this concern but within *East is East* and *Bend it Like Beckham* the urban is the dominant space and the South Asian communities are signified as being part of what defines the change from rural to urban space. In the film *Yasmin* (Peter Cattaneo, 2005), shown to acclaim on Channel Four, this is particularly powerfully rendered through the heroine's repeated journeys in and out of her small town and the claustrophobic atmosphere of the street in which she lives juxtaposed against the space and speed of her daily drive through the hills. The urban, for some South-Asian characters, becomes smothering, especially those who wish to somehow escape their lives. Yet for others, for example George Khan in *East is East* and Jess in *Bend it Like Beckham*, the urban signifies a space which represents the safety of community (although in significantly different ways for each character because Jess' urban environment is indelibly linked to her football ambitions).

The third, and one of the most significant of McLoone's list, in conjunction with his fourth thematic, is 'a (...) desire to reveal the social and political failures of independent Ireland' – for which can be read England. In *East is East* this is richly rendered through the contextualization of events with Enoch Powell's racist diatribes of the 1960s and 1970s. In *Bend it Like Beckham*, the social and political failings of England are framed through Jess' father's story of rejection on the cricket pitch: and *Anita and Me* highlights the contradictions of English sympathies through the village collection for 'starving babies in Africa'. These political concerns are then heightened through the engagement of the films with religion, McLoone's fourth thematic of Irish cinema 'especially in relation to education and sexuality'. This aspect is, perhaps, the most significant within the films problematization of the protagonists' cultural status because there is always a tension between the largely secular English culture and the religious culture of the families within the three films. Religion, as another marker of difference, is addressed clearly with scenes of worship (or its evasion) by the characters and, in *East is East* the difficulties of assimilation into the English culture are expressed interestingly through the use of the catholic parade as a cipher for the role of religious education in Britain: all ceremony and little meaning. It is only really in *Anita and Me* where religion is tackled head-on via the confused subjectivity of Meena and the role played by 'Uncle Alan' throughout the film as the comedy vicar; who ultimately departs from Tollington to save the world in his VW camper-van.

McLoone's fifth theme, and the one which brings the focus of the analysis back to the concept of nostalgia with South Asian diaspora cinema, is the 'interrogation of Irish history and Irish tradition, especially the manner in which these have been used to construct notions of identity'. In each of the three texts, the older generations are marked by their constant emphasis upon the link between the past, home and identity: history is home echoed through the stories of grandparents and suckled by the children of the films and it is not without significance that it is only once Meena's machete wielding grandmother has visited that the young girl mysteriously acquires the ability to speak Punjabi overnight.

In the hybridity of the post-national British cinema, the voices of the Other can be heard more powerfully, whether it is

Renton's rant in the Scottish hills in *Trainspotting* (Danny Boyle, 1994) or Meena plaintively crying 'I am the Others' as Anita falls head first into the river. These voices of the Other are important if British cinema is to develop a voice beyond the stereotypical forms most of the audience recognize: just as the British New Wave of the 1950s and 1960s had the ability to shape narration and influence subject matter, so has the hybrid cinema of the post-national.

Works Cited

Alexander, Karen. 'Black British Cinema in the 90s: Going, Going, Gone'. *British Cinema of the 90s*. Ed. Robert Murphy. London: British Film Institute, 2000. 109–114. Print.

Church Gibson, Pamela. 'Fewer Weddings and More Funerals: Changes in the Heritage Film'. *British Cinema of the 90s*. Ed. Robert Murphy. London: British Film Institute, 2000. 100–108. Print.

Claydon, E. Anna. 'Masculinity, Fantasy and *Bhaji on the Beach*'. *Picturing South Asian Culture in English*. Liverpool: Open House Press, 2003. 149–161. Print.

Corner, John and Harvey, Sylvia. 'Introduction: Great Britain Limited'. *Enterprise and Heritage: Crosscurrents of National Culture*. Eds. John Corner, Sylvia Harvey. London: Routledge, 1991. 1–20. Print.

Higson, Andrew. *Waving the Flag: Constructing a National Cinema in Britain*. Oxford: Oxford University Press, 1995. Print.

——. 'The Instability of the Nation'. *British Cinema, Past and Present*. Eds. Andrew Higson, Justin Ashby. London: Routledge, 2000. 35–48. Print.

Hill, John. 'British Cinema as National Cinema: Production, Audience and Representation'. *The British Cinema Book*. Ed. Robert Murphy. London: British Film Institute, 1997. 244–255. Print.

Khan-Din, Ayub, In conversation with Mark Olden, Web. 10 June. 2003. <http://www.kamera.co.uk/interviews/ayubkhandin.html>

Landy, Marcia. *British Genres: Cinema and Society 1930–1960*. Princeton: Princeton University Press, 1991. Print.

McLoone, Martin. 'National Cinema and Cultural Identity: Ireland and Europe'. *Border Crossings: Film in Ireland, Britain and Europe*. Eds. John Hill, Martin McLoone and Paul Hainsworth. Belfast: Institute of Irish Studies/British Film Institute, 1994. 146–173. Print.

Robbins, Kevin. 'Tradition and Translations: National Culture in its Global Context'. *Enterprise and Heritage: Crosscurrents in National Culture*. Eds. John Corner, Sylvia Harvey. London: Routledge, 1991. 21–44. Print.

Street, Sarah. *British National Cinema*. London: Routledge, 1997. Print.

Wollen, Tina. 'Over Our Shoulders: Nostalgic Screen Fictions for the 1980s. *Enterprise and Heritage: Crosscurrents in National Culture*. Eds. John Corner, Sylvia Harvey. London: Routledge, 1991.178–193. Print.

Filmography

Abigail's Party (Mike Leigh, 1976)

Anita and Me (Metin Hűsyein, 2003).

Bend it Like Beckham (Gurinder Chadha, 2002).

Bhaji on the Beach (Chadha, 1993).

East is East (Damian O'Donnell, 1999).

Elizabeth (Shekhar Kapur, 1998).

Happy Breed, This (David Lean, 1944).

Heavenly Creatures (Peter Jackson, 1994).

My Son the Fanatic (Udayan Prasad, 1997).

Room at the Top (Jack Clayton, 1959)

Sense and Sensibility (Ang Lee, 1996).

Shakespeare in Love (John Madden, 1998).

Trainspotting (Danny Boyle, 1994).

Yasmin (Peter Cattaneo, 2005).

4

British South Asian Cinema and Identity–II

Representing America in the films of Gurinder Chadha

E. ANNA CLAYDON

Following on from my discussion in the previous issue of nostalgia in contemporary British South Asian cinema, this article continues by focussing on the films of British South Asian and Sikh filmmaker Gurinder Chadha who first came as a director of interest with her 1989 documentary for Channel 4 'I'm British'. But a fascinating and enlightening insight into the varying kinds of identification British South Asians make with their multiple cultural influences. This was followed by *Bhaji on the Beach* in 1993, which Chadha wrote with the also then up-and-coming writer Meera Syal. Syal's semi-auto-biographical tale of being a South-Asian 'Brummie' in the 1970s was the subject of 2002's *Anita and Me*, which I also examined in the previous article but the central focus of this paper, *Bride and Prejudice*, as an adaptation of Jane Austen's classical novel of frustrated girlhood and frustrating men, *Pride and Prejudice* deals with another kind of adaptive process, not just one of South Asian to Britain but of a British text which, like so many of Austen's novels (especially *Mansfield Park*), albeit tangentially and through implicit reference, engaged with the concept of a colonial identity and culture and the possibility of postcolonialism in the immediate period of the end of the British slave trade. Consequently, the dilemmas of America and Britain are writ large in considering the 'truths' of identity in Chadha's adaptation and, it is posited, what has been lost in one country, can be found again elsewhere … at 'home', wherever that might be.

The Films of Gurinder Chadha and American Identities

Although at a first glance, Gurinder Chadha's films might appear to be simple British-South Asian comedies, they are actually much more complex in their engagements with identity and culture clashes and stand up well not only as more general 'state of the nation' studies but also as 'state of the South Asian diaspora' films. In earlier work on both *Bhaji on the Beach* and *Bend it Like Beckham* (1993 and 2002 respectively), I focussed on the tensions between British and South Asian cultural identities but what became startlingly clear, with Chadha's 2005 film *Bride and Prejudice*, was that the references to America in this and the earlier films was not so incidental: America (or Amrika, as Kholi saab always refers to it) is as much a personified character in her films as England is, through characters like Ambrose in *Bhaji on the Beach* (his name referencing to Ambrosia and his behaviour a pastiche of the English 'gentleman') and Juliet Stevenson's grotesque 'Ugly Englishwoman' as Keira Knightly's (Jules') mother in *Bend it Like Beckham*.

In this paper, whilst I shall focus on *Bride and Prejudice*, I shall discuss the development towards a discourse upon America in all three films of Chadha's South Asian identities films and how the perspective upon American identity alters for Chadha in the three movies. At the heart of these analyses will be the troublesome concept of the 'Ugly American' and its contemporary comprehension since the first Gulf War of 1991 and, especially, in the wake of George W. Bush.

Prejudices

> *Mother:* We wouldn't have these problems if we had gone to US when we had the chance; …
>
> *Father (to the girls):* Did I tell you about this Indian fellow who went to America and made it rich?

Mother (cutting across): … my brother did all the paperwork to sponsor us but, no, you didn't want to leave …

Father (cutting across): This fellow went to America and bought this huge American house and built three swimming pools in the garden: … .

Mother: … and what do we have? An old house, an old farm and new bills.

Father: … and when his father visited from India he showed him around his mansion and three swimming pools. His father asked, 'But son, why do you need three pools?' His son said proudly, 'Well, one is filled with cold water for when I feel hot, the second is filled with hot water for when I feel cold'. The father nodded and said, 'But why the third empty?' 'Well, that's for when I don't feel like swimming at all'. (*Bride and Prejudice*, 2005)

Right from the beginning of Chadha's adaptation of Jane Austen's British 'state of marriage/state of the nation' novel *Pride and Prejudice* (1813), America is identified as something for comedy and critique: where greed and stupidity encourages the wastefulness of three swimming pools and, from Darcy (Martin Henderson)'s arrival on an aeroplane into Amritsar with Bulraj and Kiran (i.e. Bingley and his sister, played by Naveen Andrews and Indira Varma), where innate snobbery exists in rejecting that which is not understood. A damning critique indeed but, in the wake of the present Iraq war and the thinly-veiled problems within the Bush administration of that time, this is, nevertheless, a belief and prejudice which is helped by many people around the world. Consequently, and initially within the film, William Darcy is established as the 'Ugly American' filled with the wealthy tourist's arrogance. As Lalita (Elizabeth, performed by Aishwarya Rai) says to him: 'You want to turn India into a theme park. I thought we'd got rid of imperialists like you'. 'I'm not British, I'm American', he replies. 'Exactly!' she retorts before stomping down the staircase. Thus, just as in the Austen's original, but with a twist, the prejudice is established. However, there are two important elements to emphasize in the initial set-up of a discourse upon America (and which can also be referenced in Chadha's earlier films). First, the desire to emigrate there and achieve American prosperity by many South Asians (especially Indians): as Kholi saab (Mr Collins, Nitin Ganatra) later puts it, from that perspective: 'UK's finished. India's too corrupt' – to succeed financially. Secondly, the changing of Darcy (seen throughout the film) to make him seem less socially and financially independent than in the novel: Catherine Darcy (played by Martha Mason), for example, becomes his mother instead of his aunt, Lady Catherine De Burgh. His social status is also altered in updating Austen's template: 'Fitz' is removed from his forename (in the original, Fitzwilliam was his mother's maiden name). This subtle change is significant because the use of 'Fitz' has long denoted families related to royalty by illegitimate bloodlines. The change from aristocrat to hotel magnate both makes Darcy more attainable, more American and also enables Bulraj and Kiran to be near aristocrats in their view of Windsor Castle and her imperious posture, which is reminiscent of the late Queen Mary. Indeed, although Kiran and Bulraj are supposed to be lawyers, they are never witnessed working whilst Darcy is seen in his management role once the action of the film moves to Los Angeles.

Thematically, both of these elements can be seen in the earlier films: America as aspiration and as land of egalitarian opportunity (although contradicting the initial prejudices in the film towards the US, these too are commonly held beliefs of 'the land of milk and honey' – ironically a phrase which originally referred to the mythical Ambrosia). In *Bhaji on the Beach*, the former is manifest through the younger girls aged around 14 or 15 – who change into westernized clothing, put on make-up and flirt with two spotty burger-joint boys who are dressed in head to toe in a pastiche of the Wild West cowboy. The clothing for the girls represents to them a freedom and maturity to be achieved but, importantly, and to be echoed later via the soccer in *Bend it Like Beckham*, it can only be fulfilled initially by hiding the behaviour from their families – especially their parents. In all three films, there is a tension between being 'traditional' and being 'modern' which is never quite resolved and never truly debated except that, ironically, Lalita is the most feminist of all

Chadha's heroines because her father is a 'Yes' man and not the 'gatekeeper' seen in other key male characters in Chadha's films: Jasminder/Jess (Parminder Nagra)'s nostaligia-ridden father in *Bend it Like Beckham* or the husband (Jimmi Harkishin) and his brothers opposed to their wives' and girlfriends' westernization in *Bhaji on the Beach*.

However, whilst the spiritedness of Chadha's heroines and their developing feminisms is appealing to the female spectator at whom these films are undoubtedly aimed, there is no doubt that none of the heroines are entirely feminist when compared to American female leads such as Erin Brokovich or Ripley or Thelma and Louise (although *Now* magazine in 1993 did describe *Bhaji on the Beach* as Britain's *Thelma and Louise*).[1] This is because, ultimately, Chadha's characters end up reinforcing normativity and tradition *but with flexibility*: Jasminder can study in the US but Jules is effectively her chaperone; Lalita can marry Darcy but it is a financially sensible marriage which Wickham (Daniel Gillies) could never have been[2]; and the heroine of *Bhaji on the Beach*, Ginder (Kim Vithana), can become more westernized (and her husband less violent) only if a *matriarchal* family unit is maintained. Repeatedly, Chadha sets up the possibility of feminism within a film, as more westernized women know it, only to find that a happy resolution has to integrate the traditional *behaviour* with feminist *values*. On the one hand, Lalita says she cannot love a stupid man who will crush her identity yet, on the other, when singing of 'Lonely Mr Kholi' she eulogizes romantic love and dreams of: (a) an English White wedding and (b) being an overseas bride.

'No life, without wife' is sung by Lalita and sisters in white pyjamas. The song starts out initially as, stylistically, a reggae piece but ends up as 1960s Motown before finally slowing to a processional classical resolution. The whole sequence can be viewed on YouTube:

> (Reggae Section)
> Lonely Mr Kholi from Los Angeles
> Came to Punjab on one bent knee
> He had a Green Cars, new house, big cash

Still made a wish with every fallen lash
For you to do the journey with him
To smile when he got home
And ask how his day had been
He wants you by his side, in joy and strife
Poor Mr Kholi
He has, no life, without wife.

(Motown)
No life, without wife.
Oh yeah, yeah, yeah, yeah, yeah.
No life, without wife.
Oh yeah, oh yeah, oh yeah.
I don't want a man who ties me down
Does what he wants while I hang around
I don't want a man who's crude and loud
Wants a pretty wife to make him proud
I don't wanna man who can't be funny
Who tells tall tales about making money

Oh Yeah …
I don't want a man who'll grab the best seat
Can't close his mouth when he starts to eat
I don't want a man who likes to drink
Or leaves his dirty dishes in the sink
I don't want a man who wants his mummy

A balding pest with too much dummy
I don't want a man who's dead in the head

Poor Mr Kholi
Aye Mr Kholi
Maybe he's good in bed … .
Ugghhhhh … .
No life
Without Wife
Oh yeah, yeah, yeah, yeah, yeah
No life
Without Wife
Oh yeah, yeah, yeah
Oh yeah, yeah, yeah

From
(http://www.nowrunning.com/film/slideshow1.asp?movieNo=1468 accessed on 23 April 2007)

What you don't want do matter no more
Soon you'll be married and ready to go
A match made in heaven just like milk and honey
You make all the Gobi he'll make the money
Everyday will be the same according to his plans
Forget what you want Mr Kholi's now your man
No life
Without Wife
Oh yeah yeah, yeah, yeah, yeah
I just want a man with a real soul
Who wants equality and not control
I just want a man good and smart
A really sharp mind and a very big heart
I just want a man not scared to weep }
To hold me close when we're asleep
Ohhh yeah … .
I just want a man who loves romance
Who'll clear the floor and ask me to dance
I just want a man who gives some back
Who talks to me and not my rack
I just want man whose spirit is free
To hold my hand, walk the world with me

No life
Without Wife
Oh yeah, yeah, yeah, yeah, yeah
No life
Without Wife
Oh yeah, yeah, yeah
Oh yeah, yeah, yeah

(http://img41.imagevenue.com/img.php?loc=loc224&image=7fe0cAishwarya_ Rai@desibabesandhunks.blogspot.com_3.jpg – accessed on 23 April 2007)

(Slower Processional)
Sorry Mr Kholi
It is not to be
My heart is set on another you see
The wandering soul I was meant to meet
Has finally come and swept me off my feet
Now I dream of what it would be like
To be an overseas bride dressed in white
To have a little home in the country
And live in the land of her majesty

The song is quite unusual in being explicitly feminist within *any* musical, Bollywood or otherwise. The spectator is left with no doubt as to what kind of man Lalita does not desire but, in its position after the introduction of Jonny Wickham and the presentation of him within the film, so far, as somewhat of a kindred spirit for Lalita, the ultimate dénouement of the song about Wickham and revealing Darcy very nearly takes away the political power of the song. Equally, the stylistic qualities of the song might be viewed as problematic in that the use of non-Indian music might be read as a disavowal of Indian culture but this is entirely erroneous. How many Bollywood films integrate Western and Eastern musical traditions within the Indian musical idiom? Chadha is merely asserting her place within this filmmaking tradition but, in making the idiom more pronouncedly Western makes the influences upon the family: America and the UK more apparent and is more inclusive of the Indian diasporic audience. Consider for example the sentimental comi-tragedy *Kal Ho Naa Ho* (Nikhil Advani, 2003), a film which is as open about the influences of Western culture on Indian women as *Bride and Prejudice* is – and debates the related issues with equal levity and heart. In this film, Roy Orbison's standard 'Pretty Woman' is the first big musical piece of the movie and the western song is fully integrated into the film stylistically through orchestration more than re-arrangement. For 'Lonely Mr Kholi', however, the orchestration is primarily Western and it only once the slower passage enters, despite its emphasis on English tradition, that a *sitar* is heard as part of the ensemble – connecting English and Indian traditions in a musical sense which ensures that the scene of Lalita becoming a 'foreign' bride is less of a disavowal of Indian identity as it might first seem. Nevertheless, how this almost universal iconography of the western bride is read seems to create a dilemma in the feminist project of the film and can be argued to articulate the confusion for many contemporary women globally; how to have everything: a job, love, a family. Ultimately, perhaps for Lalita, the only way in which she can achieve this harmony, it is implied by her rejection of Kholi, is by marrying a non-Indian. This is not a particularly useful realization within the film and again points to a rejection of tradition and Indian identity but, in creating a film about *multiculturalism* in contemporary society, narratively, irrespective of the adaptation of *Pride and Prejudice* this creates a tidy resolution for the issue of 'the difficult daughter' in much the same way the original text did by having the middle-class rural girl with limited prospects marry into upper-class cosmopolitan society.

Kholi *Saab*: Mr Collins Meets Austin Powers

The image of Nitin Ganatra, who plays Kholi, astride the circular bed with the Kholiwood sign behind him is not one which is very easy to forget but it does exemplify everything about the self-representation Kholi is presenting to Lalita and her sisters: here is the main 'Ugly American' of Chadha's film. In the 'No life, without wife' sequence, although not equal in their 'ugliness' Kholi and Darcy are both presented negatively (although there is clearly something more complex happening in the coda of the song). Kholi and Darcy represent two versions of the 'Ugly American': the neo-Imperialist and dominator (Darcy) versus the conservative evangelical comic who fails to connect with anything beyond surface detail (Kholi). Both, however, also represent variations of hyper-masculinity with Darcy referencing the darkness of the Eyre sisters' Rochester (*Jane Eyre*) and Heathcliff (*Wuthering Heights)* and with a not insignificant dash of Mills and Boon: and Kholi, albeit badly, a parody of the 'Playboy'. In creating the film's versions of the 'Ugly American', nevertheless, and typical of Chadha's methods for exploring identity, the US and UK are frequently aligned as similar yet different dreams (and dream states) for female protagonists. The nightmarish version of William Darcy is set in an anachronistic English idyll with the morris dancers whilst Kholi, against the Kholiwood backdrop references a contemporary 'Amercian idyll' – of sorts – also references a recent English stereotype, drawn on Bond and Jason King but manifested by Mike Myers: Austin Powers.[3]

Much of Mike Myer's career has been spent doing film-scale version of national parodies which, bearing in mind he spent most of his early career (in the mid-late eighties) in the UK, seem more than a little influenced by the comic characters of the then popular British comedian Russ Abbott.[4] Austin Powers, whilst referencing every Bond parody seen on film and television, also bears a passing resemblance through his physical clumsiness to Abbott's 'Basildon Bond' (the name joking about a stationary brand and punning on the activity in inactivity – creating Bond as ultimately impotent). Furthermore, Myers' extended cast of Scottish characters in the *Austin Powers* movies and *So, I Married and Axe Murderer* (Thomas Schlamme, 1993) owe a not insignificant amount to Abbott's offensive stereotype 'Jimmy' and also to children's performers 'The Crankies'[5] – who were immensely popular at the same time Mike Myers was working in British children's TV.

Within *Bride and Prejudice*, through Kholi visually referencing, albeit briefly, Austin Powers, is useful shorthand for the spectator which brings together a number of complex elements within the Kholi character. On a number of occasions within the film, Kholi disavows his Indian identity and echoes the opinion of Mrs Darcy concerning India in the US (although subtly done, this comes straight from Jane Austen): 'There's nothing you can't find in LA', he tells Lalita when he proposes to her in Amritsar and, Mrs Darcy later opines, to be challenged by Lalita, 'Well, with yoga, and spices and Deepak Chopra and the wonderful eastern things here, I suppose there's no point in travelling there any more'. Similarly, although supposedly British, Austin Powers, in performance and iconography, is an evangelist for anglophile America. Austin Powers must to get his teeth fixed in order to become more attractive: Kholi has to have access to three swimming pools. Yet this disavowal of India by Kholi is problematized by his wish to have a 'traditional' wife: something heavily criticized by Lalita and her father as hypocritical. He sells America as the land of success but also lambastes what happens to 'our women out there'. Nevertheless, rejected by Lalita, he does succeed in 'selling' America to Lalita's best friend, Chandra (Charlotte of the original) and she later tells Lalita, 'I love it here'. These confusions for the characters over their prejudices about America and yet their love of the lifestyle it can offer are frequently useful in Chadha's films because they enable an articulation of the diasporic dilemma: to leave means to reject my own culture and to embrace another yet we should not lose our identity. What *Bride and Prejudice* seems unable to decide is whether or not America represents the 'theme park' India for the Indian diaspora or simply an evolution of identity. A noticeable clue, perhaps, is in the different ways in which the UK and the US are represented as the Bakshi family travel to Los Angeles. London is introduced by a rapid montage of London landmarks *including* the Sikh temple (an image of London which is inclusive), whereas LA is established through the Hollywood sign, palm trees down Rodeo Drive, a Beverly Hills signpost and the rapping fanfare, 'Hey, must by the money'. The status is very clearly different and again the potential for affluence is manifested. Houses (and Wickham's canal boat) in London are small, pokey, whilst Kholi's version of suburbia is new, large and happily accommodates the travelling family. Again, this echoes the different representation of the UK and US in the Austin Powers films: the tight spaces of the first film's London later become replaced by the open deserts of the opening of *Gold member* with Tom Cruise as Austin Powers in the spoof trailer and Powers' teeth are fixed.

Kholi *saab*, however, is no Tom Cruise. As a comic, Nitin Ganatra, is a character actor and not typically a heroic figure. His 'Ugly American' is physically played for laughs. He is clumsy, dresses badly, gesticulates widely and has a peculiar laugh as well as messy eating habits. He uses language badly – calling Mr Bakshi 'Mamaji' when it's how he should (and later does) address Mrs Bakshi and, as pointed out earlier, constantly mispronounces America and Amrika despite his Americanized accent. Darcy meanwhile, is conventionally signalled as a character for redemption by being handsome: the spectator knows he is not the true 'Ugly American' even if the spectator has never read nor seen *Pride and Prejudice* because his is, in short, not ugly. Kholi is a comedy Indian which borders on a 1970s offensive stereotype but it succeeds because of the comic tradition of Mr Collins in Austen's original (the comedy vicar) and because Kholi's neo-conservatism, constant self-contradiction, clumsiness and mispronunciation of simple words, references the man who for many is a personification of the 'Ugly American': George W. Bush.

George Bush has provided a characterization of the American President which is, for the distanced spectator, embarrassing. Like the Deputy Prime Minister throughout the Blair government, John Prescott in the UK, Bush is not seen as somebody who can articulate himself well but whose aims for self-aggrandizement have ultimately led him into questionable decision-making processes. Just as Kholi seeks to make his family understand that American is the only way forward for personal success, so Bush's 'global policeman' routine (in imitation of his father's more articulate 'New World Order' speech of 1990) parallels the cultural imperialism debated in the film. It is not a heavily weighted parallel, between Kholi and Bush junior, in *Bride and Prejudice* but it is, nevertheless, clear that certain stereotypes are being used by Chadha to set apart Kholi (an accountant) and Mrs Darcy (who power-dresses in the style of Nancy Reagan) as Republicans and Darcy and Georgie (his sister) as Democrats (the willingness to embrace change and well-meaning (if sometimes misguided) intentions). Both Kholi and Bush take pride in their actions and talk-up their abilities but it is the fall of Darcy's pride that enables him to cease being the secondary 'Ugly American' and for Kholi to begin to be seen as more culturally integrated (and hence not so 'ugly') in the film's final dramas.

Pride

In *Bend it Like Beckham*, Jasminder's pride in her abilities lead her to secretly maintain her membership of the Hounslow Harriers football team and it is her father's finally admitted pride in her which permits her to leave, with Jules, for the soccer training schools in the US. Throughout the film, whilst David Beckham (ironically now leaving to play in LA) is the aspiration as far as ability goes for Jasminder (and his poster fulfils the role of confessor throughout the early part of the film), places at an American university are the ultimate quest for the teenager and her friend. Unlike *Bhaji on the Beach*, where the final reference to American identity is through the male strippers in Blackpool with their stars and stripes G-strings and America is much more sexualized, in *Bend it Like Beckham*, the concept of the, literally, American Dream is central to the heroine's actions and provides her motivation throughout the second half of the film. America is not criticized within Chadha's footballing film although there is some concern about the maintenance of cultural integrity explored through the family's reluctance to let Jasminder play football in the first place. Neither is America viewed as stereotypically ignorant and although there is the presence of *an* American stereotype (the coach), the film lacks the presence of an 'Ugly American' ... but this film was made in the summer before the attack upon the Twin Towers in 2001 and the resurgence of American imperialism seen in the second Gulf War.

Since those initial dark days following the attack which it feels that the world watched live on 11 September, America has staunchly defended its pride in the American identity (as basically liberal modernisers) against the pride of conflicting nations in their own identities (as generally finding pride in cultural tradition). This has created a huge debate around neo-imperialism and furthered the arguments around globalization which began over a century ago. These two positions are also central to how *Bride and Prejudice* represents the battle of wills between Darcy and Lalita. In order for both to progress, both have to compromise and in both the original novel and the film, the key motivator for this is Wickham's elopement with Lakhi (Lydia) and Darcy's subsequent admission that he did the same with Georgie (Georgiana). Three things change, however, in the film, which substantially alter the tone of Darcy's pride. First, it is established much earlier that Darcy's feelings towards Lalita are misunderstood by moving a key conversation about mistakes of prejudice to their second dance from a later scene. Secondly, when in LA and prior to Chandra and Kholi's American wedding (in a hybrid style), Lalita and Darcy evidently spend a number of days falling in love with a montage of fountain dances and beach walks complete with gospel choir and singing surfers: and, thirdly, Georgie's experience of Wickham is not an elopement but a pregnancy. The child which is not referred to and so it must be assumed an abortion took place. This updates the offence of Wickham's behaviour for Darcy more powerfully and makes his behaviour in not telling Lalita until Lakhi elopes more comprehendible for a contemporary audience. However, unlike Austen's original, the secrets cease at this point and Darcy's pride is quickly sublimated by Lalita and Darcy finding Lakhi together – and making the family much less indebted to Darcy that the Bennetts are in the 1813 novel.

In the action of removing Darcy's pride (from pride to embarrassment when his first proposes to Lalita to humility when he and Lalita find Lakhi) Darcy is transformed from the secondary 'Ugly American' into the 'knight in shining armour' and the conventional hero with the Boeing 747 as he takes the 'red-eye' to Heathrow as his white steed. Kholi himself has his 'ugliness' transmuted by the fact that he does in fact make Chandra happy. She has none of the world-weariness of Charlotte after a few months of marriage to Mr Collins in the novel and the American wedding is a very informal event only ruined by the artifice of both Mrs Darcy and Anne (her intended wife for Darcy). Indeed, by the end of the film, Kholi's ugliness is transformed from gross obsequiousness to being simply eager to please and asking Darcy if he'd 'like a beer'. Narratively, if Lalita (as the spectator knows she must) is to end up marrying Darcy, the negative representations of America must be resolved as ultimately harmless. She must subsume her own pride and compromise herself ... but does she?

In the novel, the key activity in Elizabeth's admission of love for Darcy is that she admits she was wrong and he was right about Wickham. Jane's betrayal, by Darcy, regarding Bingley, is central to her anger at the first proposal but it is brushed aside in the conclusion as an error of prejudice by Darcy. In other words, they reach a compromise by *both* being wrong about something. In Chadha's film, however, the sequence before the wedding in LA, with Darcy and Lalita falling in love, removes Wickham from the equation somewhat, as does his on-screen flirting with Lakhi throughout his visit to Amritsar. Lalita dreams about a wedding to Wickham but she is never represented as falling in love with him in the same way as with Darcy. What happens in Goa is, as she says herself of the hotel, not real and the fantasy is less important than Darcy's challenging of her expectations of him when he takes her to Mexican restaurants and flies her across the Grand Canyon. Lalita, unlike Elizabeth, never really has to admit she is wrong and thus, Lalita's pride remains unchallenged and, in Lakhi's return to the family undeflowered, unchanged. How does this affect the film as an adaptation of *Pride and Prejudice*? Well, bearing in mind the 1813 resolution to Austen's own variation on Shakespeare's *The Taming of the Shrew*, demanded the woman's subservience to her husband, *Bride and Prejudice* actually maintains the equality of the protagonists: achieving the kind of relationship Lalita sings of in 'No life, without wife'. Ironically, then, unlike Austen, for Chadha, pride is a good thing and it's prejudice that causes all the problems; and this encapsulates the position of all her films towards the complex issues of diasporic identity: have pride in who you are but don't judge those around you. Kholi *saab* spends most of the film judged by the sisters as the 'Ugly American' but he ends the film as a good husband; Darcy makes mistakes because he judges his friend's emotions falsely; and Lalita constantly chooses to misunderstand what Darcy tries to express to her. Changing the title to *Bride and Prejudice* was not just because it puns on the original title but because it diffuses the very thing Chadha sees as a strength, when balanced with kindness, throughout her films: pride.

Notes

1. *Erin Brokovich* (2001). Dir. Steven Soderbergh. *Alien* (1979). Dir. Ridley Scott and *Aliens* (1986). Dir. James Cameron more than *Alien 3* and *Alien Resurrection*. *Thelma and Louise* (1991). Dir. Ridley Scott.
2. It is interesting to note that in *Bride and Prejudice*, Lakhi (the youngest daughter), when she elopes with Wickham, *does not* marry him and is not 'spoiled'.
3. The Bond films have been parodied even before they began from *Carry on Spying* (1962 – released in the wake of *Dr No*) to *Otley* (1968) and even within themselves throughout the Roger Moore period. Jason King, meanwhile was a foppish 'hero' seen in two ATV series of the 1960s and 1970s, the latter as the main character and exemplified even further the permissive society as seen on television as spy-'medallion man'. The three *Austin Powers* films (1998–2004) have mercilessly, and cleverly, parodied not just James Bond but the entire spin-off spy films/tv series genre combining the characterisations from Bond with plots which owe more to *The Man from Uncle* and imagery from *The Prisoner.*
4. *Russ Abbott's Madhouse* was the incarnation of the *Russ Abbott Show* running throughout Myers' period of work on shows such as the

Saturday morning kid's magazine programme *No. 73* and *Wacaday*. Both were made by Thames Television.

5. The 'Jimmy' character was basically a thin version of Myers' obese Scottish thug in the *Austin Powers* movies. 'The Crankies' were/are a husband and wife team performing and father and child with the child ('Jimmy Crankie') as a Scottish version of William from the *Just William* novels of the 1940s. They also had their own ITV television series throughout most of the 1980s and were regular guests on Saturday morning television.

Filmography

Alien (Ridley Scott, 1979).

Aliens (James Cameron, 1986).

Alien 3 (David Fincher, 1992).

Alien Resurrection (Jean-Pierre Jeunet, 1997).

Anita and Me (Metin Hûsyein, 2003).

Austin Powers: International Man of Mystery (Jay Roach, 1997).

Austin Powers: The Spy Who Shagged Me (Jay Roach, 1999).

Austin Powers in Goldmember (Jay Roach, 2002).

Bend it Like Beckham (Gurinder Chadha, 2002).

Bhaji on the Beach (Chadha, 1993).

Bride and Prejudice (Gurinder Chadha, 2005).

Carry on Spying (Gerald Thomas, 1964)

Dr No (Terence Young, 1962)

Erin Brokovich (Steven Soderbergh, 2001)

Kal Ho Naa Ho (Nikhil Advani, 2003)

Otley (Dick Clement, 1968)

So I Married an Axe Murderer (Thomas Schlemme, 1993)

Thelma and Louise (Ridley Scott, 1991)..

5

Bride and Prejudice and the (Post-) National Cinema Debate

ANA CRISTINA MENDES

The primary location of Gurinder Chadha's film *Bride and Prejudice* (2004), a Bollywood-influenced adaptation of *Pride and Prejudice,* is 21st-century rural Amritsar in north-western India. In this reworking of Jane Austen's text, the Bennet family members become the Bakshis, the main cast members are Indian, the action moves between India, London, and Los Angeles, and the characters discuss post-imperialism and globalization. In the filmmaker's words, despite these updates, *Pride and Prejudice*'s 'themes have all been brought out, but with an Indian twist' (Chadha in Gritten 2004). In this Bollywoodized Austen, the Bakshis reside in a large country house beyond their means and the mother believes that the only road to financial survival is to scan the internet for suitable husbands for her four unmarried daughters. The character of Elizabeth Bennet becomes the headstrong Lalita Bakshi, while Darcy is an Oxford-educated wealthy heir to an American hotel chain, and the two meet while he is visiting India for a friend's wedding. At first, Lalita is appalled by his arrogant and condescending attitude toward India, which he finds plain and provincial, and the Indians, who he deems responsible for holding India back. The arranged marriage system that she regards as a 'global dating service', he sees as 'backward', and Punjabi dance styles are characterized by him as 'screwing a light bulb with one hand, and patting a dog with the other' (Sandhu, 2004: 24). Lalita is annoyed that snobs such as Darcy assault her country in what she considers to be a new imperialism. Indeed, she believes him to be a throwback to British colonialism since he is considering buying a beach resort in Goa. 'I don't want you turning India into a theme park', she tells him, 'I thought we'd got rid of people like you'. The two are set on a path for love, and spend the rest of the film revising their opinions of each other.

From the outset, the film's edge lies in its inclusion of Indian culture into a British canonical text, not only in the Bollywood-styled musical interludes but also in raising issues such as the economics of 21st-century cultural tourism resulting in the tourist-driven 'India without all the Indians', in Lalita's words. Nonetheless, in the context of this essay, I intend to consider not *Bride and Prejudice* thematically – and, in this respect, issues of mobility and location generally associated with diasporic filmmaking are peripheral to my investigation[1]–, but rather the *debate* around the film to focus on the ways in which critical discourses intersect to classify it as a national and/or diasporic cultural product.

Discussing a film that is defined by its filmmaker as British but by critics as South Asian diasporic entails a brief consideration of debates about identity, community, belonging, and nation in cinema studies. In the essay 'The Instability of the National' (2000), Andrew Higson suggests that we need to rethink the boundaries of British cinema from a transnational perspective. Re-working the key metaphors of travel and mobility, liminality and the diasporic, marginality and the hybrid, the critic calls into question the understanding of British film culture as a national cinema. As he himself admits, expressing the concerns many had already articulated with his concept of a British national cinema, he 'was perhaps at times rather too ready to find British films presenting an image of a coherent, unified, consensual nation' (Higson, 2000: 35). In fact, one should take into account that in recent decades 'new types of filmmaking have embraced multiculturalism, transnationalism and devolution', thus making up for 'a powerful critique of traditional ideas of Britishness and consensual images of the nation' (*ibid.*).

Underscoring the constitutional fuzziness of national cinemas (O'regan, 2002: 139), the critic puts forward a postnational model for British cinema, able to accommodate the complexities of the permeability of borders and of the fluidity of identification, and to integrate ambivalent representations of national identities in postwar Britain such as featured in filmic narratives such as *My Beautiful Laundrette* and *Trainspotting*. Following this contention, *Bride and Prejudice* might also offer us insight into what shape a postnational cinema might take. The author elaborates further on this move from 'a British cinema of consensus to one of heterogeneity and dissent':

> Some of the identities and positions explored in films like *My Beautiful Laundrette* and *Bhaji on the Beach* are surely as much either local or transnational as they are national. Given the transient and fleeting nature of many of the allegiances established in these films it seems problematic to invoke the idea of a singular, indisputable British nation, however complex and devolved – hence my preference for the idea of a post-national cinema. (Higson, 2000: 40)

As acknowledged by Higson, John Hill disagrees with the discarding of the label 'national cinema'. Hill recognizes that 'while the British cinema may no longer assert the myths of 'nation' with its earlier confidence, it may nonetheless be a cinema which is more fully representative of national complexities than ever before' (Hill, 2001: 212). This argument echoes Homi Bhabha's formulation of the Janus-faced boundary of national culture, which is 'always a process of hybridity, incorporating new 'people' in relation to the body politic, generating new sites of meaning, and, inevitably, in the political process, producing unmanned sites of political antagonism and unpredictable forces for political representation' (Bhabha, 1990: 4).

While Higson's opinion is persuasive, Hill's line of reasoning is more relevant for my purposes because, on the one hand, it highlights cinema as one of the most dynamic sites of cultural negotiation and, on the other hand, it strengthens the impact British Asian filmmaking has had on opening up the definition of national cinema. Indeed, following the commercial success and critical acclaim of films by Deepa Mehta, Mira Nair,

Hanif Kureishi, and Gurinder Chadha, the cinema of the Indian diaspora has become the object of close attention and has had the potential to capture British mainstream audiences. *Bride and Prejudice* is now set to capitalize on this growing influence in general, and on the crossover appeal of the exotic that is associated with Bollywood in particular.

At this point, I would like to address the film's positioning at the nexus of the national and the transnational, and I will try to elucidate this issue by focusing on Jigna Desai's project – *Beyond Bollywood* – published in 2004 and devoted to films in English from and about the 'Brown Atlantic' (South Asian diasporas in the United States, Canada, and Britain). Within a transnational comparative framework, this critical project interrogates and reformulates the dominant emphasis on the nation in cinema studies by positioning South Asian diasporic filmmaking as an interstitial cinema which negotiates and traffics among the two largest global cinemas – those of Hollywood and Bollywood – as well as individual national cinemas (Desai, 2004: ix). According to Desai, current South Asian diasporic films are most frequently integrated into the canons of national cinemas through the logic of cultural hybridity (Desai 36). This signals a change when compared with South Asian British films of the 1980s which were 'neither easily incorporated into the national cinema as the films openly challenged national narratives and identification processes nor were able to enter the film industry without intervention from social movements' (Desai 54). As the critic puts it, 'the shift from the eighties to the contemporary moment is the move away from an emphasis on multiculturalism to one primarily on profit' (Desai 65). In fact, since the 1990s, the British film industry, powerless to compete with Hollywood, has found itself ambivalently recognizing the role that British Asian filmmaking has played as a potential site for profit and in the promotion of its international image (Desai 39).

In this context, screenwriter-filmmaker Gurinder Chadha was the first British Asian woman to achieve access to mainstream media production in the 1980s through state-supported funding, and was in the vanguard popularizing 'Asian Kool'. *Bride and Prejudice*, her latest work, is, in fact, part of a body of 'Asian Kool' films and TV serials – including *East is East*, the BBC's satirical series *Goodness Gracious Me* and *The Kumars at No 42*, as well as Chadha's famed *Bend it Like Beckham* – which have managed to carve out an increasingly prominent niche in the cultural industries. While this is an encouraging trend, the visibility of British Asian representation in the public sphere depends on the political economy of these industries. Following Desai's theorization, this hypervisibilty has been integrated into the mainstream through the rhetoric of cultural hybridity, since late capitalist diversification supports 'plurality in constructing and penetrating its differentiated target markets' (Desai 66).

Drawing on discourses on re-Orientalization as well as on current debates in adaptation theory, Tamara S. Wagner examines how *Bride and Prejudice* redeploys both Orientalist and Occidentalist motifs by capitalizing at the same time into two burgeoning marketable genres: Bollywood film and period drama, specifically Austen adaptations. *Bride and Prejudice*, in Wagner's reasoning, pointedly explores the stereotyping exoticizing of an 'Occident' to counterpoise the problem of re-Orientalization. Wagner reassesses what she sees as the overlooked significance of the film's intricate deployment of different literary and cinematic conventions for its self-conscious juggling with re-Orientalizing elements. Much of the dilemma about the tendency to re-Orientalize a potentially truly experimental work like a Bollywoodized Austen has been created by marketing strategies, by audience expectations, and by the film's subsequent reception and prevailing criticism. Nevertheless, the interstitiality of British Asian films prevents assimilation and full co-optation of dominant ideologies; thus, '(a)lthough many of these films are read as Hollywood, British, or even Bollywood films, their disjunctures, heterogeneity, and hybridity belie this attempt to define them by their relation to these dominant cinemas' (Desai 36). Indeed, *Bride and Prejudice* is interstitial because it is 'created astride and in the interstices of social formations and cinematic practices. Consequently, (it is) simultaneously local and global, and (it) resonate(s) against the prevailing cinematic production practices, at the same time that (it) benefit(s) from them' (Naficy, 2001: 4).

It is against this critical backdrop that I position Chadha's film. *Bride and Prejudice* provides a unique overview of the debate on (post-) national British cinema, as a cultural practice that challenges monolithic understandings of nationhood, and instead gestures to a transnational ethos. Indeed, it stands as an 'attempt to make the Bollywood experience accessible to Western audiences' (Adams, 2004: 46), while at the same time it addresses itself to a strand of British cinema heritage, having been filmed at Ealing Studios, at the centre of the national film industry for more than a century. Chadha herself underscores this 'palimpsestual simultaneity between the national and the transnational' (Banerjee, 2003: 449) by defining the film as 'a combination of Bollywood and Hollywood, all tied up with a very British overall sensibility' (Driscoll, 2004: 13). In other words, what emerges at this juncture is the argument that this film serves as an interesting entry point for addressing broader debates in the study of (post-) national cinema since it represents, simultaneously, an important hybrid perspective within British cinema as well as a more global viewpoint taking in the phenomena of transnationalism and diaspora.

As a cultural product bearing out the increasing presence of the South Asia diaspora on the map of mainstream British culture, *Bride and Prejudice* can be seen as an ambivalent text, central to British Asian filmmaking whilst being re-appropriated into the multicultural heritage industry. As other 'Asian Kool' films, it has been consumed mainly by a mainstream British and a British Asian elite audiences.[2] After all, exotica has always been a marketable commodity in the West, and this film apparently illustrates Desai's contention that 'visibility can become a way to spice up culture without a compensatory interrogation or shift of values and epistemologies' (Desai 62). Moreover, Chadha participated in the London-based workshops and collectives in the 1980s, benefitting from state funding of minority film and TV productions, so her films are positioned within and work inside the mainstream.

Nonetheless, it is my contention that the aesthetics and content of the film, on the one hand, and its characterization by Chadha, on the other hand, reflect both the interstitiality associated to South Asian diasporic filmmaking, and the resultant negotiations of the institutionalization into British cinema. On the one hand, it is a hybrid film, following Laura Marks's concept, and a case in point of E. Ann Kaplan's model of diasporan aesthetics because it blends different film styles together, using a range of techniques and perspectives which merge Indian cultural influences with Western conventions; in addition, it is a hybrid film as well on the face of its articulation of diasporic cultural identity as a legacy of a colonial past. On the other hand, underscoring the complexity implicated in the notion of British cinema, Chadha wants her films to be representative of the 'new' national cinema, and *Bride and Prejudice* is no exception: 'What I'm trying to say is that Britain isn't one thing or another. It isn't just *Howard's End* or *My Beautiful Launderette.* There are endless possibilities about what it can – and is – already' (Chadha in *Sight and Sound,* 1994, quoted in Street, 1997: 107). To be sure, in an interview given in 2000 she had already stated that her first feature film – *Bhaji on the Beach* – , which preceded *Bride and Prejudice* by a decade and set up the tone for the following work, was about 'opening up what we mean about British cinema' since it was 'a very British film, made in a very British way, with Indians' (Chhabra, 2000).[3]

The dominant reception of *Bride and Prejudice* indicates an inability to locate it as part of the British national cinema. As illustrated by Desai's placement of Chadha's works within South Asian diasporic film production, most responses to the film are characterized by a puzzling consensus on its 'Indianness' – underscoring notions of translation, masala, and fusion – even if the filmmaker defines it (and herself) as British. Then, are we to see Chadha as a British filmmaker, or are we to consider her, as Gayatri Gopinath has done just last year, as part of 'a new crop of Indian diasporic feminist filmmakers' who 'are in no small part responsible for this translation of Bollywood into Hollywood, in that they act as modern-day tour guides that in effect 'modernize' Bollywood form and content for non–South Asian audiences' (Gopinath, 2005: 162)? The othering of the film by cultural critics seems to me highly problematic. What is at issue here are the ways in which both levels – the national and the transnational – interact, and *Bride and Prejudice* must be read in terms of a multiple discursive participation. In an attempt to clarify this issue, for the remainder of this paper I will trace through Chadha's description of herself as cultural producer and of her work in the media.

When asked in 2003 by an interviewer on how it felt to be the only Indian woman filmmaker in the British film industry, she stated her case rather directly: 'I consider myself more to be a British filmmaker and part and parcel of the rest of the British film industry' (Chhibber, 2003). Two years later, she asserted: 'It's so great for me to have turned things around by doing well as a British filmmaker. There's a lot to celebrate' (Arnold, 2005). During the course of another interview, Chadha clarified what she understood by the experience of the Indian diaspora she tried to translate into cinematic terms with *Bride and Prejudice*: 'I don't make Eurocentric or Indo-centric films (...). If anything, I'm diaspora-centric. (...) *Bride and Prejudice* is my way of appealing to that fact'. On a different occasion, she defined the film thus: 'It is a British film made by British finance, obviously because I am British. (...) I have been in England all my life. My links with India were through Hindi movies in the local theatres. I see myself as British-Punjabi. It works for me. (...) I never see myself as an outsider in the West'.[4] During the course of other talks, she made things even more clear about the film's origins: 'Let us remember, *Bride and Prejudice* (...) was financed by Pathe in Europe, and American rights were pre-sold to Miramax. It doesn't have Indian money in it' (Arnold, 2005); 'I had a different audience now with *Bend It Like Beckham*, a global audience and so I decided I would make a Bollywood-style British movie that would introduce the Indian film language to a global audience and open up, I hope, Indian films to audiences who were not familiar with them'.[5]

I would like to point out that adapting *Pride and Prejudice*, changing just one letter of its title and transplanting it to contemporary India, takes on a decidedly different meaning when the filmmaker in question is part of an incursion of cultural producers from the periphery into the tradition of British literary canonicity. In its post-modern ironic style, *Bride and Prejudice* can be regarded as a rewriting of nostalgic images of a romantic and pastoral England usually associated with previous Austen's adaptations to cinema and television. As Chadha remarked in interviews, she 'quite like(s) the mischievousness of taking one of Britain's great traditions and Indianising it'[6]; in her words, she 'decided that, like David Beckham, Jane Austen was another delicious English icon ripe for subversion' (Young, 2004: 34). To her, '(t)here's a sort of audaciousness about taking the most British things – football and Jane Austen – and making them Indian. It feels very cheeky taking a great English literary classic and turning it into a Bollywood-style film' (Kasriel, 2004: 23).

Against the backdrop of the booming mainstream success of the Bollywood film industry and of the hypervisibility of British Asian cultural production,[7] the thorny questions I have tried to address are the following: does *Bride and Prejudice* have the power to heighten reflexivity in a world where cultural difference is celebrated and consumed like other market commodities? How are we to understand the film, especially at a time when 'hybridity, diaspora, and postcoloniality are now fashionable and even marketable terms' (Hutnyk, 2000: 118)? Although in my mind these queries still beg further answering, it seems, to reach the conclusion of this paper, that Chadha has managed to balance a contradictory and complex positioning as a filmmaker at the nexus of national and transnational forces, politically and financially capitalizing on the alterity industry (Huggan, 2001) dominating mainstream discourse, while fleshing out the 'instability of the national', to borrow Higson's expression.

To take it one step further, *Bride and Prejudice* invites a critical perspective which questions the somewhat reductive debate around (post-) national British cinema. While it is widely acknowledged that Chadha's recent films go along the 'Asian Kool' wave, I posit that, by asserting herself as *British*, and discarding the critical labels others have devised for her as cultural producer, Chadha's ultimate subversion, adapted to this increasingly transnational and globalized age, resides in claiming her Britishness. In this way, she denies a positionality determined by the logic of hybridity and 'otherness' dominating the commodification of cultural difference and its incorporation into mainstream commercial consumption. Far from being merely a biographical detail and more than a defence of an ever more contested and fluid concept of British identity, I put forward that Chadha's assertion of her Britishness acts as a refusal to settle in the marketing niche of the postcolonial exotic (Huggan, 2001), thereby unsettling the expectations cultivated by cultural critics who, looking through nostalgic lenses at British Asian filmmaking in the eighties, are eager to dismiss her diasporic concerns as having been co-opted in the name of profit and commercial viability.

Notes

1. Also secondary to this paper is the critical analysis of existing terminology in the field of diasporic cinemas (e.g. 'migrant', 'diasporic', 'accented', 'minor', 'transcultural', and 'transnational').
2. Pnina Werbner writes that the 'overt message' of 'the new wave of British South Asian novels (...) enables these works to reach out successfully to mainstream audiences and to a small elite of British South Asian intellectuals' (Werbner, 2004, 901). What she notes seems to apply as well to the screen as to literature: '(t)he great danger of over-abstract interpretations of diasporic works is (...) one of ignoring the reality that, until recently, most high cultural works by South Asian intellectuals have been ultimately financed and consumed mainly by a mainstream English and a small secular South Asian elite audience' (Werbner, 2004, 903). Karen D'Souza and Tasleem Shakur go even further: 'How far can these comic cultural portrayals (such as *Goodness Gracious Me*, *Bhaji on the Beach*, and *Bend It Like Beckham*) which seem constructed to the sensibility of mainstream British audiences offer a social critique, or are they merely a pragmatic strategy? Why are those films hugely popular with Western audiences but not necessarily with the British South Asian community?' (D'Souza and Shakur, 2003: 90).
3. E. Anna Claydon addresses *Bhaji on the Beach* as 'representative of the new British cinema: the British cinema which has moved beyond, but not necessarily past, a concept of a homogeneous, British, English culture in which all other cultures are Othered by society and (...) towards a multiculturalism with which dominant white English culture is not yet at ease' (Claydon 2003, 149–150).

4. http://www.bollywoodmantra.com/613_bride-and-prejudice-is-not-a-k3g.html.
5. http://www.ealingtimes.co.uk/search/display.var.534220.0.0.php
6. http://www.hinduonnet.com/thehindu/thscrip/print.pl?file=2004092300730100.htm&date=2004/09/23/&prd=mp&.
7. Desai argues that this hypervisibility 'may be seen as the flip side of the invisibility that characterized racial and cultural politics earlier in Britain', and she bluntly adds that 'the burden of representation has now become the spectacle of representation' (Desai, 2004: 69).

Works Cited

Adams, Mark. 'Bolly Good'. *Sunday Mirror*. 10 October 2004. 46. Print.

Arnold, Gary. 'Director's Global Reach'. *The Washington Times*. 12 February 2005. n/p. Print.

Banerjee, Mita. "Traveling Barbies' and Rolling Blackouts: Images of Mobility in Mira Nair's *Monsoon Wedding*'. *Comparative American Studies* 1.4 (2003): 448–470. Print.

Bhabha, Homi. 'Introduction: Narrating the Nation'. *Nation and Narration*. Ed. Homi Bhabha. London and New York: Routledge, 1990. 1–7. Print.

Chhabra, Aseem. 'Chadha's Newest Wows Sundance Fest'. Web. 5 October 2015. <http://www.rediff.com/news/2000/feb/02us4.htm.>

Chhibber, Kavita. 'Gurinder Chadha Unplugged'. Web. 5 October 2015. <http://littleindia.com/march2003/Gurinder%20Chadha%20Unplugged.htm.>

Claydon, E. Anna. 'Masculinity, Fantasy and *Bhaji on the Beach'*. *Picturing South Asian Culture in English: Textual and Visual Representations*. Eds. Tasleem Shakur and Karen D'Souza. Liverpool: Open House Press, 2003. 149–161. Print.

Desai, Jigna. *Beyond Bollywood: the Cultural Politics of South Asian Diasporic Film*. New York and London: Routledge, 2004. Print.

Driscoll, Rob. 'Bend It like Austen', *Western Mail*, 6, 13 October 2004. Print.

D'Souza, Karen and Tasleem Shakur. 'From *Heat and Dust* to *East is East*: Journey from the Colonial to Post-colonial South Asian Cultural Space'. *Picturing South Asian Culture in English: Textual and Visual Representations*. Eds. Tasleem Shakur and Karen D'Souza. Liverpool: Open House Press, 2003. 77–94. Print.

Gopinath, Gayatri. 'Bollywood Spectacles: Queer Diasporic Critique in the Aftermath of 9/11'. *Social Text* 23. 3–4. (2005): 157–169. Print.

Gritten, David. 'Why I Put Jane Austen in a Sari'. *Daily Telegraph*. 20 September 2004. Print.

Higson, Andrew. 'The Instability of the National'. *British Cinema: Past and Present*. Eds. Andrew Higson and Justine Ashby. London: Routledge, 2000. 35–47. Print.

Hill, John. 'British Cinema as National Cinema: Production, Audience and Representation'. *The British Cinema Book*. Ed. Robert Murphy. London: BFI, 2001. 206–213. Print.

Huggan, Graham. *The Post-Colonial Exotic: Marketing the Margins*. London and New York: Routledge, 2001. Print.

Hutnyk, John. *Critique of Exotica: Music, Politics and the Culture Industry*. London: Pluto Press, 2000. Print.

Kaplan, E. Ann. *Looking for the Other: Feminism, Film and the Imperial Gaze*. New York and London: Routledge, 1997. Print.

Kasriel, Alex. 'Bollywood to Swoon at a New Mr Darcy'. *Evening Standard*. July 15, 23. 2004. Print.

Marks, Laura. *The Skin of the Film: Intercultural Cinema, Embodiment, and the Senses*. Durham: Duke University Press, 2000. Print.

Naficy, Hamid. *An Accented Cinema: Exilic and Diasporic Filmmaking*. Princeton: Princeton University Press, 2001. Print.

O'Regan, Tom. 'A National Cinema'. *The Film Cultures Reader*. Ed. Graeme Turner. London and New York: Routledge, 2002. 139–164. Print.

Sandhu, Sukhdev. 'Over-Scented Sensibility'. *Daily Telegraph*, 8, 24 October 2004. Print.

Street, Sarah. *British National Cinema*. London and New York: Routledge, 1997. Print.

Young, Graham. 'Film: Time for Global Domination!'. *Birmingham Evening Mail*. October 8, 34. 2004. Print.

Wagner, Tamara S. 'Foreign Fantasies and Genres in *Bride and Prejudice*: Jane Austen Re-Orientalizes British Bollywood'. *Re-Orientalism and South Asian Identity Politics*. Eds. Lisa Lau and Ana Cristina Mendes. London and New York: Routledge, 2011. 103–123. Print.

Werbner, Pnina. 'Theorising Complex Diasporas: Purity and Hybridity in the South Asian Public Sphere in Britain'. *Journal of Ethnic and Migration Studies* 30. 5. (2004): 895–911. Print.

Filmography

Bend It Like Beckham (2002) Director: Gurinder Chadha.
Bhaji on the Beach (1992) Director: Gurinder Chadha.
Bride and Prejudice (2004) Director: Gurinder Chadha.
East is East (1999) Director: Damien O'Donnell.
Goodness Gracious Me (1998–2000) BBC TV.
The Kumars at No 42 (2001–2004) BBC TV.
My Beautiful Laundrette (1985) Director: Stephen Frears.
Trainspotting (1996) Director: Danny Boyle.

6

Hanif Kureishi's *My Son the Fanatic*

Anxiety in Assimilation

PRAGYA SHUKLA

Human beings have an innate desire of being rooted and they yearn for its acceptance too. They learn the art of developing a relationship with people and place of abode in their formative phase of life. Forced by circumstances, they travel to distant lands where they are compelled to deploy their own values and individuality in order to plan a better future in the host land. Perusing Jeremiah's letter appears as if the words were being addressed to the diasporic populace:

> This is what the LORD Almighty, the God of Israel, says to all those I carried into to exile from Jerusalem to Babylon: 'Build houses and settle down; plant gardens and eat what they produce. Marry and have sons and daughters; find wives for your sons and give your daughters in marriage, so that they too may have sons and daughters. Increase in number there; do not decrease. Also, seek the peace and prosperity of the city to which I have carried you into exile. Pray the LORD for it, because if it prospers, you too will prosper. (Jer, 29: 4–7)

Migration has been an inseparable part of civilization. A new land offers economic stability but then memories of the hearth left behind haunts. The new land that had been full of hope for the migrants is nothing more than a mirage. Chitra Banerjee Divakaruni has intricately described the anxiety and pain of diasporic populace:

> ... No one told us it would be so hard here in Amreekah, all day scrubbing greasy floors, lying under engines that drip oil, driving the belching monster trucks that coat our lungs with tar. Standing behind counters of dim motels where we must smile as we hand keys to whores. Yes, always smile, even when people say, 'Bastard foreigner taking over the country stealing our jobs'. Even cops pull us over because we're in the wrong part the rich part of town. (Divakaruni, 1997: 62)

Literally meaning scattered through, 'diaspora' spotlights physical and mental displacement from a stable home and hearth. It concentrates attention on the ways in which one's place of origin or motherland continues to have a hold on those who immigrated to alien lands. Diaspora re-examines the significance of home. As individuals begin to mingle with the residents of foreign lands, they find themselves restricting and expanding their lives and identities. The study of diaspora analyses the changes and the losses of people 'dispersed' from their place of origin. Desai concluded:

> ... Thinking of the diaspora not as an empirical category but as a conceptual frame, diasporic critique brings into question, rather than assumes, the centrality of a fixed, stable home; consequently, within diasporic critique, both homeland and diaspora are understood as interrelated and mutually constituted spaces. (Desai, 2008: 207)

While Avatar Brah argues that Diaspora is: '... a space that is inhabited by those who have migrated as well as by those who have not. The concept of diaspora space foregrounds the entanglement of genealogies of dispersion with those of 'staying put' (Brah 16). Vijay Mishra states that diasporic identity is firmly located in colonial discourse and this contradiction makes it even more interesting. He further explained:

> I want to suggest that the diasporic imaginary is a condition (and 'imaginary' is the key concept here) of an impossible mourning that transforms mourning into melancholia. In the imaginary of diasporas both mourning and melancholia persist, sometimes in intensely contradictory ways at the level of the social. ... Freud – melancholia is in some ways related to

> an object-loss, which is withdrawn from consciousness, in contradistinction to mourning, in which there is nothing about the loss that is unconscious. (Mishra, 2007: 9)

Caught midst homeland and hostland, diasporas are invariably dejected and unhappy. Then the sorrow of each is different from the rest. Diasporas represent people who do not feel comfortable with their nondescript existence in an alien soil. They are caught in the web of dual territoriality. According to Mishra:

> Diasporas are people who would want to explore the meaning of the hyphen, but perhaps not press the hyphen too far for fear that; this would lead to massive communal schizophrenia. They are precariously lodged within an episteme of real or imagined displacements, self-imposed sense of exile; they are haunted by specters, by ghosts arising from within that encourage irredentist or separatist movements. Diasporas are both celebrated (by late/postmodernity) and maligned (by early modernity). (Mishra: 1)

People migrate, in spite of the distances covered; they experience a sense of nostalgia and memories of a familiar land always haunt them. Arjun Appadurai and Carol Breckenridge, for example, state that:

> Whatever their form or trajectory, 'diasporas always leave a trail of collective memory about another place and time and create new maps of desire and of attachment' ('Moving targets', i). Yet these collective memories and 'new maps' do not always serve to consolidate identities; rather, they note: More and more diasporic groups have memories whose archaeology is fractured. These collective recollections, often built on the harsh play of memory and desire over time, have many trajectories and fissures, which sometimes correspond to generational politics. Even for apparently well-settled diasporic groups, the macro-politics of reproduction translates into the micro-politics of memory, among friends, relatives and generations. (301–2)

Diaspora in films is subtle. The content is powerful and aesthetic but never direct. Like most successful works of art, they explore a profound social issue. The power of the message comes of what isn't said. It's found in a mother's furrowed brow as she struggles to hold a family together.

Diasporic films play an important role in formulating national identity and in promoting normative behaviour. Renowned authors, who have worked extensively in the theory of globalization and cultural studies, conclude: '... cinema is widely considered a microcosm of the social, political, economic and cultural life of a nation. It is the contested site where meanings are negotiated, traditions made and remade, identities affirmed or rejected' (Bhoopaty, 505).

Jigna Desai believes that 'diaspora' has become a critical means for understanding global and transnational processes. Diaspora is experienced through diasporic films, located in various diasporic spaces. Such films question and ponder over the significance of home, belonging, acceptance and citizenship. While dwelling on dislocation, citizenship, racism, diasporic films also indulge in colonialism, nationalism and capitalism.

The leading personalities of popular Hindi film industry are very conscious of their responsibilities. Producer-director Yash Chopra, during his address at the first *Pravasi Bharatiya Diwas* states: '... our moral responsibility is to depict India at its best. We're the historians of India ... . The Indian Diaspora must maintain its identity, its roots' (Chopra, 2003).

Immigrants, struggling to adjust in an alien land, enjoy the carefully crafted and floated out South Asian films, depicting an authentic lifestyle, respect for family, religion and an adorable patriarchal system. They relish the nostalgia, festivals and fasting. Deep down they understand that real homeland is much more than what is being screened. Many migrants who are struggling with income and tough living conditions feel otherwise:

> ... one has to really struggle to experience a good life in America ... and why do movies not bother to depict the struggles Indians like me go through? Just our everyday life ... it is not like the families in the suburbs who only think of us when they go to a restaurant or take a cab in the city. (Punathambekar: 158)

Diasporas experience a strong longing for familiar landscapes, smells and sounds. Without bothering much about accurate historical details, they identify and cling to the traditional values of lands, which they have left behind. Roy Chow opines:

> Nostalgia is not simply a reaching toward the definite past from a definite present, but a subjective state that seeks to express itself in pictures imbued with particular memories of a certain pastness. In film, these subjectively pictoralised memories are there for everyone to see: nostalgia thus has a public life as much as a purely private one. The cinematic image, because of its visible nature, becomes a wonderfully appropriate embodiment of nostalgia's ambivalence between dream and reality, of nostalgia's insistence on seeing 'concrete' things in fantasy and memory. (Chow: 215)

The discontent on projection of a glamorous immigrant is widespread amidst the less glamorous realities of emigration. Most people leave their motherland out of necessity. Almost everyone thinks of the advantages of going abroad at one point of their lives. Dreaming of moving away to a far off place, making a living, achieving success, is not new. When an individual lands on a foreign land in order to fulfil dreams, home and motherland become a dream. Mira Nair had once commented on filming realistic themes:

> (A) mode of exploration of what happens when you cross the colour line from one community to another (...) I want to create the unpredictability of life, that grey arena that makes us all what we are and not just the black-and-white/good-and-bad that cinema is always relegated, but that very real life we all life. That is my passion (...) to find ourselves for the first time (qtd. in Redding and Brownworth 170–2).

Hanif Kureishi, born in London in 1954, is one of the most significant British authors, filmmakers and thinkers of Asian British origin. In his film scripts, novels and essays he discusses racism, identity, fringe and post-modern lifestyles. He confesses in one of his commentaries on his works:

> From the start, I tried to deny my Pakistani self. I was ashamed. It was a curse and I wanted to be rid of it. I wanted to be like

> everyone else ... I withdrew, from the park, from the lads, to a safer place within myself ... I was only waiting now to get away, to leave the London suburbs, to make another kind of life, somewhere else, with better people. ('The Rainbow Sign', in: 'London Kills Me': 4).

Udayan Prasad has tried to capture the pain and trauma of migrants in his film *My Son the Fanatic* (1998). Scripted by Hanif Kureishi, this film bears a touching story. It is a potent character study of a man who feels his world crumbling around him by the religious convictions of his son.

Parwez (Om Puri) is an optimistic taxi driver with a wife and son who do not appreciate him much. Somewhere along the way, Farid (Akbar Kurtha), begins to drift and joins a fundamentalist Muslim sect. Once, after acquiring permission from his father, Farid invited his sect's leader into their home along with other disciples. Parwez's residence becomes home base for the fundamentalist's work. His wife starts covering her face and takes her meals in the kitchen all by herself. These new entrants help her cement the wall she had been raising between herself and her husband.

For long, filmmakers have borrowed themes from fiction while some others have an affinity for adaptation. They wish to play safe. A successful novel, they believe, will churn out a successful film too. Hanif Kureishi's novel attempts to explore the relation between a father and a son in a Pakistani family residing in England. But its adaptation by the same name wears a different look altogether. Kureishi wrote the script himself and he extended his novel in various ways. He added more characters and he breathed a change in the overall tone of the narrative. For instance, humour is resplendent in the film while it is totally absent from the novel. The film enabled Kureishi to reach a wider audience and delve deeper into moral issues that he had only touched upon in his novel. Revisiting the narration with the aim of adaptation allowed the writer to usher in changes, which is very apparent in the film. George Bluestone had aptly concluded: 'An art whose limits depends on a moving image, mass audience, and industrial production is bound to be different from an art whose limits depend on language, a limited audience and individual creation' (Berkeley: 63–64):

Adaptation involves additions, alterations and omissions. The novel *My Son the Fanatic* relates a tale spun around people and their feelings. The film, however, appears to be drenched with political, social and religious hues. The novel narrates a story of Parwez, a taxi driver, who is shattered on losing his son to the fundamentalists. Parwez had himself given up all of it in his effort to belong to the foreign land. Farid, however, finds it real tough to assimilate and he decides to turn back to where his father had begun. Each has their own response to Diaspora.

My Son the Fanatic beautifully elucidates the unexpected lifestyle of many Muslim Pakistani immigrants living in England. The film revolves around the ways in which the different generations of Pakistani Muslims, especially the youth cope with Western culture that appears to be nurtured by freedom, filth, porn and animosity for Islam. Meenakshi Gigi Durham, Associate Professor of Journalism and Mass Communication at the University of Iowa, aptly concluded:

> 'Adolescence' and 'diaspora' are terms that both invoke the metaphor of a journey: issues of border crossing, dislocations, time/space passages, and reorientation frame our understandings of both constructs. Adolescent struggles with identity can be compared with the identity questions experienced by transnational immigrants: in the liminal spaces between childhood and adulthood, or between one geopolitical state and another, the 'Who am I?' question becomes imperative. The process of constructing a self that will bridge the gaps is the defining goal of these crucial life moments. When adolescence and diaspora occur in tandem, identity formation becomes an even more complex issue. The psychological transition of adolescence, already charged in terms of gender and sexuality, is then imbricated with the conundrums of the other transition – the diaspora identity that demands delicate negotiations of race/ethnicity, nation, class, language, culture and history. For children of immigrant diaspora groups, adolescence is a particularly complex juncture, calling for a sophisticated grasp of cross-cultural dialectics and the socio-political dimensions of otherness that will mark their adult. (161)

The first generation immigrants get little time to evaluate their action. The moment they land, they busy themselves in seeking a home and livelihood. They, in fact, like the change. The second generation that are raised on these lands realize and repent the loss. They satirize their parents' false ethics, superstitious religiosity, prejudices, obsession with wealth and status.

The very values that migrants had willingly shed away to adjust and 'fall in' with the people of their 'host land' become significant for their offsprings. The youngsters have their own set of experiences that disillusions them. In the novel *Mistress of Spices* (1997), Divakaruni vividly relates the trauma of a growing boy:

> ... they took me places with them. Bought me stuff, clothes shoes food watches Nintendo games stereos with speakers to make the walls shake, even things I didn't know yet to want. They listened when I talked and didn't laugh .... They taught me how to fight howed me how to use elbow knee fist boot keys and yes, knife. And in return so little. Carry this packet here, drop off this box there. Keep this in your locker for a day. Stand on the corner and watch for. Who needs mother father school? When I'm older, maybe fourteen, I'll be with them all the time. I'll wear the same jacket, carry deep in my pocket the same switch blade with its snake flick tongue, see the same bright pull of fear in the girls' eyes and boys running. (Divakaruni, 1997: 121)

Adolescents and teenagers have a tough time in school and in the playground. If they readily accept, defeat and agree to be at the beck and call of 'old boys', they are safe, otherwise their days become traumatic and they undergo deeply distressing experiences.

The film portrays a heart wrenching conflict that many Muslim families from South Asia wrestle with when integrated into new cultures. Key issue for many South Asian households in England is to strike a balance between Islamic tradition and Western values. Parwez, raised in a religious household of Lahore, outgrew his Islamic ideologies and took up drinking and adultery in an effort to belong and assimilate in the foreign land. Farid undergoes his own set of experiences. He has a change of heart and realizes that he cannot be a part of a culture that is imbued with alcohol, drugs and pornography. He goes ahead to point out to his father that he has deviated from the path laid down by the holy *Quran*.

Farid takes up the responsibility of being a role model for the family and tries to prove that his father had deviated from the path that the Holy Scriptures required him to abide. Farid once had an English girlfriend. He had admired western music, fashion and gadgets. Now, his new found allegiance saw to it that Farid threw it all, and spent his leisure hours in reading the *Quran* and offering prayers to the Almighty.

Farid begins to recite the holy *Quran* regularly. He even begins to imbibe the teachings of Islam, under the supervision of religious leaders. He gives up his Western clothes and attires himself up in *salwar-kameez* and *kufi* hat.

My Son the Fanatic tenderly articulates a tendency of some British born Asians to revert to Islamic traditions and refuse to integrate and assimilate in the British society, a society that embraces diversity. Had Farid struggled on to mature into a Westernized Asian Briton, he would perhaps marry the girl of his choice and would have lived happily ever after. But he willingly trenched out a thorny and stony path for himself. The film depicts the repulsion of South Asian youth of British society.

> The strategy of mediating Farid's religion in piecemeal fashion, through Parwez's perspective, is significant. First, it positions the viewer with Parwez. Since each stands outside the world into which Farid is moving, audiences are encouraged to empathise with his father, as co observers of the process. Second, the progressive distancing of Farid from Parwez, which is concomitant with Farid's incremental adoption of religious rituals, emphasises the constructedness of 'fundamental' Islam. It represents a break from his immediate heritage. In a telling move, Farid learns to pray in Arabic via the medium of modern technology, in the form of an instructional video cassette. (Melanie J. Wright, 2007)

Two extended dialogues articulate the core of Farid's philosophy. In the first, he explains the reasons for his broken engagement:

> FARID: Can you put keema with strawberries? In the end our cultures, they cannot be mixed.

> PARWEZ: Everything is mingling already together, this thing and the other.
> FARID: Some of us are wanting sum what more besides muddle ... lief, purity, belonging to the past. I won't bring up my children in this country. (Kureishi, 1997)

And later, when Parwez tries to convince Farid to return to his former lifestyle, Faris responds with:

> They tell us to integrate but they live in pornography and filth and tell us how backward we are ... Their society is soaked in sex ...
> Accountancy ... is capitalism and taking advantage ...
> It is you who have swallowed the white and Jewish propaganda that there is nothing in our lives but the empty accountancy for things.
> Here Farid's Islam is positioned as separatist (a stance undermined linguistically by his Yorkshire dialect), linked to a desire for clarity and the rebuilding of a connection with the imagined past. It offers an alternative to the ideologies of assimilation and capitalism, and is anti-Semitic. When a *maulvi* from Lahore comes to stay in the family's home, a violent potential within Farid's faith is realised. There is initially some warmth in the presentation of the *maulvi*, who is shown laughing at television cartoons over breakfast ... . Under the *maulvi's* encouragement, Farid and his friends launch a campaign against the local sex workers. Firebombing of brothel house forms the dramatic climax of the film. (Melanie J. Wright, 2007)

Parwez had migrated to England with the hope of making both ends meet. He worked long hours to feed his family. When Farid befriended an English girl, Parwez was thrilled as it meant that he would finally climb up in the social hierarchy. He was always eager to please the British and behaved submissively in their company. Kureishi pointed out: '... the background to the lives of these ... people includes colonialism-being made to feel inferior in your own country' (Kureishi, 1997).

Parwez and his co-workers were frequently attacked and were often exposed to physical racial abuse. Most of them kept a cricket bat in their taxi for protection. In spite of being placed on the lowest rung of social order, in spite of being treated with contempt and disrespect, Parwez does not even think of disowning the British society. He gave up many of his practices, beliefs and habits in order to assimilate in the British society and culture. He considers himself to be a gentleman; he consumes alcohol and even develops a taste for Jazz, especially Louis Armstrong. In his effort to adjust and conform to the rules of British society, Parwez became lonelier still. His son and wife drifted away from him.

The society that Parwez is desperately trying to assimilate into was dominated by capitalism and consumerism. There was no space for warmth and understanding. He was fervently trying to belong to those who looked down upon him and eyed him with suspicion. But Parwez was not deterred. He felt his life in Britain was much better than what he had lived in Pakistan. Muslim communities living in Britain often experience such victimization. Editors of an Edited Volume have questioned the authenticity of media portrayals:

> Today, our views are too often governed by the media which portrays this faith community as a monolithic group of people, separated from society. The Muslim community's sense of belonging and integration to the mainstream society is questioned. The media choose to ignore the diversity of cultures and ethnic groups which make up Islam's religious base and which co-exist within the city and its neighbourhoods. It is this homogenising of Muslims and other religio-cultural based communities, which distorts the realities of everyday experiences. (Shakur, et al.: 2007)

Parwez's loneliness drove him to seek love and companionship in Bettina's company. He gets a chance to speak out his mind in her company. In the short story, Parwez and Bettina are just friends. In the film, the relationship culminates in a sexual relationship. Both Parwez and Bettina live on the margins and desperately yearn to belong. David Edelstein observed: '… They are playing by capitalism's rules, trying to get a foothold in a society that closely guards access to its more 'proper' ladders to the top' (1).

Parwez never regretted his decision of migrating from Pakistan to an unknown, alien land. June Thomas concluded: '… for Parwez, immigration to Britain represented a decision to prioritize materialism for spirituality ...' (Thomas: 2). Parwez was devoid of spiritualism and philosophy. All he thought of was to earn enough to feed his family, pay his mortgages. His life was bereft of philosophy and consciousness. In his robotic existence, Bettina was the only ray of hope and warmth. He was able to share his fears and inhibitions with her. Days rolled by and Parwez kept waiting for the day when his son Farid, born and brought up in the West would marry a White woman and help the family rise a rung higher in the social hierarchy. Farid's strange behaviour was a wakeup call for Parwez. After much spying and questioning, Parwez realized that his son was a lost cause. His son was clinging to the same beliefs that Parwez had discarded to start life afresh in a foreign country. Time had run a full circle and the boomerang had come back to Parwez. Parwez's human dimension is brought to the fore towards closure. His soft corner for a prostitute, his drinking bouts, offences against the laws of *Quran* make him more human and the portrait appears complete. Viewers and readers feel sorry for this man who was trying to live as best as he could: 'He had a conscience. There were a few things of which he was ashamed, but on the whole he had lived a decent life' (Hanif Kureishi, 1997).

Farid's immaturity prevents him from analysing the actions of his father in clear light. He went ahead to ascribe himself super righteousness, estranging himself from his relatives in the process. He insulted his father and fiercely defended racism and segregation. The complex, sympathetic, sexually deviant taxi driver earns a living by ferrying business travellers and sex workers. Tradition and hectic hours of work saw to it that he drifted from his family and failed to dissuade or to wield any power when his son chose to become a militant Muslim fundamentalist. Alienation and resistance to Western imperialism gives way to fundamentalism.

Farid is hounded by self-questionings arising from diasporic conditions and religious pluralism. He realized that the routine habitual practice, blind faith and rote learning laid down by the Holy text was no longer operational in his household. Therefore, the young man took charge and began to accuse his father of being a deviant. Parwez, on the other hand, had other priorities. In the new land, where he dreamt of becoming one with, Parwez was not sure about what he should believe and how to go about it. He began to segregate religiousness and religious mindedness. Jørgen Nielsen writes:

> The circumstances of migration, the situation into which Muslims have settled in European cities, and the adaptations which are being made, especially as the young grow up to be the first European Muslim generation, all impose the need to analyse. The old way has to be analysed into discrete parts so that Islam can be identified. The emphasis of the identification of Islam can be on the Qur'an and Qur'anic principles or it can be on aspects of the Shari'a tradition. In either case, one proceeds to 'reassemble' these Islamic components together with the components arising out of the migration and settlement experience into a new complex whole which functions more successfully in European urban, industrial life. As a universal religion with a long historical experience of successfully integrating into new cultures, it would be extremely surprising if Islam were not to follow exactly this kind of path also in Europe. (Nielson: 114–15)

Research by Kim Knott and Sadja Khoker has shown that there has been a shift in perception of religion and its practice among Muslim women residing in Britain. They are gradually learning to differentiate between 'religion' and 'culture', which were largely identical domain for their parents:

> Further, they are rejecting their parents' conformity to ethnic traditions, which are considered as emblematic of religiosity (such as manner of dress) while wholly embracing a Muslim identity in and of itself. Among these young women, Knott and Khokher explain, there is a 'self-conscious exploration of the religion which was not relevant to the first generation'. (Knott and Khoker: 596)

With regard to this conundrum amongst South Asians worldwide, Raymond Williams comments:

> The critical assumption here is that there are some aspects associated with past religious practice that are fundamental and essential to the continuation of the religion and others that are cultural accoutrements that are not so fundamental. Thus, the process of searching for an adaptive strategy becomes the

> attempt to distinguish what is essential in the religion and what is not. (Williams: 191)

On seeing the film and reading the text, one can but philosophize that human life has more sorrow than happiness. No matter where we go, no matter what we do, our share of both joy and sorrow follow us around. Parwez had shifted base, in the hope of leading a lavish successful life in London. Sorrow walked into his life in the garb of his son Farid, who had gradually transformed into a militant fundamentalist.

In his desire to assimilate, Parwez erased his own identity and transformed himself to be accepted in the host land. In the process, he failed to extend support to Farid. As a father, it was his moral duty to stand by his son and help him deal with inequality and prejudice. Militant Islam extends support and acts as a pillar of support for young Farid. In fanaticism, he found an escape and a shelter. His affiliation teaches him to wipe out all feelings of inferiority. In fact, he starts feeling superior.

My Son the Fanatic is a discerning and thought provoking narrative about a diasporic family struggling to assimilate in their 'new' homeland. It nudges cultural and generational conflicts to the fore. While Parwez is caught between his duties and dreams, he is also losing track as each merges with the other. However, 'conflict' and 'clash' loom large in the story but it does not actually arrive. The novel and the film are shrouded by an emotional or psychological realism. Farid is young and open to new ideas. Then what is served to him is a mishmash of retro values and Western culture, which he finds repulsive. The film and the novel project heart-rending consequences of assimilation of South Asian culture into White culture. They effectively conjure the meaningless gestures of integration sans any changes in inequity or power relationships.

Works Cited

Bhoopaty, D. 'Cinema and Politics in India'. *Political Communication: The Indian Experience*. Ed. Kiran Prasad. Delhi: B. R. Publishing Corporation, 2003. 507–17. Print.

Bluestone, George. *Novels into Film: The Metamorphosis of Fiction into Cinema*. Berkeley: University of California Press, 1957. Print.

Brah, Avtar. *Cartographies of Diaspora: Contesting Identities*. New York: Routledge, 1996. Print.

Carol, A. Breckenridge. 'Food, Politics, and Pilgrimage in South India, A.D. 1350–1650'. *Aspects in South Asian Food Systems: Food, Society, and Culture*. Eds. R.S. Khare and M.S.A Rao. Durham: Carolina Academic Press, 1986. 21–53. Print.

David Edelstein. 'Generation Gap'. Web. 16 August. 2015. <http://slate.msn.com, 1999>

Desai, Jigna. *Beyond Bollywood: The Cultural Politics of South Asian Diasporic Film*. New York: Routledge Publishers, 2004. Print.

Divakaruni, Chitra Banerjee. *The Mistress of Spices*. London: Doubleday Publishers, 1997. Print.

Gramsci, Antonio. *Cultural Themes: Ideological Material in Media and Cultural Studies Key Works*. Eds. Meenakshi Gigi Durham and Douglas M. Kellner Malden. MA: Wiley Blackwell, 2012. 9–13, Print.

Jeremiah's *A Letter to the Exiles*, Holy Bible, New International Version, 2011 by Biblica, Inc. Web. 15 July. 2015. <http://www.biblica.com/niv/>

June, Thomas. 'The First 7/7 Movie'. 16 August. 2015. <http://slate.msn.com, 1999> Web.

Kaleta, Kenneth, C. *Hanif Kureishi: Postcolonial Storyteller*. Austin: University of Texas Press, 1998. Print.

Kureishi, Hanif. *My Beautiful Launderette*. London: Faber, 1996. Print.

——. *The Road Exactly: Introduction to My Son the Fanatic*. London: Faber and Faber, 1997. Print.

Knott, K. and S. Khokher. *Religious and Ethnic Identity among Young Muslim Women*. Bradford: New Community, 1993. 593–610. Print.

Mishra, Vijay. *The Literature of the Indian Diaspora: Theorizing the Diasporic Imaginary*. London and New York: Routledge, 2007. Print.

Nielsen, Jorgen. *Muslims in Western Europe*. Edinburg: Edinburg University Press, 2004. Print.

Punathambekar, Aswin. 'Bollywood in the Indian-American Diaspora: Mediating a Transitive Logic of Cultural Citizenship'. *International Journal of Cultural Studies* 8. 2 (2005): 151–173. Print.

Roy, Chow. *Writing Diaspora: Tactics of Intervention on Contemporary Cultural Studies*. Bloomington: Indian University Press. 1993. Print.

Williams, Raymond. *The Country and the City*. New York: Oxford UP, 1973. Print.

Wright, Melanie J. *New Religion and Film: An Introduction*. New York: I.B. Tauris, 2007. Print.

7

Afghan Diaspora and Diasporic Spaces in the Cinematic Landscape of Afghanistan and Iran

IRUM ALVI

Several films made in Afghanistan raise the issue of what is home? They compel one to ask the question what is a home for the Afghan diaspora? They portray images of the Afghan in their own homes in their own country, to be precise as a place in which they live, where they have lived, and where they will live if circumstances allow them, in short images of their permanent residence. The films made in Afghanistan are perhaps a good starting point to study the issues related to diaspora as Afghanistan has been the target of wars and natural disasters causing widespread dispersal of its people. The films made in Afghanistan henceforth referred to as the Afghan Cinema, capture the various images of home, it may be the place in which they were born or grew up, the place where they live now maybe in some distant land, or the place where they even hope to live one day. The Afghan diaspora is the focal point of several films, which directly or indirectly deal with the issues of the Afghan migrants and refugees.

This paper will explores the representation of the diasporic Afghan community in films, following the progression of the depiction of diasporic themes since the beginning of cinema in Afghanistan, especially in some more recent films. Using many an image from Afghan cinema, it will investigate these portrayals in a chronological order, attempting to understand the emotions of longings for home, the nostalgia for the past and other diasporic recurrent themes in the cinema which have developed in the past decades. The paper before probing into the analysis deals with the context through which these films should be understood. The paper intends to investigate the complex concept of *Khāna* (Home), *Khānawāda/Ahle-Khāna* (Family) and *Watan* (Homeland) focusing on varied images of home captured by the Afghan films. The paper posits that for the Afghan diasporic community home indicates much more than an actual geological position or locality. It stands for much more than a house, a village, a town or even their country for them. The paper focuses on cinematic representation of the connection between Afghan diasporic community and Afghanistan, the Afghan diaspora's senses of belonging and non-belonging to the so-called 'homeland', and how these relate to issues of return to Afghanistan.

The cinema in Afghanistan captures images of what the Afghans call *'Khāna'* in *Dari* language, meaning both home and house. When the Afghan diasporas speak of *Khāna* (Home), they may be referring not so much to a place as to a feeling inspired by that place, one they have left behind. The Afghan cinema shows how home become a state of mind. It is undeniably associated with individuality: the places the Afghan diaspora labels as *Khāna* (Home) are the places which define them, the places to which they think they belong, and which they themselves own. Away from this they feel frustrated and deprived of hope and confidence, as if they have been denied the right not only to *Khāna* (Home), but also the right to grow and to become.

The word *'Khāna'* in the films evokes a symbolism which incorporates a sense of belonging, especially to a familial home, evoking metaphysical connotations. Ahmed believes 'home as a place of origin' (341) plays an important role in life. The Afghan cinema shows that it is unthinkable to reside for some major period of time in a place yet resist forming associations with it; the diaspora population resides and is shaped by the places where they stay, whether they love it or hate it seems of no consequence. Home is home. The memories of past, the home, are indelibly seared in the minds of the diaspora. The Afghans as the films show either make attempts to recreate or make efforts to escape or endeavour to build for them the home and the life they wish for.

It would be pertinent to cast a glance at the cinema and the socio-political changes and their impact on cinema in Afghanistan. Cinema entered Afghanistan at the beginning of the 20th century. Emir Habibullah Khan brought films in Afghanistan, which were shown in the royal court. The first projector, the magic box pronounced as 'mageek box' by the Afghans/Iranians was used in the years 1923–24 to show the first silent film *Paghman* to the local public. The first Afghan film, *Love and Friendship* was produced as late as 1946. *Like Eagles* (1962) was the first black and white feature film made in Kabul by Afghan filmmakers. *Run Away, Love Epic, Saboor Soldier, Ash, Last Wishes* and *Migrating Birds* were made in colour in the late 1960s.

After that, the film industry suffered a great set back as conditions were not conducive for making films. A number of films, considered B-movies due to the low production quality and audience reach, were produced in Afghanistan. The Afghan cinema captures glimpses of migration and displacement as prominent features of contemporary and modern times. The films are replete with the Afghan characters and their diasporic experiences – a direct consequence of their forming the largest refugees and migrant community in the world. The Afghans, more than any other people have wandered to different parts of the world and they amount to nearly 25 per cent of the displaced people in the world. Their long history of exile started with the Soviet intervention in the year 1979, which compelled the rural people to move to neighbouring countries, scattering throughout the host country's cities as well as rural towns. This continued till the beginning of the 1990s. The second half of the 1990s compelled more Afghans to flee in quest for livelihood and sustenance, this time due to extreme drought. Millions lived in refugee camps without the bare necessities of life and were later forced to return to Afghanistan, all these disturbing experiences have been portrayed by Afghan cinema, concentrating on the horrible conditions of the Afghan diaspora, the intolerance of the host country's government and civilians towards the Afghans, the plight of the refugee camps and the terrifying situation when these camps were closed and the Afghans were driven away. Another type of migration that Afghanistan witnessed was the emigration of the elite to Western industrialized countries, wherein a comparatively smaller group of Afghans settled in Europe, America, Canada, Australia and New Zealand. They were affluent and had contacts and resources, despite all this they were still refugees and migrants in strange lands. Khattak argues, 'Leaving home becomes symbolic of the larger insecurity where one is unable to guard against the outside and therefore is forced to abandon the most sacred of places – the home, ...' (107).

The second wave of dislocation took place from 1992 to 1996, which saw the widespread destruction of major parts of Afghanistan due to the intense fighting that broke out between the different groups of *Mujahidin*. The third wave from 1994 to 2001 began by the capture of Kabul by the Taliban, who imposed extremely severe laws on the people and equally severe punishments for not following the laws which they labelled as Islam and their interpretation of the *Shari'a*. Cinema was banned and music and photography were strictly forbidden. They even imposed a dress code for the Afghan men and women. The year 1997, when the Taliban denied handing over Osama Bin Laden saw America take a stand and bombed several training camps of Bin Laden. All these social disturbances and political upheaval resulted in the migration of the Afghans to the West in search for peace. The 9/11 saw the beginning of a war against terrorism launched by the US. The several years of war and natural calamities resulted in the biggest diaspora the world had ever seen. The impact of all this shaped the Afghan consciousness and is clearly reflected in the bleak condition of the Afghan cinema, which is as fragmented as the community it portrays.

Several films have been made in Afghanistan till date, such as *Roz Garan (Daily)* 1968 by Afghan Films, *Andarzi Mudar (Mother's Advice)* 1972 by Afghan Films, *Rozhai Dushwar (Difficult Days)* 1974 by Afghan Films, *Rabiha Balkhi (Rabiha of Balkh)* 1974 by Nazir Films, *Mujasemeha Mekhandad (The Statues Are Laughing)* 1976 by Ariana Films, *Janayat Karan (Criminals)* 1981 by Shafaq Films, *Gharatgara (Thieves)* 1981 by Aparcin Films, *Gunah (Faults)* 1981 by Ariana Films, *Tabistan*

Garm Kabul (Hot Summer of Kabul) 1983 by Afghan Films, *Parindaha-e-Mohajir/Migrating Birds* 1987 by Afghan Films and *Uruj (Ascension)* 1995 by Afghan Film.

The Afghan films deal with the social and political circumstances and depict them realistically. *Gumashta* (1991) directed by Engineer Latif and starring Saboor Toofan, Qader Faroskh, Nemat Asash, Habib Zilgai and Lina, is a knotted story about love and the influence of the lucrative opium business in Afghanistan. This film was completed in 1991 and alleged to have been lost or damaged during the war. In 2005, the film was re-discovered. From 2,000 onwards, the cinema of Afghanistan has slowly started to emerge from a lengthy period of silence. Samira Makhmalbaf, Siddiq Barmak, Razi Mohebi, Horace Shansab, Yassamin Maleknasr, Abolfazl Jalili, etc. have made a significant contribution to the cinema in Afghanistan.

Despite the fact that very few films were made in Afghanistan and these too lack technical merit, they manage to capture the images of reality of Afghan life and the images of homes and what they stand for. There are proverbs in every language about home. A popular Afghan proverb sums up what home means for the Afghans: *Khānadār rā yak khāna; bi khāna rā sad khāna* (English Translation: One home for the one who has a home; a hundred homes for the one who has none). Home is always an idealized place. The traditional attitude of Afghans towards home as captured by the films is sentimental and naïve. They desire a warm, content family home to which they may return to find a welcome, as the words *khānawāda/ahle-khāna,* meaning family, suggest. In times of wars, social and political upheaval, the home for the Afghans has become a much more complicated affair. Their perception of home has been significantly altered and ever replaced by the more pertinent questions – 'where is home?' and 'what is the meaning of home?' – for the Afghans in foreign countries.

It is pertinent to note that Afghanistan is a country destroyed by wars and the cinema of Afghanistan has shared the same fate. The films even the few that have been made by the Afghans, who may not be well trained in the art of making films have nevertheless managed to capture the images of war, poverty and destitution. In terms of content, Afghanistan's cinema is fundamentally poor. However, as far as images are concerned, it has captured lots of them despite the fact that most of the people who are involved in the area of film production in Afghanistan are low literate and have poor knowledge about cinema. The supremacy of an Islamic fundamentalist perspective towards photography, cinema and music has had a negative effect on the Afghan cinema. Economically the conditions are equally bad as there are not enough budgets for making films. This cinema is dependent on the support of foreign aids and institutions. In terms of film screening, there are fundamental problems. Afghan directors and film makers are desperately trying to rescue their industry and its inheritance. Since the Taliban were overthrown in 2001, films using Afghan settings and actors have enjoyed enormous success at home and abroad, such as *Osama* in 2003 and *The Kite Runner* in 2007, but these were made with foreign financial support. On its own, Afghanistan has only managed to make a couple of films over the last few decades but these are prove enough to that Afghanistan film industry has great potential and Afghan filmmakers have lots of stories to tell.

A short Afghan film *'The Last President of Afghanistan'* (2013) tells the story of Amir Ali and his 10 brothers, each of whom is a presidential candidate. Amir, despite being the youngest, thinks he is the one to be elected as the President because his father told him before he died that he was the one 'destined to change the world'. The film captures images of the whole city swept with a feverish condition during the elections. The film catches glimpses of the Afghans who become exiles due to their different political opinions, shared feelings similar to those of the diaspora. Amir's brothers become jealous of him, and like the biblical story of Joseph of Egypt, Amir is thrown into a dark well by them. The dark well symbolizes the political and social conditions of the Afghan people. The ray of hope still exists despite all the darkness as Ali is rescued by a girl who helps him make a comeback.

The loss of the traditional home and the loss of the sense of being at home are captured even in what are called B grade Afghan films. The social and political changes have led to the uprooting of the settled Afghan people, compelling them to migrate or be exiled, at times leaving the places where generations had lived and passed away. Instead of the home, the diasporic community finds itself forced to live in camps mostly on the outskirts of the towns in deplorable conditions; the imagery in the films of the life lived in the refugee camp is in sharp contrast with the security of the traditional Afghan home. Most importantly, the Afghan films capture the sense of homelessness felt acutely by the diaspora. The films tend to mirror the life of an Afghan who is isolated and whose existence is fragmented. He has to stand alone against the odds, a lone traveller in strange lands. He feels eternally homesick and homeless. They portray symbols of a '*dowrān-e gozashta*', a period that is no more, of memories and past. The characters are confronted with the question where is home. The 'feeling of home' is where one belongs or wants to belong according to Graham and Khosravi (130).

In *Khakestar-o-khak/Earth and Ashes,* made by Atiq Rahimi in the year 2004, we find the image of an old Afghan man Dastaguir who has to traverse long distances across Afghanistan accompanied with his grandson to inform his son that the family has been killed due to a bomb attack. It deals with '*dowrān-e gozashta*', a period that is no more. Atiq Rahimi, an Afghan born in Kabul city recalls his own horrific experiences and portrays them in this film based on his novella with the same name. He was only 17 years of age at the time when Soviet Union invaded his country, due to which he fled to Pakistan to save his life. After the end of the Taliban regime, he came back to what was once his home and filmed an adaptation of the novella, which presents very horrific images of Afghanistan on the eve of destruction when 'the dead are more fortunate than the living'. The images of the bleak landscape, a broken bridge between northern Afghanistan and Kabul, dry river-beds, a dirt track that runs across the hills leading to a coal mine, being crossed by Dastaguir who crouches against the railings of the bridge, watching the dusty road with dry eyes, waiting to hitchhike a ride to the coal mine with his grandson following him, bring to mind the images of up-rootedness and destruction and despair of the diaspora. The dust-covered apples and the stale bread convey how the bare necessities of life are difficult to procure for the Afghans during the period of war.

Dastaguir's son, Murad, entrusted Dastaguir with his young wife and his son Yassin when he left for finding work in the coal mines years ago, but the fact was that he wanted to escape and go away. The Russian Army bombed the village, destroying everything till all that remained was earth and ashes. Dastaguir's family was killed in the devastating incident while his five year-old grandson Yassin survived but lost his hearing during the bombing. However, he believes that the Russians have stolen their voices being too young to recognize the truth. He asks his grandfather if the Russians have taken away everyone's voice. He innocently asks what they do with the voices and why did he give his voice to them. The image brings to mind the mute diasporas, whose right to raise a voice has been taken away from them. The little child continues to ask questions. The most poignant being, why he was still alive, which conveys the conditions of the Afghans who ask themselves the question time and again unable to find an answer.

The cinematic images of the diaspora invite the people into the hearts and minds of the miserable lives, the desolate souls of the Afghan diasporic community who have lost everything in the war. They offer no optimism but only grief, no delight but only pain. The images depict how they have been condemned to exist and watch the world pass, to watch the wife pass, to watch the children pass, a suffocating feeling when air isn't refreshing, but becomes thick, heavy, and black and the realization that it's not the sight that has gone dim, it's the air that has grown dark. Home, for the Afghan diaspora, as their cinema depicts, is comprehensible in terms of *yadhaye maazi* which translated into English may mean memories of the past, a feeling of nostalgia (a word whose Greek origins are in the words 'nostos' and 'algi' – meaning 'return home' and 'pain'; the loss implied by the Afghan word denotes their loss of home: home exists principally in the times of yore and is apparently unachievable and even inaccessible. In the imaginations of characters on screen a house may represent home, a place infused with feelings of nostalgic longing, the scene of memories, or a symbol of a lost period; *ehsās-e bigāna*, a feeling of estrangement.

Osama (2004), by Siddiq Barmak, winner of the 61st Golden Globe Award, tells the story of woman who alters the appearance of her daughter to look like a boy and renames her Osama as she is unable to move without a male companion while *Raaz/Secret* (2004) filmed entirely in Afghanistan by producers and directors in Kabul, who attempted for the first time to produce a film independent of the government, shows ex-soldiers amidst defunct warlords.

Dain (2005), directed by Harif Bayria, starring Ahmad Jan, Harif Bayria, Akram and Hashem, is about an orphan who learns martial arts to avenge the murder of his parents. His adventure takes him to his birthplace where his ancestral enemies are waiting. In the film *Qanoon* (2005), directed by Ghafar Zalam, starring Sabah Sahar and Ahmad Zia Ghaznawi, Rabia joins the police force to serve the country and finds herself in the midst of illegal drug and organ trade, she must decide to join the lucrative drug business or fight against it. A Sayed Ahmad Waqif Al Hussaini film, *Gone with the Wind* (2005), with Masoom Qismat as the director shows a post-war Afghanistan in which a generation that has seen nothing but war and destruction. In the aftermath of the war, which has taken vast numbers of men away from their homes, leaving millions dead on battlefields, never to be welcomed home again, those who are left behind find their confidence and sense of security irrevocably shaken in a world which has become like an empty barren waste land. Home is an existential concept, and lies at focal point of the films. The Afghan hero bereft of the comforts of home lives on the margins in the post-World War Afghan cinema. The story traces the theme of pursuit of home, which for the Afghan diaspora takes top-most priority and becomes the search for the Self. Heidegger asserts in his 'Letter on Humanism' that homelessness lies 'in the abandonment of Being by beings' (218). He adds in 'Building, Dwelling, Thinking', 'The real dwelling plight lies in this, that mortals must ever search anew for the essence of dwelling that they must ever learn to dwell' (339). The films show the Afghan dwellings and in the process of learning to dwell in the real sense of the word and what Barrett calls the transitional phase followed either by total incorporation into the host society, or by a return to the country of origin (5).

The film *Love Hurts Love Takes Over* made in the year 2006 is about family, relationships and love between two strangers, their friendships, their gang lives and sacrifices, while another film made in the same year *Al Qarem* depicts the circumstances faced by the Afghan community post-9/11. Qarem and Nasir, two young Afghans living in Queens, New York, on the eve of 11 September 2001, find their lives turned into hell as hatred fills the city. The Afghan boys become innocent victims of a savage backlash against all Muslims or against anyone perceived to be a Muslim. They see bias, prejudice and hatred and wrath. The film captures the images of homelessness of the Afghan family living in Queens, before and after the historical catastrophe. The FBI agents abduct Nasir, a family friend, and try to find out why money was transferred to someone in Afghanistan during the Taliban regime. Away from home, the feeling of camaraderie takes over and the mission to help the innocent boy in distress is taken up as almost a religious obligation. The film captures harrowing images of the hate crimes carried out by the locals against those who are perceived as foreigners as some form of retaliation. All the incidents portrayed in the film are based on a true story. It shows not only the fate of the victims of homelessness but also the victimization caused by a historical tragedy. The Afghan family which was already suffering due to issues related to their immigration confronts discord that reverberated in the entire cosmopolitan city.

The film, *Wazhma/Wajma/An Afghan Love Story* (2013), written and directed by Barmak Akram, shows Kabul in winter, with snow falling from the sky. A waiter Mustafa woos a pretty student named Wajma. They have an affair, meeting secretly and enjoying a passionate relationship but always aware of the stringent Islamic rules they are flouting. Wajma learns she is pregnant, she fervently believes that her lover Mustafa will marry her but he refuses to tie the knot. The word of their disgraceful relationship gets out, forcing her father to choose between the family honour and the paternal love for his daughter. The film portrays the plight of women and their need for space and home, which for the Afghans is not limited to one place; instead circumstances have forced them to move to different locations. The film, *Unknown* (2013), portrays a woman's struggles to shoulder the responsibilities of a disabled husband and two children. She is employed by a global agency which is to close in 2014, at a time when elections are to be held and international armies are to be withdrawn. In her terrifying nightmare, the Taliban compel her to dance and offer her body to them.

Afghan film *Madrasa,* made in the year 2013, directed by Afghan filmmaker and actor Asad Sikandar, is considered to be one the most controversial movies in Afghanistan. The story deals with the Afghan diasporic community and their efforts to meet the responsibilities of educating their children. It brings to the fore the educational challenges faced by the Afghan parents outside Afghanistan, and drives home the importance of providing conditions conducive for education, despite the illegal migration. The film *Madrasa* is based on a true story like the others and depicts the real experiences of the diasporic Afghan community. The film focuses on the life of an Afghan refugee family, which has fled to Iran after the war. It shows the plight an eight-year-old Afghani girl who is not permitted to attend school due to the conditions, circumstances and laws in Iran. Her father, named Farhad, is unable to bear the pain of his innocent daughter, who aspires to become a doctor, and he does everything he can to fulfil his daughter's dream. The insurmountable and the impossible circumstances are sharply contrasted against the courage, love and sacrifices. Afghan cinema captures glimpses of the changes that take place with the passage of time as the diaspora questions where and what home stands for them. It also captures the poignant reality that the Afghans who have lost the country of origin and home fails to exist even in their own country and are compelled to live the life of exiles. This emotion of non-belonging finds expression in the films as refugees have lost the home and are compelled to flee. The loss of their homes in their own country evokes a feeling of being strangers in their own country of origin. The films portray the 'otherness' of the Afghans and their trauma due to revolutionary changes that take place in the country.

In the Afghan films we can see the sharp contrast between those who are lucky as they can have the benefit and security of a home, a privilege denied to those in diaspora. The characters in the films ruminate about the homes they have left behind. They dream of homes and family. Their dreams of home/places, imaginary or actual, offer an antidote to the loss of homes, the utopias having a therapeutic effect on the characters in distress. They also take refuge in the concept of being one, belonging to one *qawm* or nation which helps them in times of dire need. They get a strong sense of identity from the place they have left behind and it is deep and multifaceted and ensnared with a sense of belonging to the place where they grew up, the wider country – the *watan* and the nation – the *qawm*. Afghanistan's cinema gives a glimpse of their social order also which is hierarchical. It is based on gender, age, family background and class. Nawa states that the social unit is the 'extended family' (6). 'People see themselves as part of their family system, religious sect and village, but also as part of a tribe, region, and finally, country', (26) Nawa adds. A chief level of identification is the *qawm*, which is synonymous to ethnic group or tribe, but has broader connotations meaning nation.

To conclude any endeavour to describe so multifaceted a notion as home/*khāna* is necessarily burdened with challenge and vagueness. Demuth believes 'home' entails a dual meaning of both a concrete physical space and an emotional and personal space of identification and feelings of belonging (24). For the majority of the Afghan diaspora people, home means this and much more than this. It has numerous connotations, numerous countenances. The films capture the tensions of the era and a generation, which grew up with war and has seen the miseries of natural calamities. It is hard to imagine that the sense of home which is so deeply felt could be ever suppressed and set aside by the people. Afghan films may not be at par with those made in other South Asian countries so far as technical aspects are concerned, but they tell stories and these stories are our own and help understand the human condition against a human background. They realistically portray men and women who are like ourselves and who have a dream of a home, an ideal home, and whose one goal is to find a place to belong, a place to be themselves, their very own home. The question is can those in diaspora ever attain their goal of finding the home.

Works Cited

Ahmed, Sara. 'Home and Away: Narratives of Migration and Estrangement.' *International Journal of Cultural Studies* 2. 3. (1999): 329–347. Print.

Barrett, Michael. *'Let's Go Everybody.' Identity and Ambition among Angolan Refugees in Zambia*. Uppsala: Uppsala University, 1998. Print.

Demuth, Andreas. 'Some Conceptual Thoughts on Migration Research.' *Theoretical and Methodological Issues in Migration Research: Interdisciplinary, Intergenerational and International Perspectives*. Ed. Biko Agozino. Hampshire: Ashgate, 2000. 21–58. Print.

Graham, Mark and Shahram Khosravi. 'Home is Where You Make It: Repatriation and Diaspora Culture among Iranians in Sweden.' *Journal of Refugee Studies* 10.2 (1997): 115–133. Print.

Heidegger, Martin. 'Letter on Humanism.' *Basic Writings*. Ed. David Farrell Krell. London: Routledge and Kegan Paul, 1978. 189–242. Print.

——. 'Building, Dwelling, Thinking'. *Basic Writings*. Ed. David Farrell. London: Routledge and Kegan Paul, 1978. 319–340. Print.

Khattak, S. G. 'Violence and Home: Afghan Women's Experience of Displacement.' *Understanding 11 September*. Eds. Craig Calhoun, Paul Price and Ashley Timmer. New York: The New Press, 2002. 116–136. Print.

Nawa, Fariba. *Out of Bounds: Afghan Couples in the United States. A Study of Shifting Gender and Identity*. San Francisco: Aftaabzad Publications, 2001. Print..

Section B

Typology of Indian Cinema: An Accentuated Journey of Hundred Years

8

Bollywood on the Wings of Technology and its Contribution to Economy

Hundredth Year of Indian Cinema

M.M.K. SARDANA

Film has a uniquely powerful ubiquity within human culture. In 2009, across major territories, there were 6.8 billion cinema admissions (equivalent to world population) creating global box office revenues of over US$30 billion. The convergent nature of film creates consumption across a number of channels. In the same year combined DVD and blu-ray sales in the United States, Canada and European Union alone were US$32.5 billion (1.1 billion units sold). When one starts to further consider revenues and audience figures from those who consume digitally, via television, repeat view content they already own and view through illegal but vast black-market in films, the figures become truly staggering.[1]

Movies have come to be key cultural artifacts that offer a window into evolving cultural and social history. A mixture of art, business and popular entertainment, the movies provide a host of insights into shifting ideals, fantasies, and pre-occupations like any cultural artifact, the movies can be approached in a variety of ways. Cultural historians would treat movies as social documents that record the look and mood of particular social settings; as ideological constructs that advance particular historical settings; as ideological constructs that advance particular moral values or myths; as psychological texts that speak to individual and social anxieties and tensions; as cultural documents that present particular images of gender, ethnicity, class, romance, and violence; and as visual texts that offer complex levels of meaning and seeing.[2]

Cinema has been perceived to be of therapeutic value. The narrative and representational aspects of film make it a wholly distinct leisure activity. The unique properties of cinema can have positive effects on mental health because visual simulation can queue a range of emotions and the collective experience of their emotions through the cinema provides a safe environment in which to experience roles and emotions one may not otherwise be free to experience. The collective nature of narrative and visual simulation makes the experience enjoyable and controlled; thereby offering benefits beyond mere visual simulation.[3]

Film is a reflection of society, both present and past. The film and its innovations sometimes have to catch up to society but sometimes it leads society too. Movies are stories, movies are made by people who come out with ideas about something they want to say, something they want to tell someone. Movies are a form of two way communications between the narrator and society and have been that way and would continue to be that way. Amir Ullah Khan and Bibek Debroy[4] in their paper on 'Indian Economic Transition through Bollywood Eyes' have demonstrated how Hindi Films have reflected changes in India's political economy and society covering the entire span of period of Hindu rate of growth to the present globally linked era when economy has been growing rapidly. Films, more than any other form of popular culture, have been reflecting the socio-economic milieu and changes in policy. The films have been depicting economic problems of the people in a very strong way and some such examples are: *Awara* (1951), *Jagte Raho* (1956), *Naya Daur* (1959) and *Kala Bazar* (1960). There have even been comments on economic policy in films like *Johny Mera Naam* (1970), *Namak Haram* (1973), *Amar Akbar Anthony* (1977), and *Gupt* (1994). On a canvas, beginning with the period from independence, and choosing economic policy of import substitution and foreign exchange controls followed by the heady days of public sector reaching commanding heights, big dams being constructed and the Green Revolution, India's political economy has seen its twists and turns, and ups and downs. Hindi Cinema has incorporated all these trends in its own inimitable style through the idealism of Raj Kapoor, cynicism of Guru Dutt, strength of character exhibited in Dharmendra's movies like *Satyakam*, and romance in the films that follow – the heady mix that culminated in the era of angry young man. Then follows a phase of confusion and complete lack of imagination, after which one sees the happy-go-lucky recklessness of generation next. The symbolism in all this is crystal clear. Today, as the Indian Economy looks outward, Hindi Cinema goes global, too.

In pre-independent India also the Indian Cinema captured the societal, economic and political issues in a bold way even under an alien rule and without any blessing from the elitist dominated movement of Indian National Congress. In fact, Gandhi termed Cinema as 'sinful technology'.[5] Even in US there was similar vision about films at that time. The *Chicago Tribune* in its editorial observed that films were 'without a redeeming feature to warrant their existence ... ministering to the lowest passions of childhood. Amir Ullah Khan and Bibek Debroy have illustrated such initiatives in their paper. In 1921, Dhiren Ganguly commented on the Western way of life in his movie *England Returned*. This was followed by Baburao Painter's *Savkari Pash* (or The Indian Skylock), 1925, which looked at the plight of the Indian peasantry and their exploitation by money lenders. Similarly, films like *Achut Kanya* (Franz Osten, 1936), *Aurat* (Mehboob, 1940), *Roti* (Mehboob, 1942), *Do Bigha Zameen* (Bimal Roy, 1953) and *Sujata* (Bimal Roy, 1959) dealt with issues of casteism, urban dehumanization, economic and gender roles and mass migration from rural areas and subsequent plight in urban slums. Realistic portrayal of economic conditions of the people was portrayed in Chetan Anand's *Neecha Nagar* (1946) and K.A. Abbas's *Dharti Ke Lal* (1947).

Cinema in Hollywood was born in an age of reform, and many early silent movies took as their subject matter the major social and moral issues of the progressive era: birth control, child labour, divorce, immigration, political corruption, poverty, prisons, prostitution, and women's suffrage. Many silent movies dealt with dominant issues of the time in a wide variety of ways – realistic, straightforward, humourous, and sentimental. With Hollywood's bent from realism to escapism, the 1920s saw the first flowering of the major studios – The Dream Merchants – that dominated the business for decades; it started making movies which were swashbuckling and the young movie goers started dreaming of a way of life which was 'consumerist' in its approach. As early as in 1907, the American society felt threatened by the 'evil influence' of cinema and a presidential study concluded that films encouraged illicit lovemaking and inequity 'resulting in censorship'. Even the Supreme Court of United States, in 1915, ruled that films were pure and simple business and could not qualify to seek protection of the First Amendment and were not an organ of public opinion.

During the Great Economic Depression, the number of moviegoers increased as the goers could forget their worries for a couple of hours. It was a simple way of escapism. The fantasy world of movies played a critical social and psychological role in evading the harsher realities of depression-era life. In the face of economic disaster, it kept alive a belief in the possibility of individual success, portrayed a government capable of protecting its citizens from external threats, and sustained the vision of a classless American society.[6]

Hollywood's greatest contribution to the War effort was boosting morale by producing movies that were patriotic rallying cries that affirmed a sense of national purpose. Films of that period emphasized group effort and the value of individual sacrifices for a larger cause. World War II was portrayed as a people's war in which women were contributing actively by serving as nurses, riveters, welders, and long-suffering mothers, who kept the home fires burning. Leading actors and actresses entertained troops and promoted recruitment by encouraging others, with many among the fraternity volunteering themselves. Besides, it faced cuts in raw supply stock and also ceilings on costs of production. From the foregoing it is demonstrated that film clusters at Bollywood as well as Hollywood have depicted the evolving mood and aspirations of the society. The state of affairs would be similar in all other clusters as characteristically all story tellers in all mediums draw their creativity from their surrounding environments. However, the two clusters, namely Bollywood and Hollywood, are significantly distinct in their structure and approach to filmmaking and commerce surrounding their films. Though Bollywood with its enormous global impact on films, music, dances and lip-synced songs, the symbolic and emotional drama, and the wandering story line contained in a three-hour film is alien to audiences used to Hollywood products, yet it is a hugely commercial industry with an estimated annual number of globally sold tickets of 3.6 billion as compared to 2.6 billion that of Hollywood. For more than one hundred years Bollywood mainly served the home market, its export market has now been growing at an impressive rate of 16 per cent to 20 per cent per annum and is well on its ways to be integrated to global economy. Bollywood is a distinct example of a growing entertainment industry which has been essentially an indigenous industry to an emerging economy of India.[7]

The Indian film industry is built on a strong foundation – the pioneers overcame various odds and spawned new technologies capable of improving nearly every aspect of business, i.e. storing the moving images and integrating the same with already prevalent rich art forms of theatre based on mythology, dance forms and sagas of local heroes. The *tamasha* loving and theatre afficados welcome the opportunity of savouring the performance of talented artists from across distant cultural centres because it promotes cross-cultural understanding and that too at affordable costs.

India's tryst with films started on 7 July 1896, a few months after the Lumiere brothers introduced the art of cinematography in Paris in 1895. Filmmakers in the west were quick to realize the value of India as a site of filmmaking because of its natural beauty and exotic culture in their films like *Coconut Fair* (1897), *Our Indian Empire* (1897), *A Panorama of Indian Scenes and Procession* (1898) and *Poona Races '98'* (1898). The first Indian to make a film, called *The Wrestlers* (1899), was Harishchandra S. Bhatvadekhar, a stills photographer by profession. This was followed, in 1900, by *Splendid New View of Bombay* and *Taboot Procession*, both by F.B. Thanawala.[8]

J.F. Madan, who envisaged great business opportunities for Indian filmmaking, established the Elphinstone Bioscope Company in 1905. The first Indian feature film, *Pundalik* (by R.G. Torney), was made in 1912 as a result of growing demand from audiences to see Indian characters and experiences on screen. However, it was shot by an Englishman and never really received the acclaim of being an independent feature film. Instead, the honour of making the first indigenous feature film goes to D.G. Phalke for *Raja Harishchandra*, released in 1913, which was a completely Indian production and was shown as a self-contained work in its own right. Between 1917 and 1931, several many Indian silent movies were shot in Mumbai and other regions. Their content was inspired by Ramayana and Mahabharata, two of India's most well-known epics. In 1931, *Alam Ara*, India's first talkie was made – just four years after the introduction of the first talking movie, *The Jazz Singer* (1927) in New York, America. In India, sound was the transformative element that led to the rapid expansion of the nation's film industry – the most productive such industry in the world today. While in countries like Japan and France, talking movies were slow to take root. However, theatre music and songs, that play an integral part in Indian culture, found a new expression in the talkie movies. Music and fantasy have since continued to be seen as vital elements of filmic experience. Sometimes the use of music is overdone. For example, the film *Indrasabha* (1932) contained 70 songs. However, music has remained the defining element of Indian Cinema so much so that in a recent release, *LOC* by J.P. Dutta, six top singers have lent their voice to a song, which is 20 minutes long and has been picturized on eleven top actors of the Industry.

The popularity of the new medium for mass entertainment encouraged creative filmmakers and entrepreneurs supporting them to explore new ideas beyond the mythical themes to delve into social, political and gender themes. It was against this background that film directors like Bimal Roy, Raj Kapoor, Guru Dutt, V. Shantaram, Mehboob Khan made films which became popular both in India and abroad.

Indian film industry in regions like Tamil Nadu, Andhra, Bengal, Punjab, etc. also came up in quick succession to Marathi and Hindi Cinema of Bombay. Films made in the regional languages have been as good in content though varying in cinematic style and grammar. The contributions of Satyajit Ray, Mrinal Sen, Tapan Sinha, Ritwik Ghatak, Adoor Gopalakrishnan, Mani Ratnam, P.V. Rao, etc. have been everlasting and have influenced the genre of Hindi films in many ways enriching the same with their flavours. The cult of Raj Kapoor, the legendary Indian actor, remains undiminished in Russia and the Soviet Union.[9] The growth of Bollywood and Regional Cinema in India has taken place simultaneously with the growth of industry elsewhere and Indian Film Industry has been in the forefront of total production since 1960 till date. The only industry that follows India in terms of production is Hollywood, which produces 500 films per year on average and has a worldwide audience of 2.6 billion. Indian film industry produces more than 1,000 films on average in a year and attracts about 3.6 billion viewers. In terms of viewership, Hollywood was overtaken in 2004 and the dominance of Indian films on this parameter continues. Bollywood made revenue of $1.75 billion in 2006, which is only half the revenue of one Hollywood studio, Walt Disney made in 2006 – and that's saying a lot. However, while Hollywood's market inside the US has almost saturated, India's 500 million population under the age of 20 will ensure that the market in India will grow rapidly in years to come. Although Hollywood produces only a fraction of the number of films made all over the world, it garners a staggering 75 per cent of total revenues. Also, 50 per cent of earnings (expected to grow to 80%) come from the foreign markets whereas for Bollywood it is 20 per cent. Hollywood has an overwhelming domination among the top grosser all over the world, almost all the top 50 movies are made in Hollywood. It has virtually eclipsed all other film industries except Bollywood – for instance, the European film industry is cut down to one-tenth of its size since 1910.

The average cost of producing, marketing and distributing a Hollywood film is more than US$60 million and only one out of ten succeeds. At the same time Shahrukh Khan's *Ra.One* has cost $30 million dollars and is the costliest Bollywood production till date. About 50 per cent movies produced in Bollywood are never released and more than 95 per cent of those released result in losses.[10]

Historically, Bollywood as well as Hollywood both operate on full commercial basis and without state subsidies. Both the clusters produce a mix of relatively big and small budget fares followed by a relentless pursuit of blockbusters on the market with large uncertainties with mixed results. Though, Hollywood might not be in receipt of state subsidies, its export success has been positively influenced by government regulations, i.e. by creating beneficial conditions for exports of American products in industries where such exports would boost the domestic scale economies. Film has been perceived to be exactly such an industry and Hollywood exports have benefited notably from the US State Department, the Department of Commerce and various US embassies in paving the way for US film exports. While implementing Marshall Plan for the reconstruction of Europe in the post WWII period, it ensured that European countries open their markets for US film exports. State Department and Department of Commerce continued to push up their diplomatic efforts vis-à-vis the disputes that arose with the French Film Industry[11] and lately obtaining a ruling from WTO in 2009 against China on the latter's restrictive trade practices, preventing free import of Hollywood Cinema into China.[12]

Bollywood, on the other side, had been at the receiving end of the Indian Government's apathy. Despite its popularity among the masses for its entertainment value, for a long-time it did not receive any encouragement from the Government and leadership so much so that it had to traverse a period of eight decades before it was recognised as an industry eligible for availing loans from financial institutions. The state targeted it as a source of revenue by imposing excessive entertainment tax and other taxes including on raw stocks and essential imports. Consequently the industry had to fend for itself and survive. Export earnings, if any, were generated through its efforts only. Bollywood did not figure on the radar of export earning efforts of Government of India and yet on its own momentum it maintained a modest export business for less than 10 per cent of its turn over till two decades back. Bollywood industry in such circumstances remained largely fragmented and unorganised. In the initial years the studio system prevailed, i.e. where actors were employees of the studios and on its payroll. After World War II the studio system disappeared due to a combination of rising production costs caused by the war, booming land prices in downtown Mumbai where most of the studios were located, and, most importantly, the entry of a new number of independent producers after the migration of entrepreneurs and talent from the Lahore cluster after the Partition of India. Newcomers challenged the integrated production companies by staying small, outsourcing creative activities and facilities, and employing shifting freelance directors and star actors who were lured away from studios on the promise of high remuneration. These disintegrated production companies systematically targeted cross-regional Indian markets.[13] This strategy resulted in 'formula' or 'Masala' films – a cocktail of romance, drama, music and comedy along with dance-song sequences. The formula of films of that period could be summed up as 'a star, six songs, three dances'. Because of a combination of various factors and clever marketing strategies, Bollywood has not only made huge inroads into the domestic Indian entertainment market, but has also acquired international dimensions. In the star centric Bollywood films for a particular period of time a handful of male and female star actors had been and have been playing a dominant role in the mainstream cinema than in the contemporary Hollywood system. The fees charged by the handful of stars have been on the rise continuously and in today's mainstream films, such salaries may account for well over half the production budget.[14]

Unlike their counterparts in Hollywood, star actors are cast and signed through informal social relations, rather than through agents and lawyers. Mutual trust between the producers and stars is considered to be of great value; therefore, for producers of mainstream films, it is of utmost importance to maintain strong personal relations with the stars. The high demand of a few stars enhance the risk at production stage because if a star opts out or plays truant, production costs would increase to such an extent that the producer may be in dire straits. Even with changes in the industry structure, which would described in the following pages, it is considered 'safe' to cast an established star, both from the point of view of raising finances and also from the angle of box office collections. Such a state of affairs has been in existence despite the established fact that even a big star is not always a guarantee for the box office success, and hit/flop ratio of Bollywood films is remarkably equal to Hollywood films.[15] However, the influence of film stars in raising finances for production has remained undisputed. Distributors and exhibiters are the main sources of finances. The deals between the producers and financiers would be struck at different stages of production when distributors and financiers would be weighing the quality of product being developed through previews. In the segment of raising finances as well, personal relationship among the partner had been playing dominant and determining role. Uncovered finances had to be met through sources other than the chain of producers, distributors and exhibitors. Such supplementary financial sources were not legal money. Even such a supplemental funding was through extended network system rather than through legally drawn contracts.

The compulsion of means other than legal was thus a forced necessity which inevitably led to the involvement of underworld in several productions. In the nineties, many such links came to the fore in the shape of alleged links between Sanjay Dutt and the underworld and the mysterious death of actress Divya Bharti. The underworld resorted to extortion and the owner of T-Series music company Gulshan Kumar was gunned down for not submitting to extortion demands. Actor, producer and director Rakesh Roshan was fired at in January 2000. Actors, to whom underworld took a fancy, were promoted. In 2000, the film prints of *Chori Chori Chupke Chupke* were confiscated by CBI and later when the film was released, revenue generated was kept by the court; the director and producer faced imprisonment. Such instances are enough to illustrate that the Bollywood industry was murky in this decade.[16] However, in the decade of the 1990s many significant economic and technology changes were ushered in India. Indian economy was opened to global links which brought in its wake growth in Indian middle class on account of rapid economic growth. The television industry was deregulated and cable and satellite (pay channels) television network were available on domestic TV sets. With this single step Hollywood productions not only came to Indian homes, but also enhanced revenue generation for Bollywood film industry. Also, Hollywood now competed with Indian cinema. For instance, Spiderman released in 2004 earned ₹ 10 crore in the first week itself though it had to compete with the superhit film *Mujhse Shadi Karogi*. Now, Hollywood films such as *2012* and *Avatar* have set the trend of simultaneous releases in India with gross collections of 100 crore each.[17]

These two films also set the trend of release of Hollywood films dubbed in Hindi and other major regional languages, both in multiplexes as well as single screen. A stage arrived in December 2011 when Tom Cruise starrer Hollywood movie was released in India ahead of its release in US and competed with *Don 2* starring Shahrukh Khan. With the steadily increasing presence of Hollywood, Bollywood had inevitably to adopt a model which reduces its risks by bringing necessary professionalism and synergising available resources. Such an approach requires a structural change in the Bollywood industry. The urgency towards corporatization model was also triggered by the rapidly increasing number of revenue generating windows on the back of explosion in distribution and exhibition platforms in multiple manifestations like internet, mobile phones, computers, compact discs, satellite and cable channels, broad band availability – all at increasingly decreasing costs to vast population in all corners. It also has become possible to increase the number of screens from existing 13,000 to manifold with the coming up of multiplexes, where the number of screens range from 3 to 11. More screens mean that more films or prints can be shown simultaneously which raises the turnover and also lessens the lure of piracy. Even the public's willingness to pay three to four times more for their tickets in multiplexes than in single screen cinemas has created a significant avenue for multiplying revenue generation – it is indeed remarkable! Availability of multiple screens in a multiplex also opens avenues for independent producers of modest means to exhibit their work. To cap it all, distribution costs have reduced to an insignificant level as far as digital cinemas are concerned where films can be exhibited through satellite and simultaneously viewers everywhere can have the advantage of quality viewing. As more viewers flock to cinemas and multiplexes, more revenues are forecast and faster growth is projected.

The transition to digital cinema projection has entirely changed the business model of this segment for the better. When *Sholay* was released in August 1975, only four prints were in circulation – one for Delhi, one for Uttar Pradesh, and two for Bombay. A single print was screened across two cinema halls in a metro city by shuttling the reels on motorcycles from one hall to the other. The returns were slower and there was wear and tear of reels after about 350–400 screenings. This scenario can be compared with the recent releases like *Bodyguard* when over 2,000 prints were released, out of which 1,483 were digital. Four weeks into release, the movie grossed over 150 crore.[18] *Ra.One* set a higher benchmark when it released with 3500 prints. The latest films have been hitting screens all over the country far and wide, on the same day. It is anticipated that 90 per cent of screens in the next two years would be digital.

In view of such emerging advantages, it makes sense for the corporate sector to enter all three segments, namely production, distribution and exhibitions. The process of corporatization was facilitated by the recognition of films as an industry which would result in the flow of credit to this sector and also build wealth through other financial instruments as were available to other institutions. Government also permitted 100 per cent flow of FDI which is an enabling provision for the foreign companies to independently produce films across India or can enter into co-production agreements.

Over the years, corporatization has taken place in a big way and many veteran producers have set up their own corporate companies and their subsidiaries to cover various areas of film production, distribution, exhibition and many other related areas. Many established business houses have also entered the fray and that too in a significant way, and, have created interests abroad as well to boost export earnings. Some notable houses that have come into being are: 1. AGPPL; 2. Aamir Khan Productions; 3. Mukta Arts; 4. Red Chillies Entertainment; 5. Percept Picture Company; 6. Yash Raj Films; 7. Roopesh Rai Production; 8. White Feather Films; 9. Key Sera Sera Film; 10. Adlabs Studio; 11. Vishal Films; 12. Devgan Films; 13. UTV Motion Pictures; 14. Dharma Productions; 15. Pritish Nandi Communications; 16. Popcorn Entertainment; 17. Base Industries Group; 18. B.R. Films; 19. Balaji Tele Films; 20. Rajshri Films; 21 Super Cassettes Industries Ltd. (T-Series); 22. Shri Ashtavinayak Cine Vision Ltd.; 23. Madras Talkies; 24. JP Films; 25. Film Kraft Productions; 26. Excel Films; 27. RGV Productions; 28. Kaleidoscope Films; 29. India Showbiz Network Ltd.

The major and biggest effect of corporatization has been that finance was procured through legitimate means which has significantly reduced the dependence of producers on the illegal services of money lenders, and consequently, the demand for protection from the underworld has come down significantly. With corporatization there has been streamlining of the supply chain and it has become possible produce films in a definite time frame, which means reductions in costs and flow of returns is quicker. Professionalism is being shown by actors as well as the rest of the crew. A culture is fast developing where actors shoot for one film at a time and sign a film only after getting a bound script, even if they are just beginners in the industry. For example, actor Imran Khan, who is just three-films old, signs on every page of a script while signing any film. This makes binding on the director to consult the actor even if he has to change one sentence in the script.[19]

Independent producers formed groups and corporations. A new business model has come into play. Corporations who had no film making experience would collaborate with independent producers to make films. For a film production to run smoothly both the producer and the director of the film have to be the very best of friends for the relationship to work, while the corporate companies would finance as well as look after other aspects of the film. At this time, when costs have escalated because of high fees charged by actors and directors and also due to need for high-calibre publicity campaigns in expectation of raising finances from out of demand sides in advance of the actual release of films, there are hardly independent producers. Most of them have formed their own companies, or work with other corporate houses.

Even the star actors have devised strategies to provide comfort to the producers by offering to participate in the revenue generation of their productions rather than charging their hefty fees during the stages of signing and production. There have been instances when stars have collaborated with the producers without charging any money initially and signing on the condition of sharing the profits, say, 33 per cent. Thus, the producer also gets to reduce his risk considerably and on a film's success, the actor goes home laughing all the way with boxes full of money.[20]

Thus, with the liberalization of economy being linked to world economy, there has been a change in the structure of Bollywood industry at least in terms of more professionalism among actors and directors and also towards the making of films using the best technologies with inevitable optimism and confidence. At this stage of development, Bollywood industry is corporatizing itself with its traditional transactional behaviour of incorporating the social network and its acceptance of the dominance of star actors and star directors. Thus, structurally though it is tending towards Hollywood, yet it still maintains its traditional strengths in alignment with the restructured structure.

With its newly established confidence and restructured, Bollywood has taken a step forward to make its impact on the global scene by enhancing the visual impact of its presentations by adapting latest technologies from Hollywood and other global film clusters and thereby upgrading the technical base of the industry and creating a network of well-equipped and trained manpower within the country. The strategy for producing trained technical manpower in Bollywood is a farsighted one and is synergetic with the strong manpower base in India. Such a strategy has already started yielding dividends. Oscar winning special effects of *The Golden Compass* – the Hollywood blockbuster that took $370 million at the box office – were put together in 'thatched village huts in India'. The huts are replicas of rural dwellings that have been made into stylised office cubicles. They are located in the outskirts of Mumbai, from where Rhythm and Hues, the leading Los Angeles-based special effects studio outsources world-class visual pyrotechnics with the help of its 250 strong Indian staff, which hunches over computers and works overtime, thereby doing the job at a fraction of normal cost. Further since the coming of the digital technology, visual effect companies such as Prima Focus, Maya and several others are generating world-class special effects for the indigenous film industry, thereby saving them the hassle of outsourcing them at a huge cost from the west.[21]

Bollywood has been the fastest in tapping into new global business opportunities riding on a clear blend of eastern talent and western expertise to create a seamless viewing experience. Bollywood cluster and other regional clusters leveraged the benefits of what can be termed as polycentric innovation. A large number of films from the Indian clusters harnessed and networked globally distributed talent, ideas, and creativity to co-develop radically new products, services processes and even business models. Media companies in Bollywood and other clusters have since started harnessing and integrating globally distributed creativity into a coherent and synergetic innovation network. This polycentric innovation, which extends far beyond superficial Bollywood/Hollywood alliances or mere backend collaboration, is being pioneered by companies from India. Such a larger than life emanation of this big bang collaboration has been *Endhiran* (English: *Robot*), Asia's most expensive film till 2010, which was released on 1 October 2010. Produced by *Chennai* based Sun Pictures and globally distributed by HBO, *Endhiran* was the collective output of a truly international crew. Not only does this sci-fi thriller feature Bollywood style songs by Oscar winner A.R. Rahman (*Slumdog Millionaire*) and Kung fu style fight scenes choreographed by Hong Kong legend Yuen Woo-ping;, it also boasts of mind-boggling animation and special effects done by Stan Winston Studio (of *Terminator* and *Jurassic Park* fame), and eye-popping costume designs by Mary E. Vogt

(*The Matrix; Men in Black*), *Endhiran* became an embankment of polycentric innovation, cleverly blending Eastern talent with Western experience that no single region could have concocted on its own. The effort lends evidence to the fact that the monocentric film industry of the 20th century where all creative work (concept development, post production, 3D) was done in the West was shifting to a polycentric world of 21st century where new innovation hubs were emerging in India, Argentina, China and New Zealand (*The Lord of the Rings*). The creative workers in these hubs augment the capabilities of their peers in established hubs in the US and Europe by offering complementary skills, expertize and mindset as well as cost effectiveness and international aesthetics. The new polycentric mindset in the film industry is also equalled by the rapidly dropping costs of global communication, which has made real-time collaboration among creative artists across borders seamless. Now, a director in India can simultaneously review and even modify a film clip with a production designer in Hollywood via a shared digital asset management system. Creative differences between players across the globe would enable them all to learn or unlearn as per individuals' creative mind set which would finally enrich everyone and lay the new foundation for global competitiveness.

The race is already on for building a competitive global network. In India, there have been significant initiatives towards this end.

Reliance Media Works is offering integrated 3D services out of its Burbank, California facility while using a team of more than 400 3D artists in India. The sheer potential of India to offer a mass of visual effect artists makes India very attractive for filmmakers who, in the aftermath of *Avatar's* phenomenal success, are viewing to integrate ever-more complex 3D and visual effects in their films.

Prime Focus Technologies, a global production house, is creating efficiencies through the complementary skills of teams located across India, UK, Canada and US and leveraging technology strengths in India as its subsidiary. It has developed proprietary digital asset management systems.

British visual effects expert Charles Darby (*Matrix, Harry Potter and the Goblet of Fire*) has set up operations in Mumbai with Eyeqube, a special effects design studio financed by Eros International, an India-headquartered production and distribution company Darby believes that Eyeqube can produce quality work that would rival any Hollywood-London studio.[22]

Recently released film *Ra.One* offered by Red Chillies Entertainment and Eros International has further improved upon the gains of *Endhiran* (Robot) in reaffirming the capacity of Bollywood in understanding and coordinating global talent in creativity and ICT technologies, seeking international viewership and crafting business models to generate unprecedented revenues. Producers have been encouraged to take well worth risks by making investments to the tune of ₹ 150 crore. *Ra.One* movie crew consisted of 5,000 members drawn from India, Italy and the US, and was put together by more than 1,000 people working in around 15 prime studio rooms across the world. The 3D version of the movie attracted higher occupancy level than the 2D version. Due to the revived interest in 3D technology in India, the makers of the film converted some portions of the movie into 3D, with the collaboration of approximately 1,000 people. The conversion was done by Prime Focus which had earlier worked on 3D format movies like *The Chronicles of Narnia* and *Transformers*. Jeffrey Kleiser, the man behind the visual effects of 1993 Hollywood release *Stargate* was hired to supervise special effects; he led a team of 750 technicians to accomplish the task. International singer Akon was roped in to lend his voice to the songs Chamak Challo and Criminal.

Such block blustering efforts of roping in dispersed technologies enrich the Bollywood technicians' experiences and also that of the media companies which already have the vision of re offering their new-found skills globally. In a way, the spin-off effect has led to asset creation within the industry.

Ra.One already has the distinction of being the costliest movie so far produced in India. It has been released in both 2D and 3D formats across 3,200 screens in India, which include the dubbed versions in Tamil, Telugu and German. The film was premiered in Dubai, London, New York and Toronto in an effort to acknowledge the presence of South Asian communities in these countries who form the bulk of viewership abroad.

Ra.One also broke new ground in the field of publicity blitz and pre-release sales. It set apart ₹ 40 crore as publicity budget which is about 30 per cent of the total cost of the project and by Bollywood standards it has been unprecedented. The campaign aimed at domestic and foreign viewers has been the longest duration promotion in the Bollywood history and has been the most comprehensive and all pervasive among people's lives. Apart from usual presale contracts of satellite rights, music rights, etc. it launched video games with Sony Computer Entertainment Europe (SCEE) which is the full cycle PlayStation 3 blu-ray disc game developed by an Indian developer and also the first game to be dubbed by a Bollywood superstar. Besides, in collaboration with UTV digital, *Ra.One* game was launched across platforms like mobiles tablet PCs, DTH, etc. Comic serials based on the film's characters have been launched in collaboration with UTV India Games. Merchandise relating to the films is also being marketed.

Thus, *Ra.One* has not only furthered the concept of excellence through polycentric creativity, but has also opened vistas for new marketing items riding on ICT technologies which would be covering the risks on heavy investments involved. Thus, more revenue generating windows have been innovated.[23]

Hollywood and Bollywood are vying with each other; sometimes collaborating and often competing for the same market space in a healthy manner. The upcoming improvements in infrastructure in distribution and exhibition segments have encouraged Hollywood to release their Tom Cruise starrer *Mission Impossible 4: Ghost Protocol* in India ahead of its release in USA and also presenting Tom Cruise in person on this occasion. Speculations had been that this film's release was preponed to 16 December 2011 from 21 December 2011 to avoid competition with the Shah Rukh starrer *Don 2* (also scheduled for release on December 21). The veracity of such speculation apart, the fact remain that it is demonstrative of a sense of intense competition between the two clusters that have come into play. The bottom line remains that the coming together of the two entertainment clusters of Bollywood and Hollywood and their growth benefits India's economy. According to a report prepared by Pricewaterhouse Coopers (PwC) and released in 2011, Hollywood and other foreign films contributed about $60.8 million (₹ 304 crore) to India's economy in 2008–09 and it is expected to rise steadily. Hollywood has been devising innovative strategies of dubbing their releases in regional languages to increase viewership; as a result, its contribution to Indian economy would be on the rise steadily. Bollywood and regional cinemas and TV industry contributed over $6.2 billion (₹ 28,305 crore) to the Indian economy in the year 2008–09 giving employment to 1.8 million people. Thus, the film and television industry has come to contribute substantially to the overall Indian economy. The combined revenues from this segment were over US$7.7 billion (₹ 35,000 crore) in the year 2008 and would be rising to US$13 billion (₹ 60,000 crore) by 2013.

Thus, the earlier held fear that if Hollywood has, in terms of WTO principles, the liberty of distributing and exhibiting their products, it would hurt the growth of Bollywood, has proved to be misplaced. Rather, Bollywood has marketed itself as a diaspora destination riding on the skilled adaptation of ICT technologies and obtaining access to foreign techniques, and, has created a pool of skilled manpower to offer their services abroad on competitive rates. The resultant enhanced pleasure of visual presentation from Bollywood has encouraged viewers within the country and abroad to pay increased entrance fee at the box office.

There is a well-meaning point of view being expressed at this point of time that globalization has catapulted Indian films in the global market and audiences; it has altered the basic spirit of the domestic audience that was its fundamental support base. In other words, obeying the laws of finance capital of the dominant capitalist order of the West, Indian film industry transformed its aesthetics and thematic occupations. The laws of the capitalist world redefined the form and content of Indian Cinema. One of the huge manifestations of this change has been the emergence of super budget films. It is not just the crores of rupees spent on production of films that one needs to understand in this context. It has altered the sensibilities of the Indian audience and almost wiped out films made on very modest financial and technical resources and erased themes that dealt with the lives of millions of Indians who belonged to the middle and lower middle classes. The poor, the marginalized and the oppressed, of course, have been entirely liquidated. All these sections of society that had been the main patrons of the Indian Cinema for decades did not matter to the Indian Cinema of the period of globalisation, which generated its resources and tried to augment its capital from international centres. The phenomenon is true mostly of Bollywood, which parades itself as the 'National Cinema' and films made in Tamil, Telugu and Kannada, to name a few, that have always been treated as the 'Regional Cinema'. In the new economic order, both 'National' and 'Regional' cinema converged in terms of aesthetics and thematic content, caught as they were in the strong current of global capital. The mainstream Indian Cinema has been seeing its survival only by trying to match the Hollywood Cinema that, more than ever before, invaded all the markets of the world, including the strong and well-established cosmos of the French Cinema that for a long time had been signposts of good and serious cinema.

Such a view sees a great crisis of the Indian Cinema in that serious and committed filmmakers in the Indian languages find it almost impossible to cope with the demands made on them by an industry that only nourishes and promotes incredibly high budget films, on the one hand, and, on the other, the taste of an audience that relishes only spectacular, glamorous and stunning visuals and accepts only a glamourised virtual reality as the authentic representation of life. The pace, tempo, style, locale, context and experience of films are totally regulated by high-speed technology, which controls the very nature of film making. The story of the mainstream Indian Cinema is all about huge investment in expectation of heavy returns. The corporatization of the Indian Cinema is only part of the oligarchical nature and spirit of the general corporate world.

While the above criticism has its place, there are filmmakers, and there would be many, who would join their ranks and deal with themes of social justice and equality and question the economic and political choices of ruling classes and powers. There would be filmmakers who would be appalled by the plight of tribals and other oppressed classes and castes, and would protest against the unreal universe that is disseminated by the rich and powerful mainstream cinema. However, the budget available with such film makers would be limited. Technology would come to assist such group of producers to give expression to their creativity through the medium of cinema. A film like Stanley Ka Dabba was made using what is essentially a nominal still digital camera of the DSLR variety and putting it into video record model and the technique is called DSLR film making. The camera used for this film is a Canon 7D camera which costs ₹ 1,38,000 and can be rented for as low as ₹ 890 per day. The colour quality and shots in the film are as good as a movie made with an expensive camera. Telugu Movie, *Dongala Mutha*, was also shot through this type of camera. Superstar cast of the movie did not charge any fee at the stage of production and worked on terms of sharing the profits. The movie was produced on a shoe string budget. The film turned out to be a box office hit and the rates of return on the investment were phenomenal. Similar was the success story of *Stanley Ka Dabba*.[24]

Thus if a creative person has got content, technology enables him to turn out his production on his own initiative which would not have been possible earlier. It opens up new avenues of creativity for such persons and they can sell their products in a variety of ways, including by participating in specialised film festivals and gaining publicity through word of mouth. The finished product is easier to sell to an enterprising distributor than selling an idea to a film producer.

New technology application allows small budget creative filmmakers to exhibit their creations (1–10 minutes) on 3G enabled mobile phones, which represent a much greater market for film than movie theatres or PCS. If content is good, interesting, humorous, satirical, etc. it would be forwarded and may be loaded on social network giving wide publicity to the creator of such works. This would be a great way of interacting with the wide audience and getting one's talent noticed for better opportunities. Thus, with the integration of 7D type camera technology and 3G based networks, film making would get truly democratized, especially when creative persons can give visual expression to their perceptions of the world. They do not have to be slaves to big budgets.

Despite the critical view on mainstream cinema that in pursuit of redefining its success stories it is compromising with quality and sidestepping the real life situations, there have been acclaimed productions from the mainstream cinema without losing sight of revenue generation at the box office. Such movies leave behind lessons like self-confidence, motivation, leadership qualities and more, giving a drive to mainstream cinema to succeed. Some such films are *Taare Zameen Par, 3 Idiots, Chak De India, Iqbal, Laagan, Swades, Rang De Basanti, Yuva, Black, Guzarish, I am Kalam, Lakshya, Paheli,* etc. Most of these acclaimed quality movies were not lacking in revenue generation; in fact *3 Idiots* had set a benchmark for success, and, *Lagaan*, besides being a huge grosser had been among the last four films in its category at Oscar. These movies were based on India and touched the conscience of all classes of viewers.

Therefore, while constructive criticism is directed towards quality enhancement, mainstream Indian cinema has focused on its unique strengths by absorbing and adapting technologies to consolidate its position to take storytelling and scriptwriting skills to new frontiers that are recognised and appreciated by the wider audience – extending beyond our neighbourhood or Indian diasporas. In this vein, veterans like Mahesh Bhatt observe that while adoption of state-of-the-art technologies, both at the production stages and distribution chain, will certainly boost box office sales for Bollywood movies and India will expand at a projected 15 per cent compound annual rate during the next five years propelling it ahead of many established clusters of film production across the globe to become the largest film entertainment market in Asia next to Hollywood, it has to confront one blunt truth. For a country that makes a maximum number of films and has a world-class pool of skilled workers and technicians, it has absolutely nothing to offer the world market in terms of its products. According to Bhatt, we are bankrupt in our story department; he attributes the failure of Drona to the lack of storytelling techniques, though it high on special effects. Similar views have also been expressed by veterans like Yash Chopra and Shekhar Kapur.

The urgent need of the hour is to make huge investments in our storytelling skills. Bollywood would be a force to reckon with when Hollywood moguls come to India to get a script written by an Indian writer and a film directed by an Indian director. Western educated writers like Manoj Night Shyamalan have been able to compete on that turf very ably. The change that needs to happen in India is one that needs to come from within the heart of our education system and mind sets of the film entrepreneurs. The day we think in our own voice will be the day that Bollywood would break through creatively. Let's face it – Bollywood films are a big craze only with people of Asian origin. The affluent westerner just does not seem to be interested in Bollywood movies. Bollywood still has miles to go. Bollywood is on the right track and is posed for a take-off to compete with the best once it strengthens its critical thinking skills as well as scriptwriting and storytelling skills, which have universal appeal. Bollywood has created a tremendous feel-good factor about itself among governments around the world, especially in those countries that Indian filmmakers scout for exotic locales for shooting their films. The exotic locations abroad, as seen in movies, boosts tourism, trade and commerce on account of the Indian middle-class movie-goers who are eager to spend their new found disposable income by flocking to such locales. Recognising the potential of Bollywood in playing a role in boosting their economy, the host countries like Japan, Switzerland, Germany, and Australia vie with one another in extending their production facilitations to the Indian production companies. Government of India has also finally come to recognise the role that the Indian films can play in furthering friendship across the continents by offering a glimpse of the country through the entertaining media. It has signed bilateral agreements with developed and developing countries on films and some of these agreements are towards providing reciprocal incentives for film production and film co-production between the signing countries.

While the menace of piracy would get significantly reduced with the adoption of technology, government would do well to provide incentives to single screen cinemas to modernise their setups and equip them for digitized screening and creating multiple screens by offering them to avail of long-term concessional loans and tax breaks, besides providing concession on custom duties on import of related equipments. States, in recognition of the potential of film industry to create more jobs in this sector and spin-off sectors, need to soften the impact of entertainment tax particularly when the reduction in rates would be compensated by the increases in basic prices of tickets on account of enhanced facilities and visual treat that viewers would get to experience on the modernisation of theatres – as has been the experience with multiplexes where viewers have not been deterred by high ticket prices. To sum it up, one can make a statement with fair certainty that Bollywood industry and also the regional cinema industry has everything going for them – be its regulations allowing foreign investment, the impetus from economy, the digital life style and spending habits of consumers, and windows of revenue earnings enabled by advances in technology. Cash growth potential is tremendous and there are opportunities. There is tremendous good will for the industry within the country and abroad, including the foreign governments. Government on its part should be ready to remove impediments by providing necessary fiscal incentives towards modernisation and reducing the rates of taxation. The industry is well poised to provide opportunities to producers of high budget films and also those who have no assets other than creativity and the urge to go forward. There are appropriate technologies and platforms for every creative effort. Bollywood as well as regional cinema have the potential to be the star performers in the Indian Economy and they would do wonders once they improve upon their techniques of storytelling through better scripting and thus cater to a global audience which has capacity to reward the film industry immensely – but this vast potential has been virtually untapped to date.

Notes

1. Shah, Vikas S. (2001), 'The Role of Film in Society', an exclusive interview with Tom Sherak, President, Academy of Motion Picture Arts and Sciences, *Thought Economics*, June.
2. 'Hollywood as History' (undated). Available at: https://web.viu.ca/davies/HollywoodAsHistory.htm
3. Shah (2001), op. cit.
4. Khan, Amir Ullah and Bibek Debroy (2002), 'Indian Economic Transition through Bollywood Eyes: Hindi films and How they have Reflected Changes in India's Political Economy', Working Paper No. 1, Bazaar Chintan, August.
5. Free Essays (undated), 'Mahatma Gandhi and Indian Cinema'. Available at: http://essaypride.com/essays.php?free_essay=6285006&title=Mahatma-Gandhi-And-Indian-Cinema.
6. 'Hollywood as History', op. cit.
7. Lorenzen, Mark and Florian Arun Taeube (2007), 'Breakout from Bollywood? Internationalization of Indian Film Industry', DRUID Working Paper No. 07–06, Danish Research Unit for Industrial Dynamics.
8. Acharya, Sharmistha (2004), Bollywood and Globalization, a thesis submitted to San Francisco State University. Available at: www.dishumdishum.com/BollyPresentation/GLOBALIZATION.PDF.
9. Ibid.
10. Woke (2007), 'Bollywood vs. Hollywood: The Complete Breakdown', February 01. Available at: https://mutiny.wordpress.com/2007/02/01/bollywood-vs-hollywood-the-complete-breakdown.
11. Lorenzen and Taeube (2007), op. cit.
12. Baru, Sanjaya (2010), 'Bollywood's Global Market Beckons: A WTO Ruling Opening up China to Hollywood Should Help Bollywood Too', *Business Standard*, January 11.
13. Lorenzen and Täube (2008), op. cit.
14. Ibid.
15. Ibid.
16. IBEF (2013), 'Corporatization of Indian Film Industry', India Brand Equity Foundation, November.
17. Ibid.
18. Chumbhale, Ameya (2011), 'Transition to Digital Film Projection: Is the Cinema as We Knew it Coming to an End?' *The Economic Times*, October 22.

19. Khan and Debroy (2002), op. cit.
20. Ibid.
21. Bhatt, Mahesh (2008), 'Bollywood and Globalisation', *Business Line*, October 10.
22. Ahuja, Simone and Navi Radjou (2010), 'How India is Reshaping Global Film Industry', *Rediff.com: Business*, October 01.
23. Wikipedia (undated), 'Ra.One'.
24. Pulugurtha, Shiv Charan (2011), 'Democratizing Filmmaking: Movie Making Made Easy', *Gomolo*, September 06.

9

Bollywood Dreams Hand-in-Hand with the Canadian Movie Business

Interplay of Diasporic Cinema with Emotions, Creativity and Money

SHILPA DAITHOTA BHAT

The Bollywood industry as a form of visual culture developed roots in India in the beginning of the 20th century. Dadasahab Phalke was the first to have produced a film in India and from then on, the industry has been expanding by leaps and bounds and varying with changing times and advent of new technologies with the result that it is one of the biggest film industries with ever increasing market-size in the world. This essay investigates the business dimension of this gargantuan industry in the context of Indo-Canada bilateral association. Films are both cultural and commercial commodities and several Indian films have been shot in Canada capturing the scenic panorama and cultural diversity. Several Canadian film companies have opened branches in India and have benefitted commercially owing to abnormally high film consumption levels in India. Hence, a further enlarging of the Bollywood industry in conjunction with specific Canadian film technologies and business deals can enhance links between the two countries and this paper shall focus on how this area is characterized by perpetually broadening opportunities.

Incidentally, Bollywood is a nickname for the Indian film industry. The reason ascribed to its resounding success across the globe is its characteristic song and dance sequences that endeavours to encapsulate the traditional ethos of the country. Implicit in the Indian film paradigms are music and dance interwoven with themes pertaining to contemporary situations, nationalism, diaspora, history, myths, romantic entanglements and a host of other issues and thematic preoccupations. It is interesting to observe that Indian film studies have been a part of fieldwork in university courses. Dana Wilkie gives the example of DeTar, a Canadian student from Simon Fraser University who visited India and 'participated in the India film and culture field study … a 10-credit, three-month program … . The program was designed to provide DeTar and her colleagues with a deeper appreciation for Indian culture, history, religion, philosophy, gender roles, social castes, economy, and education' (49). Such educational tours have several implications. First, it provides an understanding of Indian movies, their themes and commercial aspects. Secondly, it facilitates a comparative analysis of business in Canada and India and allows the identification of opportunities in the sector. Thirdly, it forges links between students and faculty of both the countries. There is deeper engagement through educational partnerships that offer practical and theoretical opportunities for cultural appreciation.

Such educational fellowships provide hands-on experience to both the international visitors and the host country since interaction is never one-sided. It is educational and cultural since such international experiences are recorded in the theses or works produced by the visitor.

It would be pertinent to mention that India has several film industries besides Bollywood – Tamil, Kannada, Gujarati, Marathi and so on, just to name a few – but in this article the focus is on the Bollywood specifically because Hindi is a language that is understood by a large section of the Indian population and are showcased in different parts of the world.

Indian film music strikes a chord almost instantaneously in the hearts of the people and the NRIs (Non Resident Indians). In fact, it is perceived to be a uniting factor among the Indian diaspora and the proximity felt is due to the superimposition of home and abroad in these cultural commodities. It is also an industry with enormous business implications. Its profits are mammoth and the employment opportunities that it creates are remarkable. Shashi Tharoor mentions that Bollywood employs '2.5 million people' (111) and that the films are 'watched over and over again by the Indian masses' (*ibid*). The repetitive value is because of the content that is in demand since they cater to feelings of nostalgia and belonging. For a few moments, films transport the viewers to their homeland and their contemporary situation. Since the visual medium is powerful and educational and as the images are hard for the mind to resist, Indo-Canadian parents consider it good and necessary for their children to watch them. The perception is that perhaps this would allow their children a chance to savour the feeling of Home through films, which they cannot possibly experience in Canada. The watching of the movies repeatedly is cultural but then it becomes economic since there is a price to be paid for such images as they are cultural 'commodities'.

In this connection, it would be pertinent to take into consideration the views of Andrea Jezovit who analyses the popularity of Hindi movies in Canada and states that Roger Nair who owns a company in Toronto says that he 'foresee(s) Toronto as the hub of Bollywood films' (20). One realizes that the choice of a country for shooting a film is conscious and a consequence of measured calculations. Many factors work towards materializing film production. Cultural factors definitely play a vital role but then comfort in terms of adherence to laws and regulations are equally crucial. When there are legal strictures and constraints, it results in trepidation in terms of initiating business. Only a relaxed atmosphere can invite and foster both business and culture. Since, the atmosphere in Canada is conducive for filmcraft, several Indian movie producers and directors have been drawn towards the country. Besides, there is appetite for these products. The high consumption levels serve as inspiration for creativity. Capital and culture are interlinked.

Jezovit mentions that Bollywood is 'worth more than $2 billion, it produces 1,000 films yearly – twice as many as Hollywood – for a worldwide audience of 3.6 billion people' (Jezovit 20). Several successful Indian movies like *Kal Ho Na Ho* starring Shahrukh Khan, Saif Ali Khan and Preity Zinta; *Koi Mil*

Gaya starring Hritik Roshan and Preity Zinta have been shot in Canada. These are just a couple of examples. Films are cultural artifacts reflecting images of a specific society and nation and the fact that two countries figure in several movies produced from a nation, endorse that there has been a confluence of two cultures. The bilateral aspect enlivens in films. It is relevant to ponder over when a director decides that a particular country is suitable to form the background or foreground of a film. There is the requirement of genuine appreciation for the country, for its laws and its culture. Only a free mind can be creatively sturdy. The fact that there are so many films being produced by Indian directors and producers in Canada and with Canadian aspects suggests that bonds already exist between the two countries. This bond is both cultural and economic and so this has potential diplomatic reasons for intensification. It also highlights the fact that there is a people-to-people link because of the existence of the Indian diaspora in Canada many of whom are into the business. Catering to this large and growing population through Indian films, enables them to identify their 'lost homeland' that also happen to sentimentally bind them with their country. This reality of culture and capital mixture is what makes Bollywood an endearing business area.

Business and economic relations affect and trigger new cultural streams and films create a space wherein there is articulation and amalgamation of multiple perspectives. India has a huge consumer market. Approximately India has a '300 million strong middle class' (Nilekani 140) and since their aspirations have also risen, 'For global retailers, that is the dream customer' (*ibid*). The presence of a huge middle class is what has elevated the market conditions in India. Companies across the world have been eyeing India as a potential market although the Indian government has not digested this idea of being seen as a selling place. The commercialization and branding of India, in a certain sense precludes and overshadows its other resources like skilled manpower; and India is not merely a purchasing source. It has potential in other departments of trade, commerce and culture. Nevertheless, the fact that India does possess a huge market is a verity.

In the context of films, it is not sufficient if several of them are being made. What they need is an audience, which is obsessed with watching movies – in other words, in purchasing the product. That is what underlines the success of a business. The strength of India is its middle class, which is gigantic, and one that is becoming affluent on account of its ambitious people. Consequently, they are ready to purchase; and it is precisely this factor that is a precondition in business quite directly.

Deepa Mehta's film called *Bollywood/Hollywood* (2002) is set in Canada. The male protagonist incidentally is in her own words 'a dot-com millionaire who lives in Canada with his family … . He is Canadian but like most of us, he has ties elsewhere with a different culture and social mores …' (Wise, 37). The film captures the pulse of the times with the protagonist assuming a profession that is popular in India for its income-generating capacity – the field of software. The theme is contemporary. Furthermore, one of the ideas that the film touches upon is the economic dimension to the migration of people, which is accompanied by a host of intercultural difficulties. The film, therefore, captures the prevalent conditions in India. While there are references through the subplots and the characters, subtle though they may be, to the economic exigencies that constitute the driving force behind transnationalism; associated with the production of such movies is the veritable truth that they have an audience that is prepared to consume such products. The members of the diaspora create startups abroad because first, there is a suitable environment for the purpose; secondly, there is the question of earning one's livelihood. The popularity of such films can help in further exploration of the movie-making business. Diaspora themes are immensely popular. Like literature, there is scope for such plots in films. Canada's locales represent that site that Indian directors and producers are interested in and this trend can be tapped by people from both the countries.

Deepa Mehta's another movie called *Sam and Me* (1991) is also set in Canada and contains cross cultural themes. The choice of Canada as a backdrop to Indian stories is not purely because of the autonomy that exists for the production of movies but also because of the presence of the Indian diaspora. In an interview to Wyndham Wise, Mehta states clearly 'Like most things in this world, it's economics. I think distributors are waking up to the fact that here is a huge expatriate population of East Indians .... It's a huge market .... There are now enough East Indians with expendable income in North America and elsewhere' (35). The emphasis on capital is telling. Deepa Mehta here refers to three things with reference to movie business in Canada – the diaspora, the scope of the market and the disposable income of the migrant population. The role of capital underscores movie production like any other business. Capturing this at the right moment helps business ties.

The fact that the Indian diaspora enjoys movies and craves to watch them can be capitalized upon through emphasis on deeper ties between Indian and Canadian companies. There have been several Canadian companies that have evinced interest in Indian films. Jezovit's study of the Indian movie business led him to estimate that 'India's population of 1.2 billion, many of whom are devoted filmgoers, would make a huge audience for Canadian films' (Jezovit 20). The Canadian company, Discreet Logic Inc. that specializes in film technology claims that its '11-person Mumbai office is turning heads' (24) and acknowledges, 'India is one of the fastest growing markets' (24). These statements not only imply success but also indicate relief and satisfaction at having a chance to set up and continue business successfully. There is a suggestion of what might happen if there is expansion in the area. If a miniscule operation from Mumbai can create great profits, an increase in the business can create more capital.

Settling in another country is filled with apprehensions primarily because the settlers are unaware of what circumstances they might have to encounter in the new land. Though they would have done homework to understand the new country, they know that when they actually go there the situation could be different, could be unpredictable or maybe dangerous; but when they meet success, there is a sense of achievement and desire for a long-term relationship. We find exactly this and mutually in both Canadians and Indians. Again, here too, the human capital dimension in India has received worldwide attention. Owing to a high population, the consumption of films is very high. Wavefront which is a subsidiary company 'of Mountain View, Calif.-based Silicon Graphics Inc. (NYSE: $GI)' (24) in Toronto also accepts that it has had 'explosive' business growth in India. There have been efforts to explore this area. For instance, in the year 2004, there were attempts to establish 'an official co-production treaty between Canada and India' (Bracken 6). Sabbas Joseph, a director in Wizcraft International Entertainment Pvt. Ltd. (Mumbai), says that 'while 50–60 per cent of a Bollywood film is normally made outside India, North America has so far captured very little of that work, (Simon n. pag). The indication is towards the lack of utilization of existing resources. This is also because the bilateral relation between the two countries is not very strong. There has not been much research on what and how the Bollywood can be explored despite super hit movies being made. Consequently, there is less awareness and less consciousness of how collaborations in this area can be augmented. This indifference at times has been rather difficult to explain because there has been success in whatever little has been done but that has not provided fillip for further expansion.

Shashi Tharoor explores the Bollywood facet of India as one which is both at once cultural and economic. Therefore, it is doubly beneficial. Here, it is necessary to emphasize that Canada 'became the first country in the world to adopt multiculturalism as a state policy. The policy accepts and encourages all ethnic groups to retain their culture' (Sangha and Sahoo: 86). As cultural products, Indian films have always celebrated the existence and proliferation of several ethnicities, religions, festivals – aspects which are integral to the promotion of multiculturalism. The prevalence of a similar attitude in the Canadian society creates comfort levels for the creation of movies. As a tribute to multiculturalism, every May, Canada celebrates the 'Asian Heritage Month' (Sangha and Sahoo: 86). This can be seen as an example of cultural tolerance and respect. Probably, it is this policy that facilitates cultural association between Canada and Asia. These events are not insignificant as small things matter. When it comes to individuals, specifically common citizens, this is a highly sensitive issue. In India, we call the common man '*aam aadmi*' in Hindi language meaning someone who is preoccupied in dealing with his everyday struggles of life. For him/her, these little episodes of cultural sensitivity and mutual respect go a long way in restoring faith and reverence in a country's government.

Shiamak Davar is a sought after popular Indian choreographer in the Bollywood industry. His expertise in mixing various dance styles has resulted in the opening up of dance institutions throughout India. Interestingly, he has opened up branches in Toronto, Vancouver and Calgary, bringing the Bollywood dancing style into Canada too. Cori Howard mentions:

> Davar is determined to bring the Bollywood dance craze to mainstream Canadians … . The classes, set to fast-paced music and taught by a rotating crop of instructors recruited from Davar's prestigious dance institute in India, have already attracted around 500 regular participants … . In many ways, Davar's timing couldn't be better. There has of late been an insatiable appetite for all things Indian-fashion, film, jewelry, (and) food and fitness trends like yoga. (n.p.).

The opening of Indian Bollywood dance institutes in Canada can be seen as a consequence of globalization where distinct cultural products of a country are made accessible in another country. It is also an acquaintance into the cultural interests of another region. Interestingly, Davar's dance styles are not purely Indian. They are a mix of jazz, modern, belly dancing, hip-hop, the Punjabi Bhangra and a host of other dance forms that makes the art global in its aspects and appeal. The reformulations out of prevalent dance styles and fusing them makes it appear like a multicultural collage wherein every movement can be identified as emanating from a specific art stream. It is the cultural and global elements plus the commercial angle involved in the Bollywood industry that makes it an attractive terrain both in Canada and India. We, thus, find the spread of Bollywood trends in Canada.

In the year 1985, Farrukh Dhondy published an article titled 'Indian Film and its World' that appeared in the *The Moving Image* (Daedlus) stating, 'In Britain, Canada, the United States, and whatever other Western Countries where Indians are to be found, the Indian film remains an alien peepshow, an inaccessible slice of culture. Neither will it catch on in time ...' (139). It is interesting to compare what Dhondy observed in the latter half of the 20th century that prognosticated that the Indian film industry wouldn't 'catch on in time' (139), in the West, including Canada, as he refers to in the aforementioned statement. However, today it is apparent that Dhondy's prediction hasn't stood the test of time and Bollywood with all its global manifestations has successfully reached various countries and of course, in Canada too and has 'caught on in time' beyond doubt. The profitability involved is gargantuan since the themes that Bollywood films deal with are popular with the Indian and diaspora masses.

Sujata Moorthy in her essay 'Desperately Seeking an Identity: Diasporic Cinema and the Articulation of Transnational Kinship' discusses two films *New View, New Eyes* by Gitanjali Saxena and *Desperately Seeking* Helen by Eisha Marjara. *New View, New Eyes* portrays Indian images, Mumbai's urbanity and the rural areas of the country and depicts Canada from the perspective of an Indian. So there is a commingling of the personal with the global. The advantage of knowing and travelling in two countries become a part of portrayal in movies.

A movie that was produced in the year 2011 was *Breakaway* which was also dubbed in Hindi and was called *Speedy Singhs*. The film was shot in Canada and reflected the Indo-Canadian community adapting into the country. Though a commercial flop, the film is interesting for its picturing India and Canada. One of the songs, *Ni Aaja Ve*, is particularly notable for its backdrop, conflating the Taj Mahal of India with the representation of the snowy winters of Canada right before the monument and the protagonists skating on the snow. There is the harsh winter of Canada and the world famous work of art of India blended together. The coming together of the two nations happens at a cultural, artistic and heritage levels. The hero is a

Punjabi Indian whose girlfriend is a Canadian and their romantic relationship alludes to the interracial connections taking place in a society that is multicultural by nature. This is again a reference to the hybridization of cultures and people taking place in the Canadian society.

Several other movies have been shot in Canada like Neelam Sethi's *Aaj Ke Haalat* (contemporary conditions); Eisha Marjara's *Desperately Seeking Helen*, the protagonist happens to be an Indo-Canadian who travels to India to meet Helen, a Bollywood star and vamp. The protagonist's mother was killed in the Air India bomb explosion that took place in the year 1985. This historical episode has always been a painful memory for Indo-Canadians and we find reference to this in Anita Rau Badami's novel also *Can you Hear the Nighbird Call?* While the protagonist is going back to her roots, her place of origin, she is also remembering and reliving an excruciating historical incident. So, film as a commodity becomes a site not only for culture portrayal but also for the precipitation of fragments of history and memory. Reliving the Indian experience through films becomes indispensable for the diaspora. In Rohinton Mistry's short story 'Lend Me Your Light', the protagonist writes a letter to his friend describing Toronto's Gerrard Street which is like a Little India in Canada where they could 'see a Hindi movie at the Naaz Cinema' (189). So literature too is not bereft of the necessity that the Indian diaspora feels for Indian films in Canada.

In the context of the Indian diaspora, the Bollywood conceptualizes the desire for homeland for a community that has multiple affiliations. Furthermore, both Canada and India can create opportunities of investment through the motion picture – both cultural and commercial. Persistence on existing projects and ties would enable professionals of both countries to explore the area deeply. There have already been several strategic partnerships in this direction but considering the enormity of the Bollywood impact and the innumerable dimensions to it in terms of employment, investment, monetary profits and cultural representation, there is still plenty of scope for widening opportunities. This dimension has been captured by film business experts as mentioned in this article. Culturally, Indian films are acceptable and popular. Nevertheless, this area of business can be explored further.

Works Cited

Bracken, Laura. 'Hollywood North near Treaty with Bollywood'. *Playback.* (2 February 2004): 6. Web. 28 Mar. 2012.

Dhondy, Farrukh. 'Indian Film and Its World'. *Daedalus.* Vol. 114, No. 4. *The Moving Image* (Fall, 1985): 125–140. *The MIT Press (American Academy of Arts and Sciences).* Web. 27 Mar. 2012. <http://www.jstor.org/ stable/20025013.>

Howard, Cori. 'Bollywood Boogie'. *ProQuest Research Library.* Web. 27 Mar. 2012.

Jezovit, Andrea. 'Bollywood Dreams'. *Canadian Business* 80.5 (2007): 19–20. *Academic Search Premier.* EBSCO. Web. 7 Sept. 2012.

Kal Ho Na Ho. Nikhil Advani (Director). Karan Johar, Yash Johar (Producers). Dharma Productions. 2003.

Koi Mil Gaya. Rakesh Roshan (Director). Rakesh Roshan (Production). Filmkraft Productions (I) Pvt Ltd. 2003.

Mistry, Rohinton. 'Lend Me Your Light'. *Tales from Firozsha Baag.* Canada: McClelland and Stewart Ltd, 1987. Print.

Moorthy, Sujata. 'Desperately Seeking an Identity: Diasporic Cinema and the Articulation of Transnational Kinship'. *International Journal of Cultural Studies.* Vol 6 (3). London: Sage, 2003. 355–376. Print.

Nehru, Jawaharlal. *The Discovery of India.* New Delhi: Penguin, 2004. Print.

Nilekani, Nandan. *Imagining India: Ideas for the New Century.* New Delhi: Penguin, 2008. Print. 140.

Sahoo, Ajaya Kumar, and Dave Sangha. 'Diaspora and Cultural Heritage: The Case of Indians in Canada'. *Asian Ethnicity* 11.1 (2010): 81–94. Print.

Simon, Bernard. 'Bollywoods Global Drive Reaches Toronto'. FT.com (2011): Web. 27 Mar. 2012. <http://www.ft.com/cms/s/0/ cdbb6bda-9e55-11e0- 8e61-00144feabdc0.html#axzz3rvhief5a.>

Speedy Singhs. Robert Lieberman (Director). Akshay Kumar and Paul Gross (Producers). Hari Om Productions Viacom 18. 2011.

Tharoor, Shashi. *The Elephant, the Tiger and the Cellphones.* India: Penguin, 2007. Print.

Wilkie, Dana. 'Canada's Innovative Internationalization'. *International Educator* 16.5 (2007): 49. ProQuest Education Journals; ProQuest Research Library. Web. 27 Mar. 2012.

Wise, Wyndham. 'Bollywood North: An interview with Deepa Mehta'. *Take One*. September–November 2002: 32–36. General Reference Center GOLD. Web. 27 Mar. 2012.

10

Subalterns' Voices through 'Accented Cinema(s)'

A Study of Deepa Mehta's Fire and Water

SUBRATA KUMAR DAS

The term 'subaltern' meaning 'of inferior rank' is adopted by Antonio Gramsci to refer to those groups in society who are on periphery from the hegemonic power structure of the ruling classes. In describing 'history told from below', the term 'subaltern' identifies the social groups who are excluded from a society's established structures for political representation, the means by which people have a 'voice' in their society.

In the 'Preface' to the first volume of *Subaltern Studies* (1982), Ranajit Guha explained that the term 'subaltern' would be used by the authors in the series as a 'general attribute of subordination in South Asian society whether this is expressed in terms of class, caste, age, gender and office or in any other way' (vii). A subaltern is a person rendered without human agency, by his or her social status. Subaltern classes may include peasants, workers and other groups denied access to 'hegemonic' power. In India, *dalit*(s), rural, tribal, immigrant labourers and women are part of subaltern.

Some Indian female film directors living abroad make films, which are different from the traditional Bollywood films or regional films of different Indian states. These diasporic film directors are Gurinder Chadha, the British Indian filmmaker, Mira Nair, the American Indian filmmaker, Deepa Mehta, the Indo-Canadian filmmaker and others. Their films are called 'auteur' (French word for 'author') films or directors' films that reflect the directors' personal creative visions. These filmmakers believe in the primary creative importance, combined with a critical advocacy in their films. Here, a director is the sole creator of a film and thereby gives the film a distinctive individual style and theme. Sometimes, they depict the themes, which are marginal, tabooed and untouched by traditional filmmakers. Thus, the scenario(s) or the very culture that these films document appear as counter or 'punk' culture to the culture documented in mainstream popular films.

Until recently, Indian popular Bollywood films are made for male gazes. The male directors, even some female directors show the skinny, half-naked, sensual heroines in their films for male audience's gratification. Few have attempted to document the tabooed subjects of Indian cultures and mostly their films have been banned by the religious fundamentalists. Deepa Mehta, originally from Punjab, India, is such an Indo-Canadian film director and screenwriter, well known for her Elements Trilogy – *Fire* (Canada/India, 1996), *Earth* (Canada/India, 1998), and *Water* (Canada/India, 2005: 7).

These South Asian auteurs try to deconstruct the image of 'scopophilia' ('pleasure in looking') from the traditional Hollywood and Bollywood films for 'male gaze'. Laura Mulvey in her article 'Visual Pleasure and Narrative Cinema' defined 'scopophilia' as an act of pleasure in looking at the female characters portrayed as an erotic object mainly for the male observers (17). These films by Indian diasporic filmmakers like Deepa Mehta, Mira Nair and others are termed by Hamid Naficy in his book *An Accented Cinema: Exilic and Diasporic Filmmaking* (2001) as 'accented' cinema which emerges, as Naficy argues, not from 'the accented speech of the diegetic characters' within these films but from the 'displacement of the filmmakers'(4). These 'accented' films negotiate the interstitial dialogues between the home and the host societies of the filmmakers.

Thus, these films give two sites for marginalized women – a site of resistance from the part of films' characters and other being the site for the expression of that resistance for the filmmakers. I think this is also the expression of postcolonial feminism through these 'accented' cinema(s). Thus, through these films the diasporic filmmakers try to eradicate the subaltern status of women and allow them a 'space' to be heard among mainstream social phenomena. These feminist 'accented' cinema(s) not only project strong-willed and sexually assertive women but also portray women as agents of progressive, revolutionary, egalitarian social thinkers who openly show their free spirits.

In traditional Bollywood films, we almost can't get female 'voices'. In reality, women in these films are marginalized. The film critic Katey Rich, in her article 'Women on Film-Will Bollywood Best Hollywood in Opportunities for Women', argues:

> Bollywood is as well-known as its Los Angeles counterpart for giving women small space both in front of and behind the camera. But what makes Hollywood better than the Bollywood is that American media reports like the 2009 edition of Dr Martha Lauzen's Celluloid Celling Study reveal that just 9 per cent of Hollywood directors are women. However, there is no study comparable to Dr Lauzen's that Bollywood is confident to highlight the number of their female filmmakers. (Rich, n.p.)

In traditional Bollywood and even in Hollywood films, we find the traditional virtues of womanhood like that of the sacrificing, virginal, passive, and servile women. But in feminist auteur films, there are strong-willed and sexually-assertive women. Deepa Mehta's films like *Fire* and *Water*, Gurinder Chadha's *Bend It Like Beckham* (2002) and *Bhaji on the Beach* (1993), Mira Nair's *Mississippi Masala* (1991), *Monsoon Wedding* (2001) and *The Namesake* (2007) are examples of this kind of films. In this paper, I intend to study women as 'subalterns' and explore how such 'subalterns' raise 'voices' to get 'spaces' in mainstream social phenomena through Mehta's *Fire* and *Water*.

Fire (Canada/India, 1996)

Fire is the first instalment of Mehta's Elements trilogy. It is followed by *Earth* and *Water*. The film is loosely based on Ismat Chugtai's short story *Lihaaf* (*The Quilt*), published in 1942. The film portrays tradition and modernity, represented by two sisters-in-law Radha and Sita respectively and shows how the traditional values and norms are replaced by the modern outlooks of women, and thus the subsequent replacement of gender role and sexuality within a Hindu family. In an interview with to Ingrid Randoja, film director Mehta argues,

> The women's relationship represents modern India itself .... Radha is tradition bound and just waiting to blossom, but can't because of the absurdity of tradition and duty. Sita is modern India, desiring independence over tradition. Yet it's not as if she can speak her mind. She's simply a catalyst, so when she walks into the house, she makes things happen just by her presence. (Mehta, n.p.)

The story of the film revolves around two sisters-in-law of a middle class merchant joint family who develop an intimate relationship with each other due to sexual alienation from their husbands. Radha (Shabana Azmi) is barren in the family and therefore, Ashoke, her husband has taken a vow of celibacy that has lasted thirteen years. Ashoke is also studying to be a *Swami* (spiritual leader). Radha, being a traditional woman shares equal blame in their sexless marriage. After all, she is barren, not frigid, and the script makes no mention of any 'male' impotency. Radha consents to her husband's demand, but the viewers can clearly sense the burning sense of injustice consuming her.

Ashoke's younger brother Jatin is newly married by arrangement to Sita (Nandita Das), a freethinking modern woman. From the very beginning, Sita shows her counter arguments against the Hindu tradition, customs and other patriarchal social norms. In one of the scenes, she wears jeans, pretends to smoke and gives lips to Hindi film music. Thus, her bold gesture through cross-dressing may show her liberal feminism where a feminist is equated with being (like) a man. Sita's cross-dressing pushes her to claim temporary male freedom and privileges in a patriarchal family after her marriage. It reminds the audience of the familiar queer trope of cross-dressing. Studying the cross-dressing scene, Jigna Desai in her book *Beyond Bollywood* (2004) argues:

> Sita's performance, however, conveys her desire to be the new heroine of the cinema in the postcolonial moment of economic liberalization, one that incorporates the figure of the traditional heroine and the vamp into the newly married middle-class woman, one who may wear saris or jeans, the modern woman of India. Her performance and cross-dressing are queer and trangressive whether one reads as performing femininity or masculinity. (162)

Jatin has a live-in relationship with his Chinese immigrant girlfriend Julie (Alice Poon). As Ashoke is childless, he forces Jatin to get married to Sita only to have 'baby boy' in the family. Jatin continues his live-in relationship with Julie even after his marriage. Sita refuses to keep the family's unspoken plan – that she produces children to occupy her time in a loveless marriage. Here a woman is treated a commodity for baby production. Sita's 'this duty thing is overrated' (Mehta, 1996) shocks traditional Radha.

Here, the director shows the hypocrisy of male over female in a conjugal life. Jatin openly goes to his Chinese girlfriend to have sex at night, leaving Sita on her bed. Thus, during the lone hours both Radha and Sita share their pathetic life stories and come close to each other. In their intimate discussions and loneliness, they develop a desire for each other and seek pleasure in a number of ways, such as oiling each other's hair and caressing each other's bare bodies in bed. This leads to their bodily desire and Sita, being a radical modern woman, takes initiation. Thus, *Fire* comes as the first Indian film about lesbianism. It seems to be part of a new freedom in Indian films.

When Mundu (Ranjit Chowdhury), a domestic helper masturbates in front of Biji, the aged bed-ridden mother of the family, Radha catches him. He also tells her that '"hanky panky" between you (Radha) and Sita madam is not good for the family's name' (Mehta, 1996). He means that he knows of her lesbian affair with Sita and thus, threatens to get her exposed. He also gives Radha a proposal for sexual relation through his popular Hindi lyrics.

The film is also about loveless marriage between Jatin and Sita: after ejaculation, Jatin rolls over to sleep, telling Sita not to worry about the blood from her hymen: 'If you bleed, don't worry. It happens the first time' (Mehta, 1996). Here the director shows man has hidden inquiry on whether his wife was virgin or not before marriage. The film's stark contrast between the results and aims of heterosexual and homosexual relationships is another misleading cliché and biased political stance shown by Mehta. In other words, all things gay are good, and all things straight are not even as the reverse stereotype is despised.

Now the questions may come from the feminist side here: Why does Ashoke, instead of well knowing that his brother Jatin has sexual relationship with a woman, force him to get married? Why does he thus use a woman as an agent of 'baby boy' production? As a wife, Sita has every right to force her husband Jatin to stay with her. Then, why does Jatin ill-treat her for her such opposition? As these two wives are starving from conjugal sex, then what is the problem of their husbands when they are getting satisfaction through lesbian sex? Biji spits on Radha's face for her lesbian act with Sita. If Biji is justified, then, why does not she force her son to keep distance from his extra marital relationship?

The director answers these questions by the unconventional attempts that these two wives take. Sita is a rational woman from the beginning. She tries to get justification of her married life every time through argumentative ways. Therefore, she opposes Jatin's negligence towards her. Her inquisitive approaches also make Radha think over her long stance of her husband's keeping distance from her, an idea preached by *Swami*. When Sita protests against the ill-treatments of Jatin, she gets slap from him and she does the same to Jatin. Moreover, she does not stop there only. With her raised head, she leaves her husband's home. Radha also does the same, but at last. When Radha is caught by Ashoke during her lesbian sex with Sita, she is confronted by her husband. She then gives her 'voice', telling him he can get emancipation of his bodily desire from *Swami*. In anger, Ashoke abuses her calling '*randi*' (prostitute). Finally, she defies familial bonds and leaves her husband's home. Thus, through these film documentations, auteur Mehta perhaps shows the other South Asian women how to protest their husbands' coldness and callousness, their torture and torment, their patriarchal imposed rules over them. Even for sexual gratification, the director supports lesbianism if sexual gratification is not possible through husband.

The female characters portrayed feminism in these films in the three steps (Dasgupta, 1996). These are: (1) a gradual awareness of them being victims of sexual exploitation and gender discrimination in the male dominated South Asian culture, (2) the feminist consciousness of sexuality, social identity, and their needs and wants as an important part of their individual and social development, (3) the ability to challenge the norms by making a sexual-assertive decision about the choices. These types of changes are seen in Radha's character after her coming in contact with rational and argumentative Sita. Initially Radha was traditional. When doctor told her that there were 'no eggs in (her) ovary' (Mehta, 1996), she accepted her husband's celibacy silently and started leading a sexless married life. But after coming in contact with Sita, she tends to get changed. Sita always tries to emancipate herself from tradition, rituals and customs. In one of the scenes, she argues, '... we are so bound by customs and rituals. Somebody just has to press my button, this button marks tradition and I start responding like a trained monkey' (Mehta, 1996).

When Sita asks Radha if her idea shocks her, she replies in positive. In another instance, when Radha explains to Sita the need to pray for the well-being of the husbands by wives during the *Karva Chauth* festival, Sita feels disgusted and argues, 'I am sick of all these devotions. We can find choices' (Mehta, 1996). When these two wives get bodily attachment and finally commit lesbian sex, Sita wants to know if they are doing something 'wrong'. As her times progress with Sita, Radha gradually is changed and she replies that they are not doing anything 'wrong'.

From the very beginning, Sita counter-argues with Jatin regarding his keeping Chinese girlfriend, his suggestion to her keeping busy with needlework and having child. Once Jatin asks her to keep her busy having baby or get divorce from him, she replies that he is a 'pompous fool' (Mehta, 1996). On the other hand, Radha, once a devotional wife of Ashoke, starts showing her deaf ears to her husband over times. When Ashoke complains to her that Biji is not eating meal, she promptly tells him, 'Why don't you feed tonight' (Mehta, 1996)? Many times, she does not respond to her husband's calls. Finally, before leaving her husband's home, Sita tries to convince Radha that they should leave their husbands' home and begin a life of their own while saying, 'There is no word in our language to describe how we feel for each other' (Mehta, 1996). Therefore, Radha also shows her individuality and values herself, saying, 'My leaving (to Ashoke and the family) is everything to do with me' (Mehta, 1996). At last, she also leaves her husband's home and joins Sita.

I have already argued that such type of diasporic auteur films deconstruct scopophilic femininity portrayed in Hollywood and Bollywood films for the male gaze. Throughout the whole film, we notice the two sisters-in-law Radha and Sita wearing traditional dresses. They wear little makeup and their dresses are mostly not revealing skin or beauty that much. In one scene, Sita had sex with Jatin after their marriage. The scene shows the nude upper body of Jatin while Sita is still covered on top in her sari. It also shows Jatin's impassionate approach towards his bride.

Thus, Deepa Mehta's documentation examines the emotional connection of an Indian diasporic filmmaker in relation to the portrayal of femininity of her native country. Being an auteur, Mehta consciously and deliberately attempts to modify the usual emotional and patriarchal exploitation of the female body and sexuality in contemporary Indian cinema (s). *Fire* also shows the emotional transformation of two wives Radha and Sita. At the beginning, they try their best to be the all-traditional sacrificing and loving wives. However, due to their husbands' prolonged rejection and disapproval, they take a stand by desiring each other and living a life of their own.

Water (Canada/India, 2005: 7)

After well knowing the theme of this film under shooting, the shooting was forcibly stopped in Varanasi by mobs protesting what was seen as the film's disparagement of Indian Hindu culture. Although the film is set in Varanasi, it was then shot in

Sri Lanka. Though the film documents the plight of Indian widows, it was not at first released in India until Canadian Government sent it for the Academy Award in 2005 and got short listed and finally, after two years of its release in international film festival, it was released in India in 2007. Hence, such types of attempts were seen to curb the 'voices' of female film director and indirectly women's voices in the film.

Water is the third instalment of Mehta's Elements trilogy. It documents the lives of rural Indian widows in an *ashram* (secluded abode for widows) in the 1940. Set in 1938 at the time of Mahatma Gandhi's rise to prominence, the story begins when a seven-year-old Chuyia (Sarala Kariyawasam) is widowed and sent to *ashram* where the Hindu widows are forced to live their abrogated lives in miserable penury. They are considered as inauspicious and hence banned from attending mainstream social celebrations. A widow is feared and thought as a bad omen. They are expected to renounce all ornaments, cosmetics and are forbidden from looking in the mirror. But the beautiful ones, including Kalyani (Lisa Roy) are regularly sent across the river and forced to prostitute themselves with wealthy men to sustain the expenditure of their livelihood. Narayan (John Abraham), son of a *Brahmin* meets Kalyani and falls in love with her. But when Narayan's wealthy parents are informed of the relationship, their defiance of religious and cultural taboos are an invitation to tragedy of Kalyani who drowns herself with shame. Later Narayana gets to know that his father was one of the former clients of Kalyani's body.

Throughout the film, there are some scenes where the female characters show their 'voices' of resistance, protest, etc. The child widow Chuyia, traditional but finally rational Shakuntala (Seema Biswas) and few other widows of the *ashram* show such 'voices' against the social taboos against them. Chuyia is an innocent child widow. When some widows gather to hear the *slokas* (distich of Sanskrit verses) from a *pandit* (scholar and teacher, particularly in Sanskrit language), they are instructed about their destination, their refuge in secluded *ashram*. Chuyia innocently asks a *pandit, 'Admi vidhawa ka ghar kahan hai'* (where is a widower's house?) (Mehta, 2005)? This voice raises the question of society's patriarchal stance against widows. Even it is a sin to think about such secluded destination for their male counterparts. Once Chuyia is begging with other widows, but suddenly she leaves begging. As a girl, she does not like it and it is a very pathetic situation that such type of child widow is undergoing such ill and pathetic treatments only to follow the imposed taboos on her. Like Chuyia, Kalyani also stays in the *ashram* since she was widowed at the age of nine years. She did not even see her husband.

Through Chuyia, Narayan meets Kalyani and realizes the very pathetic lives these widows lead. When he confesses to his mother that he has decided to marry a widow, his mother reacts, 'What will people say!' She also adds, '*Gandhi ne dimag kharab kar diya tumhara. Ek vidhawa se shaadi, tum soch bhi kaise sakte ho? Yeh toh paap hai*' (Gandhiji has made you mad. How can you think of marrying a widow? It is a sin) (Mehta, 2005). To convince his mother, he says, '*Raja Rammohan kahte hain ki vidhawa ka punar vivah hona chahiye*' ('Raja Rammohan Ray says that the widow should be remarried'), (Mehta, 2005). When the head of the *ashram* Madhumati (Manorama), hears from Chuyia that Kalyani would get married, she protests vehemently and says, '*Vidhawa saadi nahi karti*' (A widow doesn't get married.). In protest, Chuyia says, '*Uski shaadi hogi, hum jante hain hogi*' (She will get married, I know it.) (Mehta, 2005). Thus, Chuyia shows her protest against the rigid rule that does not allow widows to get married.

Though at the beginning, Shakuntala was traditional, gradually she notices the pathetic lives of Chuyia and Kalyani, and finally shows her internal protest against the social taboos against them. Shakuntala confesses to a *pandit*, '*Punar vivah soch na bhi paap hai*' (It is sin to think about remarriage of widow.). 'But why is it so'? (Mehta, 2005). In reply, *pandit* tells her to find the answer from *bhagwaan* (God). When she learns that Kalyani is ready for marriage, she also internally cherishes the chance to get married and thus unconsciously asks Chuyia how she looks. She also asks, '*Panditji, apne toh bahut shastra padhe hain, kya isme likha hai ki vidhwaon ke shastra itna bura salook kiya jana chahiya*' (*Panditji*, you have read many scriptures; is it written there that widows should be subjected to such ill-treatment?)? This shows her internal protest against the rigid patriarchal rules. The Hindu Widow's Remarriage Act of 1856 was passed, but it was almost unknown to these widows. This law was muted by the patriarchy.

We may assume that through this film, Mehta also questions the role of Mahatma Gandhi for the welfare of widows. Narayan is a staunch follower of Gandhiji. Through his character, we notice Gandhiji's influence and his contribution to Indian society. But a deep study of Mehta's film may also show us his little role for women's amelioration. When Chuyia is molested by a *Brahmin*, Shakuntala takes her to meet Gandhiji. But Gandhiji and even his followers never cast their glances for a single moment to half dead Chuyia. Sitting in a corner, Shakuntala hears the principles of Gandhiji with her poor and pathetic looks. It deeply shows the deaf ears and blind eyes of Gandhiji in particular and of the other male followers of Gandhiji in general to the widows' miserable and pathetic lives. But at the end, there is a hope of saving the child widow Chuyia as Shakuntala is able to hand over her to Narayan. Perhaps Narayan would marry this widow and set her free from the *ashram* life.

Therefore, throughout the film we get women's concern for their 'space' in mainstream social phenomena. They raise their 'voices' against the taboos meted out over them by many sided social agents: the Hindu religious rites for widows, the imposed secluded abodes like *ashram* for widows, victims of *brahmin*(s) as a commodity for sex to sustain their livelihood, the questionable role of Mahatma Gandhi for the welfare of widows, etc. We notice Madhumati arguing that widow marriage is not possible and she is concerned for their sinful activities through such remarriage. Actually, she is deeply concerned for the societal rules for widows and the scandalous rumour through such marriage. Through the character of Shakuntala, the director also tries to show the perseveration and dedication of a widow. But being human, even a traditional and religious Shakuntala can't sustain such pathetic unworldly life.

To conclude, we may agree with Prof. Tutun Mukherjee's opinions who in her essay, 'Deepa Mehta's Film *Water*: The Power of the Dialectical Image' (2008) argues:

> The film's message is that of arousing women's emotional and social awareness and building resistance within oneself, of not succumbing to the implacable forces, and of finding plausible routes of escape. This is conveyed by Shakuntala looking back at the audience with a burning glance as the film ends. (...) It speaks of issues long neglected by the Indian society so that the widows of Mathura, Vrindavan and Varanasi seem to be the forgotten inhabitants of an oppressive and archaic world. (...) The film addresses a global audience in an attempt to alert the conscience of the world to the continued neglect of women even after the successes of feminism and the political reforms initiated by feminist ideology have secured for rights and equality for so many women around the world. (46–47)

The diasporic filmmakers like Deepa Mehta are marginalized even in their native country India by big banner and commercial filmmakers for challenging the dominant-narratives and portraying them through previously unconsidered viewpoints. Thus, from the diasporic lands, they adopt the women-centred subjects in their films and these films are the media of expression for voicing the plight as well as the progress of Indian women to the multiple audiences including the South Asian diasporic and native audiences, and Western audiences (Desai, 2004). Thus, these auteurs should be acknowledged as the spokespersons of the South Asian immigrants and diasporic communities in general and of the supressed native Indian women's voices in male-dominant Indian societies and film industry. The films attempt to transform the hegemonic, patriarchal, and male-dominant narratives and, re-imagine them from Indian women's perspectives. Besides, these diasporic film directors create a relationship between native and the diasporic generations of India through these films.

Deepa Mehta's *Fire* and *Water* are, thus, narrated almost entirely from the point of views of 'subaltern' women and therefore quintessentially give voice to women. Like any other subaltern narratives, these two 'accented' cinema(s) portray women's struggles, resistance and protests to change their social 'space' from 'periphery' to 'centre'. Thus, Mehta's films give us a kaleidoscopic social articulation of 'subaltern' women from a minority perspective.

Works Cited

Primary Sources

Mehta, Deepa. *Water* (Motion Picture). United States: Fox Searchlight Pictures, 2005.

——. *Fire* (Motion Picture). United States: Zeitgeist Films, 1996.

Secondary Sources

Dasgupta, Samita Dasgupta. 'Feminist Consciousness in Woman-Centred Hindi Films'. *Journal of Popular Culture. Summer* Vol. 30. No. 1 (1996): 173–189. Print.

Desai, Jigna. *Beyond Bollywood: The Cultural Politics of South Asian Diasporic Film*. New York and London: Routledge, 2004. Print.

Guha, Ranajit. *Subaltern Studies* (Vol. 1). New Delhi: Oxford University Press, 1982. Print.

Mukherjee, Tutun. 'Deepa Mehta's Film *Water*: The Power of the Dialectical Image'. Web. 2 January 2014. <http://www.film studies.ca/journal/pdf/cj-film-studies172_muhkerjee_deepa-mehta_ water.pdf.>

Mulvey, Laura. 'Visual Pleasure and Narrative Cinema'. Web. 4 March 2014. <http://terpconnect.umd.edu/~mquillig/20050131 mulvey.pdf>

Naficy, Hamid. *An Accented Cinema: Exilic and Diasporic Filmmaking*. New Jersey: Princeton University Press, 2001. Print.

Randoja, Ingrid. 'Deepa Mehta. Heat rises as resilient director sets Fire to film fest's Canadian slate'. Web. 11 May 1997. <http://www.now.com/issues/16/01/Ent/cover.html>

Rich, Katey. 'Women On Film-Will Bollywood Best Hollywood In Opportunities For Women'. Web. 20 December 2013.

<http://awfj.org/blog/2009/03/04/women-on-film-will-bollywood-surpa ss-hollywood-in-opportunities-for-women-katey-rich-comments/>

11

Queer Tropes in Post 1990s Malayalam Cinema[1]

RAJESH JAMES

The narrative logic of Malayalam mainstream films is usually predicated on an apparent straightness that prioritizes the heteronormative value systems of social enterprises and its cultural manifestations. Such constructs of sexuality offer interesting insights into the politics of heteronormativity in modern, contemporary Malayalam Cinema. Cinema in Kerala is quite reluctant to explore 'the love that had for so long been left out in the cold' (Griffiths: 130). But there are cases of subversive forms of queerness in contemporary Malayalam films making their presence either implicitly or explicitly in the existing categories of cinematography. These cultural texts, as Alexander Doty argues, have connotative rather than denotative queer sentiments that a culture of homophobia and heterosexism bars us from seeing (1). There are ghosts, to use Doty's phrase that inhibited the cultural texts of Malayalam cinema which are to be driven out of their closets.

This study is an analysis of post-1990s Malayalam films at a time when 'New Queer Cinema' was emerging in the West. Unlike the earlier, films after 1990s have series of queer patterns in it, though marginal. There are four recurring tropes of queer representation in Malayalam cinema after 1990s. The first pattern – closeted appearance of LGBT characters that should be brought out – acknowledges how homophobic Kerala society is and how tough it is to be out of the closet. The second trope is that of queerness as an absence or as an aberration. The third pattern is that of queer body as a comic spectacle that has less to do with the non-straight sentiments of *malayalee*[2] and more to do with how queerness is understood and metaphorized in Kerala. Such spectacular images though not directly enjoyed or appreciated on the screen, are constantly redeployed to reassure heterosexual drives of the popular audience, thereby perpetuating the superiority of a machismo. The last pattern is that of queer characters who are visibly queer with all nuances and ambiguity.

Celluloid Closets in post 1990s Malayalam Films

In his *Celluloid Closet*, a classic survey of homosexuality in Hollywood films, Vito Russo explores the stenotypes in the representation of gays and lesbians till date. Until 1980s, according to him, they were presented as an unseen danger and as the dark side of the American dream. With the enforcement of Hays Code in 1934, homosexuality became officially unspeakable and gay characters were rendered using various types of innuendo. Malayalam film industry like Hollywood, in its unique way, projected heterosexual imagination simultaneously offering limited vision of the 'actual queer life' in Kerala. In this process, the real life of Keralites with same sex desires – gays, bisexuals and some who don't align themselves with any particular sexual identity – were ignored. According to the Article 377 of the Indian Constitution, homosexuality is a criminal act. Public anathema caused by the homophobic sensibility of Keralites has also made forced filmmakers from mapping this issue. Mainstream films of the 1990s and after maintained a strange silence about queerity as if queerness is absent in Kerala or as if it constitutes purely a Western identity. Though the films of the post-1990s have got heterosexuality as its central focus, there are cases of subversive closeted metaphors which in turn challenged heteronormative conventionality of popular films.

According to Muraleedharan Tharayil, a pioneering scholar of queer studies in Kerala, 'homoeroticism in Malayalam cinema is indicated through male intimacies which are often contrasted with near absence of male desire for women' (2002: 8). Male bonding has always been an important theme in Malayalam cinema from its earliest days and it has so far been read through a heterosexist perspective that turns a blind eye towards the complex articulation of physical intimacies and desire they regularly appropriate. Films like *Harikrishnans* (1999) and *Thenkashipattanam* (2001) elaborate this by presenting men who have set up an alternative domestic system, including a child who is invariably a girl. *Thenkashipattanam* presents two men (Suresh Gopi and Lal[3]) within an alternate domestic structure with their sister Devi (Kavya Madhavan[4]).

Chakram (2003), a film by Lenin Rajendran, further extends the language of male domesticity by presenting two men falling subject to a far more unequally constituted family formation. The younger male in this film assumes a subordinate role that borders on a replication of patriarchal heterosexual domesticity. The character, Vijesh, cooks and washes for the older male Prithviraj, a popular Indian actor and even declares 'I have been serving him like a wife'. An explicit invocation of the sensual in a location of male intimacy appears in *One Man Show* (2002), in the sequence in which the hero Jayakrishanan enters his decorated bedroom on his wedding night, only to encounter his eccentric male friend Hari both in groom's attire. In his deranged fancy, Hari supposedly thinks himself as the groom who married Radhika, Jaykrishnan's wife. The situation is complicated by the presence of a lunatic (Salim Kumar[5]), also in groom's attire, who strays into the same bedroom, adding to the confusion. Hari and Jayakrishnan seem to erase the element of the erotic through exaggerated disavowal of their desire for each other, while the mad man re-inscribes it with equal vehemence by openly soliciting it. The culture of compulsory heterosexuality determines and distorts the narrative dynamics of these entire non-straight queer subtexts by a quick re-establishment of a normative order which is accomplished through a re-inscription of the main character into the heterosexual matrix that constitutes the final marriage of the hero and the heroine. Following is a close analysis of a 2011 Malayalam film called *Urumi* as an envoy of Malayalam filmic closet.

Urumi: The Warriors who Wanted to Kill Vasco Da Gama (2011): A Close Reading

As a historical fantasy film that pumps oodles of testosterone on to the screen, Santhosh Sivan's *Urumi* is a recent touchstone of closeted Kerala filmic self. Set in the back drop of fierce warrior clans of northern Kerala in the 16th century, it hubs on the cult of *Chirakkal Kelu Nayanar* (Prithviraj).[6] His target and mission is Don Vasco da Gama (Robin Prat[7]). The film is spread between the second and third visit of Gama to India and chronicles a varied version of how Vasco da Gama could have met a bloody death in AD 1524. In his task, Kelu is supported by Vavvaali (Prabhudeva)[8], his childhood friend. They remain together through thick and thin and soon find their destinies inseparably intertwined, even though they eventually fail in their mission of killing Gama. Apparently a movie set in the context of Portuguese invasion in India, *Urumi* inherently unfolds a new saga of 'friendship', untouched in the usual courses Mollywood narratives.

Amidst of its historical centredness and its cultural vivacity, *Urumi* focuses on the lively bond between Vavvali and Kelu. They are intimately intertwined and inseparable. Vavvali calls Kelu 'Changayi', a cosy expression of intimacy in Malayalm language, and doesn't want to pursue his desires apart from that of Kelu. Even though it's Vavvali who takes Kelu to his dwelling when he was thrown alone on the shore devastated, Kelu supersedes him and guides him. Although he is younger to Vavvali, Kelu calls him 'eda Vavvali' and takes decisions in his life delinquently. But Vavvali is ready to accept the choices that Kelu make for his life and finds joyance in it. When Kelu decides to fight directly against Gama, he was reluctant enough to go with him. But goes with him by saying 'if you say I will ...' (*Changayi paranga njan ceyyum*). Moreover, Kelu advices Vavvali that 'you should not go after a lady. If you go, you will be vanquished', when he gazes at Bala (Nithya Menen[9]). He never performs such (mis)behaviours thereafter. She himself asks him why he is reluctant to love to her in spite of her promptings in a song sequence: (*Enthellam paditum mindate minditum nokkiyilla ni ennittum ni enthe* ...) 'Why don't you love even after my song and my silent talk?' But Vavvali keeps silence and goes away from her.

In another scene, Bala asks Vavvali suspiciously that why he is so attached to Kelu 'mysteriously', when he explains his ligature with Kelu and he replies, 'I could have told to you not about it'. His remarks indirectly profess why he is not interested in Bala and the liaison that he has with Kelu. Moreover the name Vavvali itself is highly stereotypical since it has effeminate tone in itself. Vavvali is presented in a typical effeminate way that affords heterosexual vision of what a homosexual is like. Even though stereotypes have a contained silent discourse, it makes something invisible visible as Richard Dyer observes (6–18). By representing Vavvali as passive and effeminate, the text makes visible the apparent invisibility of gayness in his character. Moreover, the controlling .symbol of the movie is Urumi, a traditional war weapon. It is the source of Kelu's strength. As a forceful symbol, it works as his metaphorical phallus that asserts his masculinity. However, it is clear from the text that, more than the weapon, actual source of his power is his 'friend' Vavvali. He himself feels that he is able to defeat Portuguese troupes when Vavvali is with him and he has done it erstwhile. Once he is removed from his life, he fails helplessly. Urumi as the source of their power condenses and displaces their firm gay bond. Even though Kelu sexually interlaces Aracakkal Ayisha (Genelia[10]), he himself says that he has done it only to materialize his procreative motives and to ensure his race's continuity. In spite of its apparent historical zeal, the movie reflects, refracts and recreates a firm gay acquaintance of Kelu and Vavvali, though obliquely. Even though the movie is an apparent fight against Portuguese ascendancy, there is a silent stringency of war in it against the dominating heterosexist discourses and all its cultural (mal) practices.

Queerness as an Absence/Aberration

Malayalam filmscape in spite of all its progressive and dialogical trends have always been defined by spectacular paradigms reinforcing its own chosen hegemonic assumptions. Malayalam cinema after 1990s prefers and codifies an assumed brawny, macho figure. Films like *Devasuram* (1993), *Aram Thampuran* (1997), *Ravanaprabhu* (2001) align the bodies with the elusive and normative ideal of the male, fair-complexioned hefty body gratifying the egotistical masculine desires of its implicit audience. Most male bodies presented are normative and masculine. Those bodies that fail to achieve or even aspire to the assumed masculine 'normalcy' are designated as abnormal and incomplete. Such representations often create affective spectacles of pleasure, which in reverse endorse the 'normalcy' of macho figures.

The queer body is one such, spectacularly represented, constantly re-employed to establish the spectacle of queer body as absence or aberration, which satiate the egotistical, heteromasculinist cultural assumptions of a typical 'normal' Malayali. This is evident in Lal Jose's *Chandupottu (2005)*. The protagonist of the film is an effeminate young man, Radhakrishnan whom everybody calls Radha, which is a Malayali feminine name. The first half of the film explores his life as a dance teacher in a fishing village, his love affair with a young woman named Malu and eventual excommunication from the village for allegedly bringing bad omen. He is rescued and taken to a more modern beach resort where his new friends provide him training in becoming a man. The rest of the film narrates how Radha returns to his village, defeats his antagonist in a fist cuff and takes charge of *Malu* and the little boy born to her. He then enthusiastically joins a band of fishermen to go to the sea and earn a manly living. The protagonist is body and persona who signifies as a male, yet lacking masculinity. This 'lack' sets the narrative in motion and captures audience's attention. Freddie, a friend of Radha, attempts to train him in masculine manners that results in a ludicrous caricature of the hyper masculine persona of a macho male star of the 1970s. Malayalam cinema, *Jayan*, which becomes a source of slapstick humour.

In another scene, a group of men forcefully unclothe him to check whether he is a man or a woman, which actually satiates the spectator's curiosity to know the gender of an effeminate man. The narrative transforms such images of lack into a gratifying spectacle whose very continuation appears to generate and perpetuate pleasure. In the final shot of the movie, Radha jumps into the fishing boat assuming the role of a wage-earning householder as if his earlier nature was imperfect. Thus, the movie conforms to the conventions of mainstream Malayalam cinema by coercing an effeminate protagonist to fall in love with the heroine and father a child. This incident in the movie infuriated some of the queer groups in Kerala who questioned the authenticity of such representations. They stated that the film made a laughing stock of them portraying Radha as a ridiculous caricature and filed a case against the film, claiming that ever since the film came out, they faced harsher discriminations from the society. They alleged that, like Freddie and his friends in the film, people started ill-treating and even physically assaulting them to cure their effeminacy. But director Lal Jose tried to nullify the protesters by saying that that the protagonist of the movie is not a queer but just an effeminate male, a product of faulty upbringing (Tharayil: 33).

Queer Body as a Comic Spectacle

Laura Mulvey in, her path-breaking essay 'Visual Pleasure and Narrative Cinema' (1975) explores how female body becomes a spectacle of pleasure in Hollywood cinema. 'In a world ordered by patriarchal fantasies, pleasure in looking has been active/male and passive/female. The projected fantasy of male gaze determines how a female form should be stylized' (10). In his critique of the Mulvian paradigm, Richard Dyer theorized the cultural construction of masculinity as intersected to categories of identities like race, ethnicity and sexuality. Such tropes of masculinity construe certain versions of masculinity as inferior to become spectacles. Nevertheless, his speculations on masculinity had not explored how the queer body is deployed on the screen as spectacle. Queer body as spectacle has been a recurring component in the comic interludes in contemporary Malayalam films. It can be an effeminate man with squeaky walks or a macho man with feminine voice or a transgender or a cross dresser. In such cases, the character would be marginal to the narrative and function as the other celebrating the proper femininity of the upper caste heroine or the normative patriarchy of the hero. This indirectly reassures the heterosexual drives and expectations of the spectator by becoming a source of humour, providing audio-visual pleasure.

Typical of this kind is Ashique Abu's *Salt and Pepper*. The movie features Baburaj, a south Indian actor, as the chief cook who serves his master Kalidasan, an archeologist. The text replaces all the conventional masculine *goonda*[11] features of Baburaj and presents him as an effeminate male. He is spectacularly introduced in the movie with his rare demands for face creams in the background of a butcher shop which is unexpected from other hyper masculine roles which he has essayed in many films. In another occasion he is introduced to the middle aged hero in the background of a *pennukanal chadangu*[12] where he is doing a typical feminine kitchen routine of grinding flour. Babu's presence becomes a spectacle in his squeaky way of talks and effeminate mannerisms. Majority of the spectators laugh at the way he speaks and the way he walks. This particular role-reversal was celebrated in Kerala not because of its grandeur inherent comic possibilities but for Baburaj's effeminate mannerisms involved in it in spite of his macho figure and his comic way of imitating the typically feminine gestures and body language roles. By picturing an effeminate character and making his presence as a comic spectacle in contrast to a macho hero, the movie indirectly asserts superiority of a heterosexual masculine hero in contrast to an effeminate body.

Shaffi's *101 Weddings* also presents a queer character Jyothi as a foil to other masculine heroes of the movie. He is represented as a notorious other to be looked at and smiled at. The other two characters of Kunjako Boban and Biju Menon, two popular South Indian actors, become the replica of a charming suave Kerala figures. At the release of the movie, certain posters were circulated in which Jayasurya, an actor from Kerala, is imitating a Raja Ravi Varma's famous painting *Shakuntala*.[13] This spectacular representation pointed to the comic essentiality attributed to his character. The movie continuously contrasts his effeminate nature with other macho characters of the movie. His dancing steps and love for Rukhia are shot with the intention of producing smiles thereby becoming spectacles for enjoyment. Ironically enough, the character has been reviewed as one of the unique comic characters in the history of Malayalam cinema by some film reviewers of the day.

Queer Independent Films of Post 90s Malayalam Cinema

Malayalam film industry with its 80 years of filmmaking has supposedly touched the possible subtleties of everyday life in spite of all its feudal and patriarchal fervours. But it is very enigmatic the way queerity has been displaced from the main stream psyche of films. Being part of a country which has got a queer god Ardhanareeswara and lord Ayyappa who is born out of a queer bond, it is highly ironic that the general psyche of Malayali is homophobic to which the industry cater to. Mathew Kurian, in his article 'Church and Education in Kerala', explores the exclusivity of Christian education in Kerala. The convent education system in Kerala, which is a colonial import, has played a major part in determining the sexual ethos of Malayali psyche and positing homosexuality as a taboo. Since normative vision of heterosexuality gets a comfortable popularity and acceptance, it was tough for the filmmakers to ideologically destabilize it and offer an alternative perspective that heterosexuality is not the only form of sexuality. However, there are independent films, commonly called Art Cinema, which carry visible queer characters and ethos so far untouched and tabooed.

In 1978 a film named *Randu Penkuttikal* (*Two Girls*) directed by an independent filmmaker Mohanan, had discussed homosexual bond between two girls Kokila and Girija. The characters themselves project the nature of their relationship which is very revolutionary as far as the existing ethos of Kerala society are concerned though the film ends with Girija's comment on Kokila that 'homoerotic sensation was all a phase in teenagers' life and she should be married and lead a happy productive life'. Padmarajan's 1986 film *Deshadanakkili Karayarilla* (*Migrant Bird Doesn't Weep*) also depicts female bonding, though the film never explicitly claims of it being a lesbian bonding.

The release of *Sancharam* (2004), a film by Ligy J. Pullapaplly, was an epoch making event in the history of Malayalam films. The film foregrounded homosexuality as a pattern of human life and sexuality and explored the subtleties of lesbian life in Kerala uncompromisingly and blatantly. The narrative follows two childhood friends – Kiran and Deliliah –

and their coming of age lesbian love. The film depicted their blossoming love erotically as a challenge to the heterosexually groomed spectators of Kerala. The film perfectly constructed their intimate moments though not physically explicit. According to Ligy 'the film will help the young queer generation the option of going ahead in life instead of committing suicide' (http://www.afterellen.com/interview-with-ligy-pullappally). But the film was not released in the theatres of Kerala and run only in festival circles. The film had only one screening in Kerala and there was heckling reaction against it as if it is immoral and turning Kerala youth queer.

In 2013, Santhosh Sawpernika directed a film *Ardhanari* (Sawpernika) that discussed the lives of transgenders in Kerala. The movie gyrates through the inner conflicts of Vinayan, a transgender, who has got male physique and female emotions. As he becomes a butt of ridicule, shame and snide remarks from his friends and family, he goes away and reaches a place called Hamam, a community of hijras, an Indian term for transgender group in the temple town of Tamil Nadu. He becomes a hijras by staying there. But he is forced to go out of the community since he is wrongly thought to be involved in the murder of another hijras. Betrayed and misunderstood, Vinayan is mentally broken in the end. The movie ends futuristically in 2020 where Vinayan thinks about the meaning of being a hijras.

As an unconventional film dedicated to the life of hijras, it is an adventurous attempt and a welcome effort. Being an exploration of what it means to be a transgender in contemporary Kerala, the film finds the roots of transgender in Vedic god Ardhanareeswara, who is a composite of Hindu god Shiva and his consort Parvati. In a televised interview, Sawpernika said, 'There are many 'hijras' (eunuchs) in our state but sadly they are not being accepted, hence this film on 'hijadas' is for the 'hijras'. We would be really happy if a small step is made to accept 'hijras' who remain confined to themselves' (*http://www.nowrunning.com*). The film was released in the theatres of Kerala and got critical acclaim. As an attempt to educate the audience about a group that has so far marginalized and denied basic human rights (Nair 3), it glimpses the poignant lives of transgenders especially their emotional struggles and the way law treats them.

Conclusion

Cinema has become a revolutionary medium in Kerala disseminating the earlier ritualistic functions of art and offers a new political space in terms of its intellectual scope, aesthetic treatment and its political act. This is evident in the way Malayalam cinema of the post–1990s treats queer sensibilities. The increase in queer characters on Kerala film screen definitely reflects purportedly a shift in the everyday discourse of culture towards a greater awareness and understanding of queer community. Films of post–1990s reflect this ongoing queer continuum and its silent/professed existence. Diane Raymond in his article 'Popular Culture and Queer Representation: A Critical Perspective' points out three recurring queer patterns in western films. They are appearances of queer major or supporting characters, gay pretender and straight mistaken for gay (99). But in Kerala, queerness was apparently absent till 1990s with a few exceptions. But after 1990s, Malayalm cinema represents queerity in variety of tropes either denotatively or connotatively unlike previous periods. Tropes like closeted queers, queerity as default, queerity as comic spectacle and queerness in its entirety have become recurring patterns even though such images are tokenized and stereotyped. Though Malayalam cinema is still a powerful medium that spins around heterosexual patriarchal, masculine, racial and moral codes, there are subversive attempts from the margins to topple the hetronormative cultural products and its ideological formulations.

Notes

1. It is an Indian film industry based in Kerala which produces films in *Malayalm* language.
2. *Malayalee* is a popular word regionally in practice which is used to refer someone from Kerala.
3. Suresh Gopi and Lal are two popular actors in Malayalm film industry.
4. Kavya Madhvan is a popular actress in south Indian Film Industry.
5. Salim Kumar is a national award winning actor and Comedian from Kerala.

6. Prithviraj is a popular South Indian actor. He is one of the leading actors in Malayalm Cinema.
7. Robin Prat is a British actor known for his role in *Kerala Varma Pazhasi Raja* (2009) *and EK Veer Stree Ki Kahani ... Jhansi Ki Rani.*
8. Prabhudeva is a South Indian film actor and internationally known dancer Nithya Menen is a South Indian actress.
9. Nithya Menen is a South Indian actress.
10. Genelia is a Bollywood actress.
11. *Goonda* is a regional Malayalam word which is used to refer a villain.
12. *Pennukanal Chadangu* is a South Indian practice before marriage where the groom along with his family visits the bride as a way of marriage initiation.
13. It is a painting by Raja Ravi Varma. It depicts Shakuntala, a character from an Indian epic *Mahabharata*, who pretends to remove a thorn from her feet while looking for her lover Dushyantha

Works Cited

Doty, Alexander. *Making Things Perfectly Queer: Interpreting Mass Culture*. Minneapolis: U of Minnesota, 1993. Print.

Griffiths, Robin. 'Bodies without Borders? Queer Cinema and Sexuality after the Fall'. *Queer Cinema in Europe*. Ed. Robin Griffiths. Bristol: Intellect, 2008. 129–131. Print.

Mulvey, Lura. 'Visual Pleasure and Narrative Cinema'. *Screen*, 16.3 Autumn (1975): 6–18. Print.

Nair, Aparna. 'Ardhanaari: Light Falls on an Obscure World'. *Hindu*. 25 November 2012. Print.

Pullapally, Ligy. Interviewed by Sarah Warn. Afterellen, n.d., (21 July 2001). Web.

Raymond, Diane. 'Popular Culture and Queer Representation: A Critical Perspective'. *Gender, Class and Race in Media*. California: Sage Publication, 2003. 99–100. Print.

Sawpernika, Santhosh. Nowrunning, n.d.. Web. 25 November 2012.

Tharayil, M. 'Queer Bonds: Male Friendships in Malayalam Cinema'. *Queering India*. Ed. Ruth Vanita. Delhi: Routledge, 2002. 7–9. Print.

——. 'Chandu Pottu: Subaltern Masculinity and Visual Pleasure'. *Sequences 100*, Vol. 10. 2 (December 2007): 32–34. Print.

Section C

Theatricality of South Asian Diasporic/Indian Theatre: A Critical Reception

12

Diasporic Activism and the Mediations of 'Home'

South Asian Voices in Canadian Drama

NANDI BHATIA

This article[1] examines South Asian drama in Canada as a critical site of activism that addresses issues pertaining to social justice and discrimination through themes and tropes in which the home of origin has a significant role to play. Like literary criticism, South Asian Canadian drama 'has passed through its nascent stages and is now part of the theatrical life in several Canadian cities' (McGifford, 1992: xii). Despite its contribution to literature and the arts and its commitment to social activism and human rights, this drama has only recently begun to receive attention in Canadian literature anthologies such as McGifford's *The Geography of Voice* (1992), which includes two plays and devotes a couple of paragraphs to South Asian Drama in the introduction. It has, however, yet to become the object of extensive critical inquiry and interpretation. Such an undertaking is, therefore, crucial because it offers new ways of thinking about the importance of dramatic performances as social texts that enable alternative visions of the homeland, visions that render visible the entanglements of networks of power that shape nations, localities, and regions.

Critical analyses of literatures of the Indian diaspora discuss the home of origin as a subtext and a site to which diasporas aspire to return even though it remains an unachievable ideal that is refracted through nostalgic retellings of a space that remains at best imaginary. The 'diasporic imaginary', identified as 'any ethnic enclave in a nation-state that defines itself consciously, unconsciously or through self-evident or implied coercion, as a group that lives in displacement' (Mishra, 2007: 14), is, as Vijay Mishra argues, marked by a sense of loss and trauma. The need to compensate for this loss produces a return of this repressed object in diasporic narratives. Mishra provides examples of novelists and creative artists who belong to the old and new Indian diasporas: the old diasporas of indenture and classical capitalism who relocated to the Caribbean and Fiji under the British empire, and the new diasporas of transnational capital of the late 20th century, whose experiences of home are mediated through the discourse of mobility. Alternatively, some critics, as Roger Waldinger and David Fitzgerald (2012) point out, view diasporas' relationships with the homeland in terms of 'loyalty', obscuring in the process the antagonisms that may arise depending upon one's circumstances, antagonisms that produce interactions between homes of residence and those of origin and 'involve a multiplicity of actors coming together in a broad range of combinations' (1186). Refugees, for instance, may have no home or may be in a position of fighting to have a home in places from which they are displaced or where they relocate (1188).

In the case of South Asian drama in Canada, a corpus that has resulted from the efforts of playwrights, many of whom are first-generation immigrants, one does not necessarily detect narratives of melancholia, trauma, loss, loyalty or interest deemed as defining features of diasporic literatures. Rather, many of the concerns regarding issues of racism, multiculturalism, job discrimination and violence against women and other marginalized groups, concerns that constitute the subject of plays by Rahul Varma, Rana Bose, Ajmer Rode, Sadhu Binning, and Uma Parameswaran, Surjit Kalsey, Anosh Irani, and Anusree Roy, among others, are propelled by their links to the playwrights' homes of origin. Even though this home may not be the physical site of action in many of the plays, it appears in multiple dimensions and gets reproduced in terms of a productive tension that serves as the springboard for the thematic/activist content of the plays, content that negotiates the interests of minorities and migrants across home and diaspora. This is accomplished through dialogue and reflection on the enmeshment of home in contemporary diasporic contexts through a collaborative medium that attempts to bring actors, activists and spectators into partnerships for social action, a partnership sometimes encouraged through post-performance discussions which are 'another common way to connect the stage to the 'reality' outside' (High, 2011: 52) and which provide spectators an occasion to engage in conversations beyond the staged play.[2] South Asian Canadian drama's activist dimension thus acquires special relevance: first, it calls for the proliferation of a dialogue about issues of social justice through a comparative framework that examines the interconnectedness of different contexts (Canada and India in many of these plays). Additionally, it complicates critical diaspora theories, theories that link diasporic communities to home through the lens of nostalgia, longing, and belonging and focus primarily on the subtext of loss and return. This additional layer of analysis has been perhaps overlooked because drama and theatre have remained largely absent from critical discussions of the literatures of the Indian diaspora, as Aparna Dharwadker (2003) has astutely pointed out based on her survey of the field (303–305).

As the discussion that unfolds demonstrates, many of the playwrights have chosen theatre as a means of fostering discussions on politically relevant issues that address the context of Canada but whose energies are inspired by the mediations of home. The networks between home and spaces of residence which generate 'not one, but a multiplicity of imagined communities organized along different, often conflicting principles whether related to the scale of aggregation (local or national) or to the opposing visions of the community in question' (Waldinger and Fitzgerald, 2012: 1178) come alive on theatre stages through visual motifs, actors, props, and photographic collages, which confront the different trajectories of home that resurface in the immigrant imagination. Through live scenes of imagination that speak to spectators, several plays under discussion in this essay expose how, while providing emotional sustenance for some, the baggage of home may also pose challenges in the home of residence. So the questions that I raise are: How does home appear? To what end? Moreover, what does returning home teach us about the inequalities and injustices underlying the current global order? My attempt to answer these questions calls for an examination of some of the plays performed over the last 30 years or so.

Contextual Overview

At the outset, it is necessary to acknowledge that the plurality of diasporic drama in Canada defies its generalization into one particular slot; yet it is important to note that what it offers collectively is a social forum in Canada. Until the 1980s, South Asian drama in Canada was a little known field. The three companies that propelled this drama into an identifiable movement are Vancouver Saath (initiated by Sadhu Binning and other Punjabi activists in 1982), Rahul Varma's Teesri Duniya (co-founded with Rana Bose in 1981, the title translates as Third World) and Rana Bose's Montreal Serai, in 1985. Concerned with immigrant life in Canada, these playwrights laid out a clear agenda for theatre. For Vancouver Saath, which began 'as an informal discussion forum by a group of politically conscious Punjabi writers and community activists' (Binning, 1993: 22), it was critical that 'literature and art should be created for the betterment of society' (Binning, 1993: 22). Inspired by the Saaths in Punjabi villages in India, which promote friendships and solidarity without a formal or heirarchical structure through free-flowing conversations, Saath activists envisioned theatre as a particularly suitable forum for raising issues pertaining to Punjabi immigrants, namely, employment, BC's anti-labour legislation, the divisive impact of the movement for self-determination in Punjab on the Punjabi community in BC in the 1980s, and the rights of women, youth and the elderly at home and in the workplace. In this, the genres of drama and theatre acquired a centrality. Unlike Benedict Anderson's (1983) formulations regarding print culture as being central to the formation of 'imagined communities', Saath members questioned the effectiveness of print for raising critical awareness and instead found drama and theatre as more efficacious media for addressing their concerns. So, while such issues were locally addressed in journals such as *Watno Dur* and *Canada Darpan*, Saath members questioned the power of the printed word on the audience: 'We realized that most of the Punjabis were not in the habit of reading serious articles in the best of times, let alone at a time when they were simply too involved in their daily struggles to establish themselves in a new land. This realization led us to experiment with theatre' (Binning, 1993: 23). From its inception, then, the group's mandate was to form an audience-oriented theatre, one that also aimed to achieve a non-hierarchical framework through plays written and directed collectively and enacted by members from the community, many of whom had never acted before.

Affiliated with the Professional Association of Canadian Theatres, Teesri Duniya identified its ultimate goal as creating 'a shared social space in which visible minorities are recognized as different but equal' (Varma, 2009: 193–194). Since its formation, Teesri has sought to achieve this goal 'through politically engaged, high quality art that examines relevant issues, challenges audiences and supports the cause of social justice' (Varma, 2009: 194). The Serai Collective, which also runs an arts magazine *Montreal Serai* (the name given to its theatre) aims at promoting 'works that reflect and assert the diverse world we live in' so as to 'counteract exclusion, separation, and marginalization when they occur in the arts and in society at large' (Montreal Serai, 2013). The themes addressed by these groups were various: For Saath, exploitation of farm workers, gender discrimination within the family, social exclusion, racism and discrimination of immigrants based on the lack of English language proficiency were some issues that took centre stage. For Serai, multiculturalism against ghettoization became a looming concern, and Teesri dealt with topical issues in a forthright manner.

Simultaneously, and even before the 1980s, women's theatre groups proliferated in various parts of Canada. Of note are Surjeet Kalsey's contributions to women's theatre in Vancouver and Uma Parameswaran's in Winnipeg. Kalsey organized plays that foregrounded women-centred issues in Canada in the early 1980s. An actor, playwright and director with several years of experience in broadcasting, Kalsey's first play, which she wrote, *Daughters*

Behind the Palace Doors was staged in 1982 in Carpenter Hall in New Westminister, B.C. Considered a landmark production in Punjabi theatre, the play 'addressed the issue of family violence for the first time in the Indo-Canadian community through the medium of drama therapy' at a time 'when it was hard even to talk about such issues in the community' (Kalsey, n.d.). Instead of professional actors, Kalsey prevailed upon women, who had been victims of domestic abuse and sex selection, to perform in the play, offering the play itself as a site for therapeutic expression. This was a significant step in exposing imposed restrictions, regressive notions of female identity, and patriarchal attitudes that accord primacy to the male child. In this, the genre of theatre itself served as an enabling device through which women could speak, especially those who may be confined within the restrictive parameters of domestic spaces. Kalsey's other contributions include *Nirlujj Saman* (Shameless Times), a four-act play on sex selection staged in 1994, with subsequent performances in 1994 and 1995 in Abbotsford; *Poh de Agan* (Holy Fire: Lohri), a three-act play staged on the occasion of the Lohri festival in Abbotsford in 1998 to raise awareness about celebrating the birth of a girl; *Vizay ton Baad* (After Getting Visa), a one-act play that focuses on the dynamics of procuring a visa for Canada and the ways in which the protagonist's life unfolds after relocation to Canada, performed on the occasion of the Vaisakhi festival of 1997 in Abbotsford, and *Chetna* (Awareness), co-authored with Ajmer Rode, a play on 'four different issues facing the Indo-Canadian community such as drinking, wife abuse, parent-child conflict and safety of women' staged in Vançouver in 1982 and in Abbotsford in 1983' (Kalsey, n.d.). *Dhian Pardesnan* (Daughters Abroad), a three-act play 'depicting the current situation of Indo-Canadian women and their sponsors' was staged on the occasion of the Teeyan Festival in Abbotsford in 1997, and *Sat Paraiann: Ghar da Supna* (Distant Women: Dreaming of Home) was staged in Abbotsford in 1996' (Kalsey, n.d.).

As these groups attempted to establish themselves and fulfil their mandates, they looked toward India for their inspirational lessons. Likewise, the community of writers that formed Vancouver Saath initially turned to Punjabi playwright Gursharan

Singh when he visited Canada with his theatre group, Amritsar Natak Kala Kender, for its intellectual and activist energy. Together with the Punjabi Cultural Association, community members began to perform Punjabi plays, something that Saath continued when it decided to produce its first play in 1984. The first few plays used Punjab as the subject matter as in *Panjab di Awaaz* (The Voice of Punjab), Gusharan Singh's *Kursi, Morcha, te Hawa Vich Latke Log* (Chair, Battlefield and People Dangling in the Air, presented at an elementary school auditorium in Vancouver, March 1984) and *Tootan Wala Khoon* (A Well with Mulberry Trees), a play about the 1947 Partition of Punjab which sought to communicate a message against communal divisions, especially relevant in the wake of the Punjab problem in India and the demand for Khalistan which had spilled over into the diaspora (see Binning, 1993). Similarly, the opening stage directions of Rana Bose's *On the Double*, a play with a feminist theme, which shows the emergence of new forms of patriarchy in an Indo-Canadian setting, clearly states that the 'inspiration for this play was a theatre performance by a group of New Delhi women players, but in form and content the play reflects Montreal and Canadian reality' (Bose, 1999: 213). In the early years when these theatre companies were trying to get off the ground, it was theatre from home, in various languages, that served as the inspirational impetus. Varma initially wrote plays in Hindi, 'which served as a cultural unifier for the South Asian Diaspora' (Varma, 2009: 180). According to Varma (2009), Teesri Duniya:

> was launched, in 1981, with Badal Sircar's groundbreaking play *Julus* (Processions) and until 1985, produced plays in Hindi from India including: Sharad Joshi's *Ek Tha Gadha urf Aladad Khan* (A Donkey Called Aladad Khan) (1982), Anil Barve's *Thank you Mr Glad* (1983), Gursharan Singh's *Gaddha* (Pothole) and *Ahsaas* (Realization), and Kishan Chander's *Darwaze kho Dou* (Open Doors) between 1983–1984. During that period, the company also produced locally created plays in Hindi dealing with issues affecting the lives of South Asian immigrants to Canada. These plays included *Bhanumati Ka Pitara* (Pandora's Box), *Ghar Ghar ki Kahani* (Household Story, which was written by Rahul Varma) and *Nazme-Faiz* (Faiz's Poetry) by Azra Naqvi. (Varma, 2009: 180).

And Binning and other Punjabi playwrights wrote plays in Punjabi, many of which were subsequently performed in English translation.

Even though Uma Parameswaran (1998) notes that Indo-Canadian playwrights deal with '"here" Canada, and not with 'there', halfway across the world' (p. 3), her own plays returned to India through mythological stories, for example, *Meera: A Dance Drama* in order to celebrate 'Indian art traditions and at the same time to educate the outsider into our culture' (Parameswaran, 1996a: ii). Over time, the annihilation of the idea of a mythical (Hindu) India led to a plurality in the way home came to be represented and drama took on an activist dimension in the 1980s and onwards in order to address concerns shaped by multiculturalism, transnational capitalism and its local effects, violence against women, and the effects of war and displacement on women and their families. Such activism became particularly visible in South Asian Women's theatre in Toronto with the staging of South Asian Sisters in Solidarity's play *Baysharam* (Shameless, 1991), Cahoots Theatre Project's *A Canadian Monsoon* (1993), Company of Sirens' *All Whispers/No Words* (1995), 'a one-hour piece about South Asian women in Canada ... (and) their experience of violence' (James, 1998: 48) and Stree Theatre Productions' *Old Wives Tales* by Sri Lankan-born Siva Mohan Sumathy, a play that attempted to raise awareness about the civil war in Sri Lanka through a plot that 'focuses on six women gathered in a kitchen who speak candidly about the war and the effects it has on their lives' (James, 1998: 49). In 1996, *Old Wives Tales* was adapted to a theme that 'would move between Sri Lanka and Canada' (James, 1998: 49). Also significant here is the fact that the actors, directors, and artists for many of these companies belong to diverse cultural, ethnic and linguistic backgrounds.[3]

Rahul Varma's *Bhopal*

To elaborate my point further, I turn to an analysis of *Bhopal*, a play set in the Indian city of Bhopal, and the site of the biggest industrial disaster in 1984, at the American Corporation Union Carbide's pesticide factory, which claimed 3,000 lives overnight. *Bhopal* represents a watershed moment for locating home and the status of powerless groups in the larger context of transnational corporate developments. The play was first produced in Montreal in September 2001 (under the direction of Jack Langedijk) by the Teesri Duniya Theatre at the Arts Interculturels and was next produced by the Cahoots Theatre Project at the Theatre Centre, Toronto, in October/November 2003. Its Hindi translation, *Zehreeli Hawa* (Poisonous Air), was produced by Habib Tanvir's Naya Theatre, India, in December 2002, and under Tanvir's direction, it was performed in six Indian cities. Tanvir, in fact, wrote the songs in a language that drew upon the idioms of the Chattisgarhi dialect and interspersed the Hindi play with English words. Paul Lefebvre translated the play into French, after which it was produced at the Theatre Periscope in Quebec City and, under the direction of Philippe Soldevilla, performed at the Espace Libre in Montreal during 2005–2006. This expansive approach, which includes a multilingual cast of actors who performed the play in multiple languages (English, French, and Hindi) in different localities and international venues is not only inspirational but also performs a politically expedient function. It emphasizes the scope of theatrical representations by drawing in a range of viewers who speak vastly different languages (English and French in Canada and Hindi/Chattisgarhi and English in India) and intersects with local aesthetic forms to perform politically meaningful theatre. A play such as *Bhopal* then becomes the site of an emerging political consciousness that can encourage the fostering of cross-border alliances based on an identification of power relations that operate transnationally, and its far-reaching influence can be gauged by its ongoing presentation by theatre groups in Canada, the USA, and India.[4]

Dedicated 'to the victims of the Bhopal disaster', *Bhopal* was written to raise awareness about the Union Carbide disaster and its debilitating effects. Union Carbide came to India in 1905 when India was under the British rule. Known for manufacturing Eveready batteries, it moved into the production of agrochemicals in the 1960s and became 'one of India's largest manufacturers of chemical fertilizers and pesticides' by the 1970s (Varma, 2004: iii).

According to Varma, the 'company's promotional film showed healthy green crops blowing in the wind, birds singing, and men, women and children beaming with happiness as the line scrolled across the screen: 'Union Carbide' will touch every life in India' (Varma, 2004: iii). Contrary to such images, says Varma, when the Union Carbide's pesticide plant exploded on the night of 3 December 1984, the effects of the poisonous fumes that engulfed the city as a result were deadly:

> Small children fell like flies, men and women vainly scurried for safety like wounded animals, only to collapse, breathless and blinded by the gas. By morning, the death toll was more than 500, by sunset, 2,500. By the following day, numbers had no meaning. That night, Bhopal became the largest peacetime gas chamber in history … .
> Union Carbide did indeed touch many lives in India: more than 20,000 people have died so far, more than 10,000 were seriously injured, 20,000 were disabled, and thousands have suffered the ravages of respiratory diseases, madness, cancer, and other unidentified illnesses. (Varma, 2004: iii)

In Varma's words, the play represents 'global environmental issues and their ramifications for living conditions in the Third World', conditions that 'hinge on the relationship between the developed and developing worlds' and the 'unstoppable mass murder of the poor – murder which is legitimized in the name of progress, development, and the state' (Varma, 2009: 186). Home then returns in this play to display 'poverty's relationship to development' (Varma, 2009: 188) and its emergence in this form makes *Bhopal* 'a play against forgetting' (Varma, 2009: 189).

Varma zeroes in on the play's central issue through a focus on bodies – particularly of children, born and unborn, who are maimed and deformed even before birth. This is highlighted through a plot that includes a Canadian doctor, Sonya Labonte, who is skeptical of the developmental promises made to residents of a slum by Devraj Sarthi, a Non-Resident Indian who has returned to India to serve as company manager of Carbide International. The latter convinces the chief minister to grant him a licence for setting up a plant to produce an agro-chemical known as Karbide Thunder on the pretext that it would increase agricultural output and accrue profits for the country. Convinced that people, animals and babies, many of them deformed at birth, are succumbing to 'diseases unknown to medical science' because of the poison emitted by the chemical, Sonya undertakes research that serves as scientific evidence after the disaster strikes at the plant. Her research subjects include a local woman by the name of Izzat, whom she compensates financially for showcasing her deformed baby girl Zarina as exemplary of what Varma calls the 'corporate inhumanity' operative at the plant (2004: iv). The plot takes a complicated turn when the corporate manager's secretary and lover, who is carrying his child, faces the prospect of giving birth to a deformed baby. While showing the complicity of local politicians with American multinational corporations, a complicity that facilitated the disaster with fatal consequences, the play forcefully references the malformed bodies at home that continue to be affected by the policies and practices of multinational corporations with little or no accountability. Such a lack of accountability and the motivations of greed on the part of American corporations that amass their fortunes through exploitation of Third World subjects and through the complicities of local politicians interested in accruing political gains highlight the asymmetries of power between First and Third Worlds by displaying for the audience bodies that do not matter. This is especially emphasized through Izzat, who, determined to survive her acute poverty, takes advantage of the compensation offered by adversarial groups: from Sonya, on the one hand, and the company manager Devraj, on the other, from whom she takes money to hand out to villagers for erasing from public knowledge any news of their dying babies and animals. The impaired bodies represent both literal and psychic maiming through a realism that highlights bodies infected with disease in the aftermath of the disaster. The allusions to the effects on the corporeal body intensify the message of the play and thereby seek to shatter spectatorial complacency about the debilitating effects of the disaster and highlight the connections between state violence, multinational corporations and local players. This is something that Varma reinforces in his introduction: 'Even after twenty years, mothers who inhaled poisonous gas on or after the explosion are giving birth to horribly deformed babies. While still in the womb, babies are inheriting unformed limbs, melted skin, and holes in their brain tissue' (Varma, 2004: iv).

Beyond *Bhopal:* Remembering 'Home' through Gender, Caste, and Class

While Bhopal takes up the specific issue of the effects of the Union Carbide disaster, it is of importance to note that South Asian (Indian) drama in Canada is not homogenous, nor does it offer homogenizing concerns. Within what we may identify as a corpus of activist drama are plays produced, written and performed by urban first-generation professionals, by working-class groups, and semi-literate women. In these, home is remembered and enacted differently in different sociopolitical contexts. In some plays, it becomes a site of yearning for return which has emerged as a result of racism and exploitation, as in the case of an 'Old Female Worker', a character in Sadhu Binning's play, *Lesson of a Different Kind* who, because of her exploitation as a janitor who lacks a union to support her rights, dreamily longs for her home in Punjab: 'I want to sit in the winter sun on the roof-top of my home in the village and watch the little children play' (Binning, 1996: 87). On the other hand, it appears as a way of understanding the 'loss' of home in Canada, as in Varma's *No Man's Land*, where an immigrant Muslim family links the impending loss of home in Quebec in the wake of its demand for separation from Canada to the loss of the family's home during the 1947 Partition. Here home appears as an ideological space, a space of tension, and even oppression. In Uma Parameswaran's (1996) play *Rootless But Green are the Boulevard Trees*, Jayant, a child of first-generation migrants in Winnipeg, ruptures his father's nostalgia by describing his home in India as 'a sprawling, handed down untouched form from the time of the Peshwas, where you have to walk half a mile to get to the shithouse' (77). This description not only sets up a contrast with the setting of the family's home in Winnipeg with all the trappings of middle-class comfort as described in the stage directions; it also offers a foil to the home in Canada that Jayant imagines as being idyllic. As Jayant and his friends start discussing race relations and inter-generational conflicts over lunch, they soon discover that the South Asian community too is marked by intra-community tensions and hostilities, exposing the narrow conception of community that gets consolidated in a bid to protect itself from racism and biased perceptions. But underlying the reference to the Peshwas[5] is also the allusion to larger spaces and this points to the inequities of social caste.

Parameswaran's focus on caste encourages a rethinking of caste practices, which are not only operative at home, as pointed out by activists and theatre groups operating in India, but also continue to play out in diasporic spaces. Hence, this drama remembers home not only in idealized terms to construct what Rushdie (2010) calls, 'imaginary homelands' which are versions with little correspondence to the reality of the homeland. But, its preoccupation with real life characters and situations makes it an enterprise that foregrounds class, caste, gender, and race in the domain of middle-class drama and venues. For example, the performance of Ajmer Rode's *The Rebirth of Gandhi* at the Association of Commonwealth Languages and Literature Studies (ACLALS) held in British Columbia in 2007 raised the topic of caste prejudice and mistreatment of Dalits. Rather than foregrounding this border-crossing practice in terms of the ambivalence that is associated with diasporic experience and remembering, this drama engages in a diasporic activism whose themes of social justice link them to the most radical social activist theatre in India, as in Varma's *Bhopal*, and Rana Bose's *The Death of Abbie Hoffman*, a play which is adapted from Badal Sircar's *Procession*.

Remarkably, several plays, such as Varma's *Equal Wages* and Binning's *Lesson of a Different Kind*, also provide a language that addresses the gendered diaspora through a focus on female farmworkers in Binning's play, and through home-working in Varma's play, where immigrant women in Canada sew garments at home for the garment industry but do not have the protection of labour laws. Home-working, as Gayatri Spivak (1996) points out, is an urgent topic involving 'women in the transnational world', since it concerns women who 'do piece-work at home with no control over wages; and thus absorb the cost of health care, day care, work place safety, maintenance, management' (246). In such situations, suggests Spivak, the 'concept of a diasporic multiculturalism is irrelevant. ... The women stay at home, often impervious to organizational attempts through internalized gendering as a survival technique' (246). But such internalization about gendered roles also results from expectations that migrants bring into diasporic spaces. For this reason, points out Mala Pandurang (2003), in any discussion of diasporic women, it is equally necessary to focus on spaces of departure, spaces that get left out in critical accounts that focus mainly on the enigmas and difficulties of arrival. For, a discussion of the cultural expectations of home, especially with regard to gender, is crucial for understanding gender-relations in the diaspora. As the plays of Surjeet Kalsey and several plays by Vancouver Saath show, home emerges as cultural baggage that travels into the diaspora and prescribes limited and patriarchal roles for women, adding to the strains of marginalization based on colour and class, as in the case of the farm-workers in British Columbia. At the same time, showing female farm-workers fighting for their rights on the picket lines in a play such as that of Binning and Sukhwant Hundal's *Picket Line*, inspired by immigrant (Punjabi) women's demands for farm workers' rights in British Columbia in 1984, highlights the ways in which diasporic relocation creates contradictory conditions of empowerment and repression. While disempowering when patriarchal ideologies from India are rearticulated here, relocation can also be empowering as women transition from their identities as wives, homemakers, and mothers to wage earners and protectors of their labour rights.

Revisiting 'Home'

In a 2003 article, Aparna Dharwadker applauded South Asian drama in Canada for maintaining a critical distance and detachment from 'the culture of origin' and embracing 'the experience of residence in the host culture' (p. 305) in order to produce 'original' drama. 'Without this detachment from origins, diaspora theatre', argues Dharwadker, 'can only *re*-present the culture of the nation, in expatriate plays about 'home', local productions of plays from home, and full-scale imports. ... In

Canada, where the Indian expatriate communities are older, often visibly unprivileged, and entangled in post/colonial histories, an emergent culture of original playwriting and performance has offered a critique of the nation-state as well as of conditions in the diaspora' (Dharwadker, 2003: 305). However, is detachment from home possible or even necessary? Since connections between home and diasporic spaces are ever-present and lasting (manifested in all their unevenness and differentiated formulations), such an argument produces a potential disconnect between home and diaspora, which risks eliding experiences that are necessary for examining social processes in diasporic spaces and assumes that 'attachments to the home left behind are imports that inevitably fade as immigrants and their descendants gradually assimilate into a mainstream whose ties are bounded at the water's edge' (Waldinger and Fitzgerald, 2012: 1193). At a time when the climate of globalization demands a complex negotiation of local, national and global networks, plays produced by diasporic playwrights in Canada seem to be making a concerted effort to engage with the entanglement of issues at home as well as in diasporic spaces, and so they create the conditions for progressive intercultural partnerships.

In the more recent plays, home once again seems to be the central site of action: Bombay in the case of Anosh Irani and Calcutta in Anusree Roy's work. In Irani's *The Matka King*, a play about *hijras* (eunuchs), which premiered at the Vancouver Arts Club in October 2003, the protagonist Top Rani (the Head Queen), a eunuch in his thirties, who was castrated at the age of 10, says in the Prologue: 'in this city (of Bombay), no one is free. I realized that when I was ten years old. I was sent here by my father to work as a servant boy. I had dreams then. Now I can hardly remember what (the dreams) were. The truth is there is no such thing as an Indian dream' (Irani, 2007: 5). Instead of a nostalgic journey into Bombay, a city where Irani grew up and which continues to inspire him, he presents us with a horrific tale of ruptured dreams, broken hearts and social entrapment and marginalization of *hijras*, prostitutes, and the working poor. Roy's *Pyaasa*, first produced by Theatre Jones Roy at Theatre

Passe Muraille in Toronto in September 2007, presents the tragic story of Chaya, an 11-year-old Dalit girl, for whom her mother arranges employment at a local tea stall run by a woman of a higher caste, and renders visible for her audiences, Chaya's exploitation, her giving up of her dreams of continuing her school education so that she can earn money for the family, and her eventual marriage to a much older man after she is raped by the tea stall owner. And Roy's *Letters to my Grandma* is set in the pre and post-World War II period in India and in Toronto. First produced by Theatre Passe Muraille, Toronto, in November and December 2009, this play foregrounds the protagonist Molobee's discovery of her grandma's survival of the 1947 Partition through her letters, a struggle that enables Bee to deal with her own process of resettlement in Toronto. Even though the Partition, one of the most cataclysmic events of the 20th century that coincided with India's Independence and led to unprecedented material and personal loss through forced migration across the newly created borders of India and Pakistan and the violence against humanity that erupted, is not slotted in parallel terms with voluntary immigration, the play attempts to show the dislocation of immigrants whose identities are circumscribed by these historical memories, which complicate the processes of resettlement. To highlight the impact of interwoven memories, Roy's time-frame shifts back and forth between Toronto, India at the time of Partition, and in the contemporary moment, a moment in which spectators encounter the grandmother's experiences through the phone conversations and letters between Bee and her grandma. Not only do these overlapping time-frames, of historical memory and the present, show viewers how one age constructs another; they also explain the grandma's communal sensibilities, as she struggles with the idea of Bee, the granddaughter, marrying a Muslim in Toronto and subsequently accepts the fact as she begins to confront her own act of bigotry during the Partition riots, when she had a Muslim woman thrown off a jeep so she could take her place in order to safeguard her new-born child. Bee overlays these communal memories with other forms of bigotry she confronts in Toronto when people call her a 'Paki', a racist term used for South Asians.

Through an aesthetic framework that makes use of a single actor to play the different roles, the individual's multiple roles and identities are also foregrounded. Like her grandma, who posed both as a Muslim and a Hindu when the Partition carnage threatened her and her newborn baby girl, Bee too finds herself shifting into a multiplicity of roles that she has to constantly negotiate as an immigrant woman: an obedient daughter who is expected to carry out the roles and responsibilities of a Hindu woman, a young woman with independent opinions, and an immigrant faced with racism. At the very least, viewers are reminded of the value of revisiting home and its history for understanding the complexities of relationships in the present. Overall, Irani's and Roy's plays subject India and Canada to critical scrutiny and examine the effects of power networks on those living on the margins (*hijras*, bar dancers, prostitutes, and beggars). This scrutiny is especially useful at a time when images of a shining India have been promoted and pushed to centre stage in the global imagination.

Some Concluding Remarks

If the plays forcefully tackle socio-political issues, then the activism they have engendered has also not been without achievements. As Thomas Morgan Jones writes in the introduction to Roy's play, 'Anusree Roy writes plays because she truly believes that they have the power to change the world' (Roy, 2010: iii), something that is confirmed by the audience's reaction after the performance of her plays, described, as follows, by Jones:

> Following each performance, audience members were compelled to speak with Anusree. They wanted to share *their* stories and *their* personal experiences. *Letters to my Grandma* moved audiences to offer stories about their grandparents, and about their own families' experiences with war. There was one instance, following a performance of *Pyaasa*, where a woman admitted that she had spit on one of her untouchable servant's face while living in India, and tearfully asked Anusree for her forgiveness. Each conversation with each stranger spoke to a deep and meaningful connection they made with the writing. It

was as if the writing invited the audiences into Anusree's world(s) while allowing them to access new perspectives in their own lives. (Roy, 2010: iv)

Many playwrights/groups, who often operate under little economic support and have to deal with funding practices that provide financial support only if the plays fulfil a certain notion of culture that reproduces the idea of the exotic to accommodate the demands of official multiculturalism, have extended their activism to secure more funding. Teesri Duniya, for example, managed to effect reforms in the ways in which the Canada Council for the Arts parsed out funds for multicultural theatre events, funds that led to the eventual growth of the company.[6] As a result, Teesri Duniya managed to become 'one of the few culturally inclusive theatre companies in Canada' (Varma, 2009: 180) and has produced 'cutting edge political plays involving other groups' (Varma, 2009: 182).

> The moment that Teesri began to receive arts funding from the Canada Council of the Arts marks a turning point in the company's history. The result was a string of avant-garde plays which were properly workshopped and featured actors of colour who were paid unionized salaries. These plays were produced at fully equipped venues known by the theatre-going public and, until that time, exclusively used by Anglo-French companies. (Varma, 2009: 182)

Additional funding has, thus, allowed groups such as Teesri Duniya and Vancouver's Neworld Theatre to collaborate on joint productions of plays such as *My Name is Rachel Corrie* in Montreal and Vancouver, a play about a 23-year-old woman by this name, who was bulldozed to death by Israeli Defense Forces while protesting the destruction of Palestinian homes.

Even though Teesri started as a company to address the needs of the South Asian community, like many other groups in recent year, it has continued its commitment to raising awareness about global political issues by launching *Truth and Treason*, a play about the war in Iraq.[7] Such commitment shows itself again in Rahul Varma's most recent play, *State of Denial*, (2012) a play that grew out of Concordia University's History Department project, 'Montreal Life Stories', and premiered in

March 2012 in Montreal under the direction of Deborah Forde to celebrate, in its Associate Artistic Director Edward (Ted) Little's words, 'the culmination of a five-year partnership between Teesri Duniya Theatre and the Performance Working Group – one of seven research clusters comprising the Social Sciences and Humanities Research Council (SSHRC) funded project, 'Life Stories of Montrealers Displaced by War, Genocide and Other Human Rights Violations' (Varma, 2012: 3).[8] The play works with layers of gendered histories of genocides, of Armenians in Turkey in the early 20th century and in Rwanda, later in the century, to reflect upon the silence that women are subjected to as a result of brutality and violence perpetrated on communities and their bodies. Through a plot in which a Rwandan-born Canadian documentary filmmaker and researcher named Odette attempts to uncover the secret of Sahana, an elderly Turkish woman who dedicates her life to helping female Armenian survivors of the genocide, and who ships off her baby daughter to Canada for safety, Varma tackles several issues. On one level, the play examines the ethics of interviewing and collecting oral histories from displaced and vulnerable victims of war; on another level, Varma unpacks the notion of 'cultural diversity' in Canada to throw light upon the manifold reasons for which people migrate to Canada – in this case political refuge, personal survival and safety from war-torn territories. Such a trajectory, then, does not idealize the homes immigrants leave behind; rather, it exposes the fraught histories of war and power relations and presents them as global problems against which we might understand the stories of refugees in Canada and their difficulties as they wade through a maze of bureaucracy, legal issues and governmental rules. To this end, Varma expands the notion of multiculturalism from recognition of cultural diversity and co-existence to a deeper understanding of the reasons why the (unstable) national pasts of some migrants continue to haunt them (not always nostalgically) in diasporic spaces. The play seeks to achieve its aims through minimalist props and multiple characters, victims, survivors, researchers and state officials, through whose engagement with, issues regarding breaking the silence about violence, murder and rape, and the ethics of speaking and listening, a complex and nuanced understanding can emerge.

In his Writer's Statement about the play, Varma says that, as a part of the 'Montreal Life Stories' project, he 'read many testimonies of survivors of genocide' and 'books and biographies of survivors from Armenia, Rwanda, South Asia and the Balkans, and spoke to their descendants now residing in Canada' (Varma, 2012: 7). Based on these, he produced a play that 'is not a documentary but an imagined play consisting of multiple personal stories weaved into one and told through characters that come from different continents', (Varma, 2012: 7). Yet, instead of placing emphasis 'on the authenticity of the stories being performed on stage', an important element of 'verbatim theatre' or 'theatrical performances based on interview transcripts' (High, 2011: 52), Varma offers what Steven High (2011) identifies as 'a combination of verbatim and self-authored material' (52), along with post-performance discussions held with audience members after some of the shows, to engage a forum for exchange and groupthink regarding the subjectivities and lived experiences of those displaced by similar human rights violations. One reviewer, who calls the play 'highly worthwhile',[9] affirms Varma's mandate that 'in the face of such shameless denial (of human rights violations) awareness is our only hope' (Varma, 2012: 7).

In a 1998 article, Sheila James asserted that 'South Asian Canadian theatre is not a movement or a scene unto itself ... (but) grows in tandem with First Nations and People of Colour theatre communities' (46). Varma's *State of Denial* and ongoing projects by playwrights who address the implications of cross-border movements, examine the lived experiences of minorities and survivors and open up topics related to human rights through live bodies that 'function as one of the most charged sites of theatrical representation' (Gilbert and Tompkins, 1996: 203). Their work attests to the ways in which South Asian Canadian drama continues its political engagements on community, regional, national and international stages.

Notes

1. An earlier version of this paper was presented as part of a panel titled, 'Whither South Asian Drama in Canada?' at the Festival of South Asian Literature and Arts (FSALA), held from 30 September–2 October 2011, at the University of Toronto. I would like to extend my grateful thanks to the panelists, especially Rahul Varma, for sharing his insights about Teesri Duniya, to Teresa Hubel for her critical input on earlier drafts and to Chelva Kanaganayakam and Rajesh Macwan for inviting me to participate in the panel.
2. For a description of this process, see Sheila James (1998), 'South Asian Women: Creating Theatre of Resilience and Resistance'. *Canadian Theatre Review*, 94, pp. 45–50, and Sadhu Binning (1998), 'Vancouver Saath: South Asian Canadian Theatre in Vancouver'. *Canadian Theatre Review*, 94, pp. 14–17.
3. For more commentary on this issue, see Rahul Varma (1998), 'Contributing to Canadian Theatre', *Canadian Theatre Review*, 94, pp. 25–27 and Sheila James (1998), 'South Asian Women: Creating Theatre of resilience and Resistance'. *Canadian Theatre Review*, 94, pp. 45–50.
4. *Bhopal* was presented by the Masquerade Youth Theatre in association with The Madras Players in 2011 in India. (For a review of the play, see Shonali Muthalaly, 'Lots of smoke, no fire'. *The Hindu* June 27, 2011. http://www.thehindu.com/arts/theatre/article2138995.ece). Illinois State University's School of Theatre presented the play in Spring 2011 (http://www.cfa.ilstu.edu/pguithe/theatre/iisbhopal/index.html). And to commemorate the 25th anniversary of the Bhopal gas disaster, a staged reading of the play was presented on 26 March 2010, by the Association for India's Development, Theatre Rasa Nova, and Friends of South Asia (FOSA) in San Francisco, USA.
5. A titled designation in Marathi which means Prime Minister, Peshwa was created by Shivaji (1674–1680) during the growth of the Maratha empire, which ended when the British annexed it to the British empire in 1818.
6. Some examples of plays that Varma provides include 'Main Street Collective's *Divided We Stand* (1994), directed by Harry Standjofski; Jason Sherman's *Reading Hebron* (2000), directed by Wajdi Mouawad; Sylvija Jestovic's *Noah's Arc 747* (2002), directed by Paulina Abaraca; Camyar Chai, Marcus Youssef and Guillermo Verdecchia's *Ali&Ali And The Axis of Evil* (2004), directed by Guillermo Verdecchia; Nina Lee-Aquino and Nadine Villasin's *Miss Orient(ed)* (2005), directed by Sarah Stanley; and most recently,

Alan Rickman and Katharine Viner's controversial play *My Name Is Rachel Corrie* (2008), directed by Sarah Stanley' (2009: 182).

7. For information on the play see http://southasianplaywrights.org/?p=1131
8. See http://www.lifestoriesmontreal.ca
9. See http://www.teesriduniya.com/reviews.html

Works Cited

Anderson, B. *Imagined Communities: Reflections on the Origin and Spread of Nationalism*. London: Verso, 1983. Print.

Binning, S. 'Vancouver Saath: A Profile by Sadhu Binning'. *Rungh: A South Asian Quarterly of Culture, Comment and Criticism*. 2. 1 and 2 (1993): 22–126. Web. 10 June. 2011. <http://www.tru.ca/cicac/readings/ Rungh_v2_n1–2.pdf.>

——. 'Lesson of a Different Kind: *SACLIT Drama*'. *Plays by South Asian Canadians*. Ed. U. Parameswaran. Bangalore: IBH Prakashana, 1998, 85–98. Print.

——. 'Vancouver Saath: South Asian Canadian Theatre in Vancouver'. *Canadian Theatre Review* 94 (1998): 14–17. Print.

——. 'Punjabi-Canadian Literature: A Brief introduction'. *Journal of Punjab Studies* 13.1 and 2. (2006): 279–285. Web. 8 June. 2011. http://www.global.ucsb.edu/Punjab/13.1.2_Binning.pdf

Bose, R. 'On the Double'. *The Death of Abbie Hoffman and Other Plays*. Calcutta: Seagull Books, 1999. Print.

Dharwadker, A. 'Diaspora and the Theatre of the Nation'. *Theatre Research International* 28. 3. (2003): 303–325. Print.

Gilbert, H., and Tompkins, J. *Post-Colonial Drama: Theory, Practice, Politics*. London: Routledge, 1996. Print.

High, S. 'Embodying the Story: Oral History and Performance in the Classroom'. *Alt. Theatre: Cultural Diversity and the Stage*. 9. 2. (2011): 50–54. Print.

Irani, A. *The Bombay Plays. The Matka King. Bombay Black*. Toronto: Playwrights Canada Press, 2007. Print.

James, S. 'South Asian Women: Creating Theatre of Resilience and Resistance'. *Canadian Theatre Review* 94 (1998): 45–50. Print.

Kalsey, S. (n.d.) 'Stage Plays/Performing Arts'. Web. 9 June. 2011. <http://surjeetkalsey.wordpress. com/writings/stage-plays.>

McGifford, D. *The Geography of Voice: Canadian Literature of the South Asian Diaspora*. Toronto: TSAR, 1992. Print.

Mishra, V. *The Literature of the Indian Diaspora: Theorizing the Diasporic Imaginary*. Oxon: Routledge, 2007. Print.

Montreal Serai. About Serai. 2011 Web. 10 June. 2011. <http://montrealserai.com/_archives/other/About_Serai.htm. 2013.>

Parameswaran, U. 'Introduction'. *SACLIT Drama: Plays by South Asian Canadians*. Ed. U. Parameswaran. Bangalore: IBH Prakashana, 1996a. i-xxv. Print.

——. 'Meera: A Dance Drama'. *SACLIT Drama: Plays by South Asian Canadians*. Ed. U. Parameswaran. Bangalore: IBH Prakashana, 1996b. 1–8. Print.

——. 'Rootless but Green are the Boulevard Trees'. *SACLIT Drama: Plays by South Asian Canadians*. Ed. U. Parameswaran. Bangalore: IBH Prakashana, 1996c: 25–84. Print.

Parameswaran, U. 'Editorial: Drumming Towards a Better Future'. *Canadian Theatre Review* 94 (1998): 3–4. Print.

Pandurang, M. 'Conceptualizing *Emigrant* Female Subjectivity: Possible Entry Points'. *South Asian Women in the Diaspora*. Eds. N. Puwar and P. Raghuram. Oxford: Berg, 2003. 87–98. Print.

Roy, A. *Pyaasa* and *Letters to My Grandma*. Toronto: Playwrights Canada Press, 2010. Print.

Rushdie, S. *Imaginary Homelands. Essays and criticism 1981–1991*. 1991. India: Random House, 2010. Print.

Spivak, G. C. 'Diasporas Old and New: Women in the Transnational World'. *Textual Practice* 10. 2. (1996): 245–269. Print.

Varma, R. 'No Man's Land'. *Canadian Mosaic: Six Lays*. Ed. A. Ravel. Toronto: Simon and Pierre. 1995. 164–212. Print.

——. *Bhopal*. Toronto: Playwrights Canada Press, 2004. Print.

——. 'Teesri Duniya Theatre: Diversifying diversity with Relevant Works of Theatre'. *South Asian Popular Culture* 73.3 (2009): 179–194. Print.

——. Program Booklet. *State of Denial*. Presented 16 March–April at McCord Museum, Montreal, 2012. Print.

Waldinger, R. and Fitzgerald, D. 'Transnationalism in Question'. *American Journal of Sociology*. 109. 5. (2004): 1177–95. Web. 10 June. 2011. <http://works.bepress.com/roger_waldinger/25/.>

13

Sharuk and Shylock

The Creation of a South Asian American Aesthetic

NEILESH BOSE

South Asian diasporic theatre in the Americas, unlike its counterparts in other regions such as the UK, has only recently begun to develop its own aesthetic voice and tradition of dramatic literature and theatrical production. This essay examines the landmark play, Shishir Kurup's *Merchant on Venice* and its premiere production in Chicago in 2007, in order to initiate a historical discussion of South Asian American theatre history. Through an examination of this adaptation of Shakespeare's *Merchant of Venice,* its relationship to the original together with its distinctive literary qualities and a consideration of its performative manifestation, this essay argues that Kurup's play heralds the coming of a South Asian American theatre aesthetic through engagements with language and inclusion of South Asian American cultural and historical specificity into the American theatre.

Constantly having to make White America feel comfortable is a draining survival mechanism. How do we find the sound of the South Asian diaspora, here, from a home-grown all-American to a FOTB (Fresh off the Boat) and still find the 'point of entry', or in other words, White recognition? The answer is Shakespeare, but in a framework I identified with. Sharuk, just like Shylock, is really about sameness, not difference. But when we shine the light on ourselves, we find that it is easier to transcend differences between us and others, rather than think about differences within ourselves (Kurup personal interview).

'South Asian American theatre' is a term that would yield few substantive aesthetic references in the broader American performance environment, as audiences and artistes would have trouble identifying keywords, major playwrights, or established theatre institutions. Unlike other regions of the South Asian Diaspora, such as the UK or other 'ethnicized' American communities, such as the African diasporic or East Asian American, there has yet to emerge an identifiable South Asian American theatre aesthetic or institutional identity.[1]

Shishir Kurup's *Merchant on Venice*, however, functions as the first American drama to adapt Shakespeare into the South Asian diasporic context and thereby begin a conversation about the nature of South Asian American theatre and its own highly specific keywords, conventions, and points of historical reference. Other playwrights, such as Bina Sharif, Aasif Mandvi, Mrinalini Kamath, and a host of others, have written and produced plays. However, Kurup's play remains unique as it was produced as a part of both a marginal location in the American artistic environment (as referenced in the quotation above), but also within a tradition of Shakespearean production, as Kurup's training and performance worldview emanate completely from the 'West', embodied by American actor training and theatrical production.

As an actor, composer, director, and playwright Kurup's artistic life embodies a multi-disciplinary approach to the theatre. Although a prolific playwright with 14 produced plays to his credit[2], he has trained primarily as an actor. A graduate of the prestigious acting Conservatory at the University of California San Diego M.F.A. programme, Kurup has also studied with luminaries such as Anne Bogart and Tadashi Suzuki. He is a familiar face on American television and film, with frequent roles on television shows such as *Heroes*, *Surface*, and *E/R*. In addition, Kurup maintains a visible presence in the Los Angeles professional theatre community through his work as a member of the Cornerstone Theatre Company, a professional theatre organization dedicated to community-based exploration, multi-ethnic collaborations, and contemporary engagements with classic stories and plays.[3] One of the main elements of its mission includes utilizing the diverse cultural and political resources of the Los Angeles area.[4]

Kurup's multi-disciplinary work with the company includes stints as director, composer, and playwright.[5] As a playwright, six of his plays were written for Cornerstone; all were either adaptations of classic plays or community-based projects constructed in collaboration with residents of various broadly defined communities. In 1994, along with company co-founder William Rauch, he wrote *Everyman in the Mall*, an adaptation of medieval morality plays as an after-hours journey inside a contemporary shopping mall. In 1995, he adapted Herman Hesse's novel *Siddhartha* into a stage production involving residents of Watts, CA. Its work pertaining to South Asia and South Asian Americans, before *Merchant on Venice*, included *As Vishnu Dreams* (2004), a part of the 'faith-based cycle', which explored the epic *Ramayana,* through collaboration with Los Angeles-area Hindus.

Merchant on Venice is informed by Kurup's many years of artistic and community engagement in Los Angeles theatre. It was commissioned by the Audrey Skirball Kenis Theatre and his own Cornerstone Theatre Company for the LA Visions/LA Voices programme, which aimed to promote original writing about Los Angeles' diverse and multivalent social and cultural geography. Having produced three drafts from 1999 to 2005, via several workshops in Los Angeles and New York, Kurup's final script investigates the details of South Asian American life in southern California, at the intersection of Venice Boulevard and Clarington Avenue in Culver City, an area Kurup termed 'one of the densest populations of what is now America … . (meaning) everything from Thai restaurants, Hindu temples, a mosque, Sony studios …' (Kurup 'Online Interview'). This America, set in this particular corner of Los Angeles, is the backdrop for a story that retains the vitality of the events and poetic and linguistic registers of Shakespeare's original. Perhaps as a nod to his training in Western theatre traditions, Kurup maintained a close relationship with the language of the original, as he consciously worked to retain the power of the iambic flow of words and speech. He claimed that 'if you have the iamb, the way language comes out is unique and it forces your brain to work in a particular way, and, it is how Indians or South Asians talk' (Kurup 'Online Interview'); the result of their particular history with colonial and postcolonial English. Kurup aimed to merge this appreciation for language with a deep-seated exploration of South Asian American life.

Transcending mere reportage of diasporic community life, *Merchant on Venice* consciously uses form and characterization to include creative manifestations of South Asian Americana. Kurup's play also includes iambic pentameter, transfers some lines in their entirety, and creatively appropriates character and language from the Shakespearean original. Such work is by no means new to South Asians or to diasporic South Asians,[6] but Kurup's *Merchant* comprises the first attempt to comprehensively South Asian Americanize Shakespeare.

Though the play experienced several public workshops at prominent theatres, such as the Los Angeles Mark Taper Forum in 2005, its first full-scale production was staged in Chicago with the Silk Road Theatre Project from 15 September to 4 November 2007 (http://www.strp.org.). This production garnered nearly unanimously positive reviews and formed what would be the first South Asian American adaptation of Shakespeare to attract the attention of regional and national critics. As the production was named one of the top 10 plays of 2007 by *Chicago Tribune*, the *Chicago Sun-Times*, *Time Out Chicago*, and *Performink*, both the play and the production have catapulted South Asia into critical conversations about professional theatre practice in the US.

Kurup's play differs from other South Asian diasporic adaptations of Shakespeare, such as the work of Tara Arts (embodied in the many adaptations of Western classics by Jatinder Verma) and also the many non-metropolitan Shakespearean adaptations in Asia and Africa.[7] Such non-metropolitan versions, together with their accompanying critiques, tend to follow a predictable colonial-national-postcolonial framework. Kurup's drama refreshingly appears neither within nationalist frames nor in recognizably 'postcolonial' strategies, but within an emergent South Asian American diasporic aesthetic.[8] Framed by a discussion of South Asian American history, this essay examines the aesthetic and political parameters of Kurup's play through an investigation of its relations with the original, its distinctive literary qualities, and aspects of its first professional production in Chicago in late 2007.

South Asian American History

South Asian diasporic aesthetics emerge out of a history in the Americas that stretches back long before the proliferation of Bollywood cinema or South Asian-styled clothing and foods. In 1790, a Madras resident and sea captain visited Salem, Massachusetts, marking the first entry of South Asians into North America. During this era of a growing European colonial domination in South Asia and a growing rise of the American polity in the late 18th and 19th centuries, almost one thousand Indians arrived on American shores. In addition to magicians, circus entertainers, and religious mendicants and charlatans, eminent public figures visited America. Among these eminent figures was Swami Vivekananda, the 19th-century religious reformer and leader who addressed the Chicago World Parliament of Religions in 1893. During the reign of the British Empire in India, nearly three thousand Indians entered North America. Folklore includes a group of Indian slaves that found their way to Massachusetts from the 17th century, but their definitive history has yet to be written.[9]

During the 19th century, officials of the British Empire sent hundreds of thousands of indentured Indian labourers into the cane fields of Southern Africa, Fiji, and various Caribbean locations such as Trinidad and Tobago.[10] Labourers in this chain of migration did not end up in the Americas. However, a small group of farmers from the Punjab, in western India, endured a fate similar to their counterparts across the African and West Indian outposts of the empire. Many farmers in the 1890s and early 1900s, attracted by promises of work by Canadian company representatives touring India for cheap labour, immigrated to present-day Western North America. The first port of entry was

Canadian British Columbia, followed by American coastal regions in Washington, Oregon, and California. These migratory Indians sought work in lumber mills and railroads. A few thousand emigrated in the first two decades of the 20th century, forming a visible population of South Asians in the west coast. Like Chinese labourers of the same era, these labourers fought bitter anti-Asian laws that disallowed them land ownership and, at times, citizenship.[11] When work in mills and railroads often proved impossible, many of these immigrants sought to farm their own land and some managed to do so successfully. Prevented from marrying White women, as miscegenation laws were in full force at the time, and without women from their homeland, many of these labourers married Mexican women, creating a small Punjabi-Mexican community.

In addition to these farmers, political activists and revolutionaries set up the *Ghadr* (revolution) party, based in San Francisco in the 1910s. Prominent activists like Har Dayal and Taraknath Das published a newspaper and organized the South Asian community of California to oppose British colonialism. The party's constituency included the several thousand students and politically minded individuals in Canada and the US at the time. Some of these people included the Punjabi labourers who arrived a few years earlier. With links to Germany, India, and the UK, the *Ghadr* party formed a significant chapter in the history of Indian nationalist resistance to colonial rule. Given the anti-British and pro-German slant of the party, the United States heavily monitored the party's activities. By the end of World War I, the party had disintegrated.[12]

The population of South Asians in the United States remained between two and three thousand until 1965.[13] The 1965 Immigration and Nationality Act, signed by then President Lyndon Johnson, ushered in a new era of South Asian American history: middle-class professional migration and settlement. From 1965, an official preference for technically qualified South Asians allowed large numbers of migrants with English skills to settle and flourish in America. During these last 40-plus years, a slew of doctors, businessmen, lawyers, computer professionals, and other such groups have infiltrated the American social landscape. Unlike the earlier Punjabi labourers or anti-colonial revolutionaries, this wave of migrants encountered an America where citizenship and the right to own property was quite simply taken for granted. Migrants after 1965 have become South Asian Americans, assimilated and ready to construct and debate identity formation in the post–1947 South Asia of nation-states.[14] This is the America of Kurup's *Merchant*.

Active in theatre, film, and performance art since the 1980s, Kurup stands as a pioneer in South Asian American performance traditions. As a major artistic force behind the Cornerstone Theatre Company, with so many credits as playwright, actor, director, and composer, Kurup is positioned to engage with South Asian American and the varied strands of 'mainstream' American dramatic literature and production.[15] On one level, Kurup's play stands in a long tradition of adaptations of Shakespeare placed in various non-normative locales, including as predecessors: Aime Cesaire's 1969 *Une Tempéte/A Tempest*, an anti-colonial adaptation of *The Tempest* based in the Caribbean; and Murray Carlin's South African adaptation of *Othello*, *Not Now, Sweet Desdemona,* written in the same year. South Asia boasts a long and vibrant history of adaptations of Shakespeare in both English and South Asian languages such as Bengali and Marathi. For the diaspora, though, Kurup's play marks the first time that Shakespearean language, form, and character are retained in a story with South Asian diasporic characters and conflicts.

Set in Culver City's intersection of Venice and Claringdon, the play's action begins in present-day, post-9/11 America, with names, characters, and conflicts that would be immediately recognizable to a South Asian diasporic audience: wealthy, privileged elite young women, low-caste Hindu subordinates, marginalized Indian Muslims, grumbling elders, and thoroughly Americanized youth. Language, as the pivot of Kurup's theatrical vision, and as a reflection of his 'mainstream' training, remains central for the text, as his piece, like Shakespeare's, is written entirely in verse. Particular lines are transposed in their entirety,[16] and the storyline remains intact. However, both the ending and Shakespeare's presentation of Elizabethan-era anti-Semitism encounter a heavily South Asian American revision. The play includes a range of popular-cultural references from America of the last 20 years and includes a smattering of cinematic and musical references from popular South Asian films and songs. As reviews of the Chicago premiere production used terms like 'indipop' and 'polycultural deconstruction of the original', the play firmly plants itself in present day culture, politics, and art from South Asian and America, while maintaining fidelity to iambic pentameter and the narrative structure of Shakespeare's play.

Narrative and Characterization

In Sharuk's production, all of Shakespeare's characters have their South Asian American equivalents: Shakespeare's merchant Shylock, a Jew in a harshly anti-Semitic Europe, becomes Sharuk, an Indian Muslim caught in a harshly anti-Muslim, 21st century South Asian American Venice Boulevard. His daughter, Noori (Jessica) also occupies the role of demure daughter to a stern father, whereas the distressed Antonio comes in the form of Devendra, a depressed, wealthy, South Asian American Hindu businessman. His friend Jitendra (Bassanio) has found his Bollywood calling in the Indian film industry as an actor. Devendra's friends include the very same Salerio and Salarino – Yogananda and Sivananda – who counsel him in Venice. Devendra is financing Jitendra's next big film. The producer of Jitendra's first big hit happens to be a fictional and recently deceased Bipin Shah, an eminent film producer. His daughter, Pushpa, becomes a South Asian American Portia, in her mansion in Carmel, the Belmont of Kurup's piece. In the beginning the action follows Shakespeare as various suitors appear, but all are rejected by Pushpa and her Nerissa character, Kavita. As her childhood nurse, Kavita is written to come from a lower-class and possibly lower-caste background. The Prince of Morocco finds an equivalent in Murali, a dark-skinned South Indian who vies for Pushpa. He encounters the same fate with Pushpa as Morocco did with Portia.

Meanwhile, Jitendra needs to borrow money from Sharuk, and wealthy Devendra agrees to co-sign for the deal. We also see Sharuk's clown-like assistant, the counterpart to Launcelot, in

Toori, a South Indian Malayalee Hindu. Toori demonizes his Muslim boss much the way that Launcelot rains his anti-Semitism onto Shylock. Like Gobbo's ordeals when helping Jessica to deliver love letters to Lorenzo, Toori helps Noori, the sheltered daughter of Sharuk, to deliver letters to Armando, the equivalent of Lorenzo. Armando is Latino and Christian, representative of southern California, but neither Hindu nor Muslim.

In an extraordinary adaptation of Portia's suitors having to guess the substance behind the curtain – gold, silver, or lead – Pushpa's suitors have to choose between various South Asian film DVDs. If they guess correctly between Satyajit Ray's *Pather Panchali*, Girish Karnad's *Kondura*, and Bipin Shah's Bollywood extravaganza *Jab Pyar Kisi Kah Jhuta Heh*, they will win Pushpa. Jitendra, who has been in love with Pushpa ever since they met at a NetIP[17] meeting, arrives in the way Bassanio arrives to win Portia.

Like Salario and Salarino, Yogananda and Sivananda discuss a variety of fantastical events: Jitendra and Amitabh (Gratiano) are detained by the police in an incident of racial profiling, Sharuk finds out about Noori (as Shylock heard about Jessica), and Devendra has suffered at the hands of fate as his investments in Indian companies blew up in an oil tanker crash off the coast of Newfoundland. In line with Shakespeare, we then see Sharuk lament the loss of Noori and confront Devendra, forcing the Hindu businessman to pay.

Instead of a traditional courtroom, Sharuk and Devendra agree to settle their dispute in the South Asian Businessmen's Union (SABU), a makeshift diasporic organization. Led and organized by Hindus, it claims to be secular but subtly works in the name of the majority Hindu community through its *pujas* and Indian flags. The set-up of the famous courtroom scene (IV.I) remains the same as the original. The characters aim to settle their disputes just as Shakespeare's do, but the results are quite different. Just like Portia, Pushpa reveals that no blood can be shed, so a pound of flesh cannot be obtained. However, in Kurup's *Merchant*, Sharuk reveals that he has a cauterizing machine that will destroy flesh without spilling any blood. This technically should allow him to execute the agreement. As this confounds the participants, Devendra undergoes a change of heart and willingly allows the pound of flesh to be taken. The anti-Muslim Hindu crowd in Kurup's play gangs up on Sharuk, and as a non-citizen of the US, threatens to turn him into the INS.[18] Kavita, the dark-skinned, working-class servant to Pushpa, emerges with a resolution in the form of an emotional 'Tat Avam Asi' speech. In this speech, she implores everyone find empathy in the 'Other', or to realize that 'I am that' (Tat Avam Asi). This stuns all the characters and they all stumble through a resolution in a daze. Sharuk, like Devendra, has a change of heart, and relents on his mission for a pound of flesh and only asks for the principal back. The judge refuses but allows Sharuk to keep one-third of his assets, to give one-third to Armando and Noori, and to give one-third to fund the construction of a temple in Ayodhya. When asked if he is content, he replies in the affirmative, as Shylock does. Instead of an Act V with music, and a ring-back story that connects Portia and Bassanio, and Gratiano and Nerissa, we simply see Sharuk looking for Noori, missing her, and Noori singing. The play closes with Noori trying to work on her music, singing, and with Devendra and Sharuk, on stage, but without seeing each other.

Though the storyline remains intact, in several areas Kurup adapts the Elizabethan context into a South Asian American one. South Asian American references detail characters that were already sketched by Shakespeare and shape many of the archetypes of South Asian American society. These archetypes include the majoritarian Hindu community and their power, as represented in Devendra,[19] or the wealthy, palace-inhabiting girls looking for husbands in Pushpa. The marginalized that live within South Asian spaces include Murali, Kavita, and the conservative immigrant in Sharuk. As he shows how the internal diversities and contradictions of South Asian America appear within Shakespearean characters and conflicts, Kurup allows for the breadth of contemporary South Asian American culture to appear on stage.

Sameness, Difference, and Sharuk

In addition to the play's many precise South Asian American references and characterizations, Kurup introduces two major differences between his play and Shakespeare's: the anti-Muslim ideology of the 21st century as compared to the vulgar anti-Semitism of Shakespeare's late-16th century; and a conceptually different ending in which the condemnation of Sharuk does not match the punishment meted out to Shylock in Shakespeare's original.

Sharuk, as the centre of Kurup's piece, deserves a contextualization within both South Asian American and South Asian cultural and historical worlds. He appears as a visible part of the post–1965 migrant population, who often freeze their ideological positions at the time of their departure, with little connection to South Asia after their migration. Significantly he is also a Muslim and in the minority against the majoritarian Hindu community of South Asian Americans in Venice, CA. The role of the 'Muslim', as minority, as fanatic, as having questionable cultural and/or national credentials, has a long history in the South Asian socio-cultural space.

In Kurup's play, a sketch of its presence emerges for the American stage. Since the widespread rebellion against British rule in 1857 and the suspected Muslim instigation of it, the 'Muslim' has been constructed as 'fanatic' and dangerous to British colonialism.[20] Through major points in South Asian history, such as the Khilafat movement, a world-wide Islamic Universalist movement to restore the Caliph after the First World War, Muslims have been constructed by many as potential traitors or villains in dominant strands of Indian nationalist discourse. In addition, through the Muslim League, a political organization in colonial India, Muslims have often been constructed as 'threatening' to the Indian colonial and nationalist space. From 1947 onward, during the reign of the secular Indian nation-state, there have been no shortage of events that cast Islam, and Indian Muslims, as treacherous enemies to secularism and Indian nationalism: Ayodhya in 1992; or in the 21st century, in Gujarat in 2002.[21] During both of these moments of consuming communal conflict, a large part of the Hindu press portrayed Muslims as foreigners, as non-secular, and as non-Indian. Though Islam has a long, colourful, and detailed history in South Asia,[22] the precarious role of the Muslim allows for powerful and salient dramatic conflict, which Kurup exploits in his treatment of Sharuk, as Indian Muslim Shylock, at the hands of his Hindu counterparts.

The Kurup version of 'the Muslim' materializes first in the presentation of Armando and Noori, in rather different terms than Lorenzo and Jessica. There is almost no typology of Islam as an evil enemy, as we see in Lorenzo and Jessica's relationship to Judaism. Armando sees Noori as South Asian, not as Muslim, whereas the Jew-quality of Jessica and her father Shylock is paramount. Additionally, Armando is not Hindu, nor does he have anything to do with the religious culture of South Asia, so it would make sense for him to see Noori as 'desi' (of South Asian origin),[23] as opposed to belonging to a particular religion. Compare the closing monologues of Armando (II. iii, Kurup) with Lorenzo (II. iv, Shakespeare):

> Armando:
> We'll have ninitos brown and beautiful
> Who'll speak the language of both
> east and west Of pre-Columbia y
> Indus Valley
> Of jalapenoy garam
> masala Of Fateh Ali Khan y Santana
> Of sub-commandante Marcos y Gandhi,
> Of brown-skinned love tanned by a
> sun that seems to shine with more
> intensity and passion
> Upon the lands whose latitudes we share (Bose: 118)

> Lorenzo:
> If o'er the Jew her father comes
> to heaven, It will be for his
> gentle daughter's sake:
> And never dare misfortune cross her foot,
> Unless she do it under this excuse,
> That she is issue to a faithless Jew (Shakespeare 27)[24]

Armando and Noori celebrate their brownness and their Americanness, whereas Jessica and Lorenzo clearly express anti-Jewness. In Kurup's play, there is no equivalent to III.V, in which Launcelot launches into an utterly anti-Semitic diatribe. Similarly, Toori, Sharuk's assistant, does not oppose Islam and Muslims the way Launcelot and Gobbo engage with their anti-Semitic ideologies. Toori is not conspiring to help Noori become Hindu, as Armando has nothing to do with Hinduism. This situates the story in 21st century southern California and veers away from the two-dimensional conflict between religious groups in Shakespeare's play.

Another difference revolves around the characters of Shylock and Sharuk. Sharuk talks of a shared culture between Hindus and Muslims, whereas Shylock is only Jew, in a black and white world. Compare the identity-based politics of the III.I speech of Sharuk with the corresponding speech of Shylock, also in III.I:

> Sharuk:
> Our skins share the same hue! Our families the same village! Our loyalties the same flag! The ghee that fries your dal is as clarified as that which cooks our lamb. Our rites of cleansing rival your own ritual ablutions. Our call to prayer is as much a wail for God's attention as your bell-ringing pujas … . (Bose: 130–31)

> Shylock:
> I am a Jew. Hath not a Jew eyes? Hath not a Jew hands, organs, dimensions, senses, affections, passions? Fed with the same food, hurt with the same weapons, subject to the same diseases, healed by the same means, warmed and cooled by the same winter and summer, as a Christian is? If you prick us, do we not bleed? If you tickle us, do we not laugh? If you poison us, do we not die? And if you wrong us, shall we not revenge … (Shakespeare: 42)

Sharuk is crying for the shared culture of Hindus and Muslims in South Asia. This veers far from Shylock's assertion of his own dignity in a world where that is denied on absolutist terms. Hindu and Muslim history and culture in South Asia is intertwined to such a degree that they cannot be understood outside of each other. As Sharuk says, their lives are shared but inhabit a misunderstood sameness complicated by nation, by religious bigotry, and by violence. In 16th and 17th-century Europe, Jews had to assert their sameness, as Shylock had to argue.

This sameness informs Kurup's ending, which is marked by a series of intense epiphanies that mark a resolution to the actions, but not necessarily a resolution to the characters' conflicts. Unlike Shakespeare's story, everyone, at different points, in different ways, 'finds grace', in Kurup's words. Before 'grace' is bestowed upon any of the characters, Sharuk emerges as more resourceful than Shylock, as he holds a cauterizing machine that can procure a pound of flesh without spilling any blood. This obliterates Pushpa's argument. However, just before he is able to accomplish his task, he undergoes a complete change of heart. After Kavita's *Tat Avam Asi* speech, when the court is trying to deal with Sharuk, Devendra expresses his love for Jitendra, and also begs the court to have mercy upon Sharuk and give Sharuk at least his principal. The most striking difference is Kavita's *Tat Avam Asi* speech and the complete change of heart evidenced by the majority community of Hindus in the courtroom. This is not a conscious decision, as the mood seems confused as to what exactly happens when Kavita's appeal to empathy for the Other is acknowledged by SABU and Sharuk simply leaves. Kurup attempted to translate a Shakespearean, early modern version of mercy, into a modern version of empathy (Kurup personal interview).

Merchant in Production

Chicago's Silk Road Theatre Project, which produced *Merchant* in late 2007, was formed in 2003 as a theatre company dedicated to producing works by and about communities from the literal historic Silk Road, including South and South East Asia, Central Asia, East Asia, the Middle East, and the Mediterranean, along with all of their sizeable diasporas across the world. The company began partially as a creative response to the anti-Muslim and anti-Arab sentiment produced in the aftermath of the 11 September 2001 attacks in the United States. Founded by the playwright Jamil Khoury, partially of Arab ancestry, and Malik Gillani, a South Asian American arts and theatre administrator, the company began in 2003 with Khoury's own *Precious*

Stones, which depicted an Arab and Jewish lesbian couple in the Middle Eastern-American diasporic space in 1989. Over the last six years, the company has produced plays by East Asian Americans such as Velina Hasu Houston and David Henry Hwang, and Arab Americans like Yussef el-Guindi. All Silk Road's productions, including *Merchant*, have appeared in the small and intimate black box[25] Pierce Hall of the Chicago Temple Building in downtown Chicago. Silk Road commits to the production of new plays and participates in numerous initiatives for the development of original works by playwrights of Silk Road descent.

Directed by Stuart Carden, who previously directed Yussef El Guindi's *Back of the Throat* (2006) and David Henry Hwang's *Golden Child* (2007), Silk Road's production of *Merchant* maintained a contemporary *mise-en-scène*, with inflections of current South Asian popular performance culture represented by Bollywood imagery and occasional song and dance. Carden, like Kurup, retained a focus on language as the pivotal connection to the original. Elizabethan verse and rhythm were not sacrificed but rather emphasized only with words, phrases, and intonations indicative of the South Asian diasporic experience in America.

In addition to the focus on language, the production aimed to evoke contemporary American socio-political spaces such as the American Hindu, the American Muslim, and the American Latino spaces. The design team was not South Asian and was 'trained' in Bollywood aesthetics. Lavina Jadhwani, a South Asian American dramaturge, led the design team in Bollywood film screenings to get a pointed, but not overwhelming, visual feel for the South Asian diaspora through colour, costume, and dance. This popular cultural aesthetic was carried into the scenes with Bollywood characters and songs. For example, one scene included a complete visual and physical representation of Holi (the Hindu festival of springtime); South Asian Hindu sparkle and spectacle added texture to the South Asian element in the play, but remained firmly within Shakespeare's original narrative structure.

Bollywood cinema references, as a set of aesthetic and visual parameters, served as dramaturgical inspiration. *Bobby*, the 1973 love story with Rishi Kapoor as the protagonist Raja, provided partial inspiration for the character of Devendra, the Antonio character. *Kal Ho Naa Ho* (Tomorrow May Never Come), the 2003 film about a love triangle, also served as visual and thematic reference for the target emotional space of the protagonists. Part of this decision pragmatically catered to the American audiences who, in the minds of the dramaturge and director, would probably know of South Asian popular culture through films like *Bride and Prejudice* and *Monsoon Wedding*, but also the many elements of South Asian Bollywood culture – song, colour, dance, and spectacle – successfully South Asianized the characters without interfering with the spirit, language, or narrative of the original (Jhadwani personal interview).

Of the 11-member cast, only one actor (Anish Jethmalani, Sharuk) was a professional Equity actor and none of the cast members were South Asian Muslim. Eight, including Jethmalani, a South Asian American Hindu, were South Asian, and three non-South Asians of varying ethnicities – Arab American and Hispanic American among them – played various roles, with two actors portraying multiple roles. The company made interesting intra-colour casting choices: although all female characters were South Asian, two of the actors cast in these roles were Arab American, providing an interesting comment on American casting practices. The normative casting trend has been to place South Asian actors in roles labelled as 'Middle Eastern' or 'Arab', a reflection of the ambivalent racial appearance of many South Asians. Here, the trend was reversed. Of the several South Asian male roles, two actors cast in these roles were Latino Americans and a Latino American, Armando, was portrayed by a Latino American.[26]

The many points of diasporic complexity garnered nearly unanimously positive critical attention in reviews of the premier production. Called a 'polycultural deconstruction' (Jones) of the original, the play's various elements of intensely layered and detailed South Asian American conflicts and characters, the 'huge musical parody of Bollywood gestalt' (Jones) demonstrated an appreciation for the South Asian diasporic in the most vaunted of theatrical genres: Shakespeare. One critic even declared that the problems of ethics, morality, and diversity unresolved by Shakespeare's story were solved by Kurup's inventive and original change to the ending (Vitello). However, the actual novelty of its South Asian-ness was recognized as a liability for the play's longevity and ability to command wide audiences. A few Chicago critics noted that the show was mounted earlier in a 'mainstream' theatre probably because it was a 'risky, rambunctious show set in the US South Asian community and thus out of the mainstream'. One commented on how it would act as miraculous outreach to the Indian population of Queens and the 'Muslims of Brooklyn' (Weiss). These two notwithstanding, all reviewers commended Kurup for appropriating Shakespeare in a manner faithful to the core conflicts of the story, but with full appreciation for an aesthetic that includes the diasporic experience as a constituent element. Many company members in the Chicago production not only repeated the critical praise of Kurup's uncannily precise interplay between Shakespeare and South Asian America, but found unprecedented milestones in the representation of issues like internal South Asian racism (as embodied by Pushpa), something never seen before in dramatic literature (Varshney personal interview). The decision to produce *Merchant* was also made on purely artistic grounds, rather than on grounds of community representation. Jamil Khoury, the artistic director of the Silk Road Theatre Project, felt that 'the rendering of the Hindu-Muslim relationship (displayed) a much more humanizing balance, certainly more than Shylock, (often read as) an anti-Semitic caricature' (Khoury personal interview). Theatre artists, therefore, appreciated both Kurup's attention to detail and complexity as much as his attention to artistic standards.

Audience reactions were mixed, lively, and diverse. In frequent talkbacks, non-South Asians often expressed surprise and studious curiosity at Hindu-Muslim relations and the future of this play, whereas South Asian audience reactions often followed lines of religion and region. Many South Asian Hindus, according to company members, expressed outrage at the representation of such extreme bigotry against Muslims as such discrimination, according to many, was exaggerated by the portrayal of relations between Sharuk and the majority Hindu community. Some Muslim audience members voiced opposition to the portrayal of yet another stereotypical, 'angry' Muslim obsessed with his own minority identity and his own community. The issue of Noori – the counterpart to the original's Jessica – and her characterization as a young Muslim girl breaking 'free' from an oppressive religious system also garnered negative reactions. Regardless of the nature of the reactions, of all the plays produced by Silk Road, *Merchant* generated the most discussion and debate by audience members in talkback sessions in the company's history. It also drew the highest numbers of Chicago community residents (South Asians) than other plays they have produced.[27]

Conclusion

Critical appreciation of South Asian adaptations of Shakespeare has mostly focused on colonial contexts or critiques of contemporary 'interculturalism'. Such studies rely on keywords like 'hybridity' and 'tradition' that vest themselves in rigid colonial/anti-colonial, modern/traditional binaries or debates about the 'true' and 'traditional' methods of 'intercultural' theatre practice.[28] If we consider the South Asian American diaspora[29] as a condition and a location yet to be served by either the post-colonial or the post-modern attempts to make sense of Shakespeare's current manifestations, we may then find that Kurup's piece actually measures up to what Sudipto Chatterjee calls a South Asian diasporic 'critical and experiential interculturality' (Chatterjee, 113) without the divisive and powerful neo-Orientalist discursive boundaries of Shakespeare's in Asia itself. Therefore, Kurup opens up a new and potentially emancipatory critical and aesthetic space (supported by nearly unanimous critical praise) of South Asian diasporic theatre, in which South Asian American inflections do not cause critical or postcolonial dread.

Michael Neill has pointed out that 'the post-colonial condition of former colonizers differs in significant ways from that of the formerly colonized ... and of diasporic peoples from that of the metropolitans with whom they uneasily cohabit'

(Neill 114). Do diasporic South Asian Americans cohabit so uneasily? Uneasy cohabitation, which may describe historical periods in South Asian diasporic history, such as the Punjabi labour migration of the 1890s into the Americas, or the racism faced by British South Asians in the 1970s, may not best illuminate the condition Kurup explores. Such a contemporary diasporic American condition may have yet to acquire its own name. Given the lack of a high-profile diasporic intelligentsia, the South Asian America that Kurup has represented may not compare with the kinds of representations of culture by 'post-colonialists', who, according to a classic critique, inhabit a world of the 'comprador intelligentsia, a relatively small, Western-style Western-trained group of writers and thinkers, who mediate the trade in cultural commodities of world capitalism at the periphery' (Appiah: 432).

In Kurup's case, the disavowal of the West makes no such sense. The diasporic South Asian American[30] condition hardly constructs a mythic, 'non-Western' space in which to claim difference. In fact, whatever 'difference' encapsulated by South Asian American specifics occurs only within secure spaces of sameness, as the entire narrative structure, characterization, and verse are firmly 'Shakespearean'. Whereas the vibrant postcolonial and 'new' Shakespeare in Asia, Africa, and Latin America have generated a critical exhaustion, the diasporic Shakespeare, which *is* politically marginal to 'mainstream' theatre culture but *not* inflecting aesthetic form with 'cultural difference', has yet to generate sufficient reflection. However, if Kurup's highly inventive and successful *Merchant* is any indication of the future, investigation of such theatre will shape the evolving criticism of South Asian American performance.

Notes

1. Chatterjee identifies three types of performances in the South Asian American environment:

   (1) 'community' performances often in South Asian languages; (2) visiting performers from South Asia, often working in languages

other than English; and (3) South Asian American performances. See Chatterjee 111–12. He also claims that theatre about South Asians in the Americas all more or less comprise Orientalist (beginning with the early twentieth-century productions of the Sanskrit classic *The Little Clay Cart* translated and produced by Arthur William Ryder) and neo-Orientalist spectacles in twentieth-century cinema and popular theatre spectacles, like the Broadway extravaganza *Bombay Dreams*. For Chatterjee, South Asian American theatre practitioners have also not yet produced 'their messianic playwright nor (made) significant mainstream impact' (115).

2. For a complete list of Kurup's plays, see the appendix, 'List of Plays from the South Asian Diaspora', in Bose (*Beyond Bollywood*). Many of these plays, such as *Ghurba*, *Sid Arthur*, and *As Vishnu Dreams*, were commissioned by his Cornerstone Theatre Company in Los Angeles (http://www.cornerstonetheater.org). Of these plays, two have been published in anthologies. Portions of his one-man play *Assimilation* have been published in Rajini Srikanth and Esther Yae Iwanaga (*Bold Words*). The complete version of *Merchant on Venice* appears in Bose (*Beyond Bollywood*).
3. For information on the company's mission, membership, residencies, and other projects, see http://www.cornerstonetheater.org/
4. Founded in 1986 by the director William Rauch and playwright Alison Carey, the signature of the company's mission includes entering communities and creating theatre for audiences that would otherwise not have any contact with traditional theatre practices. One element of the company's activities is its 'cycle' seasons, about faith-based communities, such as the Jewish, Muslim, and Catholic communities, or geographically-defined rural communities, such as Port Gibson, Mississippi, and Marmath, North Dakota. In these projects, the company would settle in a residency to create theatre with local inhabitants or community members. These residencies would result in inventive adaptations of classics, such as their 1986 *Marmath Hamlet*, produced with residents of Marmath, or their 2003 adaptation of Hart and Kaufman's *You Can't Take it With You* set in an American Muslim family in Los Angeles as a part of its five-year 'faith-based cycle' that explored the place of religion in contemporary American society.

   In addition to creating community-engaged theatre through a mix of professional artistry and community residents in a variety of American cultural and political spaces, the company has commissioned and produced several world premiere original plays, often written for specific cycles, such as the Justice Cycle, begun in 2007 and continuing through 2010. Original plays in this cycle include Michael John Garces' 2007 *Los Illegals*, about migrant workers in southern California, and K.J. Sanchez's 2008 *For All Time*, about incarceration and criminality in contemporary America. For a complete list of Cornerstone's production history from 1986 to the present, see http://cornerstone.pbwiki.com/Cornerstone-Timeline.

5. As a playwright Kurup has contributed *Ghurba*, 1993; *Everyman in the Mall*, 1994 (with William Rauch); *Sid Arthur*, 1995; *Birthday of the Century*, 1996; *An Antigone Story*, 2000; and *As Vishnu Dreams*, 2004, for Cornerstone. He has directed *Ghurba* and *An Antigone Story* for the company and also written and directed the company's sole feature film, *Sharif Don't Like It*, 2006, a story about civil rights after 9/11 in the US. As a composer he has collaborated on *Candude, or the Optimistic Civil Servant*, 1997, and *An Antigone Story*, 2000.
6. Shakespeare in South Asia has a long history dating back to 1770, the year of the first Shakespeare performance in Bombay (currently Mumbai). For general introductions, see Lal and Chaudhuri *Shakespeare on the Calcutta Stage*; and Trivedi and Bartholomeusz *India's Shakespeare*. Regarding Shakespeare in South Asian languages, see Hasan *Shakespeare Translations* and Shankar *Shakespeare in Indian Languages*. For an historical and theoretically inflected study of the Bengal Renaissance and nineteenth-century Bengali playwrights' vexed relationship to Shakespeare, see Chatterjee *The Colonial Staged*, particularly chapter 2. Regarding the landmark 1848 production of Othello in which an Indian actor portrayed the Moor, see Chatterjee and Singh 'Moor or Less?'. In the contemporary, 'interculturalist' period, a variety of productions have sought to mesh 'traditional' Indian performance forms with Shakespeare's plays. Regarding this topic, see Zarrilli 'For Whom' and Loomba 'Local Manufacture'. A critique that predictably casts the varied types of Shakespeare in Asian sites as 'neo-Orientalist' appears in Bharucha 'Foreign Asia'.
7. See Wells and Stanton *The Cambridge Companion*, with chapters 14 and 15 about Asia and Africa respectively. Loomba and Orkin *Post-Colonial Shakespeares*, Desmet and Sawyer *Shakespeare and Appropriation* and Fischlin and Fortier *Adaptations* all investigate problems of authorship, agency, and political vocabularies for understanding Shakespeare in colonial, post-colonial, and other non-metropolitan locations.
8. The logical outcome of postcolonial 'writing back' to metropolitan centres – of nationalist constructions of aesthetics – is avoided in Kurup, as his work approximates neither the historically contested and publicly visible battles of the British Asian artistic struggle nor

the nationalist (or however 'traditionally' construed) artistic works of formerly colonized regions. 'South Asian diasporic theatre' as an academic field or practical genre has yet to acquire critical keywords or recognizable icons, as in the African or East Asian American diasporic communities. For introductions into this developing field, see Bose *Beyond Bollywood*, Chatterjee 'South Asian American Theatre', Dharwadker 'Diaspora and the Theatre', and for a recent collection of essays about British Asian theatre, Fuchs and Davis *Staging New Britain*.

9. See Rangaswamy *Namaste America*, especially chapters 1, 'The Indian *Oikumene* and Its Heartland', 15–40 and chapter 2, 'The American Context: From Pariah to Elite', 41–72.
10. For an introduction into this topic, see Tinker *A New System*. Carter and Khan *Coolitude* preserve original letters and writings by labourers themselves.
11. For example, in the case of Bhagat Singh Thind, the Indian whose naturalized citizenship was revoked in 1922 because his race was not commonly understood as white Caucasian. See Lal 'Establishing Roots' 43.
12. See Lal 'Establishing Roots' 42–48, Rangaswamy *Namaste America*, chapter 2, and Leonard *The South Asian Americans, passim*.
13. The Immigration Act of 1917, also known as the Asiatic Barred Zone Act, banned immigrants from all of South and Southeast Asia, into the United States. Revised slightly in the early 1950s, immigration from South Asia began to revive with the passage of the 1965 Immigration and National Origins Act which abolished quotas for immigrants based on nationality.
14. 'South Asia' refers to the seven sovereign nation-states of India, Pakistan, Bangladesh, Sri Lanka, Bhutan, and the Maldive Islands. During the pre–1947 periods of migration, the 'India' that migrants left was a definitive part of the British Empire and its boundaries and politics were not at all encapsulated in terms of nations or states. Additionally, from 1947 to 1971, Pakistan existed as a two entities of Western Punjab and Eastern Bengal separated by nearly one thousand miles of India. This Pakistan was radically changed after 1971, when East Bengali Pakistanis fought, on the basis of linguistic and cultural nationalism, to create their own nation-state of Bangladesh. All of these post–1947 factors (as the majority of contemporary South Asian migrants have arrived in the Americas after 1965) strongly distinguish this period of migration from nineteenth and early twentieth century diasporic politics and culture.

15. By 'mainstream' I am referring to theatrical production that not only caters to 'white' audiences but to those theatres that would not take a chance in producing a play that would require casting challenges because of ethnicity. In 2008, the Pittsburgh Irish and Classical Theatre considered mounting a production of *Merchant*, as the Shakespearean aspect of the play would surely garner an audience, but the social reality of having to employ a large cast of South Asian actors forced the company to abandon their plans (Carden personal interview). I do not have the space to historically examine the South Asian American theatre tradition in which Kurup appears as one of many playwrights, such as Bina Sharif, Mrinalini Kamath, Nandita Shenoy, Aditi Brennan Kapil, Aameera Siddiqui, and Aasif Mandvi, to name a few, who have been writing and producing plays over the last fifteen years. See the critical introduction to the US in Bose *Beyond Bollywood*.
16. For example: Pushpa/Portia, I, ii, 'the will of a living daughter curbed by the will of a dead father', Sharuk/Shylock, I, iii, 'Devendra/Antonio is a good man', Sharuk/Shylock, I, iii, 'The Muslim/Jew will grow Hindu/Christian he grows kind', Pushpa/Portia, II, vi (Kurup), II, viii (Shakespeare), 'Let all with his complexion choose me so', Sharuk/Shylock, III, i, 'You knew, none so well, none so well as you, of my daughter's flight', Sharuk/Shylock, IV, i, 'On what compulsion must I? Tell me that?' 'I am content'.
17. NetIP is an acronym for the Network of Indian Professionals, a well-known organization catering to young second-generation South Asian American professionals.
18. This element appeared in two productions viewed by the author (Lark Theatre, New York City, 2004 and the Silk Road Theatre Project, 2007). In Shakespeare's text, only Gratiano is mob-like in his anti-Semitism, whereas the others are more subtle.
19. Shakespeare's play also concerns the European transition into capitalism. Although this is implicit in Kurup's play, the social effects of economics on identities and violence does not emerge as a centre of the piece.
20. For a recent analysis of how this worked in the 19th century, see Padamsee *Representations*.
21. Both of these incidents of violence against and stereotyping of Muslims relate to a depiction of Muslims as potentially threatening to Indian secular nationalism. In Ayodhya, the birthplace of the Hindu god Ram, Hindu nationalist forces declared that the Babri Masjid was built on the remains of a temple destroyed by a Muslim

ruler, though evidence for such destruction was never found. In Gujarat in 2002, based on an altercation between Hindu pilgrims and Muslims on a train, a rampage of violence, some of which was clearly planned beforehand, was unleashed against Muslims.

22. For a historical overview of the 19th and 20th centuries, see Jalal *Self and Sovereignty*. For a discussion of pre-colonial Islam in South Asia, see Eaton *India's Islamic Traditions*.
23. 'Desi' simply refers to anyone from South Asia, in a way that does not pinpoint a specific geographical, linguistic, or religious identity. This catch-all South Asianness is most prominent in the United States.
24. All references to Kurup's text are taken from the published version in Bose *Beyond Bollywood* 93–158; all references to Shakespeare's text are taken from Shakespeare *Merchant of Venice*.
25. Silk Road's current performance space holds 99 seats.
26. For a complete cast list, see http://www.srtp.org/history/productions/merchant.html.
27. These memories are culled from interviews with dramaturge Lavina Jadhwani, 10 August 2008, and artistic director Jamil Khoury, 22 August 2008.
28. Concepts like 'hybridity' and 'tradition', often ahistorically deployed, dominate discussions of post-colonial Shakespeare, particularly Loomba and Orkin *Post-Colonial Shakespeare* and Fischlin and Fortier *Adaptations*. Rustom Bharucha *Foreign Asia* critiques contemporary Asian post-colonial Shakespeare productions but relies on predictably nativist investments in the right type of 'tradition'.
29. Owing to space constraints, I cannot examine other South Asian diasporic traditions at length or even offer comparative notes. The obvious example would be the British Asian diaspora and the many adaptations of Shakespeare, Moliere, and the range of Western classical theatre by Jatinder Verma and many others, starting from the 1970s. In the British Asian case, theatre as a political weapon (e.g. the 'Binglish' imperative to play with language and form) has simply not occurred in the American context.
30. It is certainly important to note that 'South Asian American diasporic' must be distinguished from other diasporic groups, like British Asians, as relationships to dominant metropolitan theatre cultures, and relationships to South Asia are vastly different.

Works Cited

Appiah, Kwame Anthony. 'Is the "Post"- in "Postcolonial" the "Post"- in "Postmodern"?' *Dangerous Liaisons: Gender, Nation, and Postcolonial Perspectives*. Ed. Anne McClintock, Aamir Mufti and Ella Shohat. Minneapolis: U of Minnesota P, 1997. 420–44. Print.

Bharucha, Rustom. 'Foreign Asia/Foreign Shakespeare: Dissenting Notes on New Asian Interculturality, Postcoloniality, and Recolonization'. *Theatre Journal* 56.1 (2004): 1–28. Print.

Bose, Neilesh, ed. *Beyond Bollywood and Broadway: Plays from the South Asian Diaspora*. Bloomington: Indiana UP, 2009. Print.

Carden, Stuart. Personal Interview. 2008. Web. 3 Aug. 2008.

Carter, Marina and Torabully Khan, eds. *Coolitude: An Anthology of the Indian Labour Diaspora*. London: Anthem, 2002. Print.

Chatterjee, Sudipto. 'South Asian American Theatre: (Un/Re) Painting the Town Brown'. *Theatre Survey* 49.1 (2008): 109–17. Print.

Chatterjee, Sudipto. *The Colonial Staged: Theatre in Colonial Calcutta*. Kolkata: Seagull, 2008. Print.

Chatterjee, Sudipto and Jyotsna G. Singh. 'Moor or Less? The Surveillance of Othello, Calcutta 1848'. *Shakespeare and Appropriation*. Ed. Christy Desmet and Robert Sawyer. New York: Routledge, 1999. 65–84. Print.

Desmet, Christy and Robert Sawyer, eds. *Shakespeare and Appropriation*. New York: Routledge, 1999.

Dharwadker, Aparna. 'Diaspora and the Theatre of a Nation'. *Theatre Research International* 28.3 (2003): 303–25. Print.

Eaton, Richard, ed. *India's Islamic Traditions, 711–1750*. New Delhi: Oxford UP, 2006. Print.

Fischlin, Daniel and Mark Fortier, eds. *Adaptations of Shakespeare: A Critical Anthology of Plays from the Seventeenth Century to the Present*. New York: Routledge, 1997. Print.

Fuchs, Anne and Geoffrey V. Davis, eds. *Staging New Britain: Aspects of Black and South Asian British Theatre Practice*. London: Peter Lang, 2006. Print.

Hasan, Nazmul. *Shakespeare Translations in Nineteenth Century Bengali Theatre*. Dhaka: Bangla Academy, 1995. Print.

Jadhwani, Lavina. Personal Interview. 2008.

Jalal, Ayesha. *Self and Sovereignty: Individual and Community in South Asian Islam since 1850*. New York: Routledge, 2000. Print.

Jones, Chris. 'Bold 'Merchant' Melds Bard, Bollywood'. *Chicago Tribune* 8 October 2007. Web. 14 Jan. 2009. <http://archives.chicagotribune.com/2007/oct/08/entertainment/chi-ovn_1008veniceoct08>

Khoury, Jamil. Personal Interview. 2008.

Kurup, Shishir. Personal Interview. 2005.

——. 'Online Interview'. *Chitrahar* 2007. Web. 8 Jan. 2009. <http://www. youtube.com/watch?v=v7dLKzGSbNY>

Lal, Vinay. 'Establishing Roots, Engendering Awareness: A Political History of Asian Indians in the United States'. *Live Like the Banyan Tree: Images of the Indian American Experience*. Ed. Leela Prasad. Philadelphia: Balch Institute for Ethnic Studies, 1999. 42–51. Print.

Lal, Ananda and Sukanta Chaudhuri, eds. *Shakespeare on the Calcutta Stage: A Checklist*. Kolkata: Papyrus, 2001. Print.

Leonard, Karen. *The South Asian Americans*. Westport, CT: Greenwood P, 1997. Print.

Loomba, Ania and Martin Orkin, eds. *Post-Colonial Shakespeares*. London: Routledge, 1998. Print.

Loomba, Ania. 'Local Manufacture Made-in-India Othello Fellows: Issues of Race, Hybridity, and Location in Post-Colonial Shakespeares'. *Post-Colonial Shakespeares*. Eds. Ania Loomba and Martin Orkin. London: Routledge, 1998. 143–63. Print.

Neill, Michael. 'Post-Colonial Shakespeare? Writing Away from the Centre'. *Post-Colonial Shakespeares*. Eds. Ania Loomba and Martin Orkin. London: Routledge, 1998. 164–85. Print.

Padamsee, Alex. *Representations of Indian Muslims in British Colonial Discourse*. New York: Palgrave Macmillan, 2005. Print.

Rangaswamy, Padma. *Namaste America: Indian Immigrants in an American Metropolis*. Pennsylvania: Pennsylvania State UP, 2000. Print.

Shankar, D.A., ed. *Shakespeare in Indian Languages*. Shimla: Indian Institute of Advanced Study, 1999. Print.

Silk Road Theatre Project. History, Productions: *Merchant on Venice*. 2009. Web. 14 Apr. 2009. <www.srtp.org/history/productions/ merchant.htm>

Srikanth, Rajini and Esther Yae Iwanaga, eds. *Bold Words: A Century of Asian American Writing*. Rutgers, NJ: Rutgers UP, 2001. Print.

Tinker, Hugh. *A New System of Slavery: The Export of Indian Labour Overseas, 1830–1920*. London: Oxford UP, 1974. Print.

Trivedi, Poonam and Dennis Bartholomeusz, eds. *India's Shakespeare: Translation, Interpretation, and Performance*. Newark: U of Delaware P, 2005. Print.

Varshney, Pranidhi. Personal Interview. 2008.

Vitello, Barbara. 'The Bard Goes Bollywood'. *Daily Herald*. 2007. Web. 14 Jan. 2009. <http://www.highbeam.com/doc/1G1–171910779.html>

Weiss, Heidi. 'Worldly Hindus Take on a Strict Muslim'. *Chicago Sun-Times* 1 October 2007. Web. 14 Jan. 2009 <,http://www.leekeenan.com/blog/2007/10/07/merchant-on-venice..>

Wells, Stanley and Sarah Stanton, eds. *The Cambridge Companion to Shakespeare on Stage*. New York: Cambridge UP, 2002. Print.

Zarrilli, Philip. 'For Whom Is a King a King? Issues of Intercultural Production, Perception, and Reception in a *Kathakali King Lear*'. *Critical Theory and Performance*. Eds. Janelle G. Reinelt and Joseph R. Roach. Ann Arbor: U of Michigan P, 1992. 108–34. Print.

14

South Asian Diasporic Theatre

A Critical Overview

D. SUDHA RANI

> After a three-week run in a city where Asian Americans comprise 24.5 per cent of population, this remarkable production has also remained beyond the narrow scope of the press and has gone un-reviewed and undocumented. (Uno: 324)

Roberta Uno, a theatre critic from the US, writes about the patronization of Asian American theatre in his article entitled 'Introduction: Asian American Theater Awake at the Millennium' published in *Bold Words: A Century of Asian American Writing* (2001). This is the condition of the genre of South Asian diaspora theatre across the globe for a long time. This reminds us the situation of Indian English theatre in India till recent times. Indian English drama did not establish itself for a long time before it is recognized and patronized by the urban, English speaking middle class Indians. Only when the size of the audience increased and the society began to accept theatre as a decent art form, the change in the perspective towards this art form took place. Though the genre began to develop, the criticism of this genre of literature is in its nascent stage.

While South Asian diaspora literature is rich and well established, South Asian diaspora theatre is not developed as much. Critics point out several reasons for such dwarf stage of the branch of literature. Aparna Dharwadkar, a noted critic, analyses the situation in her research article, 'Diaspora and the Theatre of the Nation' (2003):

> Moreover, while novelists often employ diaspora as the enabling condition but not the subject of narrative, immigrant playwrights can create original theatre only when they distance themselves from their cultures of origin and embrace the experience of residence in the host culture, with all its problems of acculturation and identity (303).

Nevertheless, this branch of literature is currently growing and slowly establishing itself in the host countries. It is also essential to note the significance of this critical study, which is two-fold. To begin with, South Asian Diasporic community is gaining greater importance in these countries owing to its population and their contribution to the immigrant countries. Second reason is that theatre is a more authentic form of art that expresses the human element and the issues of the human society. This paper attempts to give a critical overview of the South Asian diaspora theatre.

South Asia refers to the seven nation-states – India, Pakistan, Bangladesh, Bhutan, Nepal, Sri Lanka and Maldives Islands. Denoting the term 'South Asia', historian Neilesh Bose writes, 'Clearly the term South Asia serves only as a geographical boundary marker and not as a description of the various cultures that are included in the region' (5). Thus, the theatre of this stratum of society is highly diverse as the cultures, societies, and political scenario of so many countries are involved. It is obvious, the volume of the globe is huge and so are the parts of the globe to which South Asians continue to migrate. Unable to incorporate details of South Asian diasporic theatre in all the countries, I have concentrated on nation-states where the South Asian theatre is quite active and the publication of these plays is available like the United States of America, Canada, United Kingdom and South Africa. Narrowing down the search further, I will consider only those plays written in English and those theatre groups which have produced sizeable productions and the playwrights (from South Asian origin) writing about the community of South Asians which is in focus. Since this paper presents a critical overview of the genre, the author will not be able to go into detailed analysis of any one play and all the plays mentioned in this paper. An attempt to understand basic developmental stages, the issues presented, the formation of their hybrid identities and the 'self' of South Asian diaspora on the stage in the host countries will form focal point of this paper.

South Asian migration to United States of America started in 19th century but the initial migrants were labourers in majority. After the Indian Independence, when the young English educated Indians were looking for opportunities of migration, i.e. during 1950s and 1960s USA had taken their attention. Thus, from 1960s onwards, the student community and the professionals' community from South Asia started migrating to America. Basically, this community in America is engrossed in earning dollars; their primary aim in coming to a rich country like America. After a considerable time is taken by this community in consolidating their position, a section of them, largely young, second, third and fourth generation South Asians whose permanent settlement is in America and who identify themselves more as Americans, started opting for alternate careers in theatre, radio, television and cinema industries. While opting for theatre, two possible reasons would have prompted the choice: one being eagerness to express their 'self' on American stage and second is that this group of youngsters do not consider America as only a place to earn dollars, but they made it their home.

A group of theatre companies like, Chicago's Rasaka's Theatre, Boston's South Asian America Theatre, Chicago's Silk Road Theatre, Minneapolis's Pangea World Theatre, Pennaatak Theatre, Lark Theatre, Salaam Theatre, Disha Theatre, Shunya Theatre and many others constantly produce plays of South Asian Diaspora across the vast area of America. New York is the epicentre of this theatre activity but the whole of America is entertained by these theatre groups. Playwrights are writing plays from 1950s onwards. Playwrights from this community have been producing plays like Asif Mandvi – *Sakina's Restauarant*, Bina Sharif – *Afgan Woman, My Ancestors House, Another Journey Home*, Rehana Mirza, Gargi Mukherjee-*Our Voices*, Anuvab Pal – *Chaos Theory*, Shishir Kurup – *Merchant on Venice, Assimilations*, Alldin Ullah-*The Halal Brothers,* Taniya Hossain – *Mother in Another Language, Neighbors, Bridge and*

Tunnel Deception, Rohina Malik – *Yasmina's Necklace, Unveiled*, Dolly Dingra – *Unsuitable Girls*, Sarovar Banks's – *The Moral Implications of Time Travel*, etc. The list is quite big and same is the issues discussed and presented on the American stage.

The first generation South Asian American playwrights like Bina Sharif exhibit the longing for home and express that nostalgic feeling in plays like *My Ancestor's Home*. She writes that she is really amused that she had to leave her Muslim homeland and settle down in a liberal and democratic country, but still labelled as a Muslim woman playwright. The second and third generation immigrants like Shishir Kurup focus on the 'self' entangled in complex identities. Kurup's *Assimilations* is a demonstration of impact of racism on South Asian immigrants in the West and *Merchant on Venice* exhibits his lineage towards the Hindu-Muslim issue. *Merchant on Venice* also focuses on the common cultural background of South Asians. *Sakina's Restaurant* by Asif Mandvi is a comedy play with an inherent indication of the life and ambitions of working class South Asian migrants. A young man from India dreams to reach Ameirca, no matter whatever kind of job is offered to him there. The fascination of Indians to live in America is well exhibited in this play. Anuvab Pal's *Chaos Theory* appears to be a love story of Sunita and Mukesh but it also projects the South Asian Academic community along with their post colonial conditions.

Thus, it is evident that the South Asian American playwrights are primarily concerned about the issues of their community in America. They also exhibit their inclination of awareness about the issues related to their countries but the vigour is lacking. As they are away from their homeland they lack that seriousness towards the issues of their homelands. One of the most sensitive and important issue like Hindu-Muslim communal clashes is being dealt in lighter vein in *Merchant on Venice*. Simultaneously racism is given very serious attention in plays like *Assimilations*. Issues related to their land of migration, migrated community and issues related to identities are given prominence.

South Asian community in Canada is a little different from its counterpart in America. On the one hand, America has accepted the diasporic community from South Asia; on the other hand, Canada was hostile for a long time. So, immigrants had to focus on consolidating their homes and lives in this country. They had to bear the burden of opposition from the administration, people and simultaneously cope with the personal problems of migration and then focus on producing literature. Initially, from 1830s to 1950s the migrants were by and large labourers. Then gradually after the independence of the South Asian countries, professionals and students started migrating to this country. These young professionals started entering into alternate careers like television, radio and theatre. They wanted to address the issues related to them and voice out their problems, both personal and the concerned to community. South Asian diaspora in Canada remembers its past experiences where they suffered racism and colonialism. After a lot of struggle and outrage from this community, the attitude of the Canada government and people started changing. The population of this community is not only sizeable, but influential in more than one way currently. Analysing their population, Diana Lobb, a research scholar from Canada writes:

> Representing over a million individuals, South Asian-Canadians represented 3 per cent of the Canadian population in 2001, and their numbers were expanding at a rate of 33 per cent since the last census, a rate that far outstripped the 4 per cent rate of growth of the Canadian population (Stats Can). However, while enumerated as a single group, Statistics Canada points out that within this group are individuals with a diversity of religious and ethnic affiliations, mother-tongues, education and economic levels, and ages. This incredible difference-within is the aspect of South Asian-Canadian identity that makes it such an effective lever against not just the ethnography of settler/invader identity but also against the pedagogical narrative of the Anglo-Celtic settlers '*a priori* claim to this place. (71–72)

Theatre activity of South Asian Community in Canada primarily started with an intention to showcase the community's dissatisfaction over the living conditions and treatment they received from both the government and people of Canada. This community's theatre in Canada had a much serious ideological background in comparison to its counterpart in America. It has been playing a crucial role in the identity shaping of this community. Though the negotiation of identities was always at the heart of the genre, it realized that in this process it got transformed a lot. Writing about the importance of this genre, Ms Lobb insists on the role played by this art form and writes:

> South Asian-Canadian theatre is a particularly useful field for examining the ongoing negotiation between *Présence Asiénne*, *Présence Européenne* and *Présence Canadiénne*. What becomes obvious in examining South Asian-Canadian theatre is the caution that must be taken in attempting to identify the influence of both *Présence Asiénne* and *Présence Européenne*. *Présence Asiénne*, the vector of influence representing the connection to the ancestral homeland(s), needs to be historically situated. *Présence Asiénne* is never pure – this vector cannot be understood as representing an authentic, pre-colonial South Asian cultural influence. It is always already hybridized with *Présence Européenne*, which itself needs to be historicized in terms of what aspects (and moments) of European culture can be seen to interact with South Asian cultural realities. (130)

The journey of this genre of art started as a protest theatre, then it started displaying the issues of their counterparts in homeland *(Bhopal)* and gradually it consolidated itself as a mainstream theatre and well recognized by both the governmental agencies and people of Canada. Teesri Duniya, a theatre company, is now receiving funding from The Canada Arts Council, The Québec Arts Council, and The Montreal Arts Council. Teesri Duniya publicly announces its role in shaping the target community and its cultural identity, 'Teesri Duniya Theatre is dedicated to producing socially and politically relevant theatre that supports a multicultural vision of society, promoting inter-culturalism through works of theatre, and creating theatrical styles based on the cultural experiences of visible minorities living in Canada' (Teesri). The theatre company also works in collaboration with many Indian counterparts. Similarly, the Vancouver Sath, a theatre company that operates with naxalite ideology and East Indians focuses on the plight of the migrants. Analysing one of the plays produced by Vancouver Sath, Diana Lobb writes,

> The *Lesson of a Different Kind* that Vancouver Sath's didactic play teaches not just to Resham but to all members of the next generation brought up here is that they can redeem themselves and this society. By actively renegotiating a South Asian Canadian cultural identity grounded in conscious recognition of class oppression, the members of the next generation can begin to reorganize their society into one in which the working class has equal access to power. (151–52)

Plays like, *Komagata Mary Incident* of Sharon Pollock, *Lions of the Sea* by Jessi Thind, *Lesson of a Different Kind* by Resham Gill, *Job Stealer* by Teesri Duniya, *Bhopal* by Rahul Verma, *My Sita's Promise* and *Meera* by Uma Parameswaran are frequently produced and patronized. One remarkable feature of South Asian Canadian Theatre is, after a lot of struggle for identity and respect in the society of Canada, this art form is slowly trying to be a part of mainstream Canadian national theatre. Thus, majority of this genre is engaged in social and political change, though they continue to project issues related to this community and their counterparts in homelands.

The case of United Kingdom is different from that of United States of America and Canada. The long standing relationship of South Asian countries with that of European countries is one vital reason in shaping the diasporic literature. South Asian migration to United Kingdom is much older than colonization and it increased owing to the consolidation of British Empire in these countries. As ever, the initial migrants were servants, labour and *ayahs*. Development of literature began when educated youngsters started migrating to this country.

Interestingly, South Asian theatre in the UK began to make its appearance in a similar fashion as the English drama in India did. Touring cultural troupes used to perform for migrant Asian communities in the UK. The first one to visit was from Oudh which is arranged by two English brothers, though not much is known about these brothers and the performers. But the theatrical tradition started spreading into various regions of the UK. A theatre group emerged during World War I, namely Indian Dramatic Art Society and produced plays in English with Leftist ideology. This paved way to the vernacular theatre of South Asian languages in the UK which basically dealt with internal community dynamics. The mainstream South Asian theatre in the UK is 40 years old. Writing in the introduction to the *Critical Essays on British South Asian Theatre* 2012, the documented history of this genre, its editors Graham Ley and Sarah Dadswell opine, regarding the plight of this genre:

> The fact is that, despite its forty years of burgeoning activity, Asian-led theatre in Britain has not figured at all in prominent and supposedly authoritative accounts of the contemporary British theatre. What is remarkable about this absence is that several Asian-led companies and their leading practitioners have been well known to the theatregoers for the last twenty years, not least because 'the sector' (as it is currently known) has been required by the conditions of funding to tour widely throughout Britain. (1)

The young South Asians were eager to express their discontent over the discrimination they were facing in the society and they used theatre to express their angst. This reminds us of the English drama in India, the way it was used as a tool in the nationalist movement. Thus, the aesthetic and creative abilities of these youngsters were shaped by the urge for equality. Hence, the plays produced during 1960s and 1970s were a part of popular protest against discrimination. Interestingly, this genre in England enjoyed excellent patronization. According to Graham Ley and Sarah Dadswell, 'the primary reception of British South Asian theatre in all its varieties by audience and reviewers has not been matched by an appropriate level of secondary reception by those who might review achievements at a greater distance, from an academic or critical stand point' (1).

By 1960s, natives of England started raising their voices against these migrants and there is demarked increase in racist attacks. Tara Arts Theatre Company has toured around Britain to propagate this problem. Sudha Bhuchar (*Strictly Dandia*), Sanjaeev Bhaskar (*Goodness Gracious Me*), Ayub Khan Din (*East is East, Rafita-Rafita*) are the prominent playwrights associated with this theatre company. Tara Arts could spin the vigour in the playwrights like Hanif Khureishi (*Borderlines*), Farrukh Dhondy, Madhav Sharma (*Actors Unlimited*) who became active. Rani Murthy's Rasa Theatre Group (1998–2000) staged some of her plays like *Shades of Brown*, *Curry Tales*, *Pooja*, etc. Ruksana Ahmad produced some of the thought provoking plays like *Black Salwar*, *Mistaken* (2001), *Song for a Sanctuary* (1990), *Annie Besant in India* (2007), Kirben Pillay – *Looking for Muruga*, Jatinder Verma *2001 – A Ramayana Odyssey*, Jabine Chandri-*My Daughter's Trial* (2013), Shelley Sitas – *Calcutta Kosher* (2012), Sayan Kent and Tuyen Do – *Shared Memories*, Azma Dar – *Chaos*, Sonia Likhari – *Behna*, Gurupreet Kaur Bhatti – *Behzti* are some of the playwrights and their plays.

According to Neilesh Bose, it is from 1990s that South Asian Diasporic Theatre activity is recognized by British media and society. And it is during this time the playwrights of this sector started staging plays about a multi-folded issues like colonial, postcolonial, familial, social, cultural, political, personal to global multiculturalism. South Asian migration to this land started early and the host country enjoyed long standing relationship with these countries as all South Asian nations were British colonies. Owing to these two reasons, consolidation of this stratum of society in Britain was natural which resulted in rich artistic expressions. One prominent feature of the British South Asian Diaspora theatre is that it produced considerable number of feminist plays and popularized the angst of women of this community.

Africa as a nation has more similarities to all South Asian countries than one. The most important being, it is also one of the colonies of British. So the affiliation to this country was always part of the South Asian consciousness. But when it comes to migration, again it was indentured labourers who were displaced to Africa by the British rulers. The plight of the migrants was known to the world as Mahatma Gandhi started his freedom movement from here. Thus, the emergence of African Indian Congress is recorded but again in case of theatre by South Asian Diaspora, poor documentation and recognition plagues this art form. As the migrants are increasing in population, their attempt to consolidate their homes in dire conditions was essential to practice any art form. Thus, multi-racial theatre tradition began to develop, where Indian actors began to perform works by British playwrights (in English) for non-White audiences in Durban. Analysing this development, Neilesh Bose, a theatre historian writes:

> Indian South African theatre then started to reflect both the issues of its communities and started to use local casts. After the visit of India's Krishna Shah to Durban in 1962 (who staged Rabindranath Tagore's *The King of the Dark Chamber*), Muthul Naidoo, Ronnie Govinder, Welcome Msaomi, and others formed the Durban Academy of Theatre Arts (DATA). (366)

Gradually these actors started preparing to write, stage their plays and started theatrical companies like Durban Academy of Theatre Arts which staged plays by Muthul Naidoo, Ronnie Govinder, Kessie Govinder, etc. The diasporic South Asians identify themselves with native Africans and join hands in voicing against racial discrimination. Their intra community issues and intercommunity issues were suppressed by the fact that all of them were victims of racial discrimination. Playwrights like Rajesh Gopie, Kirban Pillay, Yugan Naidoo, are some others who contributed their plays to this sector. A keen observation of these plays reveals that these plays deal with a panorama of issues ranging from local South African society to global identity problems. One significant factor about all these plays is, the playwrights are haunted by discrimination and not displacement. *Lahnee's Pleasure* is a play by Ronnie Govinder which is staged in many locations across the country from 1972 onwards. This play exhibits the condition of Indian working class which is not even allowed to sit along with English men in a bar. Kirban Pillay's *Looking for Muruga* presents the Indian working-class life and race relations and politics of South Africa during apartheid. It focuses on the intra community issues and politics of performance also.

In spite of greater diversity, South Asian diaspora shares a few fundamental commonalities, like all these nation-states have been colonies for a long time and they got independence after a lengthy and painful struggle. They all got independence almost during the same time and started their journey of development simultaneously. The migrants from these nation-states to the specified host nation-states began with labourers and then followed by professionals and students. The journey of their theatre in the host countries began with the issues related to cultural identity, displacement and their encounters with the host nation and the citizens in the case of those who are first generation writers. In the case of second, third and fourth generation diaspora theatre personalities, the issues are more serious and certainly related to the host nation and dynamically varied but progressing towards the global issues. But this sector of literature is making its mark in the world literature and is worth paying serious attention.

Works Cited

Bose, Neilesh, ed. *Beyond Bollywood and Broadway: Plays from the South Asian Diaspora*. Indianapolis: Indiana University Press, 2009. Print.

Dharwadkar, Aparna. 'Diaspora and Theatre of the Nation'. *Theatre Research International* Vol. I. 3 (2003): 303–325. Print.

Lobb, Diana. *Canadian Literatures Beyond the Colour Line: Re-reading the Category of South Asian Canadian Literature*. PhD Dissertation. Canada: Waterloo University, 2011. Print.

Ley, Graham, Sarah Dadswell, eds. *Critical Essays on British South Asian Theatre*. UK: University of Exeter Press, 2012. Print.

James. R. Branden. 'A New World: Asian Theatre in the West Today'. *Tulane Drama Review*. Vol. 33. No. 2. (Summer 1989). Print.

Srikanth, Rajini. *The World Next Door: South Asian American Literature and the Idea of America*. Philadelphia: Temple University Press, 2004. Print.

Uno, Roberta. 'Introduction: Asian American Theater Awake at the Millennium'. *Bold Words: A Century of Asian American Writing*. Eds. Rajini Srikanth, ýEsther Yae Iwanaga. USA: Rutgers, 2001. 1–10. Print.

Webliography

Asian American Theatre Group.com www.aatrevue.com

National Asian American Theatre Festival NYC www.theatrewithoutborders.com

Silk Road theatre Project www.srtp.org

South Asian playwright's www.south Asian playwrights.org

15

Theatre for Development in Indian Context

An Introspection

PRIYAM BASU THAKUR

Theatre has its root from the ancient time of human communication. From the childhood days of theatre it caters preliterate community members' information, education, entertainment, socialization and also creates a platform for debate and discussion. The terminology development refers to 'improving the living condition of society'. In every corner of the developing world, theatre is approved as an effectual element for social change as well as behavioural change. From the period of early 1940s Western researchers used to believe that the mass media could enhance the growth of development process more effectively. In fact, the traditional media or the folk media were eschewed in the literature of development literature. But from the 1970s a new concept in development communication arena started to flourish. This new approach focused on participatory communication consisting of interpersonal and group communication. Then the necessity of traditional media for communication purpose in a complex social system was realized by the researchers because traditional media have a deep rooted entity in every culture. Marginalized people of grassroot level are also very much familiar with the various forms of folk song, dance, and drama. So it was thought that diffusing message on development through folk media which would be more approachable to the rural people who were the real target of the development communication and it would encourage them to participate in the communication process and ensure the two way process in communication. Theatre – the traditional performing art is also changing, improvising and modifying itself to the needs of the changing situation and become relevant in society. Over the decades, theatre emphasizes the themes related with the agriculture, literacy campaign, social harmony, peace building, national integration, girl trafficking, child labour, child abusing, gender discrimination, religious tolerance, women empowerment, right of sex-worker, prevention of HIV-AIDS, family planning, pulse polio, nutrition, environment pollution, etc.

Overview of Theatre

The passion to express, to communicate and to share the ideas-opinions-emotions-beliefs gave inception to performing art. Performing art has an enormous artistic value. Theatre is a major functional and spontaneous expression of performing art. Primitive men adorned their caves with wall painting, artifacts, and hieroglyphics to transmit their experience from one generation to another. Theatre emerged from age-old myth, ceremony and ritualistic activities of a culture. It has its root in ancient Greece between the 550 BC–220 BC. The Indian theatre has also a long historical value. After the development of Greek and Roman theatre, India among the other Asian countries first stepped into the 'era of theatre'. According to Shakespeare, 'theatre is a mirror of highlighting man's humanity and also a tool for understanding why man also finds it so easy to transgress that same humanity'. It is considered as a reflector of culture specific social humanity. The transition of society and culture over the thousands of years ushered theatre with an intrinsic quality of flexibility and openness. Community theatre (CT), theatre for integrated rural development (THIRD), street theatre (ST), guerilla theatre (GT), prison theatre for development (PTFD), campaign theatre, protest theatre, oppositional theatre are the new avenues with new conception transpire in the world of theatre.

Development Communication: Third World Perspective

World War II (1939–1945) reciprocated the political calibration and social structure of the entire globe. After the World War II, most of Third World countries emancipated from colonial imperialism. The emergence of United Nations (UN) commences the conventional beginning of development to less developed countries (LDC). 'Mother of Development Communication' *Nora Cruz Quebral* in the year of 1971 first coined the term 'development communication'. She defined development communication as '... The art and science of human communication linked to a society's planned transformation from a state of poverty to one dynamic socio-economic growth that makes for, greater equality and the larger unfolding of individual potentials (25–28). According to the modernization paradigm in the decades of 1950s and 1960s mass media' was considered as a prime mover in developmental process. Scholars like Wilbur Schramm, Daniel Lerner, Everett Rogers, Pye, Lakshmana Rao et al., assumed that mass media had inherent element to infiltrate into isolated traditional society and reconstitute social norms, values, attitudes of the society. But in many Third World countries monological channels of mass media failed to materialize the goal of sustainable development. Scholars in Latin America have pointed out genuine problems with the top-to-bottom conception of westernized modernization approach. By the mid–1970s the alternative ideas of dominant paradigm were put under the spotlight. Notion of development support communication, participatory communication became visible in the ground of Third World Development. Traditional media came into forefront to promote developmental issues to grassroot people more effectively than big media industry. A new trend in non-formal method of education (NFE) had drawn the attention of communication research scholars.

The Correlation between Theatre and Development: Critical Analysis

When electronic media failed to leave strong emphasis on the people of less developed countries (LDC), the re-emergence of traditional culture became necessitated. By 1970s, theatre began to work as a viable tool for popularization of education with adults and children in sub-Saharan Africa, Indian subcontinent and Latin America. The author of *History and Theatre in Africa*, Eckhard Breitinger, opines:

> The rise of Theatre for Development also marked a change in international relations. It was both the symptom and the result of the failures of 20 years of development policies that had insisted on the implantation of the materialist and technological culture of the North as the only possible road to the development, irrespective of the cultural and social environment. (24)

Srinivas R. Melkote and H. Leslie Steeves, in their book *Communication for Development in the Third World: Theory and Practice for Empowerment,* observed Brazilian educator and philosopher Paulo Freire as probably the most influential scholar to apply liberation theology in education and communication in development substance. In his notable book, *Pedagogy of the Oppressed,* Paulo Freire argues that development communication should be exercised as a dialogic process between communicator and communicate. Influenced by the Freire's academically influential work Augusto Boal developed the idea of 'theatre of oppressed' (TO). Boal conducted experimentation in August 1973 in the cities Lima and Chiclayo on the people's theatre in Peru. His objective was liberation of the viewer by theatrical performances. He used a strategy for transforming a viewer into an active participator. The four stages were:

1. Knowing the body
2. Making the body expressive
3. The theatre as language
4. The theatre as discourse

A new term, 'applied theatre', expanded throughout the world for spreading developmental ideas to marginalized people. Generally, theatre communicates with its viewer at interpersonal level and small group level of communication. Because of physical proximity, emotion, trust worthiness message content became more relevant to the viewer. Direct communication with live reality makes receiver active in communication process. Participation of local people, the use of local languages and dialects and addressing local problems increase the acceptability of theatre. Viewer feels cultural affinity with the self-development mode of the medium. As a result, they spontaneously involve with the process of communication. Dialogical theatre initiates active participation of receiver. Theatre is a very low cost medium. But it enjoys a very high popularity with powerful impact in many developing and underdeveloped nations. Developmental issues presented in a form of edutainment gives a new insight to the community members and enhance the possibility of discussion. Theatre has become part and parcel to compress the communication gap between different social classes in the unequal power relationship of complex social organization.

Theatre for Development: Indian Experience

The earliest form of Indian theatre was Sanskrit theatre which was strongly influenced by Roman and Greek theatre. It has its root in Vedic literature around 1000 AD. Theatre based on *NatyaShastra* was sophisticated in nature. Popular theatre in different regional languages also co-existed in Indian society. During the British rule Indian theatre came into direct contact with Western theatre which was based on realism. In 1920s two points of view emerged on Indian theatre. One was commercial professional theatre and other was 'non-professional' or 'new' or 'other' theatre. Sisir Kumar Bhaduri first tried to admixture these two contradictory concepts. At the same time, a new genre in Bengali literature based on realism started to evolve. A group of young enthusiast like Kaji Najrul Islam, Budhadeb Basu, Achintya Kumar Sengupta and Premendra Mitra, etc. formed *Kallol* group and they recognized Bhaduri's theatre as a model for the modern Indian theatre. The decade of 1940s witnessed a great political upsurge. The terror of World War II, rise of fascism and of course Bengal famine (1943), which led to death of two million people because of starvation and malnutrition, gave genesis of an influential theatrical movement – Indian People's Theatre Association (IPTA). The leftist intellectual all over the nation such as Khwaja Ahmed Abbas, Mulk Raj Anand, Sardar Jaferry, Rajinder Shingh Bedi, Prithviraj Kapoor, Balraj Sahani, Habib Tanvir, Utpal Dutta, Shambhu Mitra, Tripti Mitra, Bijan Bhattacharya, Salil Chowdhury, Ritwik Ghatak, Pandit Ravi Shankar, Jyotirindra Moitra, Debabrata Biswas, Hemanga Biswas, Chetan Anand, Dina Gandhi, Shaukat Kaifi, Krishan

Chander, etc. formed a strong cultural organization to spread the protest against the fascism and political violence. A Bengali drama *Nabanna,* based on Bengal famine written by Bijan Bhattacharya and directed by Shambhu Mitra and later by Kumar Roy, was a big step towards the democratization of theatre. Indian theatre with its ideological perspective adopted folk form to create social consciousness among the rural and urban people. In the post-Independence era Government of India promoted theatre for developmental activities. The first prime minister of free India Jawaharlal Nehru remarked:

> 'I am greatly interested in the development of a people's theatre in India ...'

From the 1940s street theatre played an anti-fascist role of the communist parties. Street theatre also became a part and parcel of Indian freedom movement. In a free India, street theatre evolved as a weapon against social-political-economic exploitation. Theatre activist Utpal Dutta sharply used street theatre for political awareness. During the internal emergency (26 June 1975–21 March 1976), street theatre upsurge its protest against the state-sponsored terror. Many street theatre activists were attacked, arrested and even murdered. In the time of performing a street play *Halla Bol* a great street theatre activist Safdar Hashmi was ferociously killed in Ghaziabad.

In contemporary era of globalization, neo-liberal economy created 'global village' which changes the worldwide complex social relationship. Cultural imperialism proved detrimental for diverse indigenous regional culture of Third World countries and forms a dominant culture which transfused the entire globe by powerful courtiers. But theatre remains relevant in the social context till today. Theatre persists as a major tool for empowerment of the grassroot people of India. Many theatre groups in every part of India work to give voice to the voiceless. The land of vast geographical and cultural diversity with 1.27 billion populations, only mass media is not capable to achieve the highest tryst. Regional culture especially folk theatre form for its face-to-face persuasive nature can make sure the participation of marginalized people in developmental process.

Case Study 1

Nazariya

Nazariya in Gujarat, believe that theatre is an alternative conflict resolution mechanism. It is the medium, which is known for its immense power to create question, debate and discussion among audience and the impact lasts more than the production time.

Nazariya uses theater is different forms in schools, colleges and with young people to create a culture of gender equality, communal tolerance and religious expression for social change in the city. They have experimented various forms of theatre; among them most successful was 'Forum Theatre', which gives the audience much more than just being a spectator. It initiates actual dialogue and helps in drawing solutions from the audience themselves.

Issue: Gender Discrimination

Operational area of Nazariya is Ahmedabad, mostly in the old part of the city (economically downtrodden). In various spaces, like Gomtipur, Behrampura, Juhapuraetc, they organized Forum Theatre. The issue was 'Gender Discrimination', in this form of theatre; the play stops at a crucial moment and asks audience, 'Have you been there, what would have your reaction?' People from the audience come to the stage and enacts tentative solutions on behalf of the community.

They have experimented participatory mapping along with Forum Theatre in colleges and communities on the issue of gender violence.

Nazariya experiments the approaches of participatory mapping in F.D. Girls College, where the students came up with a map where they identified areas, which according to them are harassment prone areas near their college. At first all the students were divided into groups according to the areas they come from, like: Juhapura, Jamalpur, Vatva, Saraspur, Gomtipur, Danilimda, Behrampura, Raikhad, Rakhiyal and Bombay Hotel, etc. It was a participatory process where each of the group members discussed and came up with a map collectively. The whole idea of this mapping was to identify the types of harassment they face during their travel, the reason behind such behaviour and thus identify the areas. After identifying the harassment prone zone, they spoke about the common types of harassment they face, day in and day out, identified the trend the general age group of the perpetrators and why they do this.

This mapping activity was followed by a forum theatre, where volunteers of Nazariya from college and community enacted a play where they depicted three situations of harassment (more or less similar what the student have said earlier) where each situation demanded three suggestions from the audience/students. In each situation, girls came up with multiple solutions and enacted the whole situation in front of others. From that point their next session was initiated, where they themselves developed their plan of action to stop such ill practices in their *mohalla* and how could they become more vocal about this problem.

Same activity took place in one of their community intervention area: Juhapura. It is considered as the largest Muslim ghetto in Asia. The political situation of Juhapura is volatile than in comparison to the other areas of Ahmedabad. We work on some of the IDP (Internally Displaced People, after 2002 Riot) Colonies of Juhapura where the issues of gender discrimination and religious tolerance are more prominent.

Issue: Religious Tolerance

- Another designing form was organizing rally with Forum Theatre. They organized several forum theatres in various locations of Ahmedabad, after ethnic clash broke in the North East. On the last day of theatre, they organized a rally after the event.
- They have organized a peace rally, where religious leaders actually spoke about the problem on the sphere of religious tolerance.

Case Study 2

Kolkata Creative Art Performer

Kolkata Creative Art Performer in West Bengal started their journey in 2000. Young students of this group assume that theatre can change life. Safdar Hashmi once said, 'If we can't take big theatre to the people, we can take small theatre to them'. According to this philosophy, they continue their venture of street theatre by using Badal Sircar's 'third theatre' form.

Issue: Health Communication

Pulse Polio is an immunization programme by Government of India for children from 0 to 5 years to eradicate polio and to make polio-free India. During the initial years, in many parts of Bengal, parents did not agree to take pulse polio. Murshidabad is one of the districts where this problem was very high. seventy per cent of the total populations was Muslim. Generation after generation they worked in *bidi* industry. About 80 per cent of the population was rigid that their children would not take this immunization due to lack of awareness. With the help of UNICEF Kolkata, Creative Art Performer started campaigning for pulse polio. They performed street theatre in Suti I, Suti II, Samsherganj and other blocks of Murshidabad. The impact was huge. Their performance gained highest level of mass acceptance and the situation changed dramatically. After the performances, the percentage of rigid population came down to only 2–3 per cent from 80 per cent.

These groups also effectively used street theatre to instigate awareness against the diseases like leprosy, tuberculosis, malaria, HIV AIDS, etc. In every district of West Bengal, they perform theatre for the prevention of HIV AIDS and create awareness of birth control, family planning. In three months, they have performed 914 shows in 36 districts of Bihar to disseminate the ideas of family planning by using participatory approaches.

Issue: Women Trafficking

A recent survey shows that girl and women trafficking shape a major complication in Indian society. In West Bengal, the majority of the victims of this illegal exploitation are from the district of South 24 parganas, North 24 parganas and Murshidabad. Kolkata Creative Art Performer organized street theatre in different areas of Sandeshkhali, Laksmikantapur, Sundarban and also in the districts of Howrah, East Midnapore, etc.

Issue: Alcohol and Drug Addiction

Rangabelia is a village of Gosaba block which is situated in Sundarban. The business of illegal liquor locally known as *cholai* is a common problem in South 24 parganas. In this village, Kolkata Creative Art Performer organized theatre on prevention of drug addiction and alcoholism. After watching this theatre local people took initiative to organize and perform theatre on this issue in many villages of Sundarban. This participatory approach made a silent revolution. Village people of Rangabelia with the help of local police destroyed the illegal shops of Rangabelia.

Issue: Sex Worker's Right and Health

Kolkata Creative Art Performer worked with Durbar Mahila Samanwaya Committee which is a strong organization of women's right, sex-worker's right, anti-human trafficking, HIV/AIDS prevention. On behalf of this organization, Kolkata Creative Art Performer highlighted these issues by using theatre effectively.

Issue: Child Labour

In the Dhapa Dumping Ground of Kolkata the wastes of city are dumped. Children of this 450 acres area collect scraps of plastic, metal from the mountain of garbage and sell them. It is their only way of earning. Kolkata Creative Art Performer used theatre to give slum children of this area non-formal education on their right, child labour, hygiene, etc.

Case Study 3

Ashokenagar Natyamukh

Ashokenagar Natyamukh used theatre in a different and alternative way. Their experiment on how theatre will be effective in modern educational system usher a new era. They applied theatre in formal education in a form of theatre therapy.

Issue: Pressure of Students

Ashokenagar Natyamukh adapted theatre as a weapon against illiteracy, drop-out. They devoted theatre for development of effective educational system. They performed in schools and colleges based on the topic of curriculum. By using this experimental technique they are able to eradicate the pressure of vast curriculum. In today's rat race, a student feels mounting pressure. Depression, suicidal activities rise among school and college students. Ashokenagar Natyamukh reinforced theatre in Ashokenagar Boys Secondary School, Jawhar Navodaya Vidyalaya, Haripal GD Institution, Nahata Jogendranath Mondal Smriti Mahavidyalaya, Gurudas College, Gour Mahavidyalaya, Kaliachak College, and Agrasen Mahavidyalaya. Their effort enhanced understandability and clarity of this topic. It induced student's interest about curriculum. Students achieved education, information in form of entertainment without any stress which is very significant for student's mental health.

Issue: Unprotected Children

Unprotected children throughout Kolkata face much exploitation. With the help of Humanity Association, Ashokenagar Natyamukh executed theatrical performance for street children and children of sex workers. They promoted literacy campaign by using theatre in Sonagachi, Bagmari, Ultodanga, Koley market and in many different areas in Kolkata. Their aim was to focus their problems and social right. Their participatory approach evoked a great upsurge among the unprotected children.

Conclusion

Theatre is a mechanism of social analysis which can make deep impression among the audience. The principle of participatory communicational nature of theatre is very much impressive. The need-based approaches of theatre in India empower the marginalized people of grassroot level. When mass media of India closely attached with commercialization, the years old traditional media continued work for micro-agenda. Theatrical form of communication enriches individual's development as well as community development which is significant for overpopulated country like India. Conventional theatre along with new experimentation enhances the growth of development process in India. Multiple theatre groups throughout the country deal with different issues. Plurality of expression in theatre strengthens the democratic base of India.

Works Cited

Boal, Augusto. *Theatre of the Oppressed*. UK: Pluto Press, 1979. Print.

Dharwadker, Aparna. *Theatres of Independence: Drama, Theory and Urban Performance in India since 1947*. USA: University of Iowa Press, 2005. Print.

Epskamp, Kees. *Theatre for Development: An Introduction to Context, Application and Training*. Netherlands: Zed Books, 2006. Print.

Freire, Paulo. *Pedagogy of the Oppressed*. London and New York: The Continuum, 2005. Print.

Ghosh, Subir. *Mass Communication: An Indian Perspective*. Kolkata: Sahitya Samsad, 2009. Print.

Melkote, Srinivas, Leslie Steeves. *Communication for Development in the Third World: Theory and Practice for Empowerment*. New Delhi: SAGE, 2001. Print.

Mukhopadhyay, Durgadas. *Folk Arts and Social Communication*. New Delhi: Publications Division, 1994. Print.

Odhiambo, Christopher. *Theatre for Development in Kenya in Search of an Effective Procedure and Methodology*. Germany: Eckersdorf Thielmann and Breitinger, 2008. Print.

Quebral, C. Nora. 'What Do You Mean by Development Communication?' *International Development Review* 15.2 (1972): 25–28. Print.

Sen, Geeti. *Crossing Boundaries*. India: Orient Longman, 1997. Print.

Varadpande, M.L. *History of Indian Theatre*. New Delhi: Abhinav Publications, 2005. Print.

Webliography

http://www2.warwick.ac.uk/fac/arts/theatre_s/research/jnu/resources/bengali_theatre_the_end_of_the_colonial_traditionsamik_bandyopadhyay.pdf

http://www.indiatogether.org/2011/may/soc-sircar.htm

http://nirc.nanzan-u.ac.jp/nfile/1119

http://en.wikipedia.org/wiki/Theatre_of_ancient_Greece

http://en.wikipedia.org/wiki/Theatre_of_India
http://en.wikipedia.org/wiki/Paulo_Freire
http://en.wikipedia.org/wiki/Theatre_of_India
http://en.wikipedia.org/wiki/Indian_People's_Theatre_Association
http://en.wikipedia.org/wiki/Safdar_Hashmi
http://en.wikipedia.org/wiki/Bijon_Bhattacharya
http://en.wikipedia.org/wiki/Nabanna_(drama)
http://www.cwu.edu/~robinsos/ppages/resources/Theatre_History/Theahis_1.html
http://www.spunk.org/texts/art/sp000338.html
http://www.teaterunionen.se/Pdf/Theatre%20for%20development
http://pib.nic.in/feature/fe0399/f3003991.html

Section D

Partitoned Lives in Cinema and Theatre: Recent Perspectives

15

16

Partitioned Lives and the Cinematic Quest for Redressal

MANJINDER KAUR WRATCH

The end of the British Raj in August 1947 led to the birth of two sovereign nation-states, India and Pakistan. This truncation referred to as the Partition of the Indian sub-continent was based on the assumption of a deep-rooted animosity between Muslims and Hindus. The last British Viceroy Lord Mountbatten in 1947 pushed through the hasty decision to separate the South Asian population according to religion, undermining the belief that a united India could exist in the face of diversity, rendering a crushing blow to the national *imaginaire* that advocates and preaches the mantra, 'transcend all difference', invested in the slogan 'unity in diversity'. It was beyond comprehension that how a nation built around certain common symbols and shared ideals was so easily fragmented. In fact, the majority of British India's population did not strive for or initiate the Partition, most were even oblivious to it. Muhammad Ali Jinnah and Jawaharlal Nehru, the leaders of the Muslim League and the Indian National Congress respectively took advantage of Britain's precipitous and ill-planned disengagement from India. The Partition of British India was a pre-requisite for Nehru and Jinnah both: for Jinnah the dream of a separate Muslim state, and for Nehru that of India's independence from the British colonial rule, which he would proudly proclaim on 15 August 1947.

The Partition of the Indian sub-continent in 1947 is one of the great tragedies which compels one to search for the larger meanings. Roughly a million people were butchered in murderous riots; 10 to 12 millions lost their homes and became hapless refugees. Another feature of this violence was the large scale abduction of over one lakh women by men of the other community. It was such a barbaric phase when people became temporarily insane, the absence of reason transformed kind, loving and rational beings into violent, unthinking, instinctive savages.

As a single most defining moment that affects modern national life in the most of South Asia, the Partition of 1947 has received scant scrutiny until recently when subaltern studies historians and feminists initiated the practice of studying 'history from below' or 'the underside history'. Recent works on feminist historiography draw on oral testimonies of women who lived through the carnage of 1947, capturing a hidden dimension of that experience. In mainstream historical accounts. however, there was a wilful forgetting or a subtle reframing of the Partition episode as an anomalous chapter in the nation's career. The engaging point here is: If 1947 was an aberrant moment within a grand narrative of national unity and amity, then how do we explain the recurring riots?

Urvashi Butalia takes note of this silence on the Partition. She enunciates: 'In India there is no institutional memory of Partition, the State has not seen fit to construct any memorials, to mark any particular places – as has been done, say, in the case of holocaust memorials or memorials for the Vietnam war' (Daiya: 7). Erecting memorials are acts of recognition of the suffering caused to others through no fault of theirs. Such a remembrance serves as an intervention in the history of violence, injustice, and oppression, and through it we can discern the outlines of a universal form of bonding memory that is committed to certain fundamental norms of human dignity. Jan Assmann, the main theorist of cultural memory comments in this regard by citing the case of holocaust memorial in Berlin:

> Auschwitz, the darkest chapter of German history, has long since assumed the dimension of a 'normative past' that must not and cannot be allowed to fall into oblivion under any circumstances because its importance goes well beyond the

> memories of victims and perpetrators; it has become an instance of universalized bonding memory and the founding element of a global secular religion that is concerned with democracy and human dignity. Its commandment is 'never again, Auschwitz', and this means not just that there should never again be victims of a German fascism, but that we – and this ' we' includes humanity – wish never again to be perpetrators, fellow travellers or electors of a regime that tramples on human dignity. (Assmann: 23)

Quite contrary to Assmann's critique, India's first Prime Minister Jawaharlal Nehru censored published and filmic accounts of Partition, as these were seen to incite communal conflicts. Erecting memorials with a redemptive and therapeutic resolve was a far cry in the above scenario. Kavita Daiya makes a conviction in this context; she makes it coherent that whilst censorship was practized with motives of peaceful inter-community relations, the leaders themselves failed to exercise any discretion in this regard. It has been a general official tendency to bury the truth in the name of law and order, negating the possibility of social accountability as well as affective restitution. Daiya annotates how our first President, Dr Rajendra Prasad, went up to the extent of terming the minoritized Muslim citizen-subject in India as a 'problem'. His words signal the official state discourse which favoured the ethnicization of Indian citizenship as 'Hindu', despite the country's tall claims of commitment to secular democracy. In his introduction to a collection of Mahatma Gandhi's essays, Dr Prasad asserts:

> It is remarkable how by his honest and fearless advocacy of communal unity he has enraged many of the Muslims and a negligible few among the Hindus … . This is the long and tragic history of Mahatma Gandhi's attempts to establish Hindu-Muslim unity which ended with the establishment of Pakistan on the one side and his supreme sacrifice on the other. The problem has, however, not been solved in spite of the creation of Pakistan. We have still some 40 million of Muslims in this country, spread all over the vast area of what is called India today. (qtd in Daiya: 8)

Hence, it is comprehensible from the above remarks that the leaders of the highest ranks too, irresponsibly promoted the notion that India is for Hindus. In addition, various religious minorities are welcome within the space of the nation-state as long as they accept this claim. When the state machinery itself is biased, it cannot claim to be an ethical agent of conflict resolution. Rational restitution of social order seems impossible under such leadership. Rather than finding ways of coexistence of ethnically-varied communities within the same state, our chosen representatives in their quest for easy governance found respite in agreeing to suggestions of redrawing state boundaries, so that each territory corresponds to one sovereign community. Our leaders failed to share the vision that for every Pakistan there is one Bangladesh around the corner. Partition became a reality because our leaders had failed to manoeuvre politics as an exercise of negotiation, as the technique of neutralizing tensions, as the way of creatively engaging with the aspirations of ordinary people. Not only was the country split into two halves but also the Muslim community was divided into two nations; almost all the communities were hopelessly fragmented.

The truncation of India brought along with it an unleashing of violence and death, mass reshuffle of populations, and severing of age-old roots leaving behind it a complex baggage of traumatic memories. Partition is the root cause of all our national woes. Memories of those violence-torn times of 1947 continue to shape our contemporary national experience, as we see its aftermath being enacted in the form of instances of communal riots, border skirmishes and politics of divisiveness that still categorizes and separates us in the name of regions and religions. This experience casts its long, disquieting shadow on public consciousness pushing its victims, witnesses and inheritors alike in an abyss of unspeakable sadness. But sheer silence cannot evade the morbid reality nearly 70 years after the Partition of the Indian sub-continent in 1947 for we see the redundant resurfacing of madness of hatred in the name of religion.

The anti-Sikh carnage of 1984 in the nation's capital was one such man-made calamity of interminable dimension. Similar mayhem was let loose in the form of Godhra train carnage in Gujarat and the ensuing anti-Muslim pogroms in the birthplace of Gandhi, celebrated and beheld with obeisance the world over for his psalm of truth and non-violence. Making sense of the crushing experiences requires narrative operations, creating space for memory marked by its amenability to endless revisions, to emerge as the favoured narrative organization of human experience and a timely alternative to history. Memory bears the promise of healing through recovery of our connections to the real. Bhaskar Sarkar delineates the revolutionary role of shared memories of oppression, and feels the exigency of tracking and interrogating the cultural memorialization of Partition and other traumatic genocides to offer reparations to those afflicted with it:

> In recent years, memories of suffering – of slaves, colonized subjects, displaced tribes, queer groups, and, in some cases, of their descendants – have become the basis of collective empowerment. In the place of liberal-humanist empirical suppositions, in place of essential ideals, we now espouse a critical pragmatism. This, then, is the new politics of trauma and memory that informs studies of various genocides and war atrocities, and claims of symbolic and material recompense made on behalf of the wronged of the earth. (13)

Cinematic revivification involves a cultural recall exposing traumatic experiences of the past to critical interrogation thereby opening new vistas of social transformation. This scholarly treatise through the oculus of 'reflective cinema' vis-à-vis many critically acclaimed movies, ventures to descry the pathos of sectarian violence and its aftermath, apportioned on the inculpable and vulnerable populace.

II

The field of cinema addresses the most anxious impulses of our psychic and social life. Screen representations of the Partition, the infamous 1984 anti-Sikh pogroms and the Gujarat carnage of 2002, not only foster an affective historical consciousness that supplements standard history writing but also have the potential to complicate official versions. Cinema in general has a remarkable ability to preserve and record, what happened in the past defeating the ephemeral nature of human experience. In an essay titled 'Death Every Afternoon', Andre Bazin, a film theorist, mentions about cinema's potential of mummifying time (Bazin: 30).

The theme of the Partition had a fleeting presence in the post-Independence popular cinema of the 1950s and 1960s. There were oblique and serendipitous depictions of the experience of the Partition in the form of passing allusions to character's orphan or refugee status. Most of the writers, artists and filmmakers deemed the experience to be too brutal and debilitating to be brought alive on screen. As veteran producer-director B.R. Chopra shares: 'It was such an experience, that those who lived through it could not go on living, if they were made to endure it a second time on screen'(Sarkar: 97). Only a handful of Hindi films featured explicit representations of the Partition: they included *Lahore* (1949), *Nastik* (1954), and *Chhalia* (1960) (qtd. in Jain: 235). *Lahore,* released within two years of truncation, mourns the banishment of an exile from his homeland, during the times of 1947 Partition upheaval. The film succeeds in translating on screen the nostalgia and longing experienced by the refugees who were forced to abandon their homes by the sheer turn of events.

Yash Chopra's debut film, *Dhool Ka Phool* (1959), apotheosizes communal harmony and beseeches a tangible secularism as is mirrored in the song of the movie: *'Tu Hindu Banega Na Musalman Banega'* ('You will grow up neither a Hindu nor a Muslim'), conveying the literatim of 'humanity as the biggest religion' for the young and old to follow alike. Here, I am in accord with Bhaskar Sarkar's line of thought that in acts and undertakings like this, 'cinema appropriates the figure of the foundling in a bid to go beyond the collective wound and to invoke a new order of identity' (113), as the main protagonist of the movie, an old man, brings up a foundling abandoned by his unwed mother and conditions the young boy to rise above bigoted religious affiliations, and instead embrace humanitarianism.

Chopra's second film *Dharamputra* (1961) repeats the same theme, where the abandoned son of an unwed Muslim woman raised by the Hindu neighbours, grows up to be a fanatic Hindu and tries to attack the home of his biological Muslim mother during the riots of 1947. The boy's psychic demoralization on learning the truth is brought to the fore with the aid of a montage showing scenes of riots, blood-filled streams and disoriented refugees. The film upholds the secularist ideal that religious identity is a matter of culture and is not defined by blood ties only.

The period of 1970s saw the national crisis in the form of declaration of a state of national emergency in 1975 when Mrs Indira Gandhi's government suspended most civil and political rights of the citizens in the name of governance. This intensified the unrest which was already brewing up in the people, who were frustrated with her increasingly autocratic rule. The crisis of the state nurtured further, a sense of disillusionment in the common people, who sensed betrayal by their leader and the organization. The emergence of Bangladesh through the splitting of Pakistan in 1971 revived wounds of the earlier bifurcation. These difficult times catalysed a fresh phase in the career of the nation marked by a great openness on the part of its denizens to face past traumas and engage with hitherto taboo issues, en route literature and cinema on the above subjects.

Garam Hawa (1973), based on an unpublished short story of Ismat Chugtai with a script written by Kaifi Azmi and directed by M.S. Sathyu was produced in this phase of new Indian Cinema marked by its heightened sense of realism. The movie depicts the quandary of Muslims in post-Partition India. It narrates the tale of two brothers, Salim Mirza and Halim Mirza, who live with their families and their old mother in their ancestral home in Agra. Salim (played on screen by actor Balraj Sahni) runs the shoe factory inherited from his father whereas Halim is a Muslim League activist. Soon after the Partition, Halim decides to migrate to Pakistan with his family, while Salim refuses to abandon his birthplace.

Salim's optimism is gradually shaken as he undergoes financial crisis and finds difficulty in running his family business. His son, Sikander fails to get a job despite his good academic record. Salim Mirza's factory too is set on fire. Money-lenders and banks refuse to lend him business loans, fearing that he too will go away to Pakistan. Most of his and the families problems are centred around his Muslim identity. He has to vacate his ancestral home too as Halim, the legal owner of the house has migrated to Pakistan. Salim Mirza and his family are confined to the cramped space of a rented house that too after paying a whole year's rent in advance. The film conveys how the Partition ripped apart victim communities into an abyss of alienation, making them 'exiles' in their own land, dragooning them to painstakingly and woefully live on the margins of society.

Disheartened in the above circumstances, the Mirza's are forced to leave for Pakistan. On their way to the railway station to catch the train to Pakistan, the family runs into a political procession. Several marchers of the procession are bearing red flags emblematic of their solidarity to a communist programme of an innovative breakthrough amidst these travails. The messages carried by the protestors on the placards, state their quest to fight economic injustice through amalgamation beyond the boundaries of religion and caste. The film ends on a hopeful note of a secular class struggle. Salim Mirza and Sikander are impressed with this initiative of collective action and decide to stay back in India. Salim Mirza joins the procession, instructing the carriage driver to carry his wife back home.

Another decisive turn came in the mid–1980s: militants in Punjab spearheaded a strong separatist movement demanding Khalistan as a homeland for the Sikh community and turned the venerated Golden Temple into their headquarters. Prime Minister Indira Gandhi in her bid to end terrorism sent the Army into the Golden Temple of Amritsar offending the religious sentiments of Sikhs. The violation of the sacred space angered Sikhs across the world. The effect of this action came forth in the form of assassination of Indira Gandhi by her Sikh bodyguards on 31 October 1984. Over the next few days, Sikhs all over the north India especially in Delhi became the targets of organized sectarian violence. It was in this context that the parallel cinema director, Govind Nihalini's, *Tamas*, based on an award winning Hindi novel of Bhisham Sahni by the same name was presented by the state-owned television network, Doordarshan in 1988. *Tamas* solely holds religious fundamentalism responsible for sowing the seeds of hatred and violence among otherwise peace loving people. Unfortunately, the tele-series ran into controversies, a series of petitions were filed including the one with the Supreme Court accusing the director for promoting disharmony and feelings of ill will and hatred among different communities through the serial.

The irate mobs pillaged several television stations while the artists, intellectuals and social activists backed the series and the creators. The Bombay High Court Division Bench as well as the Supreme Court ruled in favour of the broadcast and recognized the need to work through traumatic experiences in order to break recurring cycles of episodes of warring communities. The judges also acknowledged the possibility that representation of trauma may be affective as collective mourning. Here, we need to take cognizance of a quote from a legal opinion of 1971 which clearly delineates the criteria for ascertaining whether a particular cultural text promotes enmity or hatred: 'our standards must be so framed that we are not reduced to a level where the protection of the least capable and the most depraved amongst us determines what the morally healthy cannot view or read' (Sarkar: 253–54).

The 1990s witnessed strained relations between the Hindu and the Muslim communities due to attempts by Hindu fundamentalists to build a temple in Ayodhya at the site of Babri Masjid after demolishing the mosque in December 1992. In the same decade, Indian and Pakistani armies fought in the remote Kargil region for two months in the summer of 1999. Round-the-clock coverage of the war by the media fostered strong feelings of patriotism blended with anti-Pakistan sentiments in the natives, the people on the other side of the border too nurtured corresponding passions. The films of this period and the next decade not only portrayed feelings of anger and revulsion for anti-Indian sentiments shared by Pakistan's state machinery but also bear witness to the common predicament of loss experienced by the victims of state-sponsored terrorism, be it the anti-Sikh pogroms of Delhi or anti-Muslim pogroms of Gujarat.

Naseem (1995), written and directed by Saeed Mirza, nephew of the famous poet Kaifi Azmi, was produced jointly by National Film Development Corporation and Doordarshan. The film raises concerns about the dwindling future of a secular national community in India with further marginalization of the minority groups, post-Babri Masjid demolition, accompanied with rise of Hindu fundamentalism. The protagonist of the film, a teenage girl named Naseem shares a strong emotional bond with her ailing grandfather (played on screen by Kaifi Azmi). The grandfather regales his granddaughter with enchanting memories of his happy life in Agra before 1947. Naseem's elder brother Mustaq and his militant friend Zafar react angrily to his grandfather's nostalgic escapism. The film ends on a pensive note in terms of the death of the grandfather in the early hours of 6 December, concomitant with a black day which broadcasted in the world arena the conceited secularism practised in India, when Hindu fundamentalism in its bid to reclaim the mythological Ram *Janmabhoomi* demolished the Babri mosque in Ayodhya, Uttar Pradesh, sparking off another set of incidents of communal rioting. Instead of being read as the defeat of secular politics in India, the film needs to be remembered for its alive sense of 'utopian dimension of secularism' (Sarkar: 291) that persists in the memory of many like the beloved *dadajan* of Naseem.

Another cinematic venture of the same period, *Train to Pakistan* (1997) based on a popular English novel written by Khushwant Singh in 1956 and co-produced by Britain's Channel Four is blamed for its lack of freshness and originality. Set in the rural background of Mano Majra, a border village on the Indian side of Punjab, the film narrates how the village's communal amity is threatened as it comes in the grip of the Partition turmoil. The traumatic experience is heightened when one morning the villagers spot an unscheduled train as it arrives from the West loaded with the rotting corpses of Hindu and Sikh passengers.

The film failed to impress as it sounded more like a rehearsal of the same elements as were present in the novel, despite being released about four decades after the publication of the novel. On the same count, *Earth* (1999) an adaptation of the 1992 English novel, *Crackling India* by the Pakistan-born writer Bapsi Sidhwa and directed by Indian-Canadian filmmaker, Deepa Mehta with its tableau-like shots of visual representation of riots, forced abduction of the women and weary migrants on foot or in bullock carts served well the maxim, 'old wine in a new bottle'. With nothing new to offer to the canon of Partition films, the movie seemed like a recycled product assembled with raw materials gathered from Partition photographs, films, fiction and oral-histories. Both the movies, aimed at an international audience, in their allusion to other harrowing experiences like holocaust, indubitably threaten to erase the peculiarities of 1947. Such cultural repetitions tend to create a void in the discursive turn, denying a deeper understanding of the Partition fall-out in the contemporary context (Sarkar: 280–86).

A Season Outside (1998), a documentary by Amar Kanwar, brings into focus the animosity between the two sibling nation-states, India and Pakistan. The film chronicles the complex ties that bind the people of two nationalities through the 'twilight ritual' that is observed daily at sundown at the Wagah check post on the India-Pakistan border. Bhaskar Sarkar ponders over this ceremonial exercise which involves haunting exchange of looks by the members of the two armed forces, while scores of people stare each other silently across the fences: 'I will argue that footage of the twilight ritual intimates a melancholic ambivalence, an ambivalence that retains a possibility for working through – each transforming – the prejudices and expressions of belligerence to something more affirmative' (33). Surely, the deep sense of loss, palpable in the mournful eyes of people across both sides of the border demands a healing touch.

Gadar (2001), directed by Anil Sharma, manages to portray the burgeoning trend of violence during the times of Partition realistically while also staging the sprouting of love beyond the confines of religion and nationality. The audience witness at the onset of the movie how an affable bond evolves between Sakina, a rich and elegant Muslim girl studying at a convent school in Shimla, and Tara Singh, a Sikh truck driver who totes provisions to her school. Friendship further blossoms into inmost reverence as Tara Singh comes along as a seraph and rescues Sakina from an irate mob during the riot-torn times of Partition. Estranged Sakina starts living in Tara's house as her parents and brother are feared dead while on a train to Pakistan. The movie avails the regular motif of trains as 'trains of death' and 'rolling coffins' during the tumultuous times of 1947. Love surmounts differences of class and religion as Sakina reciprocates Tara's fondness and care. They stay happily married till the time Sakina establishes contact with her father way back in Pakistan, who is now the mayor of Lahore. The highly educated and liberal Muslim family is ready to accept their daughter unlike many parents of those times who exterminated or disowned their sullied daughters. But Tara Singh, the Jat labourer, is unacceptable as a son-in-law to them. Amidst pro-Indian and severe Pakistan-bashing speeches, Tara Singh lands up in Lahore and blasts his way to bring his family back home in India safely.

J.P. Dutta directed *Line of Control (L.O.C)*, produced in 2003, is based on the Kargil war of 1999 and features with an alacrity 'Operation Vijay' and 'Battle of Tololing' around the Line of Control. The movie registers a shift in sites of mourning as the inceptive anguish of Partition gets replaced by the recurrent ordeal that Pakistan has augmentedly become for India. The horrendous battle scenes, the sonority of blazing and rattling machine-guns, and roaring grenades recite the monstrosity of war. Dutta *mimeos* the icy heights and the adamantine topography that the soldiers confronted indomitably. Altogether, it is a movie backed with a detailed research on the background of war which parades both the mechanical accoutrements of it as well as articulates the human agony on being ravaged by such violence.

Way Back Home (2003) is a Bengali documentary by Supriyo Sen featuring his own parents' journey way back to Barishal, Bangladesh, their ancestral home, from where they were uprooted in 1950, in the context of mounting communal tensions. Sen, in a mood of nostalgia, documents abundantly the architectural as well as natural spaces of both Calcutta and Barishal. The old city of Calcutta with its alleys, corridors, balconies and claustrophobic staircases is shot with equal fascination, as are the green grooves, wide rivers and open fields of Barishal.

The film's finale reveals Sen's mother's search for her long-lost cousin, Kamala in Barishal, who was shunned by her family as she married her Muslim beau and converted to Islam. After a long search, Sen's mother locates Kamala's daughter Minu from whom she learns about Kamala's demise. Minu celebrates her mother's legacy and takes pride in her mother's syncretic lifestyle, despite the rising tide of Islamic fundamentalism. The movie tries to convey that in spite of the Partition and other repeated social conflagrations, secular harmony still remains an ideal (Sarkar: 297).

Khamosh Pani (2003), a film directed by Pakistani filmmaker Sabiha Sumar and produced with German and French collaboration, focuses on the 'Talibanization of Pakistan' during the reign of General Zia-ul-Haq. Ayesha, the main protagonist of the movie is a middle-aged widow who stays with her son, Salim in a small village, Charkhi of Pakistan. Salim leads a wayward life and falls prey to the extremist Islamic ideology. The arrival of a group of Sikh pilgrims to the village help in disclosing to the audiences, as well as Salim, Ayesha's true ethnic identity – Ayesha who was Veeran before the Partition belonged to the Sikh community and was abducted by a Muslim in the context of Partition. It was a regular practice during those times to target women of other communities, and to safeguard this, men killed their own women to preserve their honour. Women's purity till date is considered paramount to the strength and honour of a society. In a paradigm shift, Veeran refuses her father's demands for martyrdom at the site of the village well and chooses to live life on her own terms. Later through a dramatic turn of events, hell is let loose on Ayesha as her fanatic son abandons her on learning about her Sikh identity. She cannot bear this loss of love from her son and the rest of the village people. Broken down, she jumps into the same well she refused to jump into, 32 years earlier. The silent waters of the well swallow her.

Religious extremism forces Ayesha to make the sacrifice that she never was ready to make. The film succeeds in interweaving in its narrative the twin issues of the Partition and religious extremism. Partition is not a self-contained event; it continues to cast its sinister shadow and has far-reaching repercussions.

Pinjar (2003), directed by Chandra Prakash Dwivedi, based on a Punjabi novel of the same name, penned down by the legendary Amrita Pritam, addresses the traumatic dislocation of women in the background of religious and clan feuds during the days of the Partition of India and the period prior to it. The dislocated and abducted women's ties with their families were broken and the physical and emotional support they got from their natal homes was also appropriated. Women were doubly displaced – from the homeland and from the family. The film is a salutation to the female will for survival and celebrates Pooro's progression from being homeless to an active agency, from a skeleton to substance, from self to others. Probing the silences surrounding the gendered violence experienced by abducted women, it also discusses, the violated women's relationship to their loved ones, and their own identities in order to make sense of the inscriptions that the violence has left on their bodies and through this, arbitrate their survival. *Pinjar* acts analogous to *Khamosh Pani* in redefining parameters of honour and chastity for the abducted woman who has been merely looked at as 'a symbol of honour' since ages by patriarchy. Pooro, the main protagonist of the movie, by throwing off the mantle of victimhood, transforms not just her life, but also the lives of other women who became sacrificial lambs at the altar of honour. Gradually Pooro, a brave heart accepts her new identity, even when life gives her an opportunity to escape; she prefers to devote herself to Rashida, her Muslim husband. Pooro's acceptance of Rashida is a reflection of female loyalty as well as a challenge to socially imposed religious barriers. Pooro had been reduced to a mere skeleton – a woman without substance but her instinct for survival and her resilience transforms her into a body – an evolved woman who becomes an active agency for social change.

Amu (2005), the film by filmmaker Shonali Bose, brings alive and chronicles a realistic picture of the 1984 anti-Sikh violence. As discussed earlier, insanity ran amuck after the assassination of Prime Minister Indira Gandhi by two of her Sikh bodyguards, targeting innumerable scrupulous Sikhs on the pretext of being of the same ethnicity as the assassins. Denouncing the official narrative which proposed to sheepishly hide this pogrom under the garb of Hindu-Sikh violence and the so-called 'public anger', the movie blatantly highlights the role of the whole state machinery behind the killings. The movie makes clear its political and social concerns while narrating its main protagonist Kajori Roy's (fondly called Kaju) search for her roots. Kaju, the adopted daughter of Keya Roy, a Delhi-born, civil rights activist in Los

Angeles discovers how her Sikh father and younger brother were immolated alive by the state-sponsored goons in the riots while her mother hanged herself in a refugee camp.

Prior to a discussion of the film *Parzania* (2005), it is pertinent to sketch out a brief backdrop of Gujarat riots of 2002. Displeased with Bhartiya Janta Party's (BJP) abominable performance in February 2002, Uttar Pradesh assembly elections, the party's ascendant sister organizations – the Rashtriya Swayamsevak Sangh (RSS) and the more violent elements like the Vishwa Hindu Parishad (VHP) and the Bajrang Dal, traced the roots of party's electoral debacle in BJP's 'soft peddling of the Hindu chauvinist agenda under compulsions of coalition politics' (Varadarajan 4). This was considered as the ripe time for the party and its allied organizations to fall back on its innate and distinctive Ayodhya agenda, of forcibly constructing a temple dedicated to Lord Rama at the very site of Babri Masjid.

Hauling in Hindutva activists to Ayodhya was chosen as an 'inexpensive, theatrical way of generating a momentum' (Varadarajan 4). BJP MPs in Gujarat and other party ruled states exploited their political privileges to book complete railway coaches for this political mobilization. Local ministers were regularly seen flagging off train loads of inharmonious and boisterous activists to Ayodhya and; felicitating the triumphant flocks back.

On 27 February, during one such 'radical expedition', the bigoted activists ran rampage on the Godhra station as the Sabarmati Express carrying them waited there. The raucous activists got into arguments and fights with Muslim vendors and passengers, indulging further in grave misdemeanour of forcing Muslim vendors to utter 'Jai Shri Ram' and molesting young Muslim girls. This was followed by the retaliatory inflammation of S–6 coach of the Sabarmati Express, reducing to cinders some fifty-eight hapless passengers therein (Varadarajan: 5). This callous and heinous crime against the helpless passengers can never be justified however hard the provocation might have been. At the same time, this fateful incident reflects that how incendiary a government's selfish politics can turn out to be, rattling in process, a common man's peaceful world beyond repair.

Over the next few days the saffron organizations of Gujarat with buttress from the state machinery decided that all Muslims had to be taught a lesson. The then chief minister of Gujarat, Narendra Modi aired the same sentiments both on the floor of the state assembly and on state-run television on 28 February; an excerpt from his inflammatory address to the people of Gujarat is quoted here: 'I want to assure the people that Gujarat shall not tolerate any such incident. The culprits will get full punishment for their sins. Not only this, we will set an example that nobody, not even in his dreams, thinks of committing a heinous crime like this' (qtd. in Varadarajan: 8).

In the next 72 hours, an anti-Muslim pogrom of unimaginable proportions was unleashed. The state government's inaction delayed asking for the deployment of the Army till the evening of 28 February, and the Army's effective deployment was further prolonged till 3 March due to the lack of logistical support from the local authorities, giving free reins to the ghastly spree of death and destruction (Varadarajan: 9).

The film *Parzania* (2005), directed by Rahul Dholakia, documents with uber sensitivity, this post-Godhra ignominious chapter of our contemporary history. The movie simulates in a poignant yet brazen and forthright manner how during the communal carnage of Gujarat in 2002, the guardians of civil society – the political leaders, police and bureaucracy joined hands with the fanatic perpetrators in violating the citizenry rights of minorities to exist fearlessly in a secular democracy. Teesta Setalvad – a journalist and social activist, uprightly acknowledges in this regard: 'One of the most disturbing aspects of the large-scale anti-Muslim violence that convulsed Gujarat after 27 February is the manner in which the police force wilfully abandoned the state and its citizens to the depredations of homicidal mobs' (Varadarajan: 177).

The movie tries to universalize the pathos of 'sectarian strife' impugned on the innocent and peace-loving common people by featuring in prominence, the post-Godhra violence-torn world of the Peethawala family. The family includes Cyrus (Naseeruddin Shah) and Shernaz (Sarika) – an adorable Parsi couple and their two bubbly kids – Parzan and

Dilshad. Housed in a suburb of Ahmedabad, the Peethawala's and the other habitants of the society, strike a blissful existence, despite being from different ethnicities. The beautiful world of Peethawala's splinters under the impact of Godhra backlash, and the family's only son Parzan goes missing in the ensuing riotous confusion.

The penetrating portrayal of the family's predicament in such dire straits goads the audiences to condemn irresistibly and in all earnestness, 'partisan bestiality' of all kinds. Therein lays the *tour de force* of the movie.

The supporting cast of the movie includes Allan (Corin Nemec) – a disenchanted American scholar who happens to be in the 'land of Mahatma' to pursue his thesis on Gandhi's sterling philosophy of non-violence. Riot-ravaged Gujarat presents a violent picture instead. Disgusted with the dystopian world around him, Allan tries to attain peace by translating on paper, how the fanatical fire fuelled by a selfish government transformed Gandhi's paradise into a metaphoric wasteland. He brings out his thesis in a book form and titles it 'Parzan', as a tribute to little Parzan's innocent crusade for a utopian world full of chocolates and ice-creams; a world which had no place for violence in the name of religion. Both the films, *Amu* (2005) and *Parzania* (2005), will serve as a perduring social archive on the respective subjects, capable of shaking many coming generations from befalling into an amnesiac stupor on the above issues. Both equally discern how the domino effect of vengeance betwixt the extremists and the state machinery, apparelled as communal violence, continues to affect the common man's inter-community cordialities in the bargain, devastating the camaraderie shared by ordinary folks who want to live in peace and bonhomie.

Cinema, being a powerful means of cultural memorialization, pulls together the fragmentary experiences wallowing in an itinerary of forgetting, and reassembles them to create on screen a concrete past with tools of imaging. Borrowing words of Theodor Adorno: 'Working through' or 'Coming to terms' (Adorno 90) with the past requires an efficacious contact and articulation of it. Following the same course, the field of cinema engages a whole set of mass cultural practices through which people remember and make sense of traumatic experiences.

Concisely, cinematic mediations of the Partition and the anti-minority pogroms involve 'doing history from the present' – that is studying the traumatic and ugly past to draw lessons from it and to understand the reasons behind the contemporary crisis in the form of increasing truculence amongst various communities. Such connections with the past will beacon us to find ways of coexisting in a post-Partition India thronged with different communities, and to envisage and share a better world.

Works Cited

Adorno, Theodor. 'The Meaning of Working through the Past'. *Critical Models Interventions and Catchwords.* New York: Columbia University Press, 1998. 89–104. Print.

Assmann, Jan. *Religion and Cultural Memory*. California: Stanford University Press, 2006. 23. Print.

Bazin, Andre. 'Death Every Afternoon'. Trans. Mark Cohen. *Rites of Realism*: *Essays on Corporeal Cinema*. Ed. Ivone Marguelies. Durham: Duke University Press, 2002. 27–31. Print.

Butalia, Urvashi. *The Other Side of Silence: Voices from the Partition of India.* New Delhi: Penguin, 1998. Print.

Daiya, Kavita. *Violent Belongings*. New Delhi: Yoda Press, 2013. Print.

Jain, Jasbir, ed. *Reading Partition/Living Partition*. New Delhi: Rawat Publication, 2007. Print.

Mitta, Manoj. *The Fiction of Fact-Finding: Modi and Godhra*. Noida: Harper Collins, 2014. Print.

Sarkar, Bhaskar. *Mourning the Nation: Indian Cinema in the Wake of Partition*. New Delhi: Orient Blackswan, 2010. Print.

Varadarajan, Siddharth. *Gujarat: The Making of a Tragedy*. New Delhi: Penguin, 2002. Print.

Filmography

Dhool Ka Phool (1959), directed by Yash Chopra.

Dharmaputra (1961), directed by Yash Chopra.

Garam Hawa (1973), directed by M.S. Sathyu.
Naseem (1995), directed by Saeed Mirza.
A Season Outside (1998), directed by Amar Kanwar.
Earth (1999), directed by Deepa Mehta.
Gadar (2001), directed by Anil Sharma.
L.O.C. (2003), directed by J.P. Dutta.
Way Back Home (2003), directed by Supriyo Sen.
Khamosh Paani (2003), directed by Sabiha Sumar.
Pinjar (2003), directed by Chandra Prakash Dwivedi.
Amu (2005), directed by Shonali Bose.
Parzania (2005), directed by Rahul Dholakia.

17

'Do They Want to Turn Partition into a Gilbert and Sullivan Opera?'

Performing Partition as Uncanny Farce

ANINDYA RAYCHAUDHURI

In 1852, Karl Marx published, in *Die Revolution*, a German monthly magazine, an essay on social and political history called 'The Eighteenth Brumaire of Louis Bonaparte'. The opening lines have become one of the most commonly quoted passages from Marx's entire oeuvre:

> Hegel remarks somewhere that all facts and personages of great importance in world history occur, as it were, twice. He forgot to add: the first time as tragedy, the second as farce ... Men make their own history, but they do not make it just as they please; they do not make it under circumstances chosen by themselves, but under circumstances directly encountered, given and transmitted from the past. The tradition of all the dead generations weighs like a nightmare on the brain of the living. (Marx: 103)

As is often the case, Marx's careful triangulation of history, tragedy and farce, is deceptively complex. Marx was almost certainly not thinking of farce in its narrow theatrical sense, but his argument anticipates those made by subsequent scholars of theatre and performance. The way Marx illuminates the commonalities between tragedy and farce, for example, is echoed in Eric Bentley's work on theatrical farce:

> Farce brings together the direct and wild fantasies and the everyday drab realities. The interplay between the two is the

> very essence of this art – the farcical dialectic. If behind the gaiety of farce lurks a certain gravity, it is equally true that behind the gravity lurks a great deal of gaiety ... the surface of farce is grave and gay at the same time. (Bentley: 241–242)

While Bentley and Marx are concerned with very different things here, the interplay between the grave and the gay, or the tragic and farcical, as a dialectic force that assumes a will of its own, driving history forward, is common to both of these arguments. Marx's reading of history as almost possessing a will of its own, also recalls Barbara Freedman's account of the importance of plot in the theatre of farce:

> In farce, plot is more disturbing than content; there is something manic and uncontrolled about the way the plot unfolds ... we experience a loss of free will and control to something that 'bristles with menace', something that in turn threatens to lose control. (Freedman: 286)

In the specific case of historical farce, when theatre dramatizes history as farcical, historical forces can sometimes seem to take on a sovereign will – in depicting history as manic and uncontrolled, invisible forces and visible objects 'behave like characters' (Bermel: 25), as Albert Bermel has argued. As the line between animate, wilful human beings, and inanimate history and equally inanimate objects, gets blurred, these latter become 'would-be actors', and part of the force of the farcical dialectic comes from witnessing human beings reduced to being dominated by external forces beyond their control.

This theatrical trope of depicting history as beyond human control is particularly noticeable in the small, but diverse and interesting tradition of representing the 1947 India/Pakistan Partition on stage. As the British left India after 200 years of colonial rule, the country was divided along religious lines, with Punjab in the West and Bengal in the East divided in two. West Punjab and East Bengal formed the Islamic state of Pakistan, even though these two halves were separated by hundreds of miles of India, which had a Hindu majority but remained officially secular. Partition led to perhaps the single largest population migration in human history – with as many as 15 million crossing the newly-created borders. The level and scale of violence was unimaginable – as many as 2 million were killed and more than 75,000 women were abducted, raped and/or forced to convert (Talbot: 420). The emotional losses were also huge, as people had to leave ancestral homes – communities where they had been living since time immemorial. Most were unable to take any of their property with them; some deliberately chose to leave everything behind because they were convinced they could come back at a future date. Millions of people became destitute overnight. Returning home proved impossible, as conflict between the two states intensified, leading to multiple wars in the past six decades. In 1971, East and West Pakistan divided again, leading to further violence and the independence of Bangladesh. The shockwaves from that seismic event has radiated outwards through space and time – affecting both those who lived through the trauma, and those (like myself) who did not witness the events but carry with them the post-memory of the horrors that ensued. Every aspect of life in the subcontinent – religious, regional and political identities, community relationships, cinema, art and literature – has been indelibly marked by the events of more than 65 years ago. For so many people, Partition was and remains a defining moment, after which nothing would ever be the same again.

It is not surprising that such a formative event in south Asia would be represented theatrically, though it is surprising how rarely Partition plays as a whole have attracted critical attention.[1] This chapter, then, will look at a group of anglophone plays that attempt to negotiate the messy, painful and often horrifically traumatic transnational history of Partition. In this chapter, I will examine *Blood* (1989), by Harwant S. Bains, *Final Solutions* (1993) by Mahesh Dattani, *A Shaft of Sunlight* (1994), by Abhijat Joshi, *A Tainted Dawn* (1997) by Sudha Bhuchar and Kristine Landon-Smith, *Child of the Divide* (2006) by Sudha Bhuchar and *Drawing the Line* (2013) by Howard Brenton. Through my examination, I will study how these plays dramatize the history of Partition, and the politics that are at stake in so doing.

The cohort of playwrights I examine here represent very different traditions – from canonical British theatre (Brenton) to avant-garde Indian theatre (Dattani and Joshi). Bains and Bhuchar represent what Dominic Hingorani has identified as 'British Asian Theatre', which has not only 'facilitated the dramatization of the Asian subject onto the British stage but also redressed the lack of representation of Asian characters and actors' (Hingorani: 191). Tamasha Theatre Company, which Bhuchar and Landon-Smith set up in 1989, produced three of the plays I am examining – *A Shaft of Sunlight*, *A Tainted Dawn*, and *Child of the Divide*. For the generation of British Asian playwrights who came of age in the 1980s and 1990s, and who were often second generation Asians in Britain, the access to Partition was almost exclusively through their parents who in many cases migrated to Britain soon after Partition and before they had had a chance to begin to deal with this trauma. For all these playwrights, negotiating their post-memories of Partition is thus also an important part of coming to terms with their Asian identities. None of the playwrights have had direct, personal experience of Partition. They are geographically, temporally, generationally distanced from the trauma that they represent. Even Dattani and Joshi, who were based in India when writing their respective plays, are generationally distanced from 1947, as they were born many years later (Dattani in 1958, and Joshi in 1969). As such, it is not surprising that in many of these plays, this generational gap is dramatized on stage, with the action moving backwards and forwards between 1947, and the last two decades of the 20th century, when these plays were written. Partition is repeatedly enacted and re-enacted in and through these plays, as the violence and the trauma it caused is worked through in an attempt at therapeutic recuperation.

Perhaps consequently, these plays represent, to a greater or lesser extent, human beings as victims of wider, more powerful historical forces that constituted Partition. Some of these plays place greater or lesser emphasis on the human resistance, but generally speaking, they fit the characteristics of farce to the extent that they reflect what Jessica Milner Davis has termed the 'automatism' (Davis: 86) of characters in farce, or, in the words of Barbara Freedman:

> What is terrifying, automatic, and malevolent about plot in farce is an uncanny awareness of the automatic nature of unconscious representation; a quality of the anxiety of the ego under siege spills over onto the representation screen itself, and form becomes both manic and superego-ridden. (Freedman: 288)

A legitimate question might be raised at this point – why farce? In other words, given the fact that very few if any of the plays I am looking at can comfortably be put into the genre of farce, why do I begin my argument here?

First, as I go on to argue, many of the plays share more traits with the genre of farce than appears at first site. Secondly, Partition has been associated with farce, both in popular-interest and in academic accounts of the events of 1947. Thus, in *Empire in Retreat: The Story of India's Partition*? Rabia Umar Ali argues that: 'The hasty British departure pre-empted the partition of India that made a farce of planning for one of the most significant developments of the twentieth century' (Ali, backcover). In a recent, widely publicized article in *The New Yorker*, William Dalrymple has argued that: 'For all the elements of tragic farce in Manto's stories, and the tormented state of mind of Manto himself, the reality of Partition was no less filled with absurdity' (Dalrymple: para 36).

Dalrymple is certainly not alone in linking Urdu writer Saadat Hasan Manto's Partition writings to the counter-intuitive and illogical farce that Partition arguably was. Writing about perhaps the most famous short story of Partition, 'Toba Tek Singh', Ayesha Jalal has argued that: '... the madness of partition was greater than the insanity of all the inmates put together. But beyond partition there were other no less farcical turns in the postcolonial movement' (Jalal: 168). Ramu Nagappan has described Manto's writing as 'a fiction that smashes political notions with preposterous farce' (Nagappan: 87). Kavita Panjabi has argued that 'the deployment of religion as basis for the partitioning of the sub-continent was nothing short of a political farce' (Panjabi: 219).

The preponderance of this argument – across popular and academic conceptions of Partition is reminiscent of what Lucy P.

Chester has identified what she sees as 'the 'bumbler' school of historiography' (Chester: 6) – the view that Partition was mismanaged to such a degree, that the planning and execution descended into farcical chaos, of which the violence was a mere symptom. I should point out at this stage that this reading of history is certainly not accepted by most mainstream historiographers, but it still nevertheless retains great currency in commonsensical envisionings of Partition.

It is, thus, not surprising that when British playwright Howard Brenton decided to write a play about the high-politics that determined where the borders of Partition would be located, the play portrayed Partition as 'a farce, drenched in blood' (Brenton: 61). Of the playwrights I am looking at here, Howard Brenton is by far the biggest name, so it is no surprise that *Drawing the Line* achieved the highest profile. It premiered at the Hampstead Theatre, London, where it ran from 3 December 2013 to 11 January 2014. The play was sold out for the entirety of its run, and the final performance was live-streamed worldwide in partnership with *The Guardian*, following which Brenton participated in a live webchat with readers and viewers. Widely reviewed to general critical acclaim, *Drawing the Line* has come to be seen as a historically accurate dramatic representation of the events of 1947. 'Brenton knows how to make history manifest' (Billington: para 4), wrote Michael Billington in his review in *The Guardian* in a sentiment that was generally accepted by most other theatre critics.

Brenton's play is of particular interest to me in that it, perhaps more than the other plays I am looking at, fulfils most of the criteria of the classical farce. The characters are more caricatures than figures of any depth, the pace of action is deliberately frenetic, to mimic Radcliffe's brief stay in India, and the gradual disintegration of Radcliffe's state of mind is reminiscent of Freedman's reading of Shakespeare's *The Comedy of Errors*:

> But as the mood darkens, as it oscillates ever more rapidly between comic terror and romance, nightmare and wish fulfilment, we come to identify with the experiences of these erring creatures. We partake in an uncanny fantasy that we recognise at some level but fail to understand. (Freedman: 261)

I will have much more to say about the role of the uncanny in these plays, but, for the moment it is enough to point out how well Freedman's analysis applies to Brenton's play. Radcliffe's frenetic discussions with his advisors, the chaos of the Hindu, Muslim and Sikh judges shouting their demands at him – all show how Brenton structures his play following many of the rules of theatrical farce. As if this was not enough, Brenton has Radcliffe's advisors Rao Ayer and Christopher Beaumont actually quote from Marx:

> Christopher. Jesus Christ, crying aloud, God mighty alive …
> *He goes to the drinks cabinet.*
> Rao *enters.*
> Rao. This is my country these buffoons are tearing to bits.
> Christopher. The second time as farce.
> Rao. What?
> Christopher. History
> Rao. Oh, that bloody stuff. Pour me one. (Brenton: 69)

Radcliffe, Beaumont and Rao all recognize the futility of their actions at this point – the audience too realizes that these people are not in control. The convoluted logic of Partition has taken on a force of its own, and the narrative and structure of the play 'insists on its own meaninglessness and yet tantalizes us with the possibility of coherent meaning' (Freedman: 362).

Brenton is not content, however, to leave the farcical nature of his play merely hinted at. In a line that was widely used to publicize the play (including on the back cover of the Nick Hern Books edition that was published the same year the play premiered), Jinnah reacts thus to the announcement that the British Government had chosen Radcliffe as the Chairman of the Boundary Commission which would decide the border: 'Really? Have the British sent a fool? Do they want to turn Partition into a Gilbert and Sullivan opera?' (Brenton: 39)

The first point to make about this is that, for all of Brenton's claims of historical accuracy, it flagrantly disregards the established historic record about the process, which led to Radcliffe's nomination. Thus, Chester narrates from the official minutes of meetings between Mountbatten and Jinnah, prior to Radcliffe's nomination:

> Mountbatten informed Jinnah in confidence, that Cyril Radcliffe had been proposed ... Jinnah replied that he would need time to consider Radcliffe's suitability ... but that he 'knew of him and of the high reputation which he held at the Bar'. The next day Jinnah wrote to Mountbatten and indicated that Radcliffe would make an acceptable boundary commission chair. (Chester: 36)

The idea that Jinnah, with his extensive legal background, and his time spent at Lincoln's Inn, would not have even heard of Cyril Radcliffe, who was 'highly respected in British legal and governmental circles ... (and) was widely regarded as one of the finest minds of his generation' (Chester: 40–41) is frankly ludicrous. It might have suited Brenton's purposes as a dramatist to portray Radcliffe as a complete outsider, but, in this case, at least, Brenton has not been 'true to the characters, and the views, of the main leaders', (Wiegand: para 7) whatever his protestations to the contrary.

The reference to Gilbert and Sullivan is also a little odd. On the one hand, and in some ways, Brenton's version of the theatre of farce follows Gilbert's own Savoy Operas in a surprisingly similar manner. As Mike Leigh has written:

> ... it is their dark side, their hard edge, that so distinguishes the Savoy Operas. Perhaps they may more usefully be described as grotesque operas ... Gilbert undoubtedly anticipated the Theatre of the Absurd ... He merely holds up his mirror to the world, and reflects on its madness. (Leigh *x*)

It is easy to see that this is actually quite close to what Brenton is attempting to do in his own play. Brenton's depiction of Radcliffe suffering from diarrhoea is a case in point. In this (as in much else) Brenton recalls W.H. Auden's famous poem about Partition: 'the weather was frightfully hot,/And a bout of dysentery kept him constantly on the trot' (Auden: 804). Like Auden, Brenton derives humour from the clichéd British reaction to the tropics, and the various solutions proposed by the Indians. As Rao says, 'It's two different philosophies' 'flush right through' or 'block up' (Brenton: 52). Radcliffe's physical and psychological disintegration, as he realizes the futility of his work, is darkly comic in a way that parallels Mike Leigh's characterization of the Savoy Operas.

However, there is one very important aspect in which Brenton deviates from the structure of the Savoy Operas and from most other examples of the genre of farce. Mike Leigh has written about Gilbert's 'predilection for devices that turn you, with significant dramatic consequences, into somebody else, or into a different version of yourself ... every one of the subsequent operas ... all involve transformations of identity' (Leigh *viii*). Barbara Freedman has similarly argued that one of the ways in which 'farce is committed to the discontinuous and the dysfunctional' (Freedman: 286) is through the use of 'mistaken recognitions and mistaken timing' (Freedman: 260). There is, in farce, 'a sudden, inexplicable disjunction between personal and communal accounts of one's identity' (Freedman: 261). Similarly, Stephen Greenblatt has identified the central importance in Shakespearean farce of 'the intrigue that arises from the willed or accidental mistaking of one person here for another' (Greenblatt: 189). From the earliest origins of farce, through figures as diverse as Aristophanes, Plautus, Shakespeare, Molière, Congreve, Feydeau, Wilde, into the work of 20th century playwrights such as Orton, 'multiple mistaken identities, (and) numerous disguises' (Hutchings: 227) has, in the words of William Hutchings, been a staple of theatrical farce.

Curiously, however, for all of Brenton's desire to expose the apparently commonsensical notion that Partition was a farce, through a play that borrows devices and structures from the theatrical genre of farce, there is no room in his play for mistaken identity. Identity is absolute – indeed, that is part of the problem. Part of Radcliffe's decline is caused by the fact that the Hindus, Muslims and Sikhs in the play refuse to compromise in any way on their identity categories and the narratives that result. The most obvious example of this, and not incidentally some of the most glaring historical inaccuracies, can be seen in Brenton's depiction of the Indian judges who served on the Boundary Commission under Radcliffe. The following is an exchange between one of the Congress-appointed Hindu judges, Mehr Chand Mahajan, and the Muslim League-appointed Muslim judge, Din Muhammad:

Din Muhammad. How do we know you will not attack us?
Mahajan. India will be a peaceful democracy. Will Pakistan?
Din Muhammad. Of course!
Mahajan. Can an Islamic country be a democracy?
Din Muhammad. Can a country riddled with a vicious caste system be a democracy?
Mahajan. Insult all you want ...
Christopher. Mr Justices ...

Mahajan. Calcutta is India's
Din Muhammad. You will not get Calcutta!
Mahajan. We will! And Ferozepur!
They move to hit each other.
Christopher. Gentlemen! (Brenton: 66–68)

Throughout this discussion, the British men present – Beaumont and Radcliffe – are presented as considered, thoughtful and dispassionate, while the Indian judges are biased, stubborn and unwilling to co-operate at all in order to have a functioning boundary commission. As Radcliffe later exclaims: 'Those men are justices! Judges! How can they behave so badly?' (Brenton: 70).

If we compare this representation to the official records, as examined by Lucy Chester, the disparities are obvious. The following is her account of Din Muhammad:

> Din Muhammad was perhaps the most disillusioned with the boundary-making process. Born in 1886, he graduated from Gordon College in Lahore and served on the Lahore High Court from 1936 to 1946 ... In 1947, even before the deliberations began, he complained that the line had already been decided and that the commission itself was 'a farce'. (Chester: 57)

Mahajan, for whom Brenton merely provides the stage direction that he speaks in a 'thick accent', (Brenton: 34) had, if anything, an even more impressive judicial record:

> Mehr Chand Mahajan (1889–1967), the most distinguished of the Congress nominees, was born in eastern Punjab and joined the High Court at Lahore in 1943. In 1945, he served on the commission appointed to investigate the Royal Indian Navy mutiny .... He went on to a distinguished career in Indian

> jurisprudence, serving as Chief Justice of the Supreme Court of India in 1954. (Chester: 57–58)

As Chester admits, the judges 'were closely involved in each party's preparation of the case it presented before the commission' (Chester: 56) and that 'each party had instructed its nominees not to compromise on any important point' (Chester: 55). However, Brenton's representation is deeply inaccurate, not least because there is no recognition of the pressures these judges were operating under. As Chester writes:

> (Radcliffe's) chief Moslem colleague told him quite frankly: 'It is not that I do not wish to make modifications, but I dare not. If I did my life would be in instant danger' ... The judges were not immune from the violence that swirled around them. (Chester: 55)

The judges were not inherently unreasonable men who were blinded by their passion – they were rather men of great intellect and an impeccable legal record who were operating under great pressures of their own. Radcliffe's principal source here, it would seem, is Auden's poem again:

> Unbiased at least he was when he arrived on his mission,
> Having never set eyes on the land he was called to partition
> Between two peoples fanatically at odds,
> With their different diets and incompatible gods. (Auden: 803)

Brenton and Auden's view that partition was a result of the fanaticism of the Indian religious and political leaders, and the way they refused to yield on their respective identity-narratives, is very similar to British colonial policy in India in the years leading up to partition. As Yasmin Khan has written:

> The experience of colonial rule had doubtless stirred up these divisions and added to a sense of separation, especially among elites. Reminders of religious 'difference' were built into the brickwork of the colonial state, a Muslim traveller would be directed to the 'Mohammedan refreshment room' at a train station and drinking taps on railway platforms were labelled 'Hindu water' or 'Muslim water' ... Generations of European administrators, travellers and scholars foregrounded the

> 'spiritual' in all their interpretations of India and, in their eyes, Hindus, Muslims and Sikhs were inescapably separate and mutually incompatible ... All this backfired catastrophically as religious boundaries, both more porous and less sharply defined in an earlier age, now hardened. (Khan: 19–20)

My point of interest is not so much Brenton's disregard of the established historic record – he is not a historian, and does not intend to create a historically accurate account of Partition, even if such a thing were to be possible. I am more interested in what this account of Partition does to Brenton's theatrical world-view, especially in terms of his use of the conventions of farce. In other words, by portraying the Indians in his play as absolutely fixed and certain in their own respective identities, Brenton has no room for that most common of theatrical devices in farce – mistaken identity. Identity in this world has hardened to the point where even Jinnah, famously non-observing in his personal life, is heard to say: 'I can only pray that a divided India is the will of Allah' (Brenton: 40). Brenton exploits and reinforces one Indian stereotype after another – from Lord Krishna to the *Bhagavad Gita* – Indians are spiritual, and fatalistic, but most of all, always and ultimately devout and religious – so that there is never any danger of mistaking a Hindu for a Muslim or vice versa.

When it comes to the representation of Partition in plays written by South Asians, however, things are very different. An obvious example is Mahesh Dattani's play *Final Solutions*, which is mostly set during the communal riots that engulfed large part of India in 1992, after Hindu fanatics destroyed the Babri mosque in Ayodhya. The characters of the play are haunted in many ways by their experiences and memories of Partition, and Dattani's play charts the various reactions of people as they are forced to examine their own prejudices when two Muslim men, Bobby and Javed, seek refuge from the violence on the streets, in the house of Ramnik and Aruna Gandhi's Hindu family. Dattani's drama charts a complex web of inclusion and exclusion, borders being erected and then demolished, boundaries between communities reinforced and transgressed, as historic relationships between a Muslim and Hindu family are explored with a complexity that is completely absent from Brenton's narrative. At the heart of this complexity are the sometimes-contradictory ways in which people engage with their own and other identity categories. Javed for example, narrates his involvement in communal violence as a feeling of comfort in numbers:

> On the bus, there were at least a dozen of us ... of them. It is so clear, isn't it? Anyone sitting at home, sipping tea and reading the newspapers, will say that it is obvious that a minority would never start a riot, we are too afraid, that it had to be politically motivated. Try telling it to a thousand devotees swayed by their own religious fervour, united by their fantasies of persecution, constantly reassuring themselves that this is their land by taking out processions. (Dattani: 205)

The gap between 'of us' and 'of them' is crucial. As an exchange earlier in the play between Bobby and Javed on the one hand, and the Gandhi couple Ramnik and Aruna, on the other, shows the dynamic between individual and collective identity is nuanced and complex:

> Javed. Those bastards!
> Bobby *(to Javed)*. Javed.
> Javed. *(looks at Ramnik)*. Sorry.
> Ramnik *(annoyed)*. Why are you apologizing to me? Of course they are bastards. They beat you up, didn't they?
> Javed. What I meant was, they are your own ...
> Aruna. He thinks we're all the same!
>
> Ramnik. How dare you suddenly join forces? In my house.
> Bobby Only because we were being clubbed together ... *(looks at Aruna and away)* unreasonably. But why do you feel I'm being ...?
> Ramnik. You resented being clubbed together. (Dattani: 183–185)

The gap between 'of us' and 'of them' is represented by the gap between feeling powerful in unity, as part of a wider community, and between feeling clubbed together as part of a homogenous 'them' within which there is little or no individual agency. Dattani allows his characters to express their agency both in terms of choosing to club together, and to stand apart. This agency is reflected in the dramatic structure of the play, as Dattani employs the chorus to represent this fluidity of identity, in stark contrast to Brenton's more hardened approach. This can be seen from the stage directions at the start of the play:

> The Mob/Chorus comprises five men and ten masks on sticks. The masks are strewn all over the ramp. The player 'wears' a mask by holding the stick in front of him. At more dynamic moments, he can use it as a weapon in a stylized fashion. There are five Hindu masks and five Muslim masks. The Mob/Chorus become the Chorus when they 'wear' either the Hindu or the Muslim masks. But when referred to individually, they remain Chorus 1, Chorus 2, etc. The players of the Mob/Chorus do not belong to any religion and ideally should wear black. (165)

The chorus demonstrates the promise and peril of identity categories poignantly at numerous times throughout the play. For example:

> Chorus 1. What must we do? To become more acceptable? Must we lose our identity? Is that what they want? Must we tolerate more? Does our future lie in their hands? Is there anyone more insecure than us? (208)

The plot of *Final Solutions* is, in many ways, similar to Abhijat Joshi's *A Shaft of Sunlight* – both are centred on Hindu families, where apparently liberal and open-minded people are forced by the communal violence in 1990s India to face up to their family's culpability in the violence of 1947. The Gandhi family in *Final Solutions*, is, we learn by the end of the play, living off the proceeds from the shop they own and run, the shop they bought 'at half its value (after) they had it burnt in the name of communal hatred' (226). *A Shaft of Sunlight* centres on Safina, a Muslim woman, who has married Bimal, a Hindu man. Their family takes the form of that very Hindu form of secularism which, as Bimal's mother Shanta demonstrates, hides an insidious and virulent form of Islamophobia. The roots of the violence that engulf their city in the present of the play, and of the prejudices that fan the violence, once again lie in the events of 1947. Like Bobby and Javed, Safina is unable to easily articulate an identity outside of the politics of partition. Born a Muslim, married into a Hindu family, Safina remains an outsider. '… because in this house there is no place for my past' (Joshi: 17), she says, 'I'm a minority in my own house' (32). Especially, but not exclusively, for the women in these two plays – Shanta and Safina in *A Shaft of Sunlight*, and Daksha/Hardika, Aruna and Smita in *Final Solutions*, their identity is never really within their control. This is especially the case for Daksha, who is renamed Hardika after her marriage. Daksha as a young girl, and Hardika as an elderly woman both occupy the stage at the same time, personifying the temporal and causal link between the violence of 1947 and the violence of 1992. Her journey from Daksha – a young girl who is a fan of Muslim singer Noor Jehan, and who confides to her diary her dislike of her in-laws and her desire for friendship with a Muslim family – to Hardika, who is deeply suspicious of Muslims who killed her father in 1947 and who, she thinks, should all go to Pakistan, reflect the lack of control all these individuals feel in the face of overwhelming societal pressures. Partition is more than a political legacy; it is a personal legacy that means one would be 'very foolish … to think you can create your freedom' (Dattani: 220).

Partition as a painful inheritance is further explored in Harwant S. Bains's *Blood*, which tells the story of Partition through the figures of Manmohan and Balbir. The play opens in the middle of hellish violence. Young Balbir witnesses his father being murdered, and the dead body of his mother being raped. From the fields and villages of Punjab, through immigration with his adopted brother Manmohan to Britain and life in a bedsit in London, to Balbir's rise up the ranks of organized crime, both the brothers, their family, and the next generation remain in the grip of this original sin – Partition is in their blood, and whatever Balbir does, he is taken inexorably towards his death at the hands of the man who may or may not be his son. The play ends with Manmohan cremating his brother's body, and lamenting the literally bloody inheritance that has blighted their whole lives:

> This is the field, my brother, my blood, where we sat and played and made our life-long promises. This is the field where you planted the seed for a money tree to grow. It grew into our

hearts my brother. (*Pause.*) It poisoned our blood. (*Pause.*) I will scatter your sacred ashes in the river. You will nourish the soil ... (*Slowly.*) ... I loved you ... (Bains: 47)

Manmohan's lamentation recalls Amrita Pritam's famous poetic evocation of Waris Shah, as she laments the pain that Partition has caused her beloved Punjab:

O friend of the sorrowing, rise and see your Punjab
Corpses are strewn on the pasture,
Blood runs in the Chenab.
Some hand hath mixed poison in our five rivers
The rivers in turn had irrigated the land.
From the rich land have sprouted venomous weeds
How high the red has spread
How much the curse has bled! (Pritam: 93)

It is, perhaps, because of this generational distance that these plays are so deeply inter-textual. Writing about her selection of dramatic and cinematic texts, Jisha Menon has described how:

The mimetic practice of adaptation allows the artist to embed creative difference by retelling a story that is similar but not identical to the original ... Mimetic semblance points not only to the doubleness of characters within these stories but also to the palimpsestic doubleness of the narratives themselves. (Menon: 18)

I have already discussed above how Brenton, in his play, has dramatized Auden's poetic account of Radcliffe's role in partitioning India, and how Bains evokes Pritam's poetry in the closing moments of his play. *A Tainted Dawn* takes its title from a famous Urdu poem by Faiz Ahmed Faiz. The play as a whole is structured as a series of dramatic vignettes, all adapted from various short stories. For Daksha/Hardika in *Final Solutions*, and therefore for the audience, the main access to the events of 1947 is provided by Daksha's diary – for the playwrights, actors, audience – for all of us who have any connection to Partition, this connection is only ever textual and hence always already mediated.

One of the more poignant examples of doubled, palimpsestic stories that tell of doubled, palimpsestic identities, is the story of Pali and Altaf, which, perhaps appropriately, appears in a couple of different iterations in these plays. The story originally appeared in a short story by author Bhisham Sahni, whose writings on Partition has achieved great critical and popular attention. Sahni's story centres on Manohar Lal and Kaushalya, who get separated from their son Pali while attempting to flee the violence of Partition. Pali is found and looked after by a childless Mulism couple, Shakur and Zenab. Under pressure from community and religious leaders, they have him converted to Islam and rename him Altaf. Eventually, Manohar Lal tracks him down. Shakur and Zenab agree to give up the boy they have come to consider their own son, on condition that Manohar Lal brings him back for Eid each year. Crossing the border back to India, however, Manohar Lal faces the same pressures that Shakur and Zenab faced, and is forced to put his son through a re-initiation ceremony that marks his re-entry into the Hindu faith. Stuck on either side of the border, the two pairs of parents are left helpless in the face of overarching societal norms to conform, leaving the reader to wonder how the child Pali/Altaf could ever grow up to accommodate both these aspects of his character. The Pali/Altaf story has been dramatized twice – first as one of the vignettes that formed *A Tainted Dawn* by Sudha Bhuchar and Kristine Landon-Smith, and then nine years later as a full-length play *Child of the Divide* by Sudha Bhuchar. In all three versions of the story, the dramatic focus is on the lack of individual control in the face of external, overwhelming historical and political forces. The ignorant innocence of these characters makes their border-crossings more poignant and more pointless, but also robbing them of any sense of transgressive agency. Their helplessness in the face of overwhelming external pressure is matched by the lack of control that these playwrights experience in trying to tell the story of Partition in new ways. Partition repeats itself endlessly, and the narratives too, repeat themselves, almost beyond authorial control. Familiar stories, familiar experiences are rendered unfamiliar through this repetition, as the physical home of the domestic or the national, the conceptual home of identity categories, and the discursive home of history and narrative, are all rendered deeply, terrifyingly unstable.

Through this telling and re-telling, this manic and uncontrollable repetition and doubling, this deeply unfamiliar familiarity, Partition becomes uncanny. The uncanny is, in Nicholas Royle's words:

> ... a crisis of the proper: it entails a critical disturbance of ... the very idea of personal or private property including the properness of proper names, one's so-called 'own' name, but also the proper names of others, of places, institutions and events .... It can consist in a sense of homeliness uprooted, the revelation of something unhomely at the heart of hearth and home. (Royle: 1)

As Pali/Altaf crosses and re-crosses the border, becoming in turn Hindu, Muslim and Hindu once again, he has to learn everything anew – his name, his appearance, the names he has for his parents. Inanimate objects acquire just as much if not more power than human beings. When he is Altaf, he depends on his 'red rumi cap' and 'white muslin kurta' to be able to pass as an insider. When he is Pali, these markers become symbols of the offensive threat he poses to the societal fabric. The plot of both *Final Solutions* and *A Shaft of Sunlight* hinge on objects of great importance that may or may not have been destroyed – a sacred divine chariot, and a wall that is also a shrine, respectively. These objects which are constantly spoken about but never seen, which are thus both present and absent, drive forward the frenetic plot just as much as any individual character. In *Drawing the Line*, the objects that take on this willed determinative role are the maps. The play was advertised using a shot of a map and, in performance, the stage-space seems to be gradually being taken over by rolls and rolls of maps. Far from Radcliffe being in charge of the map and the cartographic delineation that he has apparently come to India for, the maps in fact take charge and haunt Radcliffe as he spirals out of control, into physical and psychological destruction: 'Radcliffe (*aside*). Extraordinary. To have no control over yourself. Makes you aware of your inner being, in a queasy kind of way' (Brenton: 64).

Brenton's Radcliffe descends into a hallucinatory world populated by a clichéd, Orientalist vision of Lord Krishna, who gives him the illusion of control, while undermining his agency at the same time. In *Final Solutions*, on the other hand, it is a small statue of Krishna, which determines lines of inclusion and exclusion. Aruna and her affective attachment to the object that is the idol determines where she will allow Javed and Bobby as Muslims to go, which water pot to touch, and what food to eat. In the climax of the play, as Bobby lifts up the idol in the ultimate act of rebellion, what he reinforces, paradoxically, is an extra-human, deeply uncanny force, that renders human activity even more meaningless:

> Your God! My flesh is holding Him! Look Javed! And He does not mind! He does not burn me to ashes! He does not cry out from the heavens saying He has been contaminated! ... Look how He rests in my hands! He knows I cannot harm Him. He knows his strength! I don't believe in Him but He believes in me. He smiles! He smiles at our trivial pride and our trivial shame. (Dattani: 24)

What should be a moment of human resistance to externally imposed reactionary norms becomes a lament of individual helplessness in the face of wider, almost supernatural forces. Krishna's idol is similar to Daksha's diary. Initially presented as evidence of a young girl's coping strategy it becomes, by the end of the play, just another example of her ignorance, and powerlessness.

The maps, the wall, the shrines, the clothes, the diary – they all represent what Douglas Bruster has identified as a central characteristic of theatrical farce:

> Comedy generally, and farce in particular, often feature a misplaced object, or objects, the finding of which leads to a recognition and brings on, finally, the story's denouement. Movable objects like rings, letters, and articles of clothing come to be invested with a narrative value replicating itself uncannily in the larger world of reading and interpretation. (Bruster: 63)

Imparting a sovereign will to inanimate objects, or abstract forces of history, then renders these plays, and the Partition that they represent as uncannily doubled – controlled and frenetic, meaningless and yet logical. In Barbara Freedman's words:

> The interplay of logic and absurdity, transgression and innocence, meaning and mistake, suggests that the play ...(works) to disperse and deny the meaning of one original, meaningful plot that can be retrieved. (Freedman: 263)

The results, while no doubt dramatically effective, rely on the recycling and reinforcing of a particular, and particularly insidious narrative of history. By rendering Partition as an abstract historical force that is beyond the control of any of the individuals on stage, these plays are reinforcing the historical narrative that Gyanendra Pandey has described as the way history 'produc(ing) the 'truth' of the traumatic, genocidal violence of Partition and ... elid(ing) it at the same time' (Pandey 45) According to Pandey, the nation-state creates its own narrative of Partition, paradoxically, by making it non-narratable. In constructing the violence surrounding Partition as inexplicable, the nation-state and its official narrative of history can be absolved of the responsibility of having to explain it, or having to account for the experience of those who lived through it, and their memories of partition today. Partition occurs in the passive voice throughout – in a Beckettian non-space, played by Beckettian non-actors, such as the three hellish figures who come in and out of the narrative in *Blood*, or, indeed, Brenton's hallucinatory Krishna. The history of Partition is, thus, moved to a non-human sphere, removing all sense of agency on behalf of the human characters. Partition, then, is inscribed as ghostly, non-human, unreal. In this non-space, human bodies are endlessly violated, the lines between the human and the non-human are consequently erased, and meaning and logic do not apply. This non-space produces great theatre, but ultimately relies on a flawed, and deeply problematic reading of the Partition that is being represented on stage.

Note

1. Notable exceptions include Jisha Menon, *The Performance of Nationalism: India, Pakistan, and the Memory of Partition*. Cambridge: Cambridge University Press, 2013 and Nandi Bhatia, *Performing Women/Performing Womanhood: Theatre, Politics, and Dissent in North India*. New Delhi and Oxford: Oxford University Press, 2010

Works Cited

Ali, Rabia Umar. *Empire in Retreat: The Story of India's Partition*. Oxford: Oxford University Press, 2012. Print.

Auden, W.H. *Collected Poems*. Ed. Edward Mendelson. New York: Vintage, 1991. Print.

Bains, Harwant S. *Blood*. London: Methuen, 1989. Print.

Bentley, Eric. *The Life of the Drama*. New York: Athenaeum, 1966. Print.

Bermel, Albert. *Farce: A History from Aristophanes to Woody Allen*. New York: Simon and Schuster, 1982. Print.

Bhatia, Nandi. *Performing Women/Performing Womanhood: Theatre, Politics, and Dissent in North India*. New Delhi & Oxford: Oxford University Press, 2010. Print.

Bhuchar, Sudha, Kristine Landon-Smith. *A Tainted Dawn*. London: Nick Hern Books and Tamasha Theatre, 1999. Print.

Bhuchar, Sudha. *Child of the Divide*. London: A&C Black 3PL, 2007. Print.

Billington, Michael. '*Drawing the Line* – A Review'. *Guardian*, 10 December 2013. Web. 24 July. 2015. <http://www.theguardian.com/stage/2013/dec/10/drawing-the-line-review>

Brenton, Howard. *Drawing the Line*. London: Nick Hern Books, 2013. Print.

Bruster, Douglas. *Drama and the Market in the Age of Shakespeare*. Cambridge: Cambridge University Press, 1992. Print.

Chester, Lucy P. *Borders and Conflict in South Asia: The Radcliffe Boundary Commission and the Partition of Punjab*. Manchester: Manchester University Press, 2009. Print.

Dalrymple, William. 'The Great Divide: The violent legacy of Indian Partition'.

New Yorker, 29 June 2015. Web. 24 July. 2015. <http://www.newyorker.com/magazine/2015/06/29/the-great-divide-books-dalrymple>

Dattani, Mahesh. *Collected Plays*. New Delhi and London: Penguin, 2000. Print.

Davis, Jessica Milner. *Farce*. London: Methuen, 1987. Print.

Freedman, Barbara. 'Reading Errantly: Misrecognition and the Uncanny in *The Comedy of Errors*'. *The Comedy of Errors: Critical Essays*. Ed. Robert S. Miola. New York: Garland, 1997. 261–297. Print.

Greenblatt, Stephen. *Learning to Curse: Essays in Early Modern Culture*. New York: Routledge. 2007. Print.

Hingorani, Dominic. *British Asian Theatre: Dramaturgy, Process and Performance*. Basingstoke: Palgrave Macmillan. 2010. Print.

Hutchings, William. 'Joe Orton's Jacobean Assimilations in *What the Butler Saw*'. *Farce*. Ed. James Redmond. Cambridge: Cambridge University Press, 1988. 227–236. Print.

Khan, Yasmin. *The Great Partition: The Making of India and Pakistan*. New Haven and London: Yale University Press, 2007. Print.

Jalal, Ayesha. *The Pity of Partition: Manto's Life, Times, and Work across the India-Pakistan Divide*. Princeton and Oxford: Princeton University Press, 2013. Print.

Joshi, Abhijat. *A Shaft of Sunlight*. London: Nick Hern Books, 1999. Print.

Leigh, Mike. 'Introduction'. *The Savoy Operas: The Complete Gilbert and Sullivan*. London: Penguin, 2008. Print.

Marx, Karl. 'The Eighteenth Brumaire of Louis Bonaparte'. *The Collected Works of Karl Marx and Frederick Engels. General Works 1844–1895. Volume 11*. London: Lawrence and Wishart, 1975. 100–198. Print.

Menon, Jisha. *The Performance of Nationalism: India, Pakistan, and the Memory of Partition*. Cambridge: Cambridge University Press, 2013. Print.

Nagappan, Ramu. *Speaking Havoc: Social Suffering and South Asian Narratives*. Seattle: University of Washington Press, 2005. Print.

Pandey, Gyanendra. *Remembering Partition*. Cambridge: Cambridge University Press, 2011. Print.

Panjabi, Kavita. 'Partition Violence: Self-Reckoning and the Structuring of a Modern Subjectivity'. *Cartographies of Affect: Across Borders in South Asia and the Americas*. Eds. Debra A. Castillo and Kavita Panjabi. Delhi: Worldview, 2011. 217–240. Print.

Pritam, Amrita. *Selected Poems*. Ed. Khushwant Singh. New Delhi, Bharatiya Jnanpith, 1982. Print.

Royle, Nicholas. *The Uncanny*. Manchester: Manchester University Press, 2002. Print.

Talbot, Ian. 'The 1947 Partition of India'. *The Historiography of Genocide*. Ed. Dan Stone. Basingstoke, Hampshire and New York: Palgrave Macmillan, 2008. 420–437. Print.

Wiegand, Chris. 'Live Webchat: Howard Brenton on Drawing the Line'. 14 January 2014. Web. 24 July. 2015. <http://www.theguardian.com/stage/2014/jan/07/live-stream-howard-brenton-drawing-the-line>

Contributors

THE EDITORS

Ajay K. Chaubey is Assistant Professor in English at the Department of Sciences & Humanities, National Institute of Technology, Uttarakhand. Prior to this, Ajay shared his knowledge and experience in the premier institutions of Uttar Pradesh, Rajasthan and Delhi. His major publications include the volumes on V.S. Naipaul and Salman Rushdie followed by two other volumes on the literature of the Indian Diaspora. Ajay loves to travel extensively and this devouring desire impelled him to attend, partake and present research papers in conferences, symposia and workshops held in India and England. He is a Life Member of academic organizations, viz. IACLALS, AESI and Sahitya Akademy, New Delhi, among others. He is also the member of International Research Networks like 'Writing, Analysing, Translating Dalit Literature', promoted and promulgated by Nottingham Trent University, Nottingham and Emma University, France and 'South Asian Diaspora International Researchers' Network' (SADIRN), functioned by academicians of Monash University, Australia and independent researchers of South Asia.

Ashvin I. Devasundaram is Lecturer in World Cinema at Queen Mary University of London and author of *India's New Independent Cinema: Rise of the Hybrid* (Routledge, 2016) – the world's first book on new Indian 'Indie' cinema. He is Programming Adviser to the London Asian Film Festival (LAFF), Creative Director of the Edinburgh Asian Film Festival (EAFF), and a BBC Academy Expert Voice in Cultural Studies and Visual Arts. Ashvin will be introducing the first UK university curriculum module on new independent Indian cinema at Queen Mary University in 2017. Ashvin has delivered the prestigious Annual Dadasaheb Phalke Memorial Lecture 2015 at the Indian High Commission's Nehru Centre in London. He is on the Editorial Board of peer-reviewed *The South Asianist*, Journal of South Asian Studies, University of Edinburgh. Ashvin is also on the Advisory Panel for BFI India on Film – a major initiative charting India's cinema heritage and history – part of the UK-India Year of Culture 2017.

THE CONTRIBUTORS

Ana Cristina Mendes has been a researcher at the University of Lisbon, Centre for English Studies (CEAUL/ULICES) since 2005. Her areas of specialization are postcolonial and migration studies, with an emphasis on the cultural industries and exchanges in the global cultural marketplace. She has recently been pursuing research in the subfields of poverty studies (slumming), visual arts, cinemas and literatures of the Asian emerging economies. Her publications include the co-edited book *Re-Orientalism and South Asian Identity Politics* (2011), the edited collection *Salman Rushdie and Visual Culture* (2012), and the monograph *Salman Rushdie in the Cultural Marketplace* (2013).

Anindya Raychaudhuri is a Lecturer in English. He was previously British Academy Postdoctoral Fellow, first at UCL and subsequently at the School of English, University of St Andrews. His primary research interest is in the cultural representation and collective memory of war and conflict. He is also interested in postcolonial and diasporic identities and cultures. He is the author of a monograph, *Narrating Partition: Agency, Memory, Representation* (OUP, 2016).

D. **Sudha Rani** is an Associate Professor at the Department of H&S, VNR Vignana Jyothi Institute of Engineering and Technology, Hyderabad. She has been an active researcher interested in cultural studies and performance studies. She is the first research scholar to work on all full length plays of Mahesh Dattani. Besides more than six books, she has presented and published many research papers. Her latest paper, 'Cultural Memory Transmission Among Madigas: A Study of Adijambava Mahapuranam' may be accessed in volume 4 of SAARC Culture journal.

E. **Anna Claydon** has published a small number of works on British South Asian films, particularly the work of Gurinder Chadha, and is particularly interested in issues of hybridity and identity. She also works on film music, seriality, and disability in the media and has a forthcoming book *Analysing Film* (Palgrave Macmillan) aimed at students and researchers understanding film from an intercultural and adaptive perspective. She works at the University of Leicester in the UK.

Irum Alvi, PhD and M.A. (Gold Medalist), is presently working as Faculty in HEAS (English) Department, Rajasthan Technical University, Kota. She is the In-Charge, Professional Communication Skills and Assistant Dean, Applied Sciences. Dr Alvi has been quite dynamic as she has not only organized national and international seminars, conferences and workshops, but also has been Resource Person, Guest Speaker and Keynote Speaker at several academic forums. Her area of interests is Communication Studies and Soft Skills apart from Indian, American and World Literature. Being multilingual in Persian, Dari, Urdu, etc. she writes research articles, papers and poems and has also been the Editorial Committee Member of the University newsletter, the college magazine and brochure, etc.

M.M.K. Sardana is presently a Visiting Fellow at the Institute for Studies in Industrial Development (ISID), New Delhi. Earlier he was in the Government of India, as an IAS officer, from where he retired in 2004 after holding several senior positions. As a Visiting Fellow, he has been making studies on contemporary issues bordering on policies of the government.

Manjinder Kaur Wratch is working for her doctoral degree on partition literature from University of Jammu. Earlier she has served as Faculty of English Language and Literature at various institutes of the country. For her MPhil dissertation, she worked on the legendary Punjabi and Hindi author, Amrita Pritam. Additionally, She has made many presentations at various national and international conferences and has contributed more than 15 research papers for many anthologies and journals – national as well as international.

Nandi Bhatia, Professor in the Department of English at the University of Western Ontario and currently Associate Dean of Research, Faculty of Arts and Humanities, works on film, theatre, and literatures of India and the British Empire. She is the author of *Performing Women/Performing Womanhood: Theatre, Politics and Dissent in North India* (Oxford University Press, 2010) and *Acts of Authority/Acts of Resistance: Theater and Politics in Colonial and Postcolonial India* (University of Michigan Press and Oxford University Press, 2004). Additionally, she has edited a collection of essays titled *Modern Indian Theatre* (Oxford University Press, 2011) and has co-edited with Anjali Gera-Roy, *Partitioned Lives: Narratives of Home, Displacement and Resettlement* (Pearson-Longman, 2008). Additional work includes an edited special issue of *TOPIA: Canadian Journal of Cultural Studies* on 'Bollywood and the South Asian Diaspora', a guest edited issue of *Feminist Review* on 'Postcolonial Theatres' and a co-edited special issue of *Fashion Theory*.

Neilesh Bose is an Assistant Professor of South Asian history at the University of North Texas. He holds a PhD in South Asian history from Tufts University. Other publications include his edited anthology, *Beyond Bollywood and Broadway: Plays from the South Asian Diaspora* (Indiana University Press, 2009) and his joint (with Sudipto Chatterjee) translation of Utpal Dutt's Bengali *Maanusher Adhikare*, as *Rights of Man* (Seagull India, 2009). His research interests include modern South Asia, Bengal and Bengali Muslim studies, imperialism, diasporas, and decolonization. Conversations with generous scholars and artists such as David Morrow, Sudipto Chatterjee, Jatinder Verma, Sarah Dadswell, Don Weingust, Jamil Khoury, Anish Jethmalani, Lavina Jadhwani, Stuart Carden, Pranidhi Varshney, and of course, Shishir Kurup himself have assisted in the development of this essay.

Pragya Shukla is Assistant Professor at the Department of English and Foreign Languages, Central University of Chhattisgarh. Her area of interest are Feminist Studies, Film Studies and Narrative Techniques. Her doctoral thesis was on 'A Comparative Study of the Fictional Works of Githa Hariharan and Shashi Deshpande'. Apart from research papers, she dabbles her hand in writing poetry and short stories also.

Priyam Basu Thakur has been associated with the Department of Journalism and Mass Communication of Rishi Bankim Chandra College and Acharya Prafulla Chandra College of West Bengal as a Guest Lecturer from 2012–2014. Currently, she is a PhD scholar and has joined the Department of Mass Communication and Videography, Rabindra Bharati University as a Junior Research Fellow. Her research interests include Audio-visual Media (Television), New Media, Traditional Media, Media Effects Research.

Rajesh James is Assistant Professor of English in the Postgraduate Department of English, Sacred Heart College, Thevara. He is a budding documentary filmmaker from Kerala with number of acclaimed films to his credits. His film *Zebra Lines* (2014) was officially selected in the competition section of IDSFK, VIBJYOR, and Leipzig International Documentary Film Festivals. He has published in Phillip Drummond' (ed), *The London Film and Media Reader 3: The Pleasures of the Spectacle* and various other Indian journals.

Rekha Sharma is a doctoral student in the School of Communication Studies at Kent State University, USA. Her research interests include political communication in news and popular culture as well as media related to government conspiracy theories. Her recent work focused on exploring the political effects of infotainment programmes, messages about war in animated cartoons, and the use of YouTube in the 2008 US Presidential Primary and General Elections.

Sanjena Sathian is Atlanta-bred, now California-based senior editor and writer at a digital startup magazine called *OZY*, which she joined about eight weeks after its launch. She has been a student journalist for student international political magazine, the *Yale Globalist*, which took her around the world, managing a talented group of young reporters. Sathian studied English literature at Yale, focusing on writing. She studied literary long-form journalism and wrote two award-winning theses: a creative thesis in fiction and an academic thesis on the novels of Zadie Smith and their creation of a modern public sphere in the city of London.

Shilpa Daithota Bhat is Assistant Professor in Ahmedabad University, Gujarat, India. She is the first recipient of Lorna Marsden International Visitor Fellowship to York University, Canada (2015). A Commonwealth Fellow to the University of Toronto, she was also a recipient of the Pacific Asia Network of Canadian Studies to Korea University. She has travelled to McGill University, University of Western Ontario, University of Toronto and University of York, Canada, for research. Her areas of interest are South Asian Narratives, Diaspora and Postcolonial Theories, Canadian Studies and Children's Literature. She is the author of *Indians in Victorian Children's Narratives: Animalizing the 'Native',* 1830–1930 (Lexington Books, 2017).

Subrata Kumar Das is an Assistant Professor of English at Vishweshwar Singh Janta College, Rajnagar (affiliated to Lalit Narayan Mithila University, Darbhanga, Bihar, India). He is pursuing Ph.D. from the UGC-Centre for the Study of Indian Diaspora, University of Hyderabad, India. He worked on Jhumpa Lahiri's *The Namesake* (2003) for his MPhil dissertation. He has worked as Associate Editor for the *Journal of Literary Aesthetics*, published by Guru Nanak Khalsa College for Women, Ludhiana, Punjab (online) and National Press Associates (print), New Delhi, India. He has presented many scholarly papers in national and international conferences, seminars and workshops. He has published ten papers on diasporic literature, diasporic cinema and other areas in national and international journals and edited books. His areas of interest lie in literary theories, especially Postcolonial Literary Theories, different areas of Postcolonial Literature: Indian Diasporic Literature and Films, Cultural Studies, Graphic Novel, Romantic Literature and Translation Studies.

Index